Tanja Rabl

Private Corruption and its Actors

Insights into the Subjective Decision Making Processes

PABST SCIENCE PUBLISHERS
Lengerich, Berlin, Bremen, Miami,
Riga, Viernheim, Wien, Zagreb

Bibliographic information published by Die Deutsche Nationalbibliothek
Die Deutsche Nationalbibliothek lists this publication in the Deutsche Nationalbibli-
ografie; detailed bibliographic data is available in the Internet at <http://dnb.ddb.de>.

DR. TANJA RABL
University of Bayreuth, Chair of Human Resource Management, 95440 Bayreuth,
Germany, Tel. ++ 49 (0) 921-55-2953, Fax ++ 49 (0) 921-55-2954,
E-Mail: tanja.rabl@uni-bayreuth.de

© 2008 Pabst Science Publishers, D-49525 Lengerich
Printing: KM Druck, D-64823 Groß-Umstadt

ISBN 978-3-89967-525-2

Acknowledgment

A journey is easier when you travel with company, and in this journey I had the best of company. This book is the result of nearly four years of work whereby I have been accompanied, supported, and inspired by many people. I would like to acknowledge with great appreciation their contributions and assistance.

First and foremost, I would like to express my deep and sincere gratitude to my academic advisor Prof. Dr. Torsten M. Kühlmann, Chair of Human Resource Management at the University of Bayreuth, Germany. He inspired me to work on the corruption topic, which is one of the core interdisciplinary research topics of the Faculty of Law, Economics, and Business Administration of the University of Bayreuth, Germany. I am grateful for the freedom he gave me in working on the topic, for the support and advice in all my research efforts, and for the fruitful discussions. I highly appreciate that he encouraged and enabled me to submit papers to international conferences and journals. For me, this was both personally and professionally enriching. The feedback of the international community on my presentations and papers always motivated me to continue my work and helped to improve it.

I also warmly thank Prof. Dr. Herbert Woratschek, Chair of Services Management at the University of Bayreuth, Germany. When I presented my research topic to him, he immediately was enthused and declared his willingness to take the role as second referee of my dissertation. Moreover, I am also indebted to Prof. Dr. Bernhard Herz, Chair of Monetary and International Economics and Vice President of the University of Bayreuth, Germany, who has agreed to serve on my dissertation committee. I greatly acknowledge the burden and extra efforts they both took as reviewers of my work and members of the dissertation committee.

This study could not have been conducted if there were not some sponsors. I, therefore, thank the foundation "Wertevolle Zukunft", the Business Keeper AG, the Telekom AG, and the ABB AG for the financial support for this research project.

I am very grateful to my colleagues who have accompanied me during my time working at the Chair of Human Resource Management at the University of Bayreuth, Germany, and not only were coworkers but also established a social environment that has made my time in Bayreuth enjoyable: Ludwig Merker, Philipp Dengel, Elisabeth Prechtl, Philipp Schauwecker, Kathrin Heckner, Antje Schramm, and Nadine Schoberth. I owe a huge debt of gratitude to two of them: Ludwig Merker always gave me his advice and practical support when I needed it, may it be in IT affairs, in strategic questions, or in research questions. I always could be sure to find a good idea or a good solution together with him. I thank him for all his time and efforts. He also aided the development of my dissertation. He offered me the possibility to gain some of my empirical data during "CampusLive," a recruiting initiative for future students that he initiated for the Faculty of Law, Economics, and Business Administration at the University of Bayreuth, Germany. Philipp Dengel, now managing director of the Bavarian University Centre for China, was a fantastic colleague on whom one always could rely in daily work matters supporting each other. It was my pleasure to discuss teaching and research ideas with him. I enjoyed working with both of them a lot and thank them for this "dream teamwork".

My warm thanks are also due to the secretaries at the Chair of Human Resource Management at the University of Bayreuth, Germany, especially to Petra Hammon and Katrin Stark, as well as to all the students who worked for and with me. In the process of gathering the data for my dissertation, I am much obliged to Larissa Hammon. In supporting me in all IT questions, I am very grateful to Christopher Kühn.

Many friends have accompanied me on my way and have taken care that I do not forget that there is a life besides work. I owe them great thanks.

I would not have been able to achieve all this if there were not my family and my parents. For their understanding, their support and their encouragement, they deserve far more credit than I can ever give them.

Bayreuth, July 2008   Tanja Rabl

TABLE OF CONTENTS

LIST OF FIGURES

LIST OF TABLES

LIST OF ABBREVIATIONS

English

§	paragraph
§§	paragraphs
%	percent
AACSB	Association to Advance Collegiate Schools of Business
ANOVA	analysis of variance (univariate)
AT	attitude
AVE	average variance extracted
BI	Business International
BPI	Bribe Payers Index
C	client
CA	corrupt action
chap.	chapter
corr.	corrections
CPI	Corruption Perceptions Index
df	degree of freedom
EC	European Commission
ed.	edition
Ed.	editor
Eds.	editors
EFMD	European Foundation for Management Development
e.g.	example given
EQUIS	European Quality Improvement System
et al.	et alii (and others)
etc.	et cetera (and so forth)
F	computed value of F-test
f^2	effect size
FDI	foreign direct investment
GCR	Global Competitiveness Report
GD	desire to achieve a private or professional goal
GDP	gross domestic product
GF	goal feasibility
GI	goal intention
GLOBE	Global Leadership and Organizational Behavior Effectiveness
GNP	gross national product
GR	goal realization
HP	holder of a powerful position
ICRG	International Country Risk Guide
ID	desire to achieve a private or professional goal through corrupt action
IGO	intergovernmental organization

II	intention to achieve a private or professional goal through corrupt action
IMF	International Monetary Fund
Jr.	junior
LISREL	Linear Structural Relations
MANOVA	multivariate analysis of variance
n	number in a subsample
N	total number in a sample
NAE	negative anticipated emotions
NGO	non-governmental organization
no.	number
OAS	Organization of American States
OECD	Organisation for Economic Co-operation and Development
p	probability
p.	page
PAE	positive anticipated emotions
PBC	perceived behavioral control
PETS	Public Expenditure Tracking
PLS	Partial Least Squares
pp.	pages
q^2	predictive relevance
Q^2	Stone-Geisser's Q^2 of redundancy
QSDS	Quantitative Service Delivery Survey
r	correlation coefficient
R^2	R-Square; coefficient of determination
SD	standard deviation
SEM	structural equation modeling
SN	subjective norm
t	computed value of t-test
TI	Transparency International
Trans.	translator(s)
UN	United Nations
US	United States
Vol.	volume
WTO	World Trade Organization
z	a standard score; difference between one value in a distribution and the mean of the distribution divided by the standard deviation
α	Cronbach's alpha
η^2	eta squared; measure of effect size
χ^2	computed value of a chi-square test
κ	Cohen's kappa
ρ	Dillon-Goldstein's rho

German

BDI	Bundesverband der Deutschen Industrie e.V.
ca.	circa
d.h.	das heißt
EUBestG	EU-Bestechungsgesetz; Gesetz zu dem Protokoll vom 27. September 1996 zum Übereinkommen über den Schutz der finanziellen Interessen der Europäischen Gemeinschaften
IBES	Inventar berufsbezogener Einstellungen und Selbsteinschätzungen
IntBestG	Internationales Bestechungsgesetz; Gesetz zu dem Übereinkommen vom 17. Dezember 1997 über die Bekämpfung der Bestechung ausländischer Amtsträger im internationalen Geschäftsverkehr
Nr.	Nummer
max.	maximal
PIA	Persönlichkeitsinventar zur Integritätsabschätzung
PIT	Psychologischer Integritätstest
StGB	Strafgesetzbuch
z.B.	zum Beispiel

1   Introduction

> *In an office, in one of these big modern skyscraper buildings: David Molton, top marketing manager, is in a meeting with Brian West, the chief executive officer of a small consulting firm. The atmosphere is very relaxed. For years, David's company has been doing business with Brian's consulting firm regarding the sponsoring of sports events.*
>
> *The two men are discussing which of the upcoming events might be a good deal for David's company to sponsor, when Brian discreetly mentions that his consulting firm urgently needs orders.*
>
> *"David, maybe you can help me out? You would get provisions if you conveyed some further sponsoring contracts to my firm."*
>
> *"Well, let me think. It would be no problem to advise our suppliers to also sponsor sports events and to persuade them of what an effective marketing tool this is. I already have toyed with that idea myself."*
>
> *"That would be great. And I promise, it will pay off for you. We will derive your provisions from the advertising revenues."*
>
> *"Yeah, of course, why not get some additional income for my efforts?" David laughs. "I don't see any risk. Negotiating with you was always my responsibility."*
>
> *"And your provisions will be paid to your private account, so that they will not occur in any of your company's documentation," Brian adds.*
>
> *"You're right. And why should my company have a problem – it's an investment in our good business relationship. You always offered very good service on good terms. And maintaining good business relationships with our partners is even one of the top priorities in our mission statement."*
>
> *"Don't forget, your company will benefit, too. You will sponsor the most important sports events; there is no better advertisement for your company than that," Brian emphasizes.*
>
> *"Absolutely. So, why not? Where's the problem? Let's do it."*
>
> *"Perfect."*
>
> *(Source: the author)*

1.1   Motivation and Goals of the Study

In recent years, corruption has become one of the most widely discussed topics worldwide in the public and among business practitioners, as well as among researchers. While primarily corruption in the sectors of politics and public administration was discussed, in the meantime private corruption, that is, corruption in and between companies, has become topical as never before. Corruption is experienced as a serious problem worldwide that not only affects politics, society, and economy (Transparency International (TI), 2007b), but also affects companies themselves. European citizens see corruption as the most worrying form of white-collar criminality (European Commission (EC), 2004a; EC, 2004b). Taking the example of Germany, this does not astonish: Over the past years, many spectacular corruption cases with the involvement of companies were reported in the media. You could find headlines like "Corruption – Helix of temptation" (Buchhorn, 10/2005), "Welcome in the baksheesh republique" (Brost & Storn, 30/2005), "Self service in DAX companies – Corruption is top priority" (Hinze, 2005, July 19), "Always new names, new figures, new sites – A net with thick knots" (Leyendecker & Ott, 2006, December 13), and "Culture of purchasability" (Münchau, 2006, December 20).

Corruption may take many forms: Actors pay commissions for alleged services, make illegal rebates and discounts, or give outright gifts of money or gratuities. Corporations often do not keep records of the illegal discounts and rebates. Instead, they conceal kickbacks from government agencies through false invoices, bills of lading, and accounting entries. They make payments by deposits in secret bank accounts or through phony consulting firms or dummy firms, which are set up solely for this purpose. The parent corporation can write off bribe money as a legitimate business expense and can claim it knew nothing about the payoffs. Bribes paid to influence purchases include paid vacations, the use of corporate recreational facilities, expensive dinners, theater tickets, provisions for call girls, and expensive gifts (Clinard, 1990, pp. 133 – 135; Coleman, 1998; pp. 39 – 40).

Corruption in one form or another has been present throughout history (Bardhan, 1997; Deflem, 1995). It can be found everywhere, in every society (Freisitzer, 1981) and every economic system (Krug, 1997), even if the manifestations (Noack, 1985, p. 9), the frequencies (Bannenberg & Schaupensteiner, 2004, p. 12; Freisitzer, 1981; Noack, 1985, p. 9), the hierarchical levels (Noack, 1985, p. 9), and the degree of cultural capture (Bannenberg & Schaupensteiner, 2004, p. 12) change. The list of companies involved in corruption is long; they no longer can be counted on one hand. The detected cases pervade various sectors, among them the automobile industry (e.g., BMW, DaimlerChrysler, Faurecia, Hyundai, Lear, Opel, Porsche, Skoda, VW), the electrical industry (e.g., Infineon, Philips, Siemens), the finance industry (e.g., Commerzbank), the energy industry (e.g., Linde, Thyssengas), the communication industry (e.g., Samsung, Telekom), the pharmaceutical industry (e.g., Ratiopharm), the furniture industry (e.g., Ikea), the security sector (e.g., Heros), or the retail sector (e.g., Bauer, Rewe). Corruption in and between companies is as old as the concept of business relationships (Pitt & Abratt, 1986). It is a "universal phenomenon with roots that stretch far back into human history" (Coleman, 1998, p. 38). In the meantime, in some economic sectors, corruption is carried out as part of everyday business policy (Schaupensteiner, 2004). It is accepted as normal business practice in many segments of the economy (Coleman, 1998, p. 38). In most countries between 2 and 10% of the total order value are paid as bribes, in some countries even more (Bannenberg & Schaupensteiner, 2004, p. 13).

Referring to the example of Germany again, it is obvious that corruption is no longer an exceptional case there; Germany can no longer claim its superiority over other societies (Schaupensteiner, 2004). Rather, corruption is regarded in Germany's public opinion as a mass phenomenon. In the 2007 annual report of the worldwide networked "coalition against corruption," Transparency International (TI) (Eigen, 2003), Germany kept its 16th place from the years before in the 2007 Corruption Perceptions Index among 163 countries (TI, 2005; TI, 2006; TI, 2007c) after it continuously improved its position from the 20th to the 15th place in the years 2000 to 2004 (TI, 2000; TI, 2001; TI, 2002; TI, 2003; TI, 2004). With this result, Germany only achieves the West-European mean (TI, 2007a). Nevertheless, as valid studies of the dark field are lacking, statements about increasing corruption as a form of white-collar crime are not easy to obtain. But an increasing awareness and increasing prevention and control definitely contribute to a higher detection rate (Bussmann, 2004).

With the "corruption eruption" (Glynn, Kobrin, & Naim, 1997, p. 8) in the mid nineties, ignorance of the phenomenon has been replaced by a strong sensitization. There is a broad global interest for anti-corruption efforts worldwide. The reasons are manifold (for a summary see Hotchkiss, 1998; Johnston, 2000, August; Pearson, 2001; Tanzi, 1998; Williams & Beare, 1999). In the business context, especially, the globalization and growing competitiveness of the world economy, an increasing international integration in economic and trade arenas, growing expectations regarding accountability and transparency, and the changing nature of the media seem to be important motivators (Johnston, 2000, August; Pearson, 2001; Tanzi, 1998; Williams & Beare, 1999). Moreover, movements to ban international corruption by both domestic legislation (e.g., the US Foreign Corrupt Practices Act), by international agreements of intergovernmental organizations (IGOs) like, for example, OECD, OAS, IMF, World Bank, and WTO (e.g., the OECD Convention on Combating Bribery of Foreign Public Officials in International Business Transactions and the OAS Inter-American Convention Against Corruption), and voluntary standards by non-governmental organizations (NGOs) like, for example, Transparency International (e.g., TI Anti-Corruption Handbook) (Hotchkiss, 1998; Johnston, 2000, August) reduced the tolerance for corruption.

This growing awareness of the corruption phenomenon also initiated a lot of interdisciplinary research that tries to examine corruption from different perspectives. Economics, sociology, social psychology, criminology, political science, and business ethics have made important contributions to our understanding of corruption and its causes and consequences (Amundsen, 1999; Andvig & Fjeldstad, 2001; Brünner, 1981a; Williams, 2000). Most research addresses political and public corruption, while private corruption, that is, corruption in and between companies, is still a neglected topic. Moreover, there is only little research that focuses on the person who acts corruptly. While there are a few data on personal characteristics and motives of corrupt actors, the interrelation of behavioral components causing a person to act corruptly has only rarely been investigated. That is why the present work aims at examining the person-based components of corrupt action in interaction with a specific situational context, namely the business context. My primary concern is to answer the following questions: What makes decision makers in companies act corruptly? Which motivational, volitional[1], emotional, and cognitive aspects play a role? How does their interplay lead to corrupt action? To answer these questions, I developed and empirically validated a model of corrupt action using an experimental simulation design combining a business game with a standardized questionnaire. Additionally, I investigated a number of selected personal and situational factors in relation to this model of corrupt action. Furthermore, I examined both the reasons given for a corrupt and non-corrupt decision as well as the rationalization strategies used by corrupt actors. As the empirical study was conducted in Germany, all country-specific aspects regarding corruption refer to the German context.

Thus, in summary, the present work makes a contribution to existing research in that it

- provides a literature review on the corruption phenomenon focusing on private corruption;

- offers insights into the subjective decision making processes of corrupt actors by providing an empirical validated model of corrupt action;

- examines the influence of a number of important personal and situational factors on the model of corrupt action;

- gives a picture of the frequently used reasons for corrupt and non-corrupt behavior;

- outlines the most frequently used rationalization strategies of corrupt actors.

The study also has important practical implications. Based on the results, it deduces recommendations for (human resource) management to prevent and combat private corruption.

1.2   Structure of the Study

The present work is organized into seven chapters, which follow the classical linear format starting with a theoretical part, continuing with an empirical part, and concluding with a discussion of results and implications. This shall help the reader to follow the deduction of the research question and the research hypotheses, to under-stand the development of the theoretical model, and to be able to relate to the methods and analyses used to come up with results that have both theoretical and

---

[1] Volitions are processes that determine which motivational tendencies should be realized. They seek to initiate action and realize the formed intention (Heckhausen, 1989, p. 17).

practical implications. The structure of the work is outlined in figure 1. A short description of each chapter's content is provided in the following.

Chapter 1 introduces the work by providing an overview of the motivation for the study as well as the work's research interest and focus.

Chapter 2 gives a literature review on the state of the art in corruption research. First, it tackles the problem of defining corruption. It outlines the main aspects of the corruption concept leading to an overall definition of corruption. After that, corruption is distinguished from related concepts and described as a classification of white-collar crime, deviant workplace behavior, and unethical behavior. A comparison of different forms of corruption follows. Then, the chapter summarizes the various causes of private corruption, including environmental, organizational, and personal factors. Following a similar structure, it outlines the consequences of private corruption for the environment, the organization, and the person. A presentation of theoretical approaches that describe the corrupt relationship follows. After that, the chapter examines the variety of theoretical approaches that have been used to explain the corruption phenomenon. The literature review closes with an overview on the problem of the normalization of corruption in organizations, including the description of rationalization and neutralization strategies.

Chapter 3 presents the theoretical framework and the research hypotheses. After deducing the research question, the research model is developed. The relevant reference models and theories are examined, followed by a discussion why they seem to be appropriate. The chapter closes with a description of the model of corrupt action. The relationships between the relevant person-based components of corrupt action described in the model are formulated as research hypotheses.

Chapter 4 introduces the methods used for empirically testing the model of corrupt action derived in Chapter 3. Following the discussion of the problem of an empirical investigation of corruption, the research design is described. Chapter 4 offers information on the research methods used for data collection, on the sample, as well as on the procedures followed in the study. It also discusses the relevant quality criteria. The chapter ends with a description of the techniques of analyses used to analyze and interpret the data gathered in the study.

Chapter 5 presents the results of the study. First, the results on the model of corrupt action and its evaluation are described. Further explorative results on sociodemographic and situational influence factors, on the reasons for the respective behavior, and on the rationalizations for corrupt behavior follow.

Chapter 6 discusses the empirical results in the light of the literature and gives an overview of managerial implications. It also addresses the limitations of the study and outlines avenues for future research.

Chapter 7 gives an overall summary of the work and outlines the work's contribution.

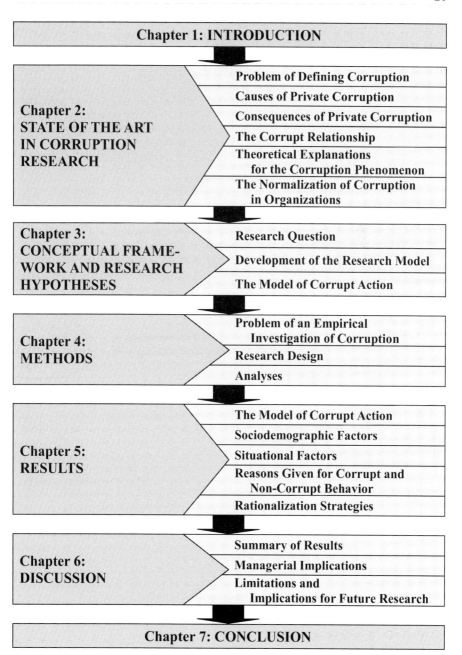

Figure 1:   The Structure of the Work

As the present work focuses on private corruption, please note that throughout the work the terms "company," "enterprise," "firm," and "organization" are used alternatively, always referring to a for-profit organization.

2 State of the Art in Corruption Research

There is a broad body of interdisciplinary research on corruption – a fact that on the one hand allows deeper insights into the phenomenon, but on the other hand makes it difficult to find a common denominator. Nevertheless, this variety of research approaches to corruption enables us to get a picture of its various facets. In the literature, there is a main focus on political corruption and on (international) public (including private-to-public) corruption. As my work aims at throwing light on private corruption in a national context but only little research has been done in this area, the following review of corruption research concentrates on those aspects relevant to my topic, also trying to transfer research results to private corruption where possible and necessary. The literature review starts with a discussion of the various attempts to define and conceptualize corruption. A reflection of the various causes and consequences of private corruption and a description of the corrupt relationship follows. Then, the review summarizes several major theoretical attempts to explain the corruption phenomenon before closing with a look at the normalization of corruption in organizations.

2.1 Problem of Defining Corruption

As corruption is a complex and multifaceted phenomenon, it is hard to define it in a short and precise way. The adjective "corrupt" has been borrowed from the Latin word "corrumpere" (Krug, 1997, p. 2; Scholz, 1995, p. 31). According to its linguistic origin, corruption characterizes actions such as "spoil, weaken, distort, erode, undermine, bribe, ruin, destroy" (Grieger, 2005, p. 3). The term is already used in the bible with a core meaning centered around injustice (Génaux, 2004). Despite a variety of definitions circulating within the sciences dealing with corruption (e.g., economics, law, sociology, social psychology, criminology, political science, theology), there is no universal conceptualization (Andvig & Fjeldstad, 2001). Various approaches to the phenomenon exist, each with a specific focus, be it the violation of legal norms, of moral values, or trust (Pies, Sass, & Meyer zu Schwabedissen, 2005).

2.1.1 Common Aspects of Definitions

Nevertheless, out of the number of definitions the following common dimensions of corruption can be derived (see Rabl & Kühlmann, 2006, November; Rabl & Kühlmann, 2008):

(1) Exchange

Corruption is based on the interaction between at least two partners (Alemann, 2004; Ashforth & Anand, 2003; Deflem, 1995; Getz & Volkema, 2001; Heidenheimer, 2002; Höffling, 2002, p. 25; Lapalombara, 1994; Maravic, 2006; Schwitzgebel, 2003; Warburton, 2001), between a supplier/corrupter and a recipient/corruptee, the person who induces or initiates the corrupt exchange and the person who accepts it (Deflem, 1995; Küchler, 1997; Neugebauer, 1978, p. 6; Schmidt, 2004, pp. 3 – 4; Streißler, 1981; Van Duyne, 2001). It is an exchange of benefit and reward that comes off voluntarily and takes place by mutual agreement (Engerer, 1998; Park, 2003; Schmidt, 2003; Van Klaveren, 1989). As the corrupt exchange aims at the successful realization of personally defined goals, it is an strategic interaction (Deflem, 1995).

(2) Violation of norms

Corruption is immoral behavior (e.g., Brasz, 1970; Van Duyne, 2001) that includes the deviation from legal norms[2] (e.g., Argandoña, 2005; Brünner, 1981b; Deflem, 1995; Eliasberg, 1951; Fischer, 1981; Freisitzer, 1981; Hacker, 1981; Khan, 1996; Luo, 2002; Neugebauer, 1978, p. 7; Nye, 1967; Schmidt, 2003; Streißler, 1981; Zimring & Johnson, 2005) or from moral values[3] (e.g., Argandoña, 2005; Brünner, 1981b; Brasz, 1970; Fischer, 1981; Freisitzer, 1981; Hacker, 1981; Schmidt, 2003; Streißler, 1981). For a decision on whether a conduct is corrupt or not from either a legal or moral point of view, local variations in law and culture have to be considered (Zimring & Johnson, 2005).

(3) Abuse of power

Corruption is seen as "criminality of the powerful" (Hardt, 2001, p. 50; see also Zimring & Johnson, 2005, p. 4). Corrupt actors utilize the authority, position, and/or knowledge entrusted to them for the sake of their advantage (e.g., Ashforth & Anand, 2003; Brasz, 1970; Brünner, 1981b; Clinard, 1990; Fischer, 1981; Freisitzer, 1981; Hardt, 2001; Huntington, 1989; Khan, 1996; Lambsdorff & Teksoz, 2002; Lapalombara, 1994; Neugebauer, 1978, p. 7; Noack, 1985; Nye, 1967; Pies et al., 2005; Pitt & Abratt, 1986; Rose-Ackerman, 1975; Rose-Ackerman, 2001; Schmidt, 2003; Tanzi, 1995a; Tanzi, 1998; Treisman, 2000; Van Duyne, 2001; Warburton, 2001; Zimring & Johnson, 2005). The application of power is a precondition for the success of corrupt action (Clinard, 1990; Luo, 2002; Van Duyne, 1999).

---

[2] Zimring and Johnson (2005) argue that only a legal standard can provide a definition of corruption that qualifies both analytically and morally as a crime, and thus allows a comparison with other offenses. The German criminal law does not know the term "corruption", but understands the acceptance and grantage of a bribe in business relationships (§§ 299, 300), the malpractices in office regulated in §§ 331 to 335 (acceptance and grantage of an advantage or a bribe) in addition to § 108b (bribery of electors) and § 108e StGB (bribery of members of parliament) as corruption (Bannenberg & Schaupensteiner, 2004, p. 25). Donations within the scope of socially accepted societal or business practices are in accordance with the commandment of courtesy or are accepted by the law of custom. A rule of thumb is that allowances up to the value of ten euros are not objectionable, while cash returns are not tolerated at all by law (Bannenberg & Schaupensteiner, 2004, p. 26). Regarding international corruption, in Germany the Law for the Combat of International Corruption (IntBestG) and the EU Bribery Law (EUBestG) are relevant (Schmidt, 2004, p. 4).

[3] Many processes identified as corrupt by the society are not seen as corrupt by (German) criminal law, like, for example, spoils system or nepotism (Bannenberg & Schaupensteiner, 2004, p. 29).

(4) Absence of direct victims

Corruption does not produce victims directly. Rather, there are only offenders who are involved in the corrupt act, and all gain an advantage by acting corruptly (Schmidt, 2004, p. 2; Zimring & Johnson, 2005). Victims are only found outside the corrupt relationship (Arnim, 2003; Hacker, 1981) – the reliable competitor who is squeezed out of the market by the corrupt competitors, the consumer who pays an exorbitant price, the tax-payer who pays exorbitant taxes, or the citizen who is at the mercy of a dishonest system, for example (Arnim, 2003). The real victims of the corrupt interaction are often unaware of the harm done to them (Deflem, 1995). As within the corrupt relationship no individual victims exist, this has direct consequences for detection[4]. Without a victim who makes a report, the judiciary is not able to intervene, and offenders who turn in themselves voluntarily are rare (Bannenberg & Schaupensteiner, 2004, p. 37; Zimring & Johnson, 2005).

(5) Secrecy

Corruption prospers in secrecy (Argandoña, 2005; Bannenberg & Schaupensteiner, 2004, p. 37; Brünner, 1981b; Fischer, 1981; Gorta, 2001; Graf, 2000; Hacker, 1981; Luo, 2002; Schmidt, 2003; Schwitzgebel, 2003; Van Duyne, 1999; Warburton, 2001). Corrupt actors form an intimate, close, and conspired community (Rügemer, 1996, p. 11) in which they secretly agree on the illegal aims and advantages of their exchange relationship (Hardt, 2001, p. 21). Apart from situational constraints, the possibility to continue the corrupt action mainly depends on the unimpaired victims' trust (Hacker, 1981; Warburton, 2001). The secrecy is also a reason for the difficulties in the detection, analysis, and measurement of the corruption phenomenon (Bannenberg & Schaupensteiner, 2004, pp. 37 – 40; Engerer, 1998).

When one combines these aspects, this leads to the following definition of corruption, a definition similar to the one also used by the German Federal Criminal Police Office:

Corruption is deviant behavior which manifests itself in an abuse of a function in politics, society, or economy in favor of another person or institution. This abuse of a function occurs on one's own or the other's initiative in order to achieve an advantage for oneself or a third party. As a result, a damage or disadvantage to politics, society, or economy is expected or does actually appear. The corrupt actions are kept secret in mutual, amicable agreement (Rabl & Kühlmann, 2008, p. 478; see also Rabl & Kühlmann, 2006; Rabl & Kühlmann, 2006, November; Vahlenkamp & Knauß, 1995, p. 20).

---

[4] In Germany, there is a large dark field of at least 95%, this means, out of 100 cases only five are detected (Bannenberg & Schaupensteiner, 2004, p. 38).

2.1.2 Corruption-Related Concepts

The difficulty in defining corruption also arises from a number of corruption-related concepts that are partially overlapping and at times interchangeable. In the following, I only sketch those concepts that identify some basic varieties of corruption that are also relevant in a business context (see Rabl & Kühlmann, 2006, November).

Bribery represents the essence of corruption; it can be understood as corruption per se. It is the payment in money or kind that is given or taken in a corrupt relationship. Many equivalent terms to bribery like kickbacks, baksheesh, sweeteners, grease money, facilitating payments, and pay-offs are all notions of corruption in terms of the money or favors paid to employees in private enterprises, public officials, and politicians. These are payments or returns needed or demanded to make things pass swiftly, smoothly, or more favorably through the private, state, or government bureaucracies (Amundsen, 1999; Andvig & Fjeldstad, 2001; Argandoña, 2005). Bribery must not be confused with gift giving. While a bribe implies reciprocity, a gift does not (Tanzi, 1998). A gift aims at expressing esteem, appreciation, gratitude, or good will, but not at obtaining a direct benefit (Argandoña, 2005).

A special variety of corruption is favoritism. In this case, power is abused to favor friends, family, and anybody close and trusted, which results in biased decisions regarding state or company resources. Another term used for favoritism based on social network ties is cronyism. Khatri, Tsang, and Begley (2006) define cronyism as a "reciprocal exchange transaction where party A shows favor to party B based on shared membership in a social network at the expense of party C's equal or superior claim to the valued resource" (p. 6). While horizontal cronyism occurs either intra- or interorganizational among peers, vertical cronyism occurs only within an organization in a superior-subordinate relationship (Khatri & Tsang, 2003). Cronyism is a subset of corruption that differs from the corruption concept in regard to the exchange aspect: Cronyism includes only reciprocal exchange because it includes just a favor given without explicitly specifying the return obligation. Corruption, in contrast, also includes a negotiated exchange where the parties agree on the terms of exchange with the benefits being readily apparent. Cronyism specific to family members is called nepotism. It is a special form of favoritism in which an office holder prefers his proper kinfolk and family members (Khatri et al., 2006).

Corruption is often accompanied by offenses that represent separate corpi delicti like, for example, embezzlement[5]; extortion[6]; fraud[7]; tax fraud; infidelity; anti-competitive arrangements; betrayal of industrial secrets; false certification; falsifica-

---

[5] Embezzlement is a theft of resources by people who are put to administer it (e.g., when disloyal employees steal from their employers) and a misappropriation of funds (Amundsen, 1999; Andvig & Fjeldstad, 2001). Embezzlement is clearly distinct from corruption because it does not include the interaction and exchange aspect, although it is a form of power abuse for private gain. Nevertheless, it is sometimes included in broader definitions of corruption (Amundsen, 1999; Andvig & Fjeldstad, 2001).

tion of documents, balance-sheets, or accountancy; cartelization; price fixing; money laundering; pseudo-payments for works/services not received; and wages for ghost workers (Rügemer, 1996, p. 48; Schmidt, 2004, p. 5).

There are some conceptions of corruption that explicitly include some of the offenses mentioned above – for example, those used by two[8] of the three major conventions, namely the Council of Europe Convention and the UN Convention[9]. There are other conceptions like, for example, the ones used by Transparency International[10] and the World Bank[11], which give a broad definition of corruption as the abuse of public or private office for personal gain. They do not specify which offenses exactly should be included in their conceptualization. It has to be carefully noted that these broader conceptions neglect important elements of a narrower definition (e.g., exchange, interaction of at least two partners).

2.1.3 Corruption – A Form of White-Collar Crime

Corruption or related concepts like bribery and illegal kickbacks are often treated as forms of white-collar crime (e.g., Clinard, 1990; Pies et al., 2005; Reasons, 1982; Sutherland, 1940; Weisburd & Waring, 2001; Zimring & Johnson, 2005). As in the case for corruption, no precise definition of white-collar crime exists (Weisburd & Waring, 2001, pp. 7 – 18; Vaughan, Gleave, & Welser, 2005, August). White-collar crime is defined by characteristics of the offender and of the offense itself (Zahra, Priem, & Rasheed, 2005). Edwin Sutherland, who introduced the term to the academic world (Geis, 1992), based his definition on the characteristics of the offender. He defines white-collar crime as "a crime committed by a person of respectability and high social status in the course of his occupation" (Sutherland, 1949, p. 9). Geis (1992) also argues that white-collar crime involves the "abuse of power by persons who are situated in high places where they are provided with the opportunity for such abuse" (p. 47). Reasons (1982) sees it as a "crime committed by a person in a position of trust for his or her personal gain" (p. 59). Herbert Edelhertz, in contrast, focuses on the work context defining white-collar crime as "an illegal act or series of illegal acts committed by nonphysical means and by concealment or

---

[6] Extortion is money and other resources extracted by the use of coercion, violence, or the threats to use force (Amundsen, 1999; Andvig & Fjeldstad, 2001). Although extortion is basically seen as a corrupt transaction (Amundsen, 1999; Andvig & Fjeldstad, 2001), it does not include the amicable exchange relationship based on mutual agreement inherent in corruption per se.

[7] Fraud is an economic crime involving some kind of trickery, swindle, or deceit (Amundsen, 1999; Andvig & Fjeldstad, 2001). Fraud is a much broader term than corruption that covers both bribery and embezzlement (Amundsen, 1999; Andvig & Fjeldstad, 2001). While corruption is an exchange relationship, fraud can be committed as a solitary act (Van Duyne, 2001).

[8] The OECD Convention focuses on different kinds of bribery offenses (Organisation for Economic Co-operation and Development (OECD), 2007).

[9] For a detailed list of included offenses see OECD (2007).

[10] See TI (2005, p. 24) or http://www.transparency.org/news_room/faq/corruption_faq.

[11] See Tanzi (1998, p. 564) and Wei (1999, p. 4).

guile, to obtain money or property, to avoid the payment or loss of money or property, or to obtain business or personal advantage" (Edelhertz, 1970, p. 3). The US
National White Collar Crime Center provides a "consensus definition" (Coleman,
1998, p. 7) of white-collar crime: "White collar crimes are illegal or unethical acts
that violate fiduciary responsibility of public trust committed by an individual or
organization, usually during the course of legitimate occupational activity, by
persons of high or respectable social status for personal or organizational
gain" (Helmkamp, Ball, & Townsend, 1996, p. 351). White-collar crime does not
require that the act is punished, only that it is punishable (Stitt & Giacopassi, 1993,
p. 59). From these definitions, it became apparent that white-collar crime has similar
characteristics to corruption. White-collar crime is also characterized by an abuse of
power, a violation of legal norms or deviation from societal norms, an abuse of business instruments, social harmfulness, exertion within an occupational activity,
secrecy, the absence of physical violence, monetary or natural profit or private or
commercial advantage as aim, and the involvement of individuals who are otherwise
considered respectable members of society (Löw, 2002; Zahra et al., 2005).

Clinard and Quinney (1973) divide white-collar crimes into occupational crime and
corporate crime. Occupational crime "consists of the offenses committed by individuals for themselves in the course of their occupations and the offenses of employees
against their employers" (Clinard & Quinney, 1973, p. 188). As an occupational
crime, corruption against the organization may, for example, include self-dealing or
padding expense reports (Grieger, 2005; Zahra et al., 2005). Corporate crime, in
contrast, "consists of the offenses committed by corporate officials for their corporation and the offenses of the corporation itself" (Clinard & Quinney, 1973, p. 188).
The term "organizational crime" is broader and includes both corporate and non-
corporate crimes (Coleman, 1998, p. 12). As corporate or organizational crime,
corruption on behalf of the organization may, for example, include bribery (Grieger,
2005; Zahra et al., 2005). Thus, what applies for white-collar crimes also applies for
corruption: There are corrupt acts in which either an individual is the only one who
benefits and the organization is the victim, or in which the organization is the beneficiary and others in society are the victims, or in which both the organization and the
individual acting on behalf of the organization are beneficiaries and others in society
are the victims (Zahra et al., 2005).

2.1.4 Corruption – A Form of Deviant Workplace Behavior

In the literature, corruption is not only labeled as white-collar crime, but also often
regarded as a kind of deviant workplace behavior (e.g., Grieger, 2005; Robinson &
Bennett, 1995). Robinson and Bennett (1995) define deviant workplace behavior of
employees as "voluntary behavior that violates significant organizational norms and
in doing so threatens the well-being of an organization, its members, or both" (p.
556). They provide a two-dimensional configuration of deviant workplace behaviors.
The first dimension, the organizational-interpersonal dimension, represents the target
of the deviant behavior. It ranges from deviant behavior aimed at the organization to

deviant behavior primarily directed at a member of the organization. The second dimension represents the severity of the deviant behavior. Deviant behavior on this dimension varies on a continuum from minor to serious forms. This configuration results in four classifications of deviant behavior: production deviance, political deviance, property deviance, and personal aggression (Robinson & Bennett, 1995; see also Appelbaum, Deguire, & Lay, 2005, and Litzky, Eddleston, & Kidder, 2006). If it includes accepting kickbacks, corruption, on the one hand, can be classified as property deviance, which represents "those instances where employees acquire or damage the tangible property or assets of the work organization without authorization" (Robinson & Bennett, 1995, p. 565). In this form, corruption is deviant behavior directed at the organization with high severity (Robinson & Bennett, 1995) and having negative effects on an organization's bottom line (Litzky et al., 2006). On the other hand, if it includes showing favoritism, corruption can be classified as political deviance, which represents "engagement in social interaction that puts other individuals at a personal or political disadvantage" (Robinson & Bennett, 1995, p. 566). In this form, corruption is deviant behavior directed at members of the organization with low severity (Robinson & Bennett, 1995) and generating costs to the organization resulting from inconsistent service quality, dissatisfaction, and perceptions of unfairness (Litzky et al., 2006).

2.1.5 Corruption – A Form of Unethical Behavior

As the vast body of literature on ethical behavior in organizations shows, it is generally assumed that corruption represents a form of unethical behavior. Empirical studies (e.g., Mitchell, Lewis, & Reinsch, Jr., 1992; Vitell & Festervand, 1987) found corruption or related concepts like bribery or giving kickbacks to be judged as unethical behavior. Thus, "the antithesis of ethics versus corruption is obvious" (Zekos, 2004, p. 644). In contrast to deviant behavior, which focuses on the violation of organizational norms, unethical behavior deals with the breaking of societal rules (Appelbaum & Shapiro, 2006). The focus on business ethics has generated interest in trying to define what is unethical (Mitchell, Daniels, Hopper, George-Falvy, & Ferris, 1996). Unethical encompasses more than illegal (Mitchell et al., 1996) because ethics is a more general set of moral principles or values (Lynch, Lynch, & Cruise, 2002; Mitchell et al., 1996; Pelletier & Bligh, 2006) that determines what is good or bad, right or wrong, with moral duty and obligation or without (Mitchell et al., 1996; Pelletier & Bligh, 2006; Roozen, De Pelsmacker, & Bostyn, 2001). Thus, illegal behavior partially overlaps with unethical behavior: "Some action could be illegal and ethical and there are certainly legal behaviors which could be seen as unethical" (Mitchell et al., 1996, p. 441). Corruption is both illegal and unethical behavior.

A deontological viewpoint based on the recognition of duties applying Kant's categorical imperative[12] allows corruption to be classified as unethical because due to the universal duty of renouncing corruption regardless of the consequences of its exercise, corruption and its means, despite plausible positive ends, are wrong (Salbu, 2001). From a teleological point of view, an ethical actor aims at maximizing net social utility. The rule utilitarian conducts this social cost-benefit analysis taking into account all cases, the act utilitarian only considering a particular situation. Regarding the harmful consequences of corruption (see chap. 2.3, p. 59), only in the second case is a moral justification of corruption plausible (Salbu, 2001).

2.1.6 Forms of Corruption

The number of attempts to categorize different forms of corruption also contributes to the difficulties in conceptualizing the phenomenon. In this work, I only discuss categorizations of corruption that help to clarify corruption in and between companies (see for further distinctions Amundsen, 1999, and Shleifer & Vishny, 1998).

(1) Public versus private corruption

A frequent classification especially relevant to my research is the functional distinction between public and private corruption. While public corruption occurs when the person being corrupted holds a public office, regardless whether the corrupting person is a private or public official, private corruption occurs when bribes are demanded or supplied by employees of companies (Brünner, 1981b). It is

the type of corruption that occurs when a manager or employee exercises a certain power or influence over the performance of a function, task or responsibility within a private organization or corporation. Because he has a margin of discretion, he can choose to act contrary to the duties and responsibilities of his post or job, and thus in a way that directly or indirectly harms the company or organization, for his own benefit or for that of another person, company or organization (Argandoña, 2003, p. 255).

The most obvious situation of private corruption is the negotiation of contracts in which the negotiator offers or demands an extra in return for the order (Van Duyne, 2001).

---

[12] A first formulation of the Kantian categorical imperative is: "Act only in accordance with that maxim through which you can at the same time will that it become a universal law" (Kant, 2002, p. 37).

(2) National versus international corruption

National corruption refers to corrupt acts that are confined to the territory of a single country. International corruption includes corrupt acts of parties belonging to different countries, corrupt acts with payments to another country, or payments through intermediaries in another country (Argandoña, 2005).

(3) Isolated versus systemic and situational versus structural corruption

Based on the dimensions of corruption frequency (isolated versus systemic) and stability of the corrupt relationship (situational versus structural) Höffling (2002, chap. 2) distinguishes the following forms:

(a) Isolated situational corruption: These are corrupt acts committed reactively when the situation offers an opportunity. They are not intended to be repeated. Mostly, only a few persons are involved. They only have a superficial acquaintance with each other. The risk of failing when initiating a corrupt transaction is comparatively high. Against the background of the normative attitude of the social environment, corruption is seen as deviant behavior that has to be disapproved (see also Bannenberg, 2002, pp. 97 – 103, and Bannenberg, 2003b, who terms this type of corruption "single case corruption," "corruption by opportunity," or "bagatelle corruption").

(b) Isolated structural corruption: Corruption of this type is limited to strong, long-term relationships. The corrupt acts are planned in advance, take longer time to realize, and are intended to be repeated. Only some few actors are involved who invest a great deal of effort to keep their behavior secret and have a big trust in the willingness to cooperate with each other. Both parties depend on keeping the secrecy and trust because corruption does not comply with the expectations of the social environment (see also Bannenberg, 2002, pp. 103 – 108, and Bannenberg, 2003b, who terms this type of corruption "grown relationships").

(c) Systemic situational corruption: This form of corruption originates in an environment where corruption is normality. The corrupt exchange can be conducted with an unknown partner without high risk of rejection and prosecution. Corruption is public practice ("petty corruption").

(d) Systemic structural corruption includes corruption occurring in long-lasting social relationships. The social environment does not regard the abuse of a function for personal gain as deviant behavior, but accepts, excuses, and even facilitates it. Often, corruption is associated with other crime, like, for example, tax fraud. Under these conditions, corruption tends to spread; corruption networks and corruption cartels develop. Imitators are easy to find. It is difficult to leave the network. A number of possibilities to justify the corrupt behavior exist (see also Bannenberg, 2002, pp. 108 – 111, and Bannenberg, 2003b, who terms this type of corruption "networks" and "organized white-collar crime").

(4) Personal versus collective corruption

On the one hand, corruption can occur as deviant behavior of a single actor within an organization (Brief, Buttram, & Dukerich, 2001; Brünner, 1981b), which is called "personal corruption" or "corruption in the group" (Brünner, 1981b, p. 681). On the other hand, if corruption is tolerated by the group and group-specific structures and institutions advance corruption (Brünner, 1981b), "collective corruption" (Brief et al., 2001, p. 471) or "corruption of the group" (Brünner, 1981b, p. 681) occurs. When collective efforts are taken to establish corrupt relationships or networks, this may result in corruption penetrating the organization and becoming part of its structure (Grieger, 2005).

(5) White versus grey versus black corruption

Heidenheimer (2002) named three categories of corruption according to social perceptions in the context of several sorts of political systems that seem to be also relevant for corruption within the private sector:

(a) White corruption: White corruption indicates that corrupt behavior is tolerated by the majority (Alemann, 2004; Heidenheimer, 2002; Zimring & Johnson, 2005). There is no wish to punish corrupt conduct (Zimring & Johnson, 2005).

(b) Grey corruption: In the case of grey corruption, corruption is regarded as reprehensible according to accepted moral standards, but nevertheless the involved actors are lacking any sense of doing something wrong (Alemann, 2004; Heidenheimer, 2002). Thus, there are some people who want corrupt action to be punished, while others do not, with a majority being ambivalent (Zimring & Johnson, 2005).

(c) Black corruption: Black corruption exists when corruption is generally condemned and punished as a severe violation of moral standards and the law (Alemann, 2004; Heidenheimer, 2002; Zimring & Johnson, 2005).

(6) Demand-driven corruption (passive corruption) versus supply-driven corruption (active corruption)

The initiative to corrupt acts can either be demand-driven and come from the person who receives the payment or supply-driven and come from the person who pays. Active corruption is the offense committed by the person who promises or gives the bribe as contrasted to passive corruption, which is the offense committed by the person who receives the bribe (Argandoña, 2005; Manandhar, 2005, p. 6).

(7) Market corruption versus parochial corruption

Market corruption is a competitive type of corruption with a high degree of transparency where the identity of the partner is irrelevant. Parochial corruption is a transaction with few potential contractors and restricted competition where the identity of partners matters due to limited entry and exit (Lambsdorff, 2002).

(8) Grand versus petty corruption

Corruption is differentiated in respect to whether it involves large payments and large effects (grand corruption) or whether it involves facilitating payments (petty corruption) (Argandoña, 2005; Manandhar, 2005, p. 5).

(9) Debiting and crediting corruption

In regard to public corruption, Pies (2003) distinguishes between debiting and crediting corruption, depending on the effect of corruption on the company. In the case of debiting corruption, the company is forced to pay a higher price than the official one for the bureaucrat's service. Thus, the company is debited compared to the case without corruption. A conflict of interests exists. The company is the victim. Crediting corruption occurs when a bureaucrat and a company secretly agree on a lower price than the official one. The company has lower costs than in the case of corruption. A harmony of interests exists. Third parties are the victim. Regarding private corruption, I assume most cases to be cases of crediting corruption, except cases where one of the partners has monopoly power.

2.1.7 Summary

The multidisciplinarity of corruption research, in addition to the variety of catego- rizations of corruption, allow no universal conceptualization of the phenomenon. This work is based on the corruption definition outlined on page 25, which summa- rizes the main characteristics of the phenomenon. As the empirical part examines the German case, all country-specific aspects of the definition – this means the legal norms and moral values – refer to Germany. The focus of this work is on private corruption where bribes are demanded or supplied by employees of companies.

2.2   Causes of Private Corruption

Research on the causes of corruption has almost exclusively focused on public and political corruption, in addition to international corruption. Thus, in the following, I provide a framework of factors with a relevant influence on private corruption.

All criminal behavior – and therefore also corrupt behavior – requires both motiva- tion and opportunity (Albrecht, McDermott, & Williams, 1994; Baucus, 1994; Coleman, 1998, p. 176; Finney & Lesieur, 1982; Löw, 2002; Maravic, 2006; McKendall, DeMarr, & Jones-Rikkers, 2002). The literature argues that the motiva- tion and opportunity to engage in corruption are the product of three factors, varying from situation to situation in shape and effect: environmental, organizational, and personal factors (Ashforth & Anand, 2003; Grieger, 2005). A person (respectively an employee) always acts within a certain organization, and an organization always acts within a specific environmental context. Thus, although my research solely focuses on the person who acts corruptly, in the following, I outline how all of these three factors – environmental, organizational, and personal – may determine an individu- al's corrupt behavior.

2.2.1 Environmental Factors

"Corruption corrupts" (Andvig & Fjeldstad, 2001, p. 91). Thus, private corruption is more likely if the organization acts in an environment that is prone to corruption. The environmental factors that have an influence on private corruption can be divided into four sectors: culture, law, society, and economy. As the political factors identified in the literature are only relevant for political and public corruption, they are neglected in the following, but referred to if conclusions can be drawn for aspects concerning private corruption.

Culture

The prevalence of corruption in different countries differs widely (Gaviria, 2002). Should one ask businesspersons, they would assert that in some countries, doing business is even impossible without acting corruptly (Getz & Volkema, 2001). This is due to the varying tolerance of corruption from country to country (Getz & Volkema, 2001). As Andvig and Fjeldstad (2001) state: "The borderline for acceptable behaviour is not universal" (p. 59). What is seen as corruption in one culture may not be seen as corruption in another. This is called the "cultural relativity" (Collier, 2002, p. 7) of corruption. The same behavior is perceived differently – once it is endorsed, once it is tolerated, and once it is prosecuted (Fleck & Kuzmics, 1985). Several empirical research findings underline the culture-boundedness of corruption (e.g., Cherry, 2006; Johnson, Kaufmann, McMillan, & Woodruff, 2000; Killias & Ribeaud, 1999; Park, 2003; Su & Richelieu, 1999; Treisman, 2000; Tsalikis & LaTour, 1995).

A typical example demonstrating this cultural relativity is the guanxi-phenomenon in China (Chan, Cheng, & Szeto, 2002). Guanxi involves "relationships between or among individuals creating obligations for the continued exchange of favors" (Dunfee & Warren, 2001, p. 192). While for some, especially Westerners, guanxi can hardly be distinguished from corruption (Chan et al., 2002; Dunfee & Warren, 2001; Steidlmeier, 1999; Su & Littlefield, 2001), others, especially the Chinese from their own cultural perspective, defend the ethicality and morality of guanxi, regarding it as necessary for establishing trust and long-term relationships (Chan et al., 2002; Dunfee & Warren, 2001; Steidlmeier, 1999). Fan (2002) argues that guanxi allows corruption to flourish. Millington, Eberhardt, and Wilkinson (2005), in contrast, only found a weak relationship between illicit payments and the established understanding of gift giving within guanxi networks. Luo (2002) outlines nine differences between corruption and guanxi:

> Guanxi is an ingredient of social norm, whereas corruption deviates from social norm. [...] Guanxi is legal, whereas corruption is illegal. [...] Guanxi essentially builds on favor exchange, whereas corruption mostly involves monetary exchange. [...] Guanxi involves implicit, social reciprocity, whereas corruption pertains to explicit, transactional reciprocity. [...] Guanxi does not involve any lawful risks if it fails, whereas corruption is linked to high legal

risks and uncertainties. [...] Guanxi builds on a long-term orientation, whereas corruption deals with a short-term transaction. [...] Guanxi does not specify a time limit, whereas corruption often requires timeliness. [...] Guanxi builds on trust, whereas corruption is based on commodity. [...] Guanxi is transferable, whereas corruption is not (pp. 412 – 414).

Corruption may be the result of cultures and cultural value systems that tolerate, rather than condemn, corrupt activities (Beets, 2005). The norms and values of a specific culture influence the individual's behavior (Grieger, 2005). As cultural values also influence decisions on whether to act corruptly or not, they have to be considered in the study of corruption (Getz & Volkema, 2001). Some empirical studies investigated relationships between universal cultural dimensions and corruption. Corruption was significantly and positively related to the following of Hofstede's (1980) dimensions:

- to power distance (Davis & Ruhe, 2003; Getz & Volkema, 2001; Husted, 1999; Sanyal, 2005), "the extent to which the members of a society accept that power in institutions and organizations is distributed unequally" (Hofstede, 1984, p. 83);

- to uncertainty avoidance (Getz & Volkema, 2001; Husted, 1999), "the degree to which the members of a society feel uncomfortable with uncertainty and ambiguity" (Hofstede, 1984, p. 83);

- to masculinity (Davis & Ruhe, 2003; Husted, 1999; Sanyal, 2005), "a preference in society for achievement, heroism, assertiveness, and material success" (Hofstede, 1984, p. 84);

- to collectivism[13] (Davis & Ruhe, 2003), "a preference for a tightly knit social framework in which individuals can expect their relatives, clan, or other in-group to look after them in exchange for unquestioning loyalty" (Hofstede, 1984, p. 83).

Mallinger, Rossy, and Singel (2005) using the GLOBE study's dimensions (House, Hanges, Javidan, Dorfman, & Gupta, 2005) also found a significant relationship between corruption and uncertainty avoidance defined as "the extent to which members of collectives seek orderliness, consistency, structure, formalized procedures, and laws to cover situations in their daily lives" (Sully de Luque & Javidan, 2005, p. 603). But in contrast to the studies using Hofstede's dimensions, they found that the greater the uncertainty avoidance, the less likely corrupt practices occurred. They argue that in countries showing high uncertainty avoidance, specific policies and procedures for conduct in addition to a well-enforced legal environment contribute to a reduction of corruption. Getz and Volkema (2001), in contrast, explain their contrary finding arguing that an individual may use corruption to

---

[13] In Husted's (1999) study, individualism failed to be significant due to the fact that it was highly correlated with the gross national product (GNP) per capita that also entered the regression model.

circumvent the imposed rules. Martin, Cullen, Johnson, and Parboteeah (2007) also based their study on the cultural dimensions used in the GLOBE study (House et al., 2005). Contrary to the finding by Davis and Ruhe (2003), they found a negative relationship between corruption and in-group collectivism addressing the degree of group cohesiveness and loyalty (Gelfand, Bhawuk, Nishii, & Bechtold, 2005). Davis and Ruhe (2003) explain the positive relationship of corruption with collectivism by multiple competing values in collectivist societies rather than one single standard that applies to everyone as well as by staffing and appraisal procedures relying on seniority and personal connections rather than on performance. Martin et al. (2007), in contrast, argue that more individualistic societies are more likely to engage in corrupt activity because of their stronger drives for success at the expense of the collective. Additionally, their results underline that other environmental factors moderate the effects of cultural dimensions on corruption. In their study, high levels of welfare socialism and political constraints offset the power of achievement motivation and in-group collectivism in leading to corrupt action, while high levels of welfare socialism but not political constraints enhanced the corruption-reducing effect of humane orientation.

Another cultural aspect determining corruption is religion. Several empirical studies found that countries with lower perceived corruption followed the Protestant traditions rather than being dominated by hierarchical religions (La Porta, Lopez-de-Silanes, Shleifer, & Vishny, 1999; Paldam, 2001; Sandholtz & Koetzle, 2000; Treisman, 2000). Treisman (2000) explains this by the fact that office holders may have less coverage through hierarchy. La Porta et al. (1999) argue that Protestant societies keep to social norms encouraging their members to denounce malfeasant actors.

Furthermore, the country's colonial history was found to play a role in determining its actual level of corruption (Serra, 2006; Swamy, Knack, Lee, & Azfar, 2001; Treisman, 2000). Swamy et al.'s (2001) and Treisman's (2000) results showed former British colonies as well as the United Kingdom to be less corrupt. The experience of British rule imprinted in these societies may have created a respect for the rule of law and procedural justice.

There is mixed evidence for the impact of ethnic and linguistic fractionalization on corruption. While Treisman (2000) found no relationship, La Porta et al.'s (1999) and Alesina, Devleeschauwer, Easterly, Kurlat, and Wacziarg's (2003) results showed ethno-linguistic diversity to be associated with corruption.

Law

Besides cultural determinants, weaknesses in a country's legal sector are relevant for the occurrence of private corruption. Ali and Isse (2003) found judicial inefficiency to be related with corruption. This judicial inefficiency can be a consequence of political instability (Damania et al., 2004)[14]. A breakdown of the legal order creates legal uncertainty, which in turn promotes corruption, especially in developing countries (Ades & Di Tella, 1996; Heberer, 1991, p. 29; Heberer, 2001; Sanyal, 2005). Corruption does not only tend to be greater in countries with a unstable legal framework (Lambert-Mogiliansky, 2002). Rather, often a complex legislation (Lambert-Mogiliansky, 2002) and a lack of transparency in laws provide a fertile ground for corruption (Tanzi, 1998). Laws written in the lawyers' professional language are difficult to understand, sometimes remain unclear, and thus provide scope for interpretation (Tanzi, 1998).

The tax deductibility of bribes in some countries was shown to determine the propensity to act corruptly (Sanyal & Samanta, 2004a). If there is the possibility for companies to count the costs of corruption to the costs of doing business, and thus benefit from reduced tax liability, this advances corruption.

Another facilitating factor is a lack of law enforcement (Nye, 1967; Sanyal, 2005). In this context, a lack of an independent and impartial judiciary even fosters corruption (Manandhar, 2005; Sanyal, 2005). The fact that penalties are seldom applied as specified in the law and that the administrative processes up to punishment are slow and cumbersome (Tanzi, 1998) makes its contribution. The greater the time gap between the illegal behavior and the penalization, the lower the efficiency of sanctions (Steinrücken, 2004). As subjective perceptions about the probability of punishment are formed by observing past rates of punishment (Sah, 1991), a deterring effect only occurs when there is both a communicated risk of detection and a consequent sanction (Bussmann, 2004).

The penalties' structure is also relevant. Tanzi (1998) theoretically argues that on the one hand, higher penalties may reduce the frequency of corrupt acts, but on the other hand, they may lead to higher bribes paid and demanded in the corrupt acts that still occur. In addition to the theoretical arguments (Borner & Schwyzer, 1999; Lui, 1986), there is also empirical evidence that the motivation to act corruptly increases with a lower degree of penalty (Abbink, Irlenbusch, & Renner, 2002; Goel & Rich, 1989). Studies on other unethical behavior also underline this finding (Buckley, Wiese, & Harvey, 1998; Carnes & Englebrecht, 1995). To be effective, penalties for corruption have to be proportional to the bribe in the case of the corruptee and proportional to the additional gain achieved through corruption in case of the corruptor (Streißler, 1981). But high penalties fail when corrupt actors see themselves as gamblers in a lottery (Cadot, 1987) and when there is a low probability of being adjudged and of early penalization (Steinrücken, 2004). According to Vogt (1997, p. 53), the risk of getting a medium penalty depends on the probability of

---

[14] In Damania, Fredriksson, and Mani's (2004) study, judicial inefficiency was discovered as a mediator variable in the relationship between political instability and corruption. This finding was also confirmed by other authors (e.g., Serra, 2006; Treisman, 2000).

being detected, the probability of being accused, and the probability of being sentenced.

Society

A third set of environmental factors determining corruption concerns a country's society. It is often stated that a decay of moral norms and values is responsible for the increasing number of corruption cases (Heberer, 2001; Morgan, 1998). Bunz's (2005) study confirmed such a societal change in values for Germany: German leaders observed an increasing tendency to individualism and egoism, a lack of public spirit, a greed for money, a lack of security and orientation, a lack of morale, and a lack of leadership examples. Although morale was seen as important for the functioning of both economy and society, the leader's moral awareness was judged as decreasing or at least as changing. Thus, the negative examples given by members of higher social levels foster corruption (Freisitzer, 1981). Bussmann (2004) argues that it is not a general erosion of values in society, but rather a fragmentation of norm validity and its context sensitive application that encourages crimes like corruption. The higher the perceived corruption, the more likely is real corrupt action (Cabelkova & Hanousek, 2004).

A country's press and media play an important role for the perception of corruption and therefore also for the level of corruption. Ahrend (2002), Brunetti and Weder (2003), and Treisman (2000) found that a free press effectively deterred corruption. A free press gives both the mission and the right to the exposure of unethical offenses (Treisman, 2000). Graeff (2004) showed that not only the independence of media, but also the extent of media usage, measured by the number of Internet hosts and expenses for information and communication, decreased the corruption level. This press and media influence also provides public control, whose absence promotes corruption (Heberer, 1991, p. 29; Heberer, 2001; Priddat, 2004).

Especially in countries where there is a loophole regarding corruption, society and its morality is an important control instrument. If corruption is not condemned by public opinion, it spreads because corrupt actors' behavior is not regarded as deviant (Krug, 1997, p.139).

The characteristics of a country's population are also related to perceived corruption. Beets' (2005) results showed that those nations with a higher level of perceived corruption had a relatively rural population, smaller percentages of middle-aged citizens (15 to 64), fewer citizens either employed or seeking employment, larger households, higher fertility rates, shorter life expectancies, and larger percentages of national consumption attributable to the wealthiest citizens. They also accepted economic aid from other countries. Mocan's (2004) study also confirmed the relationship between a country's unemployment rate and corruption. Corruption was also found to be higher in less educated societies where human development was inhibited (Ali & Isse, 2003; Beets, 2005; Emerson, 2006; Espejo, Bula, & Zarama, 2001; Sanyal & Samanta, 2004b; Treisman, 2000). Changes in the human development scores, particularly for developed countries, were associated with changes in the corruption level, showing that in developing countries, other culture-related factors were more important (Sanyal & Samanta, 2004b). Furthermore, corruption was found to be lower in countries with a higher degree of female participation to public life (Dollar, Fisman, & Gatti, 2001; Swamy et al., 2001).

Social and economic inequality also count among the important determinants of corruption (Heberer, 1991, p. 29; Heberer, 2001; Husted, 1999; Smelser, 1985). Income inequality, especially, was found to promote corruption (Goel & Rich, 1989; Jong-sung & Khagram, 2005; Sanyal, 2005). Jong-sung and Khagram (2005) argue that inequality also adversely affects social norms regarding corruption and people's beliefs about the legitimacy of rules and institutions, thereby making it easier for them to tolerate corruption as acceptable behavior.

Economy

The most important environmental factor relevant for private corruption concerns a country's economy.

First, the structure of the economic system plays a role. A highly complex economic system offers the opportunity for corruption because of the greater number of important decisions that have to be made that also affect others' property and interest (Zimring & Johnson, 2005).

Second, corruption is related to both the wealth and the growth of a country's economy. Several empirical studies found a positive relationship to economic adversity and poverty (Beets, 2005; Getz & Volkema, 2001), in addition to a negative relationship to economic growth (Mauro, 1997; Paldam, 2002; Serra, 2006; Treisman, 2000) mostly measured by using the gross domestic product (GDP) per capita.

Third, countries with large endowments of natural resources are more susceptible to corruption. Such resources create opportunities to exploit the associated rents. This behavior may have spillover effects to other segments of the society (Ades & Di Tella, 1999; Leite & Weidmann, 1999).

Fourth, lacking openness to trade was found to increase the level of corruption (Ades & Di Tella, 1999; Sandholtz & Gray, 2003; Sandholtz & Koetzle, 2000; Treisman, 2000; Wei, 2000a). Even low foreign direct investment (FDI) flows in the past positively affected corruption (Kwok & Tadesse, 2006). It is argued that corrupt practices can perpetuate themselves more easily in closed economies (Sandholtz & Gray, 2003) because domestic firms are cut off from foreign competition (Ades & Di Tella, 1999) and therefore have less to gain from curbing corruption (Wei, 2000a) and benefit from higher rents (Treisman, 2000). Countries integrated into international society do not only face economic pressures but also norms that legitimate and stigmatize corruption (Sandholtz & Gray, 2003).

Fifth, the extent of economic competition is associated with corruption. Empirical studies showed that higher competition lowered the level of corruption (Ades & Di

Tella, 1999; Clarke & Xu, 2002, Emerson, 2006) because of an increased supply, lower rents, and the possibility to switch to other suppliers if a bribe is demanded (Ades & Di Tella, 1999; Laffont & N'Guessan, 1999; Rose-Ackerman, 1978; Shleifer & Vishny, 1993; Streißler, 1981). This contradicts theoretical arguments. Only perfect competition in a perfect market with a great number of small suppliers and demanders, complete market transparency, and homogeneous products prevents corruption (Rose-Ackerman, 1978, pp. 200 – 209; Streißler, 1981). If some of these conditions are violated, trying to change them to approach the ideal may increase the level of corporate corruption (Rose-Ackerman, 1978, p. 208). Monopolistic or oligopolistic markets are especially conducive to corruption when either the demander or the supplier is alone or very powerful among few in the market (Streißler, 1981). Kugel and Gruenberg (1977) argue: "Since oligopoly markets are characterized by a lack of price competition, international payoffs become a kind of nonprice competition" (p. 36). The same is true for a market of inhomogeneous goods with lacking information about the goods' prices and qualities and therefore no standard market price (Rose-Ackerman, 1978, p. 201; Streißler, 1981). Under such conditions, high competition leads to the fact that not the best offer but the bribe decides who gets the contract (Geis, 1997): The greater the competition, the greater the need to act corruptly (Clinard, 1990, p. 132; Coleman, 1998, p. 201). Thus, corruption occurs where the market and competition cannot develop sufficiently (Ockenfels, 1997). Empirical evidence on ethical decision making also showed mixed results regarding the level of overall business competitiveness (Ford & Richardson, 1994). But both Hegarty and Sims (1978) and Martin et al. (2007) found higher corruption under increased competition or increased perceived competitive intensity.

Sixth, according to empirical results, the smaller the economic freedom and the higher governmental restraints and interventions, the more likely is corruption (Ades & Di Tella, 1997; Ali & Isse, 2003; Paldam, 2002; Park, 2003; Sanyal & Samanta, 2004a; Sanyal & Samanta, 2004b). Corrupt payments between firms are used to circumvent government regulations. The restriction of private transactions (e.g., price controls, rationing) by legislation creates payoff opportunities and thus provides corrupt incentives (Rose-Ackerman, 1978, p. 206). But Sanyal and Samanta (2004b) showed that changes in economic freedom resulted in changes in perceived corruption for developed countries but not for developing countries.

Seventh, if one company in a market acts corruptly and is successful, its behavior finds imitators (Krug, 1997, p. 67). Thus, once corruption is experienced as a successful means to achieve advantages, its attractiveness is enhanced (Coleman, 1998, p. 204).

Finally, certain industries are more prone to commit illegal acts (Baucus & Near, 1991) like corruption. The construction, engineering, commodity, and equipment industries are especially vulnerable because of the scale of the venture, strong competition, and increased likelihood of corrupt payoffs (Lane & Simpson, 1984).

While in Ford and Richardson's (1994) and Loe, Ferrell, and Mansfield's (2000) reviews two of the three reported studies relating industry type to ethical decision making did not result in significant findings, in O'Fallon and Butterfield's (2005) review only one study out of nine produced no significant finding. In Martin et al.'s (2007) study, in contrast, industry was no significant determinant of corruption. Due to the fact that different industries were examined in various studies, no overall conclusions can be drawn (O'Fallon & Butterfield, 2005). Daboub, Rasheed, Priem, and Gray (1995) summarize five ways the industry type may influence the commission of illegal acts – by industry culture[15], by organizational isomorphism (imitating behavior through observation of and interaction with other firms in that industry), by the pressures exerted by the industry, by the industry's structure (market perfection or imperfection), and by the industry's vulnerability to regulation, monitoring, and opportunity for misbehavior.

2.2.2 Organizational Factors

Besides the number of environmental factors described above, there are also various factors in and around the organization that influence whether corruption occurs or not.

Organizational Characteristics

A first set of organizational factors concerns characteristics of the organization like the size of the firm, the type of the organization, and the organizational performance.

Many researchers claim that there is a relationship between firm size and illegal or unethical behavior, although the results regarding the nature of this relationship are mixed (Coleman, 1998, pp. 206 – 207; Daboub et al., 1995). Nevertheless, empirical studies hint at a detrimental effect of organizational size on ethical decision making (Ford & Richardson, 1994; McKendall et al., 2002; O'Fallon & Butterfield, 2005). Holtfreter (2005) found that corruption took place in larger organizations. Browning and Zabriskie's (1983) empirical study also revealed that respondents from larger firms were more likely to accept gifts and favors from ex-suppliers. It is argued that larger organizations open more possibilities to bribe. The bigger the organization, the greater is the anonymity and impersonality (Coleman, 1998, p. 207), the more frag-mented are responsibilities for important tasks (Coleman, 1998, p. 207), the more difficult is the control and thus the probability of being detected (Streißler, 1981), and the greater are the resources to easily absorb the costs of illegal action (Baucus & Near, 1991; McKendall et al., 2002). Clarke and Xu's (2002) study, in contrast, showed that small enterprises generally pay higher bribes than large enterprises. Martin et al. (2007) accordingly found a negative relationship between firm size, measured as number of employees, and corruption. Even managers from smaller firms asked in Vitell and Festervand's (1987) study believed that unethical practices

---

[15] Ford and Richardson's (1994) review showed that industry ethical standards were not related to an individual's ethical beliefs and decision making behavior.

were more common in small organizations. An argument may be that small firms may lack professional expertise to circumvent regulations (Coleman, 1998, p. 207).

Furthermore, the organization type seems to play a role. Clarke and Xu (2002) found that newly created (de novo) firms paid higher bribes. Among the reasons given is that they perform better than state-owned enterprises, especially in transition economies. They also have less well-developed relationships, so they compensate risks by demanding higher bribes (Clarke & Xu, 2002). Supporting this argument, in Martin et al.'s (2007) study, the percentage of state or government ownership of a firm was negatively related to corrupt activity.

The organizational performance also appears to be related to corruption. Holtfreter's (2005) study showed that corrupt organizations were profit-making companies. According to the studies conducted by Clarke and Xu (2002) and Svensson (2003), more profitable enterprises paid larger bribes (Clarke & Xu, 2002) and were demanded higher bribes (Svensson, 2003). Martin et al. (2007) found higher sales revenues to be positively related to corruption. This contradicts research on white-collar crime and illegal behavior, which mostly found economically depressed firms more likely to violate the law (Coleman, 1998, p. 206; Daboub et al., 1995; McKendall et al., 2002). Nevertheless, despite an organization's overall well-being, financial constraints may increase a firm's propensity to corruption as, for example, Martin et al.'s (2007) study showed.

Organizational Structure

Besides general organizational characteristics, an organization's structure, in both its structural complexity and decentralization, is a further determinant of corrupt action.

Structural complexity may serve as an enabling factor by creating opportunities to act corruptly (Grieger, 2005). High organizational complexity can contribute to illegality because it decreases communication, coordination, and managerial control, and allows the "abdication of a degree of personal responsibility for almost every type of decision" (Clinard & Yeager, 1980, p. 4).

An additional aspect related to corruption is decentralization. While empirical research on organizational decentralization is rare and inconclusive (McKendall et al., 2002), there are studies showing a positive relationship between decentralization on the macro-level and corruption (e.g., Treisman, 2000). Nevertheless, it is argued that decentralization in organizations allows greater freedom and flexibility in decision making, reduces and fragments accountability because more people are involved in decision making (Clinard, Yeager, Brissette, Petrasehk, & Harries, 1979, p. 7), and thus impedes good choices and increases law violations (McKendall et al., 2002). Corruption emerges in such fragmented systems because they generate "control leaks" (Espejo et al., 2001, p. 144). It is the result of a lack of necessary cohesive forces and organizational identity (Espejo et al., 2001).

Organizational Procedures

A number of further factors is related to procedures practiced in organizations. Relevant aspects include the democratic freedom in an organization, the power distribution, the established control mechanisms, and the reward structure.

Although democracy was not studied on the organizational level, there is empirical evidence on the macro-level that the level of corruption decreases with an increasing level of democracy (Emerson, 2006; Lederman, Loayza, & Soares, 2001; Sandholtz & Koetzle, 2000) or longer exposure to democracy (Treisman, 2000). Paldam (2002) argues that the effect of democracy is ambiguous because it varies with the length and the strength of the transition to democracy. Applying these results to organizations, according to Sandholtz and Koetzle (2000) one may argue that the more extensive democratic freedom in an organization, the greater is the deterrent to corruption.

As definitions of corruption show (see chap. 2.1.1, p. 23), the abuse of entrusted power is an important characteristic. Klitgaard (1998) has conceptualized the opportunity for corruption in a formula: Corruption equals monopoly plus discretion minus accountability (p. 75). Thus, corruption should decline with reduced monopoly and discretionary power of employees (Azfar, Lee, & Swamy, 2001). When an employee is the only person charged with performing a task, this employee has monopoly power with respect to the task and is able to extort payment without worry that a competing employee will step in to perform the task at a lower or no cost (Adamoli, 1999; Shleifer & Vishny, 1993). Furthermore, increasing discretion increases corruption (Adamoli, 1999; Bayar, 2005; Gorta, 2001; Morgan, 1998; Tanzi, 1995b; Tanzi, 1998; Tirole, 1986). The fewer the decision makers, the higher their discretionary power (Adamoli, 1999). When employees are given considerable discretion, they have opportunities to give favorable interpretations of organizational rules and regulations to other businesses in exchange for illegal payments (Tanzi, 1995b) and can allocate resources at their disposal, providing more advantages to some than to others (Adamoli, 1999). Different types of formalization, such as formal labor contracts, job descriptions, written evaluations, or policies and procedures manuals can reduce the autonomy of employees, thereby reducing the opportunities for corruption (Tirole, 1986). But rigid rules and precise formal procedures allowing no discretion may also incite noncompliance (Tanzi, 1995b) and increase the corruption value because the costs for the buyer and the opportunities to act corruptly for the seller increase (Adamoli, 1999). In case of a high specialization and separation of functions, corrupt transactions are more likely to occur and to go undetected (Getz & Volkema, 2001). Moreover, as the level of responsibility of decision makers, and therefore their accountability, decreases, the opportunities for corruption increase (Adamoli, 1999; Morgan, 1998).

Corruption is also facilitated by insufficient or lacking control mechanisms (Andvig & Fjeldstad, 2001; Bannenberg, 2003a; Fiebig & Junker, 2004, pp. 109 – 110). Institutional imperfections in monitoring allow corrupt employees to act without fear of being held accountable (Rose-Ackerman, 1999, p. 52 – 59). The lower the probability of detection, the higher the likelihood that corruption occurs (Andvig & Moene, 1990; Azfar et al., 2001; Carrillo, 1999; Lui, 1986; Macrae, 1982). Tight supervision by superiors increases the risks of corrupt behavior and decreases its attractiveness (Carrillo, 1999; Carrillo, 2000). It is the more effective, the bigger the stakes (Carrillo, 2000). But in case of promotions, tight supervision can be detrimental because it may not only deter agents from being corrupt, but also decrease the incentives for supervisors to monitor (Carrillo, 1999). Holtfreter (2005) found that more corruption cases are detected in organizations with anonymous reporting systems and internal audits. Despite the very few studies examining or supporting the effects of internal controls on illegal behavior by corporations, it has become widely accepted that internal controls in the form of ethical compliance programs make a positive difference (McKendall et al., 2002). Schulze and Frank (2003) found a two-fold effect of monitoring on corruption in their experiment: On the one hand, monitoring reduced corruption through deterrence. On the other hand, it destroyed the intrinsic motivation for honesty. Thus, the net effect on overall corruption was a priori undermined and surveillance increased overall corruptibility (Schulze & Frank, 2003).

The procedural aspects mentioned above all determine another aspect relevant for the likelihood with which corruption in organizations occurs: the probability of being detected. The risk of detection decreases with increasing individual scope of decision in addition to lacking control and monitoring, with increasing exclusiveness of the actor's position, with an increasing number of actors involved, as well as with an increasing size of the bribe (Vogt, 1997, pp. 51 – 52). The motivation to close a corrupt contract increases when the risk of detection decreases (Borner & Schwyzer, 1999; Carrillo, 1999; Carrillo, 2000). For this relationship, there is empirical evidence for corrupt behavior (Goel & Rich, 1989) and for other unethical behavior (Buckley et al., 1998; Carnes & Englebrecht, 1995). In their experimental bribery game, Abbink et al. (2002) found the penalty threat to significantly reduce corruption, although discovery probabilities were typically underestimated.

An organization's reward structure also influences corrupt behavior. Hegarty and Sims (1978) found that individuals could be conditioned to behave unethically under appropriate contingencies. When subjects were rewarded for paying kickbacks in their experiment, unethical behavior was higher than when subjects were not rewarded. Several reviews of empirical research on ethical decision making also underline this. Most of the studies reported in the reviews of Ford and Richardson (1994), Loe et al. (2000), and O'Fallon and Butterfield (2005) showed that rewards for unethical behavior induced such behavior, while sanctions prohibited unethical behavior.

Thus, the deterrence effect of penalties and punishment (see chap. 2.2.1, p. 37) has an important role in the context of private corruption. Individuals in organizations are more prone to act corruptly in the case of weak punishments and low penalties within the organization (Carrillo, 1999; Carrillo, 2000). Corrupt behavior occurs in all those cases where there is no deterrence by the threat of punishment (Bannenberg, 2003a), like, for example, by the danger of being suspended from the job or being fired (Carrillo, 2000). Bayar (2005) argues that especially in the case of a high posterior probability of facing corrupt actors increasing fines only limitedly prevent corruption. When an intermediary is used, fines do not decrease incidences of corruption cases at all, but increase the usage of intermediaries instead.

In addition to the mechanism of punishment, the rewards created by recruitment, promotion, and renumeration are relevant for corruption. Merit-based recruitment and merit-based promotion were found to be associated with corruption (Andvig & Fjeldstad, 2001; Morgan, 1998; for merit-based recruitment also Rauch & Evans, 2000). Furthermore, the arrangements of renumeration also have a determining effect. Professionals working on a fee-for-service basis have numerous opportunities to persuade clients to consent to profitable but unnecessary procedures, while those working on salary have little to gain from such activities (Coleman, 1998, pp. 208 – 209). Commission-based motivations to promote products or services lure corrupt cooperation (Luo, 2002). Many corporations also have profit-sharing programs for top-level executives and managers that are intended to align management interests with the owners' value maximization goals. These profit-based mechanisms create a huge amount of pressure and opportunity for individual managers to act corruptly (Chen & Tang, 2006). There has been some speculation in the literature on whether high wages decrease incidences of corruption or not (Frank, 2004; Tanzi, 1998). On the one hand, it is argued that high wages reduce the number of corrupt acts (Andvig & Moene, 1990; Cadot, 1987; Carrillo, 1999; Carrillo, 2000; Hotchkiss, 1998; Tanzi, 1998; Theobald, 2002; Van Rijckeghem & Weder, 2001) because they raise the opportunity costs of corruption when detected, for example, losing one's job or being charged penalty payments (Cadot, 1987; Carrillo, 1999; Carrillo, 2000; Frank, 2004; Tanzi, 1998). This argumentation is supported by the finding of Schulze and Frank (2003) in a controlled experiment that fixed higher wages only decreased the propensity to act corruptly when corruption was detected and the payment could be lost. On the other hand, high wages may lead to higher bribes on the part of those continuing to act corruptly (Carrillo, 2000; Tanzi, 1998) because their greed is not eliminated (Tanzi, 1998) and they still compete with others for rewards (Litzky et al., 2006). Thus, while high wages may reduce the number of corrupt acts, the total amount of corruption money paid may not necessarily fall (Tanzi, 1998). So the beneficial effect of the wage rise is offset (Carrillo, 2000).

Organizational Culture

Organizational culture in general plays an important part in determining decisions (Coleman, 1998, p. 206) and therefore also in determining corrupt decisions (Gorta, 2001; Luo, 2002). Organizational culture is

1) a pattern of basic assumptions, 2) invented, discovered, or developed by a given group, 3) as it learns to cope with its problems of external adaptation

and internal integration, 4) that has worked well enough to be considered valid and, therefore 5) is to be taught to new members as the 6) correct way to perceive, think, and feel in relation to those problems (Schein, 1988, p. 7).

In particular, Schein (1988) views culture as comprising three levels: observable behaviors and artifacts, values, and underlying assumptions. Aspects constituting an organization's culture and relevant for corruption include organizational goals in addition to an organization's ethical climate, which is reflected in the handling of corrupt incidences, in ethical guidelines, in leadership, in the kind of social pressure, and in the perceived corruption level in the organization.

The goals set by an organization in its mission statement may determine corruption. The maximization of profit and shareholder value has a central importance to contemporary business, but may also favor corruption (Banfield, 1975; Coleman, 1998, pp. 204 – 205; Kochan, 2002). The profit goals of the firm may prevent managers from pursuing their own code of moral and human values if they possess no utility in the context of profit maximization (Michelman, 1983). Unethical behavior arises because people feel under pressure to compromise personal standards to achieve organizational objectives (Bowman, 1976; Carroll, 1975). The managers' first duty is to their firm and not to themselves (Michelman, 1983). But managers know that a decline in profitability also poses a direct threat to their careers (Coleman, 1998, pp. 204 – 205). In Rosenberg's (1987) study, 33 out of 46 participants voted to make the bribe payment. 21 of these recognized a need to subordinate ethics in favor of achieving the firms' goals.

The willingness to act corruptly also depends on an organization's ethical climate (Peterson, 2002) and moral tone (Coleman, 1998, p. 195); this means, on its ethical system, its attitudes towards ethical and unethical behavior, and its handling of ethical issues (Coleman, 1998, p. 195; Peterson, 2002). Both Loe et al.'s (2000) and O'Fallon and Butterfield's (2005) reviews support the notion that ethical climates and cultures have a positive influence on ethical decision making. Murphy, Smith, and Daley's (1992) study showed that the chief ethics manager's attitude toward ethical issues influenced the company's giving of gifts, but not the acceptance of gifts. As corruption is a criminal offense closely connected to licit activities that have a positive social value, there often seems to be an attitude of general acceptance of corrupt practices in organizations (Adamoli, 1999).

This is reflected in the absence of reporting of corrupt incidences. A company's stockholders and top management do not want to know about cases where bribes are paid to obtain lucrative deals (Rose-Ackerman, 1978, p. 191). This behavior is tolerated because its elimination is too costly (Rose-Ackerman, 1978, p. 190). Many companies shrink away from making corrupt acts public because they fear for their goals and fear negative headlines (Köpf, 1997, pp. 82 – 83; Scholz, 1995, p. 15). Thus, the organizational history in dealing with reports of corruption influences the occurrence of corruption (Gorta, 2001).

Corruption may also be the result of lacking or ineffective guidelines, codes of conduct, or codes of ethics. In high pressure, high-velocity environments individuals make up their own rules and create their own rationale for what is acceptable (Cameron, 2006). Companies are more vulnerable to corruption when they have no policies to guide them in such situations (Lane & Simpson, 1984) and when individuals feel ambiguity about what the expectations of behavior are in these situations (Litzky et al., 2006). Thus, both ethics and virtues can serve as "essential fixed points in a sea of chaotic change and uncertainty" (Cameron, 2006, p. 321). Because ethical standards may be unstable, however, they must be supplemented by virtuous standards – "universal aspirations that focus on the best of the human condition" (Cameron, 2006, p. 321). One advantage of ethical codes is that they provide clarification of usually unstated precepts that should guide ethical conduct (Gellerman, 1989). But in organizations, there often exists a double moral with ethics declarations as fig leaf and behavioral standards that are not asserted (Bannenberg, 2003a). Despite few exceptions, the reviews of Ford and Richardson (1994), Loe et al. (2000) and O'Fallon and Butterfield (2005) showed that the majority of studies support the idea that the existence of a code of ethics is positively related to ethical decision making raising the general level of awareness of ethical issues. Nevertheless, the awareness of an ethical code is no guarantee of its impact on individual decision making (Maes, Jeffery, & Smith, 1998). The perceived usefulness of ethics codes was found to be positively related to the degree of familiarity with the specific contents and intentions of the code (Wotruba, Chonko, & Loe, 2001). Only well-communicated codes help improve ethical behavior (Weeks & Nantel, 1992). Furthermore, codes have to be written in simple terms (McDonald, 2000). Abstract behavioral guidelines facilitate corruption (Bannenberg, 2003a). Unclear sets of standards combined with a non-contingent reward system were found to be associated with reports of client improprieties like, for example, kickbacks for orders (Mitchell et al., 1996).

In many cases, corruption results from defective leadership practiced in organizations. Continuing unethical behavior in the workplace is linked to the lack of a moral leader in an organization (Appelbaum & Shapiro, 2006). Corrupt behaviors are advanced to upper hierarchy levels (Bannenberg, 2003a). Leaders who engage in unethical practices serve as bad examples (Gorta, 2001) and often create an atmosphere of allowance that is conducive to the existence of deviant behavior that parallels that of the leader (Trevino & Brown, 2005). Top corporate leaders are able to persuade their subordinates to engage in illegal activities, often without specifically ordering them to do so, because their position in the organization gives them control of rewards and punishments that are important to those below them (Coleman, 1998, p. 195). Van Duyne (2001) even speaks of corruption as a "leadership disease" (p. 14). If leaders are successful, they are deprived of negative feedback no matter what they are doing. An aversion to independent minds in the organization and a circumvention of the principle of accountability and transparency arises. This results in a kind of virtual ownership of the organization, where the leaders determine what is responsible management. They build a court of followers with the same opinions and values rewarding persons at will. This has been called "Caligula appointments" (Van Duyne, 2001, p. 90), which may result in favoritism (Van Duyne, 2001). While Murphy et al.'s (1992) study showed that leadership did not influence ethical behavior (giving gifts or favors to/accepting gifts or favors from customers in exchange for preferential treatment), Ford and Richardson's (1994) review showed mixed results regarding the top management's influence on ethical behavior. Defective leadership also may play a role in another respect. First, if managers violate their employee's trust, this may lead to severe deviant acts (Litzky et al., 2006). Second, lack of trust of managers in their employees often becomes a self-fulfilling prophecy in that employees act out negatively in an effort to retaliate (Litzky et al., 2006). Third, corruption may be the result of an unfair treatment of employees (Bilitza & Lück, 1977; Henle, 2005; Litzky et al., 2006). When employees feel that they have been treated unfairly, these feelings often lead to a desire for retaliation or some other negative behavior to restore the balance or get even (Litzky et al., 2006).

Grieger (2005) hypothesizes that corruption in organizations is mediated by groups. The stronger and more cohesive groups are, the more influence they exert on the suppression or on the encouragement of both individual and collective deviant behavior. Corruption depends on the behavior of peers and colleagues and thus is the result of social pressures (Gorta, 2001; Litzky et al., 2006; Wirl, 1998). Ford and Richardson's (1994) and Loe et al.'s (2000) reviews showed support for the importance of the person's peer group in determining a person's ethical decision making behavior. Osgood, Wilson, O'Malley, Bachman, and Johnston (1996) also found that people who tended to spend a lot of time with peers were more prone to take part in deviant activities.

"Corruption breeds corruption" (Carrillo, 2000, p. 3). Thus, the level of perceived corruption in an organization has an influence on corrupt behavior. The higher the perceived fraction of corrupt employees in an organization, the higher the number of corrupt employees (see Andvig & Moene, 1990). Higher degrees of corruption in the organization's upper levels also encourage corruption in lower levels (Cadot, 1987). A history of previous wrongdoing is also associated with increased occurrence of illegal behavior (Baucus & Near, 1991). Corruption evolves in organizations when corrupt actors serve as role models to others (Vaughan et al., 2005, August). If everyone believes everyone else is corrupt, corruption becomes a part of the culture (Cabelkova & Hanousek, 2004). Such subcultures in organizations provide a network of communication informing about opportunities, techniques, and motivations for corrupt behavior (Coleman, 1998, p. 209). Thus, corruption is the result of learning processes during the professional development (Bilitza & Lück, 1977). The process of socialization shapes managers to the corporate image (Coleman, 1998, p. 197). Corruption, therefore, emerges from the "discrepancy between the lived experience in organizations and socially derived normative expectations" (Kayes, 2006, p. 51). With an increasing number of corrupt actors, eventually internalized moral feelings of guilt decrease (Andvig & Fjeldstad, 2001). Moreover, when many others are involved in corruption, the loss of reputation for each employee decreases (Andvig & Fjeldstad, 2001) and the probability of being revealed is lower due to the strained capacity of internal and external investigation units (Andvig & Fjeldstad, 2001; Andvig & Moene, 1990; Lui, 1986). The perceived corruption level of an organizations also affects agents interacting with that organization. The higher the perceived corruption in an organization, the more probable it is that a person dealing with that organization will offer a bribe. High corruption perception does not only entice employees in the organization to think that there is nothing wrong with accepting bribes, but also encourages people outside the organization to believe that they must pay bribes to cooperate with this organization (Cabelkova & Hanousek, 2004).

2.2.3 Personal Factors

Although there are various environmental and organizational factors enabling or even encouraging corruption, corrupt action is always undertaken by a person. Thus, there are a number of personal factors, like sociodemographic factors, personality traits, values and attitudes, and motives contributing to whether individual corrupt behavior occurs or not.

Sociodemographic Factors

A number of sociodemographic factors were studied for their determining influence on corrupt behavior.

Many empirical studies in the business ethics literature investigated differences between men and women in ethical decision making (for an overview see e.g., Ford & Richardson, 1994; Loe et al., 2000; O'Fallon & Butterfield, 2005; Robin & Babin, 1997; Roxas & Stoneback, 2004) and revealed contradictory findings (Dawson, 1997). Often, no differences were found between males and females, but when differences were discovered, females were more ethical than males (O'Fallon & Butterfield, 2005). Studies investigating sex differences in corrupt behaviors also revealed mixed results: Some business ethics studies found sex differences (e.g., Chen & Tang, 2006; Deshpande, 1997; Deshpande, Joseph, & Maximov, 2000; Loo, 1996; Loo, 2003; McCabe, Ingram, & Dato-on, 2006; Poorsoltan, Amin, & Tootoonchi, 1991; Stanga & Turpen, 1991; Weeks, Moore, McKinney, & Longe-necker, 1999), and some did not (Ekin & Tezolmez, 1999; Hoffman, 1998; Kidwell, Stevens, & Bethke, 1987; Kohut & Corriher, 1994; Lund, 2000). While there were a number of economic micro-data studies confirming a positive relationship between corruption and male sex (e.g., Gatti, Paternostro, & Rigolini, 2003; Mocan, 2004, p. 16; Swamy et al., 2001), economic experimental studies also revealed inconsistent results. While Schulze and Frank (2003) found differences at least in the risk condition, Frank and Schulze (2000) and Hegarty and Sims (1978) did not. Criminological research examining real cases supports this picture. Holtfreter (2005), who surveyed certified fraud examiners on corruption cases, found corruption equally likely to be committed by males and females. But in her analysis of court cases, Bannenberg

(2002) observed that corrupt actors were predominantly male (pp. 216 – 217). Weisburd and Waring (2001, pp. 24 – 25) obtained the same result in their analysis of a sample of convicted criminals. But these criminological results have to be viewed with caution: The low proportion of women involved in corruption reflects their underrepresentation in the higher circles of corporate decision making. Thus, men and women cannot be assumed to have the same opportunities for corruption (Coleman, 1998, pp. 211 – 212).

Another relevant sociodemographic variable is age. Studies relating age to unethical behavior also delivered inconsistent results and found either no significant age differences, a positive, or a negative relationship (for an overview see e.g., Ford & Richardson, 1994; Loe et al., 2000; O'Fallon & Butterfield, 2005). Mocan's (2004) economic micro-data also provided evidence for a complex relationship between age and corruption: Individuals who were 20 to 39 years of age were more likely to be asked for a bribe in comparison to those who were younger than 20. Individuals who were 60 years and older were less likely to get involved in corruption (p. 16). Gatti et al. (2003) found older individuals to be more averse to corruption. This is consistent with the results of the business ethics studies conducted by Deshpande (1997) and Lund (2000): Not only did older managers (40 plus) judge corrupt behavior more unethical than younger managers (Deshpande, 1997), but older individuals also reacted more ethically in situations involving bribery (Lund, 2000). Age also seems to have an indirect influence on corrupt behavior as increasing age is linked to higher levels of moral judgment (Rest, 1986) and lower levels of Machiavellianism[16] (Hunt & Chonko, 1984), both of which are related to lower levels of corruption (see p. 54 for moral judgment and p. 53 for Machiavellianism). But regardless of actual behavior, age was shown to relate to greater sensitivity to ethical dilemmas (Dubinsky, Jolson, Michaels, Kotabe, & Lim, 1992; Ruegger & King, 1992).

Related to the question whether age has an influence or not is the question whether students differ from professionals or managers in regard to corrupt behavior. The literature on ethical decision making provides mixed evidence for employment versus student status (Ford & Richardson, 1994; O'Fallon & Butterfield, 2005). In O'Fallon and Butterfield's (2005) review, three out of seven studies found students to be less ethical than practitioners. Nevertheless, due to the mixed results, one should be cautious with a generalization for all decisions having an ethical component and the conclusion that students generally are less ethical than professionals (Harris & Sutton, 1995). Regarding corrupt behavior, there are few studies showing students to be more willing to engage in such behavior than their professional counterparts (e.g., Kohut & Corriher, 1994; Wood, Longenecker, McKinney, & Moore, 1988). But interestingly, in Poorsoltan et al.'s (1991) study, students expressed strongly negative attitudes toward bribery and kickbacks to achieve personal or business goals. Accordingly, Chen and Tang (2006) found that when students considered a situation

---

[16] Arlow's (1991) study showed that those under the age of 24 had significantly higher Machiavellian scores than those aged 24 or over.

to be unethical, they were less likely to engage in corruption. Thus, whether there are differences between students and professionals in regard to their propensity to corrupt behavior remains unclear.

Furthermore, education, employment, and work experience seem to have an influence on corrupt behavior. Although the reviews of Ford and Richardson (1994), Loe et al. (2000), and O'Fallon and Butterfield (2005) report mixed findings, the majority of studies that revealed differences indicated that more education, employment, or work experience was positively related to ethical decision making.

While Browning and Zabriskie (1983) found that respondents with less education viewed taking gifts and favors to be less unethical than those with education, Deshpande (1997) found no differences between those with graduate education and those with non graduate degrees. In Mocan's (2004) study, individuals who were more educated were more likely to be targeted for bribes (p. 16).

In addition, Gatti et al. (2003) found employed individuals to be more averse to corruption. In Weeks et al.'s (1999) study, individuals in later career stages appeared to possess higher ethical judgment regarding corrupt behavior than individuals in earlier career stages. Arlow (1991) additionally found a negative relationship between the length of work experience and Machiavellianism, a variable positively related to corruption as will be discussed later (see p. 53).

The type of education does not appear to have an influence on ethical decision making (Ford & Richardson, 1994; O'Fallon & Butterfield, 2005). Merritt's (1991) results showed that when judging the behavior of others, business students were more likely to accept unethical behavior than non-business students, but regarding the reports of their own intended behavior, there were no significant differences. When examining corrupt behavior, results are inconsistent. In their experiment on corruption, Frank and Schulze (2000) found that economics students were significantly more corrupt than others. In Schulze and Frank's (2003) experiment, students of economics showed higher levels of corruption in the non-risk treatment indicating that they behave more self-interested, but this differences disappeared in the presence of possible detection. Davis and Welton (1991) found a tendency over time for students to change their attitudes about ethical behavior, but argue that the causes (value transmission, value clarifications, moral development, or moral action) are difficult to determine. Although the rational self-interested calculation is seen as economists' skill (Arlow, 1991; Carter & Irons, 1991), Yezer, Goldfarb, and Poppen (1996) – in contrast to Frank, Gilovich, and Regan (1996) – argue that there is no evidence that the exposure to economic training increases unethical behavior.

Although the type of education does not seem to make a difference, the type of job in which one is employed obviously does so. Vahlenkamp and Knauß' (1995) empirical study showed that the following positions and departments were judged as most endangered and prone to corruption by business representatives: purchasing, processing in the supply department of producing companies, logistics, awarding of building contracts, planning, development and calculation (of technical constructions and products), security and security officers, the control sector, and control officers (pp. 40 – 41).

An individual's power and decision scope in the job also has an influence on the vulnerability to corruption (Fiebig & Junker, 2004, p.110 ; Rügemer, 1996, pp. 24 – 25). Bannenberg (2002) observed that corrupt actors were ambitious, social climbers, and had high professional competence and power and decision scope in their position (pp. 216 – 218; see also Bannenberg, 2003a). It is argued that the larger the decision competence and the higher the organizational rank, the more intensive are the efforts for corruption and the higher are the bribes (Rügemer, 1996, p. 25; Van Duyne, 1999). This is confirmed by Roozen et al.'s (2001) results, which revealed that a high level of responsibility in the company contributed to a negative ethical attitude of employees. Akaah (1996), in contrast, found no differences in regard to organizational rank in the judgments on bribery. An interesting note is that in Callan's (1992) study, the top management was more likely to have attitudes against cronyism and giving advantage to others. Carroll (1978) argues that higher levels of management may themselves feel no pressure to behave unethically, but can put extreme pressure on lower level managers to meet corporate goals at the expense of personal standards of morality.

A further sociodemographic factor relevant for corrupt behavior is an individual's wealth. Wealthier individuals were found to be more likely to engage in corruption (Gatti et al., 2003; Mocan, 2004). Hunt and Laszlo (2005) argue that bribery is more attractive to both parties when the client is richer. Their study revealed a positive relationship of both bribery incidence and value with household income. Hunt (2004) showed that the rich paid the most bribes and the poor the least, while in the middle range, bribery was insensitive to income. These findings are supported by Bannenberg (2003a), who identified the typical corrupt offender to be without debts and to value societal status as well as a high standard of living (Bannenberg, 2003a). As people's wage contributes to their income and wealth, it is also important to take into account the discussion of the wage level's influence on corrupt behavior, which revealed inconclusive results (see chap. 2.2.2, p. 45).

There is little research examining the relationship between marital status and corruption. Mocan's (2004) study showed that single individuals were less likely to be asked for a bribe than were married individuals (p. 16).

Personality Traits

Besides sociodemographic characteristics that relate to a person's vulnerability and propensity to act corruptly, the question arises what the corrupt actor's personality is like.

Coleman (1998) states that "white-collar offenders are psychologically 'normal'" (p. 178). They are socially unobtrusive (Weisburd & Waring, 2001, pp. 70 – 71) and do not have symptoms of a major psychiatric disorder (Coleman, 1998, p. 178). Rather, the typical white-collar crime offender resembles the normal successful manager (Bussmann, 2004) with attributes useful for both legal and illegal business (Gottfredson & Hirschi, 1990, p. 195; Löw, 2002, p. 65).

One of the most frequently examined personality variables in relation to unethical and corrupt behavior is the locus of control. The concept relates to the individual's expectation regarding the instance being responsible for the consequences of one's behavior. It distinguishes between internals, who attribute consequences of their behavior to themselves and their own behavior, and externals, who attribute consequences of their behavior to external people or circumstances (Rotter, 1966). From the reviews of Ford and Richardson (1994), Loe et al. (2000), and O'Fallon and Butterfield (2005) it can be concluded that the findings in regard to ethical decision making are mixed. Several studies reported no significant differences. Those that found differences consistently reported that internal locus of control was positively and external locus of control was negatively related to ethical decision making. This is also supported by studies examining corrupt behavior. Cherry and Fraedrich's (2000) results allow the conclusion that managers with an internal locus of control exhibit harsher judgments of bribery and less intention to pay a bribe. Accordingly, Hegarty and Sims (1978) found that an external locus of control was significantly related to paying kickbacks.

A second widely studied personality trait relating to a person's propensity to act corruptly is Machiavellianism. It refers to a person's tendency to deceive and manipulate others for personal gain (Christie & Geis, 1970; Bowyer, 1982, p. 201). The reviews of Ford and Richardson (1994), Loe et al. (2000), and O'Fallon and Butterfield (2005) allow the conclusion that Machiavellianism is negatively related to the ethical decision making process. Hegarty and Sims (1978) accordingly found people high on Machiavellianism to be more likely to pay kickbacks than people low on Machiavellianism.

There are a number of other personality characteristics mentioned in the context of white-collar crime and also applicable to corruption. White-collar offenders are described as extraverted personalities. In Collins and Schmidt's (1993) study, offenders scored higher on social extraversion, with the possibility of the effect on white-collar crime being mediated by extra-curricular activity. Another characteristic of both white-collar criminals (Smettan, 1992, pp. 25; Wheeler, 1992) and corrupt actors (Vogt, 1997, p. 60) is high risk preparedness. They both show high career and success orientation (white-collar criminals: Simon & Hagan, 1999, pp. 145 – 146; Löw, 2002, pp. 67 – 68; corrupt actors: Berg, 1997, p. 59). While egocentrism was identified as characteristic of white-collar criminals (Coleman, 1998, p. 179), Levine (2005) attributes the qualities of pathological narcissism to the leaders of corrupt organizations because their greediness and sense of personal entitlement reflects their search for admiration by others. Furthermore, low conscientiousness (Litzky et al., 2006; Stauffer, 2003), low emotional stability (Litzky et al., 2006), low agreeableness (Litzky et al., 2006; Stauffer, 2003), and cynicism (Litzky et al., 2006) can help predict deviant or unethical behavior, but it is questionable whether these relationships also apply for corrupt behavior.

Values and Attitudes

In addition to sociodemographic factors and personality traits, values and attitudes influence an individual's propensity to corruption.

Despite a few notable exceptions, Loe et al.'s (2000) and O'Fallon and Butterfield's (2005) reviews conclude that research generally suggests a positive relationship between cognitive moral development or ethical judgment and ethical decision making. Levine (2005) argues that corrupt conduct reflects primitive moral thinking rather than a rejection of morality.

Furthermore, a person's value orientation plays a role in whether a person is likely to act corruptly or not. According to the reviews of Ford and Richardson (1994), Loe et al. (2000), and O'Fallon and Butterfield (2005) research reveals fairly consistent findings in regard to value orientation. While idealism[17] and deontology[18] are generally positively related to ethical decision making, relativism[19] and teleology[20] as well as other factors, such as economic orientation are generally negatively related. Hegarty and Sims (1978), for example, found that individuals with high economic and political value orientation were more likely to pay kickbacks. Regarding the influence of religion, the results of the three literature reviews (Ford & Richardson, 1994; Loe et al., 2000; O'Fallon & Butterfield, 2005) predominantly suggest a positive relationship between religion and ethical decision making.

Corruption is also influenced by the attitudes and subjective norms towards that behavior. Powpaka's (2002) findings (see chap. 2.5.4, p. 79) suggest that besides the negative influence of perceived choice, both the attitude toward bribe giving and the subjective norm positively influence the intention to bribe. The attitude, in turn, is positively affected by perceived necessity of the bribe and negatively by perceived unethicality of the act. Subjective norm, on the other hand, is positively influenced by perceived support of the act by top management. There also exists a positive relation between attitude and subjective norm. Wated and Sanchez (2005) found that managers with a negative attitude toward bribery were more likely to discipline corrupt employees. Managers' subjective norms did not have a predictive effect.

---

[17] Idealism describes an individual's attitudes towards the consequences of an action, and how the consequences affect the welfare of others (Forsyth, 1980).

[18] Deontological moral philosophies stress the methods and intentions involved in a particular behavior. Fundamental is the inherent rightness or wrongness of behaviors (Ferrell & Gresham, 1985; Fraedrich, 1993).

[19] Relativism describes the extent to which an individual rejects moral rules or principles (Forsyth, 1980).

[20] Teleological moral philosophies deal with the moral worth of behavior determined totally by the consequences of the behavior. Acts are morally right or good if they produce some desired end (Ferrell & Gresham, 1985; Fraedrich, 1993).

Nevertheless, some studies discovered an inconsistency between values or attitudes and behavior. Pitt and Abratt (1986) and Miller (2006) observed (intents for) corrupt behavior, although corruption and corruptive practices were condemned. Moreover, corrupt actors were found to be not previously convicted and to not show deviant moral concepts. Nevertheless, they were observed to not be aware of the illegal and unethical character of their action and to have strong tendencies of justification and neutralization. They denied personal responsibility and the immorality of their behavior as well as the resulting harm (Bannenberg, 2002, pp. 353 – 354; Bannenberg, 2003a; Bannenberg & Schaupensteiner, 2004, pp. 59 – 63; Darley, 2005; Schaupensteiner, 2004). These findings are congruent with characteristics identified for white-collar offenders (e.g., Coleman, 1998, pp. 188 – 194; Simon & Hagan, 1999, pp. 141 – 143) as well as with the justification and neutralization strategies of corrupt actors reported by Ashforth and Anand (2003; see chap. 2.6.1, p. 87).

Motives

The question arises why employees and managers in companies act corruptly. The motives for corrupt action are manifold. Individuals may aim at achieving private objectives, organizational objectives, or a mixture of both (Grieger, 2005).

One motivator for a white-collar crime like corruption is the financial self-interest (Bannenberg, 2003a, Bannenberg & Schaupensteiner, 2004, pp. 58 – 59; Deflem, 1995; Fiebig & Junker, 2004, pp. 112 – 113; Hacker, 1981; Levine, 2005; Löw, 2002, p. 66; Smettan, 1992, pp. 27 – 29). This includes the desire for financial gain as well as the "fear of falling" (Coleman, 1998, p. 182), the desire to protect what one already has (Coleman, 1998, p. 182). The wish to enrich oneself especially motivates financially well-situated people (Hacker, 1981); their greed makes them want even more, the more they already have (Levine, 2005; Löw, 2002, pp. 67; Wheeler, 1992). The attractiveness of the opportunities for corruption depends on the economic value of the benefit of the corrupt exchange (Coleman, 1998, p. 207; Vogt, 1997, pp. 54 – 61). In the case of high-value contracts, 3 to 5% are paid as provisions (Scholz, 1997, p. 8), which may even reach 15 to 20% in international business (Scholz, 1997, p. 4). The higher the size of the bribe, the more likely is corrupt action (Borner & Schwyzer, 1999; Carrillo, 1999; Carrillo, 2000). Schilling (2004) argues that both the level and the sort of the price determine whether a person is likely to act corruptly. "Every person has his/her price" (p. 101).

Not only the benefit in terms of money, but also the achievement of symbolic values and benefits can be a motive for corruption (Hacker, 1981). Often there are other advantages for the corruptee than money; this may include houses, aircrafts, cars, boats, motor cycles, real estate, villas and cottages, take over of maintenance and repair, furniture, antiques, electrical equipment, parcels of shares, pleasure and study trips, participation in congresses, vouchers, discount prices, invitations to luxury restaurants and to the red-light district, interest-free loans without refund, excessive charges for partly fictitious contracts, certificates, consultancy contracts and secondary employment, kickbacks or shareholding of patents (Bannenberg & Schaupensteiner, 2004, pp. 69 – 77; Rügemer, 1996, pp. 23 – 24; Schaupensteiner, 2004). Bannenberg (2003a) observed that personal advantages can not only be material, but also immaterial including, for example, power, prestige, and status.

So another motive for corrupt action is career ambition (Bannenberg, 2003a; Bannenberg & Schaupensteiner, 2004, p. 59). Individuals may engage in corruption to get ahead in the company (Clinard, 1990, p. 131). They pursue the goal of success by trying to prove themselves in, for example, winning in the economic competition (Coleman, 1998, p. 182; Graf, 2000, p. 28), thereby gaining recognition and personal entitlement (Graf, 2000, p. 28; Levine, 2005).

The strive for power is another motivating force (Bannenberg, 2003a; Bannenberg & Schaupensteiner, 2004, p. 59; Graf, 2000, p. 28). Case studies of Dunkelberg and Jessup (2001) on illegal or unethical behavior showed that despite the power they already had, all individuals studied were driven by the desire to have even more power. They also acted as though they believed they were above the rules because of their status and position.

Frustration in the job due to, for example, lacking recognition or missed career chances (Bannenberg & Schaupensteiner, 2004, p. 59; Fiebig & Junker, 2004, Löw, 2002) may also motivate corruption. In their laboratory experiment, Schweitzer, Ordonez, and Douma (2004) found that people with unmet goals were more likely to engage in unethical behavior than people attempting to do their best.

A number of other motives are thrill seeking (Fiebig & Junker, 2004), excessive demands at the work place (Bannenberg & Schaupensteiner, 2004, p. 59), revenge as a reaction to maltreatment (Fiebig & Junker, 2004, pp. 114, 116; Löw, 2002, p. 68) and dissatisfaction (Löw, 2002, p. 68; Sims, 2002). Aquino, Lewis, and Bradfield's (1999) research revealed a direct relationship between negative affect like anger, hostility, fear and anxiety and deviant behaviors.

Besides these private motives there also may be a number of organizational motives that drive the individual who acts on behalf of the organization to corrupt action. An important motive is to gain advantages over competitors (Clinard, 1990, p. 131; Priddat, 2004). Advantages for the person who submits a corrupt offer include the achievement of contracts, enabling of cartel agreements, other advantages in business competition, achievement of permissions and concessions, the allocation of subsidies, the payment of fictitious and excessive bills, the betrayal of business secrets, the achievement of insider or confidential information, the avoidance of prohibitions and controls, the saving of fees or residence permits for employees, smooth order processing or manipulation in commissioning (Bannenberg & Schaupensteiner, 2004, p. 50; Rügemer, 1996, p. 25; Schaupensteiner, 2004; Schmidt, 2004, p. 17).

2.2.4 Summary

There is a vast body of research on the causes of corruption. Nevertheless, there are some restrictions: First, the causes identified in the literature mainly refer to political and public corruption. Thus, this work attempts to report those causes also relevant for private corruption. Second and accordingly, there is rare empirical evidence for the reported factors in regard to private corruption. If there are empirical studies, they either refer to other types of corruption in the case of environmental and organizational factors or more broadly to white-collar crime and unethical behavior in the case of organizational and personal factors. Third, empirical research on the motives of corrupt action is especially scarce. Thus, there is a need for empirical support for the causes of private corruption outlined above. Figure 2 summarizes the potential causes of private corruption.

Environmental Factors			
Culture	**Law**	**Society**	**Economy**

• Cultural relativity
• Cultural dimensions:
  ⋗ Power distance
  ⋗ Uncertainty
    avoidance
    (Low/high?)
  ⋗ Masculinity
  ⋗ Collectivism
    (Low/high?)
• Tradition of
hierarchical religions
• Non-British colonial
history
• Ethno-linguistic
diversity
	• Judicial inefficiency
	• Complex legislation
	• Lack of transparency
	• If so:
	  Tax deductibility of
	  bribes
	• Lack of law
	enforcement
	• Low penalties
		• Decay of moral norms
		and values
		• High perceived
		corruption level
		• Absence of public
		control
		• Characteristics of
		population, e.g.,
		high unemployment
		rate, low education
		• Social and
		economic inequality
			• Complex economic
			system
			• Economic adversity
			• Large endowment of
			natural resources
			• Lacking openness to
			trade
			• High economic
			competition in
			imperfect markets
			• Lack of economic
			freedom
			• Imitation effects
			• Vulnerability of
			certain industries

Organizational Factors			
Organizational Characteristics	**Organizational Structure**	**Organizational Procedures**	**Organizational Culture**

• Firm size
(Large/small?)
• De novo company
• Profitable company
	• High organizational
	complexity
	• Decentralization
		• Lack of democratic
		freedom
		• High discretion
		• Insufficient control
		• Low risk of detection
		• Low deterrence by
		punishment
		• Merit-based
		recruitment and
		promotion
		• Profit-based
		renumeration
			• Profit goals
			• Corruption-friendly
			climate:
			  ⋗ Lacking report of
			    corrupt incidences
			  ⋗ Lacking guidelines
			  ⋗ Defective
			    leadership
			  ⋗ Peer pressure
			  ⋗ High perceived
			    corruption level

Personal Factors			
Sociodemographic Factors	**Personality Traits**	**Values and Attitudes**	**Motives**
• Male employee • Younger employee • Education (low/high?) • Low employment and work experience • Vulnerability of certain types of jobs • High power and decision scope • Wealthy employee • Single employee	• External locus of control • Machiavellianism • Extraversion • High risk preparedness • Pathological narcism	• Primitive moral thinking • Relativistic and teleological value orientation • Corruption-friendly attitude • Corruption-friendly subjective norm • Neutralization/ Rationalization	• Financial self-interest • Material and immaterial benefits • Career ambition • Strive for power • Frustration in the job • Search of thrill • Excessive demand • Revenge • Dissatisfaction • Gaining advantages over competitors

PRIVATE CORRUPTION

Figure 2:   The Causes of Private Corruption

2.3   Consequences of Private Corruption

Just as the causes of corruption are complex and varied, so too are the consequences (Pearson, 2001). These consequences of corruption are discussed controversial (Heberer, 2001). Whereas some researchers have attempted to defend corruption as a pragmatic action that actually accelerates economic development and benefits the society in which corruption occurs, others have asserted that corruption has negative consequences (Rose-Ackerman, 1999). On the one hand, regarding its positive effects summarized in the "efficient grease hypothesis"[21], Pies et al. (2005) term corruption as "invisible hand" (p. 32) because corruption is a reaction to bad governance and encourages action to overcome artificial regulations. In this respect, corruption "oils the mechanism" (Tanzi, 1998, p. 578) or "greases the wheel" (Tanzi, 1998, p. 581). On the other hand, the metaphor of the "invisible fist" (Pies et al., 2005, p. 36) is used to describe the unproductive distribution fights to which corruption can lead. Resulting in bad governance it distorts the actors' behavior and causes inefficiency[22] as well as worse societal results. Corruption can be seen as "sand in the wheels of commerce" (Cuervo-Cazurra, 2006, p. 808). Now the latter of these contrary views is widely accepted (Rose-Ackerman, 1999, pp. 3 – 4, 225 – 229). In the following, an overview of the consequences corruption has on the environment, the organization, and the person is given. Corrupt actors' behavior does not only affect themselves and their organization, but it also affects the environment surrounding the organization. Like for the causes of corruption, most of the literature refers to political or public corruption. Thus, only those effects and results out of the vast body of research are reported that are relevant for private corruption.

2.3.1 Consequences on the Environment

An individual's corrupt behavior most seriously affects two sectors of the environment: a country's society as well as its economy. These effects are often interwoven and not clearly distinguishable.

Consequences on Society

Widespread corruption damages both a society's rules and values. It leads to a disrespect of, and contempt for, the rule of law (Azfar et al., 2001; Coleman, 1998; German, 2002; Guerrero & Rodriguez-Oreggia, 2008; Mauro, 1995). The practice of corruption results in a habituation effect (Engerer, 1998), creates a climate of corruption (Coleman, 1998, p. 39; Hunt, 2004), and is destructive to the public morale (Andvig & Fjeldstad, 2001; Heberer, 2001; Lane & Simpson, 1984; Mauro, 1998b; Schaupensteiner, 2004; Wiehen, 1998) because it harms a social and democratic

---

[21] The "efficient grease hypothesis" is especially relevant for public corruption and political corruption (see e.g., Huntington, 1968, pp. 59 – 71; Leff, 1964; Lui, 1985).

[22] A relationship only relevant for public corruption is that bureaucracy expecting bribes introduces overregulations and slows administration processes to maximize the possibilities for corruption (Myrdal, 1968, pp. 951 – 955).

society's core values (Bannenberg & Schaupensteiner, 2004, p. 42). The tolerance of corruption may encourage more people to engage in corruption over time (Rose-Ackerman, 1999, p. 16). Thus, corruption endangers a society's structure and stability (Mauro, 1995; McFarlane, 2001).

Moreover, corruption weakens the general trust and confidence in the functionality of the legal order and in the economic system (Andvig & Fjeldstad, 2001; Espejo et al., 2001; Pies et al., 2005; Rose-Ackerman, 1999, pp. 97 – 99; Theobald, 1990, pp. 130 – 131).

Furthermore, corruption creates inequality by systematically favoring the rich and powerful (Bardhan, 1997; Cederblom & Dougherty, 1990, p. 155; Davis, 2002; Gupta, Davoodi, & Alonso-Terme, 2002; Johnston, 1989, Klitgaard, 1988, p. 41; Mo, 2001). Corruption is especially likely to increase income inequality (Gupta et al., 2002; Mo, 2001; Tanzi, 1998). Empirical studies underline this (e.g., Mauro, 1995; Li, Xu, & Zou, 2000). The people who receive the bribes are not necessarily those who should have received any compensation at all in a fair market (De George, 1993). There is an unjustified enrichment of corrupt actors (Bausch, 2004). As the advantages of these individuals are at the expense of others, corruption produces a negative overall welfare (Priddat, 2004).

Consequences on Economy

There are a number of literature reviews on the economic impact of corruption (see e.g., Rose-Ackerman, 1999; Tanzi, 1998; Wei, 1999).

In general, it is widely agreed on that corruption damages a society's economic development (Azfar et al., 2001; George, Lacey, & Birmele, 2000; Kaufmann, Kraay, & Zoido-Lobaton, 1999; Klochko & Ordeshook, 2003; Mauro, 1995; McFarlane, 2001; Morgan, 1998; Pies et al., 2005; Shleifer & Vishny, 1993; Wei, 1999) by lowering basic indicators (Kaufmann et al., 1999; Morgan, 1998; Wei, 1999).

One of these indicators is economic growth measured as the growth of the GDP, which is lowered by corruption (Azfar et al., 2001; Bardhan, 1997; Klochko & Ordeshook, 2003; Manandhar, 2005, p. 11; Shahabuddin, 2002; Tanzi, 1998; Treisman, 2000). There is some empirical evidence supporting either a direct effect (e.g., Poirson, 1998; Soon, 2006) or an indirect effect (e.g., by the path of invest-ment: Lambsdorff, 2003; Mauro, 1995; Mauro, 1997; Pellegrini & Gerlaugh, 2004; Tanzi & Davoodi, 1997; by the path of political instability and the level of human capital: Mo, 2001; by the path of the quality of institutions: Mocan, 2004, pp. 22 – 25) on economic growth. Corruption primarily has impact on the accumulation of capital, but does not clearly affect the productivity of capital. This may be the reason why a direct link between corruption and growth is not clearly observed (Lambs-dorff, 1999). But the pathways whereby corruption affects growth are rarely spelled out in the literature (Gaviria, 2002).

Among these channels through which corruption can slow down economic development and economic growth (Morgan, 1998) are the following:

Reduced investment: Empirical results show that corruption lowers investment and, consequently, economic growth (e.g., Brunetti, Kisunko, & Weder, 1998; Brunetti & Weder, 1997; Campos, Lien, & Pradhan, 1999; Knack & Keefer, 1995; Mauro, 1995; Mauro, 1997; Pellegrini & Gerlaugh, 2004; Lambsdorff, 2003). Wedemann (1997) questions the generality of these findings, arguing that the correlation between corruption and investment might be strong for countries with little corruption, but loses power for countries with higher levels of corruption. He therefore concludes that certain kinds of corruption might have more significance for investment decisions than the overall level of corruption as such. An inability to predict the effects of a corrupt payment reduces levels of investment (Campos et al., 1999). This means that if businesses are able to forecast and estimate the level of corruption to include it in their calculations as a measurable expense, and if they know that corruption has a positive effect, it does not impede investment. But if corruption is unpredictable, so that a paid bribe is no guarantee that services are rendered and no more bribes can be expected later, corruption is economically damaging (Amundsen, 1999). Such uncertainty can deter investment and hinder economic development (Goudie & Stasavage, 1997; Tanzi, 1998). Corruption does not only lower investment, but also changes the composition of investments. As it destroys legal certainty, it results in a short-term orientation with a preference for more liquid investment forms, which can be withdrawn more quickly and are less vulnerable to exploitation (e.g., portfolio capital, bank credits) instead of illiquid investment (e.g., direct investment) (Rose-Ackerman, 1999, pp. 32 – 35). Depending on the corruption level, Wei and Wu (2001) found a significant change of the ratio of FDI and bank credits toward more short-term and more liquid engagements. As a "discount on local takeover synergies" (Weitzel & Berns, 2006, p. 786), local corruption affects foreign and domestic acquirers alike.

Reduced foreign direct investment: There is predominant empirical evidence for a negative relationship between corruption and FDI[23] (e.g., Davis & Ruhe, 2003; Habib & Zurawicki, 2002; Smarzynska & Wei, 2002; Soon, 2006; Wei, 2000b; Wei & Shleifer, 2000; Zhao, Kim, & Du, 2003). The effect of corruption on FDI thereby depends on the country of origin of FDI. On the one hand, Cuervo-Cazurra's (2006) study showed that corruption resulted in relatively lower FDI from countries that have signed the OECD Convention on Combating Bribery of Foreign Public Officials in International Business Transactions. On the other hand, Cuervo-Cazurra (2006), Habib and Zurawicki (2002), and Wu (2006) found that investing countries that are more exposed to corruption in their home markets are relatively less sensitive to corruption in foreign markets, which results in relatively higher FDIs. Furthermore, corruption affects not only the level of FDI, but also its composition.

---

[23] Wheeler and Mody (1992) did not find a significant relationship between perceived risk in the host country (including corruption) and the size of FDI.

Widespread corruption leads to the foreign investors' preference for an association with local partners in the form of joint ventures because of the importance of their knowledge about how to deal with corrupt agents. In the absence of corruption wholly-owned subsidiaries are preferred, especially when intangible assets are wished to be protected (Smarzynska & Wei, 2002). The reason for the depressing effect of corruption on FDI is that corruption represents a source of economic risk and uncertainty to foreign investment, and thus stands in contradiction to the market requirements of stability, security, and predictability (Williams & Beare, 1999). It acts as an irregular tax on business, increasing costs and distorting incentives to invest (Kwok & Tadesse, 2006; Mauro, 1995; Shleifer & Vishny, 1993; Tanzi & Davoodi, 1997; Wei, 2000b) so that investors fear losing their investments (Shahabuddin, 2002; Vogt, 1997, pp. 117 – 119). Thus, corruption reduces capital accumulation and lowers capital inflows (Lambsdorff, 1999; empirical evidence in Lambsdorff, 2003). Decreasing investment also means disadvantages for the citizens of a country because incomes decrease, jobs disappear, and the transfer of technology stagnates (Pies et al., 2005).

Reduced international trade: Corruption does not only impede economic development by creating a barrier to investment, but also by distracting international trade (Manandhar, 2005, p. 11; McFarlane, 2001).

> By forcing producers and consumers to pay higher costs in order to engage in the transaction, corruption functions as a transactional barrier. As such, corruption imposes additional costs on market actors with the effect of deterring market exchanges from ever taking place (Sutton, 1997, p. 1438).

Bribes function as an unofficial tariff on export, prevent open markets, and restrict the benefits of trade agreements (Shahabuddin, 2002). Li et al. (2000) found corruption to be associated with lower levels of foreign trade. Nevertheless, the empirical relationship between trade barriers and corruption appears surprisingly weak (Andvig & Fjeldstad, 2001).

Destruction of jobs: Another factor impeding economic development and only relevant for international corruption (Köpf, 1997, pp. 91 – 92) is the destruction of jobs (Bannenberg & Schaupensteiner, 2004, p. 42). If corruption is the standard competitive practice in international business, competitors not willing to meet this standard will lose business and therefore jobs for workers at home (Lane & Simpson, 1984). Corrupt activities of companies in foreign countries also suppress domestic companies in the market who do not have the same corrupt potentials, but comparable services. This costs jobs and the profit flow to the foreign country (Vogt, 1997, p. 126). Furthermore, if extensively high prices had to be paid for former contracts due to corruption, companies can conclude fewer contracts in the future, which leads to fewer jobs (Köpf, 1997, p. 91; Rügemer, 1996, p. 86).

Increased unofficial economy: Corruption increases the level of unofficial economy (Bannenberg & Schaupensteiner, 2004, p. 42; Caiden, 2001), which is also empirically shown (Friedman, Johnson, Kaufmann, & Zoido-Lobaton, 2000; Johnson et al., 2000). Firms use different strategies: They keep profits down and hide revenue (Rose-Ackerman, 1978, p. 201) using "off the books" accounts and secret bank accounts (Sanyal, 2005) or setting up firms in unofficial economy (Rügemer, 1996, pp. 91 – 92). Thus, corruption leads to other crimes such as money laundering (Theobald, 1990, pp. 125 – 126) and tax fraud (Gupta et al., 2002). In the worst case, corruption opens the door to organized crime (German, 2002; Wiehen, 1998).

Reduced tax revenues: Corrupt activities diminish the state's tax revenues for several reasons. First, when corruption destroys jobs (see paragraph above), the dismissal of employees has negative consequences on the state income due to tax deficits and expenses in form of unemployment compensation payments[24] (Vogt, 1997, p. 107). Second, lacking citizens' trust in the functioning of the legal order and the economic system (see chap. 2.3.1, p. 60) leads to a lower tax moral (Vogt, 1997, p. 120). Third, as described above, companies undertake efforts to keep bribe payments and corrupt incomes secret and move into unofficial economy. Thus, financial resources necessary for the payment of bribes, in addition to corrupt incomes, are not accounted for correctly and the correct tax is not paid (De George, 1993; Vogt, 1997, p. 121). This leads to decreasing tax revenues (Gray & Kaufmann, 1998; Kaufmann, 1997; Krug, 1997, p. 62). Fourth, corruption causes higher cost prices and increased expenditures, which are often shifted to the end-consumer. Consequently, there are higher tax obligations for the end-consumer to cover the costs arising through corruption (Krug, 1997, p. 62; Wiehen, 1998). This may result in less consumer spending and therefore in less tax revenues for the state (Vogt, 1997, pp. 107 – 108). These negative effects superpose the possible benefit the state may have when the corrupt company's additional operative success and additional profit and the corrupt employee's spending of achieved material advantages lead to the payment of taxes (Vogt, 1997, p. 88).

Misallocation of talent: As corruption provides more lucrative opportunities than productive work, it creates a suboptimal allocation of talent, which in turn affects economic growth (Acemoglu & Verdier, 1998; Baumol, 1996; Kaufmann, 1997; Murphy, Shleifer, & Vishny, 1991; Tanzi, 1998): Talented and highly educated individuals are more likely to invest their energy in activities with the potential to pursue profit and collect lucrative graft than to accept the more modest financial rewards of truly productive activities (Kaufmann, 1997; Murphy et al., 1991; Tanzi, 1998).

---

[24] Tanzi and Davoodi (1997) found that corruption increases public spending. Research on public corruption shows that corruption alters the composition of public expenditures and leads to lower expenditures for education and health (Mauro, 1998a; Tanzi, 1998), but higher investments in capital-intensive "white elephant" projects with no economic benefit (Kaufmann, 1997; Manandhar, 2005, p. 63; Shahabuddin, 2002). Thus, one may conclude that increasing expenses for unemployment compensation payments may reduce the public resources for an investment into education and health.

Misallocation of resources: There is a discussion in the literature on whether corruption increases efficiency or inefficiency of resource allocation. On the one hand, it is argued that in the bidding for contracts, the most efficient and lowest cost firm is able to pay the highest bribe and thus wins the contract, thus improving allocative efficiency (Beck & Maher, 1986; Frank, 2004; Getz & Volkema, 2001; Leff, 1964; Lien, 1986), especially when the agent has little manipulation power (Burguet & Che, 2004). But on the other hand, the highest bidding capability often does not stem from cost efficiency, but is often associated with substandard quality (Azfar et al., 2001; Kaufmann, 1997). Thus, tenders are diverted away from the best and most suitable supplier (Geis, 1997; McFarlane, 2001). In the worst case, this may result in buying a worse service for a higher price (Vogt, 1997, pp. 45 – 47). Moreover, decisions are biased to inappropriate technology and activities causing costs to the economy. As, for example, more expensive products are less likely to have a commonly known price, they offer more possibilities for kickbacks (Shleifer & Vishny, 1993).

Distortion of competition: Corrupt transactions distort competition (Compte, Lambert-Mogiliansky, & Verdier, 2005; Emerson, 2006; George et al., 2000; Heberer, 2001) because they erode equal opportunities for buyers and sellers on the market (Ockenfels, 1997). The object of an illegal payoff is often not subjected to competitive bidding. Given the need for secrecy in the corrupt partnership, corrupt agents may reduce the risk for detection by considering only a small number of partners (Kaufmann, 1997; Rose-Ackerman, 1999, p. 12). There is a higher willingness of colluding with established firms than to bring new, innovative firms into the circle (Alam, 1990). As they are also often credit-constrained and therefore unable to pay bribes, the market entry of innovative firms is impeded (Murphy, Shleifer, & Vishny, 1993). Corruption especially favors big companies that have the necessary money and methods of payment for corruption (German, 2002; Rügemer, 1996, p. 90; Vogt, 1997, p. 133). This may lead to a concentration of economic power and monopolization, resulting in lower quality of the offered products and an impossibility to get higher quality substitutes (Vogt, 1997, pp. 133 – 134). Corruption entices companies to seek competitive advantages not by entering the market competition with a good price-performance ratio, but with good relations (Pies et al., 2005). The corrupt actors also reduce competition in the market by reducing transparency in their aim to keep corruption secret. So a denatured market develops in which part of the actors are not able to make offers because they do not know the business contents and conditions (Rose-Ackerman, 2001; Vogt, 1997, pp. 44 – 45). Honest businesses lose out in obtaining contracts because of their refusal to acquiesce to corrupt practices (Ades & Di Tella, 1996; Krug, 1997, p. 77). Corruption also undermines competition by facilitating collusion in price between competing firms (Burguet & Che, 2004; Compte et al., 2005). It thereby generates a price increase that goes far beyond the bribe received (Compte et al., 2005). If bribes are thought of as a sort of illegitimate tax (Sandholtz & Gray, 2003) and are budgeted in prices (Rügemer, 1996, p. 80) to cover increased costs for the production and sales of products and services (Vogt,

1997, p. 108), this also leads to increased prices (Rügemer, 1996, p. 80; Schulze & Frank, 2003). When the costs are shifted to the end-consumer, the buying power is reduced. This can lead to inflation in economically instable countries (Shahabuddin, 2002; Vogt, 1997, p. 113).

Erosion of useful regulations: Corruption erodes useful regulations because it masks regulations that assure the functioning of competition or the security of consumers (Kaufmann, 1998; Klitgaard, 1988, pp. 39 – 40)

Danger to business ethics: When corruption gradually spreads, it leads to a corrupt market and to a deterioration of business morality (Hunt, 2004; Van Duyne, 1999). Thus, it discourages good business practices (McFarlane, 2001) and endangers business ethics (Bannenberg & Schaupensteiner, 2004, p. 42). Even honest market partners may be animated to corrupt participation (Lambsdorff & Nell, 2005).

2.3.2 Consequences on the Organization

Luo (2002) presents an organizational perspective of corruption. He argues that corruption represents a firm's evolutionary hazard, strategic impediment, competitive disadvantage, and organizational deficiency in the long run.

Evolutionary Hazard

Corruption represents an evolutionary hazard to a firm because of its effect in regard to five aspects:

Low firm growth: Although there may be gains from a specific transaction or deal, they may be significantly outweighed by the combined organizational losses when looking at an overall organizational effect of corruption (Luo, 2002). Fisman and Svensson (2007) showed that corruption negatively influenced firm growth. A 1% rise in the rate of bribery payments translated into a 3.3% drop in firms' annual rate of growth. This adverse effect of bribery on firm growth was more than three times greater than that of taxation on growth. McArthur and Teal (2002) found that firms encountering high corruption generated an output per employee that was 18% lower in average compared to firms in an environment of low corruption. Despite these strong results, Reinikka and Svensson (2002, 2006) stress that in reality some firms may still benefit from corruption.

High costs: Corrupt transactions involve financial costs that directly attenuate a firm's growth potential. The size of these costs varies among different deals and depends on demand and supply (Luo, 2002). A quantitative assessment of the costs of corruption is difficult. In general, cost increases due to corruption are likely to be in the range of 15 to 40% of the contract value (Wiehen, 1998). Often the expenses for bribes cannot be compensated by making contracts more expensive, but have to be borne by the companies (Pies et al., 2005). The burden of these costs is likely to fall on the small enterprises because they operate in a far more competitive market than large ones, so that they have greater difficulty in passing the costs on to their customers (Tanzi, 1998). Furthermore, corruption causes transaction costs: initiation costs in the search for a suitable corrupt partner, which is time consuming and has to be undertaken discreetly; negotiation costs in the negotiation on the bribe; control costs to keep the transaction secret and to control the receipt of the bribe; and adaptation costs in longer-lasting corrupt relationships (Vogt, 1997, pp. 95 – 99). Moreover, corruption may become a standard operating procedure in the company over which one may lose control (Lane & Simpson, 1984).

High risks: Corruption results in high risks for all actors involved. The degree of risks depends on a corrupter's willingness, power, position, experience, and network (Luo, 2002). It includes the risk of detection and punishment as well as the risk of contracts not being fulfilled (Goudie & Stasavage, 1997). Because of its illicit nature, actors have no recourse in the courts to demand fulfillment of the corrupt agreement, so that it is not assured that the promised return service is delivered (Lambsdorff & Nell, 2005; Shleifer & Vishny, 1993). Furthermore, there is the financial risk that the price of the stock will fall when stockholders who are unsatisfied with the company policy sell their stock and potential buyers also evaluate company performance (Rose-Ackerman, 1978, p. 198). Corruption also endangers the future of a company because it withdraws freedom of action. As it makes companies dependent on some customers while others are neglected, they are vulnerable to blackmail (Then, 1997).

Punishment: When corruption is detected, not only the individual corrupt actor, but also the corrupt organization will be punished. Such institutional punishment includes an often long-lasting reorganization of the firm in the effort to rebuild business connections and reputation. It brings along a removal of corrupt top managers, a rectification of operational and financial policies, a cancellation of institutional membership in industrial associations, as well as a placement of auditors into management decisions or board meeting. Even the disciplinary punishment of individuals (see chap. 2.3.3, p. 68) affects the organization. If corrupt managers quit their jobs, the organization loses the customers and networks connected with them (Luo, 2002).

Negative reputation: Furthermore, corruption damages a company's reputation (Lambsdorff & Nell, 2005). Reputation can already be damaged by speculation and suspicion, independently from legal conviction and the evidence of facts (Pletscher, 1999). The loss of reputation can result in a negative change of the company's situation in the sales market, resourcing market, labor market, and capital market (Pies et al., 2005). Companies may be marked as poorly managed, producing defective products, and unable to ensure customer service (Luo, 2002). They may lose customers and suppliers whose trust is impaired and who have to worry about their own reputation (Bundesverband der Deutschen Industrie e.V. (BDI), 1997; Pies et al., 2005). It also may get more difficult to acquire skilled labor on the market (Pies et al., 2005). Thus, once the market tags a company with this negative image, it will be difficult for the company to survive and grow (Luo, 2002).

Strategic Impediment

Corruption also means a strategic impediment for organizations, which is reflected in a misallocation of resources and a deterrence of capability building.

Resource misallocation: Corruption involves financial resources, human resources, and time resources, resources whose strategic allocation should ensure an organization's competitive advantage (Luo, 2002). Corruption alters allocation decisions towards more inefficient outcomes (Schulze & Frank, 2003) and hard-to-detect activities (Shleifer & Vishny, 1998). In accordance with accounting laws and standards, the spending of money for corruption cannot be recorded as production costs or operational expenses, but rather is undertaken secretly without exposure in the open accounting book (Luo, 2002). Furthermore, enormous time is lost by corrupt actors in negotiating, ensuring the secrecy of the corrupt deals, and guarding against the risk of nondelivery of returns, which comes at the expense of a firm's productivity (Kaufmann, 1997). The positive relationship between corruption and spending of time is also empirically shown (Kaufmann & Wei, 1999; Svensson, 2003).

Capability building deterrence: Corruption creates a climate where dynamic capability mechanisms like organizational learning, knowledge upgrading, and continuous innovation are obstructed. Corruption is seen as "a substitute for innovated technological and organizational skills" (Luo, 2002, p. 417) that allows a quicker and more effective accomplishment of organizational goals than the development of dynamic capabilities (Luo, 2002).

Competitive Disadvantage

Apparently, corruption may support the sale of products and services and result in a competitive advantage (Krug, 1997, p. 38; Vogt, 1997, pp. 43 – 44). All competitors are damaged except the one who gets the contract (Pies et al., 2005). Besides the fact that in a corrupt market a company may sometime be the loser itself, this obvious presumption of a competitive advantage deceives: Corruption does not only hinder firm growth as shown above, but also substantially reduces firm competitiveness (Gaviria, 2002). A firm's competitive position in the market is hurt by the dishonesty and untrustworthiness that are related to corruption. Dishonesty and unreliability destroy business networks because business partners avoid corrupt firms. Furthermore, corruption harms the trust on which long-term relationships with suppliers, buyers, distributors, and other firms are based. The consumers' confidence in a firm's service and their loyalty are eroded, which contributes to a competitive disadvantage (Luo, 2002).

Organizational Deficiency

Corruption is not only caused by organizational deficits, but also results in organizational deficiency. As top managers are often involved in corruption and therefore in violation of business ethics and arms-length business principles, they serve as bad role models resulting in mismanagement, problematic leadership, and a lack of business morality. Thus, an organizational culture is created that contemns innovation, transparency, effective information flow, and productive collaboration (Luo, 2002). So employees are inspired to defalcation (Lambsdorff & Nell, 2005). Moreover, the higher the frequency of corruption, the higher the propensity to replicate such acts (Andvig & Moene, 1990). Even young generations' attitudes may be affected when there are no incentives for integrity and honest behavior (Tirole, 1996).

2.3.3 Consequences on the Person

Although corrupt actors' behavior substantially harms the environment and the organization, it is primarily they themselves who have to bear the consequences. Corrupt actors have to accept the responsibility for their decision and action (Lane & Simpson, 1984).

Thus, they have to face both legal punishment according to the country's law as well as disciplinary punishment (Luo, 2002). This may include fines, jail sentences, or the loss of employment (Lane & Simpson, 1984). The costs of being suspended because of corruption are not only the managers' jeopardized future careers (Rose-Ackerman, 1978, p. 199) and the foregone future wages (Carrillo, 2000), but also include the loss of the company's trust in the employee (Löw, 2002), a loss of reputation (Carrillo, 2000; Lane & Simpson, 1984), the dishonor of a shameful action (Carrillo, 2000), a social stigma that in its degree depends on the prevailing norms and expectations within the culture (Treisman, 2000), embarrassment, and psychological suffering (Lane & Simpson, 1984). Corruption also undermines self-respect because corrupt actors create networks of systematic deception and therefore compromise their characters in countless ways (Cederblom & Dougherty, 1990, p. 154). It impairs employees' moral (Levi, 2000), leads to a lacking sense of wrongdoing (Reichmann, 1997), and encourages repeat offenses (Levi, 2000).

2.3.4 Summary

As for the causes of corruption, there is also broad research on the consequences of corruption, but with similar restrictions. The literature especially focuses on environmental consequences in regard to political and public corruption. Outlined above are those that also may apply to private corruption. Figure 3 summarizes the potential consequences of private corruption. Theoretical literature in regard to organizational and personal consequences of corruption is scarce, and empirical research on these aspects is predominantly missing. Thus, the consequences of private corruption described here need to be empirically supported.

Consequences on the Environment

Consequences on the Society:
- Damage to a society's rules and values
- Weakening of the general trust and confidence in the functionality of the legal order and the economic system
- Increased inequality

Consequences on the Economy:
- Damage to economic development and economic growth
  - Reduced investment
  - Reduced foreign direct investment
  - Reduced international trade
  - Destruction of jobs
  - Increased unofficial economy
  - Reduced tax revenues
  - Misallocation of talent
  - Misallocation of resources
  - Distortion of competition
  - Erosion of useful regulations
  - Danger to business ethics

Consequences on the Organization

Evolutionary Hazard:
- Low firm growth
- High costs
- High risks
- Punishment
- Negative reputation

Strategic Impediment:
- Resource misallocation
- Capability building deterrence

Competitive Disadvantage:
- Reduction of firm competitiveness
- Destruction of business relationships
- Loss of customers' and suppliers' trust

Organizational Deficiency:
- Mismanagement and defective leadership
- Lack of business morality
- Obstacle to innovation, transparency, effective information flow, and productive collaboration
- Animation of employees to defalcation
- Danger of a replication of corrupt acts

Consequences on the Person
- Legal and disciplinary punishment
- Loss of employment
- Loss of company's trust in the employee
- Loss of reputation
- Social stigma
- Psychological suffering
- Damage to self-respect
- Impairment of the employee's moral

PRIVATE CORRUPTION

Figure 3: The Consequences of Private Corruption

2.4   The Corrupt Relationship

Besides the vast body of research on the causes and consequences of corruption, there also are two major attempts in the literature that try to describe the different states of the corrupt relationship: the sociological approach as well as the New Institutional Economics approach.

2.4.1 The Sociological Approach

Höffling (2002, chap. 5) provides a five-phase model (see figure 4) in order to describe the corrupt relationship and to understand the dynamics of corrupt action:

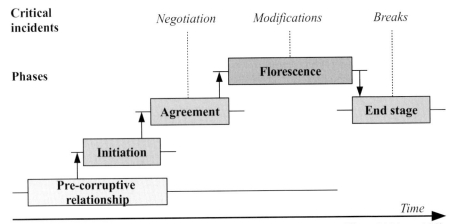

Figure 4:   Phases of the Corrupt Relationship (adopted from Höffling, 2002, p. 118)

- Phase 1: The pre-corruptive relationship

  Often, long-lasting, pre-corruptive, and legal relationships are the base of corruption. These can be business, amicable, or kinsmanlike relations. In this first phase, corruption intentions do not yet exist (Höffling, 2002, pp. 115 – 116, 119 – 122).

- Phase 2: Initiation

  In the initiation phase, at least one partner aims at corrupting or being corrupted (Höffling, 2002, pp. 116, 122 – 127). Once one partner has taken the decision to make a corrupt approach, this partner attempts to convince the other to be part of the corrupt action (Warburton, 2001). To keep the scope of rejection as small as possible, the partner is brought into a situation of dependence (Höffling, 2002, pp. 116, 122 – 127). This involves power from both partners' point of view (Warburton, 2001). If the corrupted partner takes the initiative, this is indicated by a declaration that a service so far provided without demanding a return service will not be continued without an advantage being granted. If the corrupting partner takes the initiative, "feeding" with presents, from small to quite expensive, that constrict the receiver's action scope when accepted is a popular strategy (see also Fiebig & Junker, 2004, pp. 119 – 123). This way, the receiver gets into a debtor position. The beneficiary demands the unidirectional advances as corrupt action (Höffling, 2002, pp. 116, 122 – 127). These attempts can only be successful if the following conditions are met: There is a trustful connection between the two partners. One of the partners has a resource the other partner wants or needs, is dependent on, and cannot easily obtain another way. Both partners see the possibility to conduct the transaction in secret and perceive a low risk of punishment (Warburton, 2001).

- Phase 3: Agreement

With the phase of agreement on the exchange modalities of service and return service, the corrupt relationship in the narrow sense begins. The mode, time, and place of the corrupt exchange are negotiated. It is anchored in the consciousness of both partners that they agreed to a moral dubious exchange (Höffling, 2002, pp. 116 – 117).

- Phase 4: Florescence

In the phase of florescence, the corrupt relationship is established and routinized. The agreements are secretly transformed into action. Modifications of the relationship are also possible, like, for example, changes in the exchange relation or the inclusion of further actors (Höffling, 2002, p. 117, pp. 127 – 138).

- Phase 5: End stage

The end stage of the corrupt relationship is reached when the participants have exchanged service and return service according to the agreement. They continue to keep their transaction secret (Höffling, 2002, pp. 117 – 118, 138 – 142). The two actors are now tied together in such a way that continuing trust is required (Warburton, 2001). Often the corrupt relationship stabilizes, and the corrupt action is repeated (Höffling, 2002, pp. 117 – 118, 138 – 142). Each partner now has the power resource of information regarding the other partner's previous corrupt transactions. Such a corrupt dyadic exchange also can mark the beginning of the establishment of a corrupt network (Warburton, 2001). Nevertheless, in this final phase, there is also the danger that the relationship breaks up, either because one of the partners decides to cancel the cooperation, or because the corrupt transaction is detected (Höffling, 2002, pp. 117 – 118, pp. 138 – 142).

In the process of a corrupt relationship, different relationship patterns are observable. The typology of these relationship patterns is based on the following structural characteristics of corrupt relationships (Höffling, 2002, chap. 6):

- Initiative, which addresses the question of the role allocation (active, passive) at the beginning of the corrupt relationship;

- Dominance, which describes who controls and determines the corrupt transaction and its modalities;

- Rigor, which describes how much the dominating party enforces its views and aims in the corrupt relationship;

- Routinization, which refers to the degree of the development of routines in the corrupt relationship;

- Duration of the corrupt relationship, which addresses the stability of a corrupt relationship;

- Exclusiveness, which describes whether corrupt activities are limited to two partners or whether corrupt relationships to further partners exist;

- Testimonial behavior, which refers to the willingness to report about the corrupt relationship in a criminal procedure.

According to these characteristics, Höffling (2002, chap. 6) identifies four relationship patterns (see table 1):

- Entanglement pattern: The basic principle of this pattern is the entanglement of the holder of a powerful position by the client. The client tries to create a feeling of obligation on the side of the holder of a powerful position by suitable payments in advance, so that the holder cannot refuse later expected services. The client relies on the principle of reciprocity without acting with too much rigor.

- Harmony pattern: The central characteristic of this pattern is the partners' correspondence, which is based on harmonizing interests. The relationship is marked by equality.

- Habituation pattern: This pattern is described by the habituation of the holder of a powerful position to the conveniences of the corrupt relationship. The holder more and more gets used to the corrupt benefits and gradually grows into the role of the demander.

- Coercion pattern: The dominating characteristic of this pattern is the coercion of the client by the holder of a powerful position abusing the dependency. The demands and expectancies in regard to return services are clearly communicated.

Table 1:   Four Relationship Patterns (adopted from Höffling, 2002, p. 149)

	Entan-glement pattern	Harmony pattern	Habituation pattern	Coercion pattern
Initiative coming from	Clearly C	Rather HP	Rather C	Clearly HP
Dominance in the course of the relationship	Clearly C	Rather C	Rather HP	Clearly HP
Rigor in the behavior of the dominating party	-	--	+	++
Degree of **routinization** of corrupt transactions	--	-	+	++
Duration of the corrupt relationship	--	-	+	++
Exclusiveness of the relationship · for the holder of a powerful position · for the client	 + -	 + +	 - -	 - +
Testimonial behavior · of the holder of a powerful position · of the client	 ++ --	 + -	 ++ +	 -- ++

C = Client; HP = Holder of a powerful position
Strength of the structural characteristics in relation to each other:
-- = very weak; - = weak; + = strong; ++ = very strong

2.4.2 The New Institutional Economics Approach

There are also attempts using the New Institutional Economics approach to describe the corrupt relationship focusing on the transaction costs that occur before, during, and after the relationship and that have to be taken into account by the persons willing to participate in corrupt action (Lambsdorff, 2002; Lambsdorff & Teksoz, 2002). Transaction costs include the costs of searching for partners, determining contract conditions, enforcing contract terms, and keeping corrupt transactions secret (Lambsdorff, 2002; Lambsdorff & Teksoz, 2002). A significant indirect association exists between the level of transaction costs and the level of mutual trust among the contract partners. The less trust among corrupt partners, the more time, effort, and money must be spent to organize the corrupt exchange (Lambsdorff & Teksoz,

2002). Corrupt transactions are less vulnerable to opportunism[25] when embedded in legal relationships (Lambsdorff & Teksoz, 2002) or relationships based on kinship or friendship (Rose-Ackerman, 2001). Thus, corrupt contracts are relational contracts (Lambsdorff & Teksoz, 2002).

Lambsdorff (2002) distinguishes three phases in the corrupt relationship:

- Phase 1: Contract initiation

  First, one has to search for a potential partner for the corrupt transaction (Lambsdorff, 2002). This requires information on whether the potential partner is able and willing to provide the requested service. This information can be gained by three means: by a public but disguised information distribution (e.g., spreading rumors about the potential corruptibility of oneself), by an organized advertisement via middlemen, or by direct information provision to well-acquainted business partners. The best opportunity for corruption arises between business partners with established legal relationships. In this case, corruption takes place as "already existing relationship deteriorate into illegal relationships" (Lambsdorff, 2002, p. 225).

  Second, once a corrupt partner is found, the contract conditions have to be determined (Lambsdorff, 2002). The partners have to negotiate the value of the bribe as well as the type of return and have to specify the conditions of the corrupt transaction as concretely as possible to avoid later excuses of one partner. They may also agree on how they conceal their illegal payments (Lambsdorff, 2002).

- Phase 2: Contract enforcement

  In a next step, the enforcement of the corrupt contract has to be ensured because the exchange of corrupt services often does not take place at the same time, thus offering the possibility to refuse the provision of the return or to alter the negotiated services. As corrupt transactions are not legally enforceable, other mechanisms to secure them have to be found (Lambsdorff, 2002):

  One possibility is to use so-called hostages, "valuable asset[s] given by someone who might profit from opportunism to those on the other side of the contractual agreement, who are in a position to be harmed by opportunistic behavior" (Lambsdorff, 2002, p. 229). These hostages are kept in the case that a proposed service is not delivered by the corrupt partner. Such hostages, for example, can be resources from a linked legal relationship, which are owned by someone else and serve as safeguards against opportunism in the corrupt relationship (Lambsdorff, 2002).

  A second possibility is to establish a good reputation as a trustful partner dealing honestly. As the delivering of this information is difficult to realize for the

---

[25] Opportunism is a behavior that is characterized by "a lack of candor or honesty in transactions, to include self-interest seeking with guile" (Williamson, 1975, p. 9).

corrupt partners themselves, middlemen[26] may be used who can publicly disclose their past record, link the parties involved, and guarantee the corrupt deal (Lambsdorff, 2002).

A third possibility is the repetition of relationships by dealing with old partners. The expectation of future deals and the possible damage of losing them serves as a deterrent against opportunism in current transactions (Lambsdorff, 2002).

Another possibility to enforce contracts is vertical integration. There are two ways of realizing this: On the one hand, the corrupt partners can form a new company under common ownership and control. Then, the common aim of raising their firm's profit minimizes the risk of opportunistic behavior. On the other hand, the provider of corrupt services can be given hierarchical control rights by, for example, offering this person a position on the firm's board. This reduces the probability of a refusal to provide the promised payment (Lambsdorff, 2002).

A last possibility offers social embeddedness. Being a member of a social structure created by, for example, organizational links, does not only help to spread information of corrupt opportunities, but also ensures a trustful environment with no incentives to behave opportunistically (Lambsdorff, 2002).

• Phase 3: The aftermath

After the fulfillment of mutual claims and the exchange of services and return, the corrupt transaction is ended. Nevertheless, due to the mutual dependence, each partner has the means to impose harm on the counterpart. Thus, two different situations may arise (Lambsdorff, 2002):

First, there is the risk of denunciation and extortion. Either one of the corrupt partners may wish to take revenge or to ease conscience, or well-informed third parties may denounce participants if they need not fear prosecution. The last may be the case when prosecutors offer witnesses a reward in exchange for inside information, when private agents bid for such information to squeeze corrupt competitors out of the market, or when media pay tip-offs to report on scandals (Lambsdorff, 2002).

Second, a fulfilled corrupt transaction also has consequences on following contract designs. It is difficult to reject further corrupt agreements because the declaration of corrupt payments becomes troublesome and more suspicious. Furthermore, as the expected penalties rise with further corrupt transactions, this leads to demands of higher bribes. Moreover, the risk of exposure can serve as a means to enforce corrupt contracts and to avoid denunciation. This can also be achieved by engaging middlemen who will take the full blame in the case of detection (Lambsdorff, 2002). However, this includes the risk that middlemen may not serve the clients' interest, perhaps demanding higher fees or conducting

---

[26] Bayar (2005) found that the existence of middlemen increased the incidences of corruption.

reverse bribery on one of the corrupt partners (Rose-Ackerman, 1978, pp. 193 – 194).

2.4.3 Summary

The literature provides two approaches that describe how a corrupt relationship between two actors originates, develops, terminates, or extends. While both approaches consider the dynamics in this relationship, the sociological approach additionally focuses on the structural characteristics of the corrupt relationship; the New Institutional Economics approach, in contrast, additionally discusses the transaction costs that may arise in the course of the corrupt relationship.

2.5   Theoretical Explanations for the Corruption Phenomenon

The interdisciplinary literature on corruption provides a number of theoretical attempts to explain the phenomenon, partly drawing on established theories. These theoretical contributions can be divided into two groups:

(1) Theoretical approaches that primarily focus on the explanation of the accomplishment of corrupt interaction: for example, principal-agent theory or social exchange theory;

(2) Theoretical approaches that primarily focus on the explanation of the determinants of corrupt action: for example, anomie theory, theory of planned behavior, social learning theory, neo-institutionalism, or agent-centered institutionalism.

In the following, theoretical approaches applicable for the explanation of private corruption are reported. Approaches referring to other types of corruption like, for example, Collier's (2002) institutional choice framework to explain political corruption and Aultman's (1976) approach integrating role theory, anomie theory, and social learning theory to explain police corruption are not outlined.

2.5.1 Principal-Agent Theory

A popular approach in the economic research thread to explain corrupt behavior is the principal-agent theory (Andvig & Fjeldstad, 2001; Banfield, 1975; Klitgaard, 1988; Husted, 2007; Pies et al., 2005; Rose-Ackerman, 1978).

According to this theory, corruption includes at least three actors: the principal, the agent, and the client (Klitgaard, 1991). In an organization, every individual, except those at the bottom, can be seen both as principal (as superior looking downwards) and as agent (as subordinate looking upwards). The executive board at the top are agents of the organization as well as principals of those below them (Grieger, 2005).

The principals (e.g., the supervisors) delegate those tasks they themselves cannot fulfill due to lack of time, competence, or costs to agents (e.g., the employees) who are provided with all necessary resources, especially the power of decision (James, 2002; Pies et al., 2005). This relationship consists of an incomplete or relational contract (Husted, 2007), which explicitly or implicitly regulates the duties of both parties (Husted, 2007; Pies et al., 2005).

The principals need to rely on the fact that the agents do not misuse the provided scope of discretion – except when they tolerate or even encourage it, which might be the case for some agents making corrupt offers (Pies et al., 2005). The agents can act opportunistically (Kidder, 2005) and break the contracts with their principals, abuse power and trust by closing a hidden contract with a client. The agents promise to use their scope of decision in the clients' favor and the clients pledge themselves to give a reward (Pies et al., 2005). The clients can act in their own name, as agents of another principal, or as autonomous middlemen who act on behalf of a principal or an agent (Homann, 1997). It is assumed that both agents and clients are motivated by self-interest (Kidder, 2005; Schilling, 2004). This implies that their decision to behave corruptly is a rational choice decision that is based on calculations of potential personal gains and losses that may result from their behavior (Klitgaard, 1988, pp. 69 – 70). On the one hand, they take into account the perceived constraints (e.g., the likelihood of detection, the probability and size of penalties, transaction costs) as opportunities to act corruptly; on the other hand, they consider the expected benefits in the light of their individual preferences (Grieger, 2005).

The core of the principal-agent-client problem lies in asymmetric information. On the one hand, prior to the contract, the principals lack knowledge about whether the agents are honest or dishonest and whether they have hidden motivations to obtain certain resources (problem of adverse selection). On the other hand, after contracting, the principals have poor information about the agents' and the clients' either productive or corrupt activities (problem of moral hazard) because actions are taken hidden from or unobserved by the principals (Andvig & Fjeldstad, 2001; Husted, 2007).

Pies et al. (2005) assess this scheme with three actors too simple to reconstruct most of the corruption cases. They argue that often there is not only one client on the demand side, but many competing clients. To get the contract in a corrupt market it is necessary to pay a bribe higher than the competitors. They model the decision of the client on whether to act corruptly or not using a pay-off matrix (see figure 5).

Four different combinations of strategies are possible, resulting in four different states, which are evaluated by the clients. A higher number indicates that this state is considered better than the states with lower numbers. The best solution for client A is to act corruptly while client B acts honestly. The second best solution is when all clients act honestly in a fair competition, because there are no costs due to detection, punishment, or reputation loss. If everybody participates in the corrupt competition, the chances to get the contract are the same for all, but everybody has to take the risks related with corruption. The worst case for client A is to act honestly while client B acts corruptly. The same is true for client B. Both clients will decide on the strategy to act corruptly to achieve the highest pay-off for themselves. Thus, the state in quadrant 3 will result with a pay-off of "2" for both. An equilibrium is achieved from which no client will deviate. This reflects the dilemma of corruption: Although there is a better state for all, it cannot be achieved.

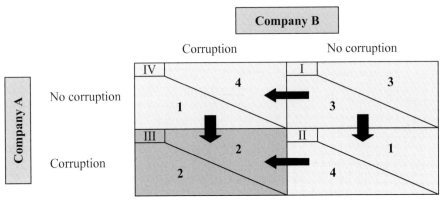

The numbers 1, 2, 3, 4 indicate the pay-offs in monetary units.

Figure 5:   The Dilemma of Corruption (adopted from Pies et al., 2005, p. 144)

2.5.2 Social Exchange Theory

The social exchange theory often applied by the sociological researchers contains potential to explain corrupt behavior, but up to now it is only applied to one form of corruption, namely cronyism (Khatri, Tsang, & Begley, 2005, August; Khatri et al., 2006). The theory argues that social exchange involves a series of interactions that generate obligations (Emerson, 1976). These interactions are independent and contingent on the actions of another person (Blau, 1964, chap. 4). They evolve over time into trusting, loyal, and mutual relationships (Cropanzano & Mitchell, 2005).

According to social exchange theory, corruption can be seen as a kind of social exchange where corrupt actors form social relations based on the benefits and costs they provide one another. They expect the relationship to be rewarding because both partners involved in the social exchange transaction possess a resource the other desires. As exchange relations are reciprocal, corrupt relationships disintegrate over time if this reciprocity is broken (see Blau, 1964; Cook & Whitmeyer, 1992; Emerson, 1972a; Emerson, 1972b; Homans, 1961; Khatri et al., 2005, August; Molm, 1994; Thibaut & Kelley, 1959).

2.5.3 Anomie Theory

Anomie theory, which also comes from a sociological tradition, represents another approach to explain corrupt behavior (Maravic, 2006), related white-collar crimes like fraud (Riahi-Belkaoui & Picur, 2000; Zahra et al., 2005), or white-collar crime in general (Löw, 2002, pp. 35 – 36). It is rooted in the work by Emil Durkheim in the year 1893 (Löw, 2002, p. 35), which defined anomie as "a state of normlessness or lack of regulation, a disorderly relation between the individual and social order" (Riahi-Belkaoui & Picur, 2000, p. 36). Robert Merton, a criminologist that applied Durkheim's definition of anomie to modern industrial societies with emphasis towards the United States, specifically redefined the term. Anomie refers to a situation in which there is an apparent lack of fit between the culture's norms about a person's goals and the culture's norms about the appropriate means to achieve those goals (Merton, 1949, pp. 125 – 149). Deviant behavior and therefore also corrupt behavior occurs as a form of what he calls innovation strategy, when people perceive socially acceptable means of goal achievement as either ineffective or impossible for them (see Riahi-Belkaoui & Picur, 2000; Zahra et al., 2005). Whether people behave corruptly depends on the degree to which they would like to realize certain goals within the framework of legitimated norms. The greater the goals' intensity, the smaller the acceptance of norms, the smaller the perceived possibility to achieve the goals by legitimated means, and the bigger the perceived possibility to achieve the goals by illegitimated means, the bigger is the probability that a person commits a white-collar crime like corruption (see Löw, 2002, p. 36). Cloward and Ohlin (1960) emphasize that formal structures prevent people from achieving socially demanded success symbols, therefore leading to deviant as well as corrupt behavior (Maravic, 2006).

2.5.4 Theory of Planned Behavior

A psychological theory stemming from attitude-behavior research that is widely used to explain unethical behavior (e.g., Bobek & Hatfield, 2003; Chang, 1998; Fuku-kawa, 2002; Leonard, Cronan, & Kreie, 2004; Randall & Gibson, 1991) is the theory of planned behavior (Ajzen, 1991; for a detailed description see chap. 3.2.2, p. 96).

Powpaka (2002) applies this theory to explain managers' decisions to bribe (see figure 6), whereby he replaces perceived behavioral control by perceived choice. He argues that high perceived behavioral control over bribe giving may not increase the intention to bribe as suggested by Ajzen's (1991) model. He found that managers' intention to bribe is positively influenced by their personal attitude toward the act and negatively by their perceived choice. The attitude toward bribe giving is positively affected by the managers' perceived necessity of the act and negatively by their perceived unethicality of the act. The subjective norm is positively influenced by the perceived support managers would receive from top management, and by the attitude toward bribe giving.

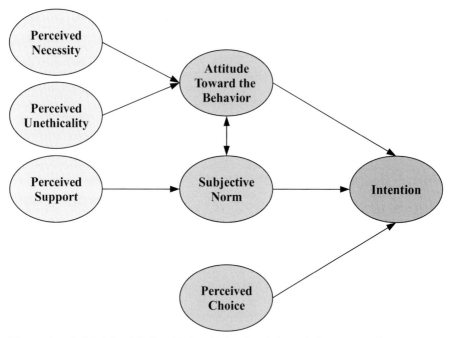

Figure 6:   A Model of Bribe Giving Behavior (adopted from Powpaka, 2002, p. 230, model b)

2.5.5 Social Learning Theory

Vaughan et al. (2005, August) use the social learning theory (Bandura, 1977) generally and the theory of differential association (Sutherland, 1949, chap. XIV) more specifically to explain the spread of corruption. According to social learning theory, individuals can learn by observing the behavior of those around them (Bandura, 1977). Differential association refers to how differential exposure and interaction generate "normative definitions favorable or unfavorable to illegal or law-abiding behavior" (Akers, 2000, p. 76). Thus, employees in organizations learn that corrupt behavior is expected and how corruption is carried out (Vaughan et al., 2005, August).

Vaughan et al.'s (2005, August) social learning model of corruption is depicted in figure 7. Before engaging in behavior, actors observe their social environment. It provides them with hints on how corrupt and non-corrupt behaviors are distributed and which payoffs are associated with each behavior. Actors then interpret these observations to figure out the cultural norms of their environment. Based on these interpretations, they make decisions on whether to act corruptly or not in the future.

Their behavior results in payoffs, which may lead to explicit pecuniary or implicit non-pecuniary rewards including status. As synonymous with the influence as a role model, individuals themselves shape the observation and learning process of others.

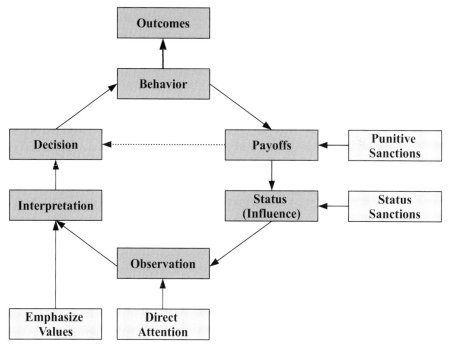

Figure 7:   A Social Learning Model of Corruption (adopted from Vaughan et al., 2005, August, p. 16)

The model includes four points of intervention for organizations in determining the individual's corrupt or non-corrupt behavior (Vaughan et al., 2005, August):

- Directing attention of observations: Organizations can focus observation on corrupt actors by publicly recognizing individuals who achieve particularly good results, even if their performance resulted from corrupt behavior. Conversely, organizations may focus observation on non-corrupt actors by recognizing particularly upstanding behavior, regardless of performance.

- Emphasizing values: Organizational culture may shape the interpretation of behavior observations. If descriptive statements show that corrupt behavior is rewarded in an organization, this contributes to a spread of corruption, while clearly stated sanctions for corrupt behavior diminish corruption. Through organizational culture, organizations can re-interpret the behaviors of actors and cast them in ways that reduce the "fitness" of corrupt actors as role models.

• Punitive sanctions: An organization may reduce the payoffs achieved from corrupt behavior by punitive sanctions. These may reduce growth in status either directly or indirectly, although individuals who consistently act corruptly still may achieve a higher net status.

• Status sanctions: An organization can undertake efforts to reduce the status of offenders in order to reduce their attractiveness as role models.

2.5.6 Neo-Institutionalism

The neo-institutionalistic view on corruption stresses the role of the institution, which influences the agent's behavior (Maravic, 2006). According to the "calculus approach" (Hall & Taylor, 1996, p. 7), institutions affect behavior "by providing actors with greater or lesser degrees of certainty about the present and future behavior of other actors" (p. 7), by enforcement mechanisms for integer behavior or penalties for corruption, for example. They alter the actors' expectation about others' reactions to their own action. Following the "cultural approach" (Hall & Taylor, 1996, p. 7), institutions affect behavior by establishing criteria and principles that agents use to build their preferences and to interpret the world. They provide a network of routines, symbols, and scripts, which serve as moral or cognitive templates for interpretation and action. For the survival of an organization, legitimacy is more important than efficiency. This legitimacy is achieved by copying formal organizational structures, also called "isomorphism" (Hasse & Krücken, 2005, p. 23). Maravic (2006) argues that corrupt practices in organizations are part of a legitimation strategy where, for example, the superior's behavior or typical business practices are copied. According to March and Olsen (1989, see p. 38 for the key arguments), corrupt behavior follows a logic of appropriateness. The employee's role is defined by shared assumptions about what is due to occupants of other roles like, for example, the supervisor. Corrupt action therefore reflects an adaptation to structures of corrupt routines institutionalized in organizations and justified by the experience. But corruption may also occur because of conflicting and ambiguous rules, which cause uncertainty.

2.5.7 Agent-Centered Institutionalism

Maravic (2006) uses the agent-centered institutionalism – a combination of neo-institutionalism and rational choice – to explain corruption. Based on the works of Quah (1989) and Scharpf (1997), Maravic (2006) distinguishes three action dimensions that determine each other:

• Motivation to act corruptly: The first dimension describes the factors that guide actions within organizations like, for example, formal and informal rules or the organization's mission statement. They determine what is considered as corrupt. This dimension influences an actor's decision to deviate from the rules or to keep to them and therefore reflects the motivation to act corruptly or not ("Do I want to deviate from the organization's norms, rules, and values?").

• Opportunity to act corruptly: The second dimension describes the factors that enable corrupt behavior like, for example, extensive competencies, high freedom of action, and monopoly power over resources ("Is it possible for me to act corruptly when regarding my competencies, position, and responsibilities?").

• Lacking limitation to act corruptly[27]: The third dimension describes the factors that prohibit or prevent corrupt behavior like, for example, monitoring, control, and penalty systems ("Do I manage to overcome hindering factors like control and sanction mechanisms?").

These three dimensions, in all possible combinations, constitute eight different situations reflecting four different risk states: no risk for corruption, low risk, high risk, or actual corruption. The eight constellations are shown in table 2.

Table 2:   Action Dimensions, Situations, and Risk for Corruption (adopted from Maravic, 2006, p. 119)

Situations	Action dimension I: Motivation	Action dimension II: Opportunity	Action dimension III: Lacking limitation		Degree of corruption risk
I	No	No	No	=	No risk
II	No	No	Yes	=	Low risk
III	No	Yes	No	=	Low risk
IV	No	Yes	Yes	=	High risk
V	Yes	No	No	=	Low risk
VI	Yes	No	Yes	=	High risk
VII	Yes	Yes	No	=	High risk
VIII	Yes	Yes	Yes	=	Corruption

2.5.8 Theory of Structuration

According to Grieger (2005), the theory of structuration by Giddens (1984) provides an explanation for collective corruption. The theory balances the two extremes of

---

[27] This third action dimension identified by Maravic (2006) cannot be clearly distinguished from the second action dimension. Rather, they both describe the contrary facets of the same dimension, namely the scope for action that is either enabled or restricted.

agency and structure, which is referred to as the duality of structure: Social structures enable social action, and social action creates those structures. Structures are the rules, procedures, and norms that govern an agent's behavior. As agents have knowledge of their society on which they refer in their interaction, they in turn produce structure as the condition for their future action. This recursive interaction of agent with structure is called structuration (Giddens, 1984, chap. 1).

Organizations represent the structuration of relationship between social actors. According to the theory of structuration, organizational structure with its rules, procedures, and norms enables and restricts interactions and therefore determines whether actors in the organization act corruptly or not. Based on the image of their potentially corrupt social environment, actors themselves produce corrupt structures leading to an institutionalization of corruption. Thus, Grieger (2005) concludes that corruption in organizations is both action and structure and "can be conceptualized as been tied up in the fabric of producing and reproducing the organizational process through actions" (p. 17).

2.5.9 Summary

As corruption is a phenomenon investigated by different disciplines, there are also various approaches to theoretically explain the phenomenon from different perspectives: the economic perspective (principal-agent theory), the sociological perspective (social exchange theory, anomie theory, neo-institutionalism, agent-centered institutionalism, and theory of structuration), or the psychological perspective (social learning theory and theory of planned behavior). The theoretical approaches either predominantly focus on the explanation of the accomplishment of corrupt interaction or on the explanation of the determinants of corrupt action. Due to the complexity of the corruption phenomenon, it is difficult to arrive at an overall theory explaining all aspects.

2.6   The Normalization of Corruption in Organizations

Often, an individual's corrupt behavior is both cause and consequence of a normalization of corruption in the organization[28]. Normalization means "institutionalized processes by which extraordinary situations are rendered seemingly ordinary" (Ashforth & Kreiner, 2002, p. 217). A single corrupt act often "set[s] in motion a cascade of further corrupt actions [like a] tornado of corruption" (Darley, 2005, p. 1181) that gathers force and pulls in more of the organization's members. In the following, these normalizing mechanisms that favor the spread of corruption are described.

---

[28] For the following see also Rabl & Kühlmann (2008, May).

2.6.1 Rationalization and Neutralization Strategies

Once corrupt action has been undertaken, individuals use different rationalization tactics to justify[29] their acts of corruption (Aguilera & Vadera, 2005, August; Ashforth & Anand, 2003). According to identity theory, individuals aim at seeing themselves in a positive light (Ashforth & Kreiner, 1999). Rationalization strategies allow corrupt offenders to view themselves as moral and ethical individuals, which frees them from any pangs of conscience that would hinder them from further corrupt engagement (Anand, Ashforth, & Joshi, 2005). Thus, a technique of rationalization is also considered a technique of neutralization (Sykes & Matza, 1957), "a device that enables individuals to violate important normative standards but to neutralize the definition of themselves as deviant or criminal" (Coleman, 1998, p. 188). It defends offenders both from self-blame and from social criticism and protects the actor's self image (Sykes & Matza, 1957; Vitell & Grove, 1987).

Corrupt individuals do not abandon societal values; they only construe situations differently (Sykes & Matza, 1957). They do not completely reject conventional norms, and do not feel that the norms they may be violating should be replaced, but they hold that they do not apply under special circumstances (Sykes & Matza, 1957; Vitell & Grove, 1987).

Rationalization strategies reject negative interpretations of corrupt acts, thereby neutralizing the potential stigma of corruption. They can be used by an individual in isolation and become far more potent when institutionalized in the collective (Ashforth & Anand, 2003). Most of the techniques of rationalizations are culturally learned and socially reinforced (Coleman, 1998, p. 193; Vitell & Grove, 1987). Organizations not only supply their members with a set of appropriate rationalizations, but also help to isolate them from contact with those who would judge their corrupt behavior harsher. Corrupt offenders apply and adapt existing rationalizations to their own behavior (Coleman, 1998, pp. 192 – 193). The successful use of a particular technique may lead to the technique's use in subsequent situations of a

---

[29] Justifications are one common category in the social psychological research on accounts, on explanations for organizational misconduct (Konovsky & Jaster, 1989; Szwajkowski, 1992). Szwajkowski (1992) provides an overview of common classifications (e.g., Schönbach, 1980; Scott & Lyman, 1968; Semin & Manstead, 1983). He argues that the literature on accounts can be organized into a 2 x 2 matrix framework. The first dimension centers on whether or not the actor admits that some net harm is done by the act, and the second consists of whether or not the actor admits responsibility. When both are admitted, the account is a concession, while denial of both constitutes a refusal. Admitting responsibility but not harm equates to a justification, and the opposite condition is an excuse. Thus, according to these classifications, justifications are "accounts where someone accepts responsibility for their behavior, but denies any pejorative interpretations of their behavior" (Konovsky & Jaster, 1989, p. 392). Konovsky and Jaster's (1989) study demonstrated that business men and women were more likely to defend their questionable behavior by using excuses and justifications than to openly concede errors of judgment and behavior.

similar nature (Vitell & Grove, 1987). Thus, rationalization techniques contribute to the spread of corruption in and across organizations (Wellen, 2004, October).

Rationalization techniques may be prospective or retrospective in nature. Prospective rationalizations are future oriented and calculative, providing a rationale for future commission of corrupt behavior and therefore functioning as ex ante determinants[30]. Retrospective rationalizations are past oriented and defensive, providing a post hoc justification for involvement in corrupt behavior (Ashforth & Anand, 2003; Coleman, 1998, p. 188; Shover & Bryant, 1993; Sykes & Matza, 1957).

Höffling (2002, chap. 8.3) identifies nine conditions that enable the use of such techniques of rationalization and neutralization:

(1) Norm of reciprocity: Corruption is a social exchange relationship that includes trust and reciprocity. As it is related to the social expectation of "tit for tat," which is a legitimate practice in all areas of life, it provides a possibility for neutralization.

(2) Useful side effects: The experience of positive side effects of corruption neutralizes corrupt action.

(3) Goal conflicts: Corrupt situations often represent a dilemma between personal and organizational values and goals. Actors do not take the decision in favor of their own person, but in their responsibility for the company, a fact that enables neutralization.

(4) The partner's responsibility: As corruption is an interaction between at least two partners, it can be neutralized by the delegation of responsibility to the partner, thereby making use of the preventive effect of "not knowing". It is not only a post hoc attribution of initiative, but also serves as a kind of exoneration.

(5) Controlled environmental conditions: Neutralizing is the awareness of not being able to either cause or avoid what happens. It reflects a kind of powerlessness against pressures for conformity, informal rules, and controlled procedures and ways of behaving.

(6) Processes of adaptation: Individuals have the preparedness and the will to adapt to the group. The permanent confrontation with the common business practices makes individuals question their own normative standards and may give rise to neutralization.

(7) Individual differentiation: Corrupt actors themselves can choose suitable criteria to distinguish between acceptable and unacceptable behavior in adaptation to the environment. So long as this individually set border is not crossed, there is no reason to question the legitimacy of one's own behavior.

---

[30] Rabl and Kühlmann (2008, May) showed – based on the data gathered in this study – that relationships of rationalization strategies with important person-based determinants of corruption were lacking. Thus, is is questionable whether rationalization strategies possess potential as ex ante determinants of corrupt behavior.

(8) Social recognition of alternative interpretations: Corrupt acts often are declared as sideline jobs, and bribes as charges or favors. The social recognition of the legitimacy of these alternative interpretations allows the corrupt actors to trivialize the behavior in front of themselves.

(9) Abstraction of victim and damage: Corruption is criminality without victims where both partners are offenders. Thus, the actors can easily ignore the consequences of their corrupt acts to the public. Rather, they restrict the effects of corruption for themselves to "You scratch my back and I'll scratch yours."

Based on the work of Sykes and Matza (1957)[31], Ashforth and Anand (2003) propose eight types of rationalizations for corrupt behavior, which reflect the conditions outlined above:

(1) Legality: Corrupt actors excuse their behavior arguing that as it is not labeled specifically wrong, it is not actually illegal and therefore has to be okay (Ashforth & Anand, 2003).

(2) Denial of responsibility: Corrupt actors construe that they had no other choice than to participate in corrupt activities due to circumstances that are beyond their control, like, for example, management orders, peer pressure, financial strains, deception, or everybody else's behavior (Anand et al., 2005; Ashforth & Anand, 2003; Ashforth & Kreiner, 1999). They see themselves as a "billiard ball" (Sykes & Matza, 1957, p. 667), which is helplessly propelled into new situations. Such a rationalization, for example, may amount to "What can I do? My arm is being twisted" (Anand et al., 2005, p. 11).

(3) Denial of injury: Corrupt actors are convinced that their behavior has not caused any harm to anyone because, for example, the organization is insured or the actual damage is slight (Anand et al., 2005; Ashforth & Anand, 2003; Ashforth & Kreiner, 1999). They may argue: "No one was really harmed" (Anand et al., 2005, p. 11). Corrupt actors also may render the corrupt act less offensive by comparing it to more extreme forms (Anand et al., 2005; Ashforth & Anand, 2003; Ashforth & Kreiner, 1999), arguing "It could have been worse" (Anand et al., 2005, p. 11).

(4) Denial of victim: Corrupt actors refute that there is a victim by one of three ways: First, they may argue that the violated party deserved what has happened (e.g., "They deserved it", Anand et al., 2005, p. 11) so that the corrupt act is a form of revenge (Ashforth & Anand, 2003; Ashforth & Kreiner, 1999). Second, they may argue that the "victim" volunteered to participate and therefore is not a victim at all (e.g., "They chose to participate", Anand et al., 2005, p. 11). Third, they may either deny the victim's individuality through depersonalization, arguing that the victim is only an interchangeable member in a group, or they may deny the

---

[31] From the rationalization techniques outlined in the following, techniques 2 to 6 were identified by Sykes and Matza (1957).

victim's humanity through dehumanization, arguing that the victim is an object or of a lesser species (Ashforth & Anand, 2003; Ashforth & Kreiner, 1999).

(5) Social weighting: Corrupt actors use two practices that moderate the salience of their behavior. One practice is the condemnation of the condemner, which impugns the legitimacy of those casting the actor and the actor's behavior as corrupt (Ashforth & Anand, 2003; Ashforth & Kreiner, 1999). They may respond to potential condemners: "You have no right to criticize us" (Anand et al., 2005, p. 11). Another practice is selective social comparison, where the actors compare themselves with others who appear even worse (Ashforth & Anand, 2003; Ashforth & Kreiner, 1999), arguing, for example: "Others are worse than we are" (Anand et al., 2005, p. 11).

(6) Appeal to higher loyalties: Corrupt actors argue that universalistic ethical norms have to be sacrificed to realize higher-order values (Ashforth & Anand, 2003). This rationalization may amount to "We answered to a more important cause" (Anand et al., 2005, p. 11).

(7) Metaphor of the ledger: Corrupt actors rationalize that they are entitled to act corruptly because of their accrued credits (both actual or anticipated) in regard to time and effort in their job (Ashforth & Anand, 2003) arguing, for example, "We've earned the right" (Anand et al., 2005, p. 11).

(8) Refocusing attention: Corrupt actors deemphasize, compartmentalize, or suppress knowledge of their acts in favor of more normatively redeeming features of their work (Ashforth & Anand, 2003).

2.6.2 Process of Normalization

There are three major approaches that provide insights into how corruption is normalized in organizations, becoming part of the organizational structure: the approach by Ashforth and Anand (2003), the approach by Brief et al. (2001), and the approach by Darley (2005). They all outline the social influences[32] that contribute to the spread of corruption in organizations.

The Approach by Ashforth and Anand (2003)

Ashforth and Anand (2003) develop a widely cited model that explains how corruption becomes normalized, "that is, become[s] embedded in organizational structures and processes, internalized by organizational members as permissible and even desirable behavior, and passed on to successive generations of members" (p. 3). In their approach, they bridge the gap between the individual and the organization as units of

---

[32] Wellen (2004, October) proposes a social influence framework to explain how corruption starts out as isolated deviated incidences enacted by a minority and may become the standard procedure in the organization conducted by a number of employees. The author emphasizes the stronger perception of deviant behavior of minorities than normative behavior of the majority that generalizes to the group as a whole, more for individuals with low organizational commitment than for highly committed individuals.

analysis (Grieger, 2005). The authors identify three pillars that underlie the process of normalization and that are mutually reinforcing and reciprocally independent (Ashforth & Anand, 2003):

(1) Rationalization means "the process by which individuals who engage in corrupt acts use socially constructed accounts to legitimate the acts in their own eyes" (Ashforth & Anand, 2003, p. 3). Common rationalization techniques used to justify corrupt practices have already been described in chapter 2.6.1 (p. 87). They abet the malleability of the language, which is reflected in an agentless passive style, in analogies and metaphors, in euphemisms, in labels, and in jargon corrupt actors may use to deny the immoral implications of their behavior.

(2) Socialization means "the process by which newcomers are taught to perform and accept the corrupt practices" (Ashforth & Anand, 2003, p. 3). Cohesive corrupt groups often create a "psychologically (if not physically) encapsulated social cocoon" (Ashforth & Anand, 2003, p. 26). This social cocoon represents a relatively closed microcosm where cognition, affects, and attitudes to corrupt behavior are shaped and which fosters the identification with the group and its ideologies. Veterans serve as role models for newcomers, who are encouraged to imitate their corrupt behavior. While corrupt behavior is reinforced, doubt and hesitancy is punished. Socialization within the social cocoon may take three mutually reinforcing routes by which newcomers are seduced into corruption: In the route of cooptation, rewards subtly induce newcomers to skew their attitudes toward corrupt behavior. In the route of incrementalism, newcomers are induced to gradually escalate their corruption. This fosters cognitive dissonance, which can be resolved by invoking rationalization techniques that support an attitude change. In the third route toward corruption, compromise, newcomers are induced to engage in corruption through attempts to resolve dilemmas, role conflicts, and other intractable problems, therefore also fostering an attitude change. Such socialization may also involve a kind of coercion that can be expressed by the demand for loyalty and obligation as well as by the fear of the group's repression or punishment.

(3) Institutionalization means "the process by which corrupt practices are enacted as a matter of routine, often without conscious thought about their propriety" (Ashforth & Anand, 2003, p. 3). The institutionalization process consists of three major phases: In a first phase, a permissive ethical climate encourages an initial corrupt decision or act. In a second phase, corruption is successfully incorporated in the organizational memory and embedded in organizational structures and processes. In a third phase, corruption becomes routinized as a kind of normative prescription, which is adapted to in processes of habituation and desensitization and which is enacted mindlessly.

The Approach by Brief et al. (2001)

Brief et al. (2001) provide another approach to the normalization of corruption in organizations. They describe the processes that result in officially sanctioned corporate corruption, the endorsement of ethically questionable behavior of a collective of employees that is rooted in moral disengagement. The three relevant and overlapping processes are the following:

(1) Sanctioning describes "the implicit or explicit endorsement of a corrupt corporate practice by an authority figure who likely has engaged in amoral reasoning" (Brief et al., 2001, p. 473). Employees are either directly ordered to engage in corruption (explicit sanctioning) or encouraged to such questionable engagement by emphasizing the ends and disregarding the means (implicit sanctioning). The setting of high performance standards, attractive rewards for goal achievement, and harsh punishments for goal failure, in addition to the management's disinterest in the means of goal achievement, make employees see corruption to be condoned in their organization. Sanctioning is a result of amoral reasoning, because corrupt behavior does not cause managers to experience value conflicts. Rather, they adhere to a value system that places corporate success above all other concerns and therefore overlook the ethical implications of their business decisions.

(2) Compliance describes "the initial obedience of organizational members to the authorization to engage in a corrupt practice" (Brief et al., 2001, p. 473). Managers frame situations so that subordinates do not deliberately consider the ethical implications of their decisions, but see corruption as a practice demanded by role requirements and obligations and comply to the management's authorization to corrupt engagement. There are two reasons for this compliance: First, the legitimate authority of hierarchically superior managers creates potential for obedience among subordinates. One prerequisite is that the subordinates collectively believe that the exercise of authority is justified. Subordinates have to accept their superiors' claim that they have the right to give orders by the virtue of their position. They often do so because they perceive superiors to have the power to punish disobedience. A second prerequisite is that the group of subordinates is convinced that disobedience is punished. Another prerequisite is that the subordinates collectively perceive hierarchical obedience as necessary for organizational health and therefore good for individuals and society. Second, the division of labor within an organization contributes to compliance because discrete subtasks limit the discretion of subordinates.

(3) Institutionalization describes "the means by which the collective wrongdoing becomes part and parcel of everyday organizational life" (Brief et al., 2001, p. 473). The means are manifold. One circumstance for the institutionalization of corruption is when organizational members adhere to directives whose moral or ethical implications are invisible to the actors. This occurs when jobs are fragmented and practices highly standardized and routinized. Attention then is

focused on the details of the job, on effective task performance, and adherence to the rules associated with the functional role rather than on moral considerations of the consequences of one's actions. Another circumstance enabling ongoing corruption is when the potential consequences of this behavior are known to the actors. Corruption then becomes institutionalized "through the collective inter-pretation of 'ethically loaded' activities" (Brief et al., 2001, p. 484), which constructs a reality that justifies corrupt behavior. It is likely that a deviant ethical culture emerges. Shared values, norms, and beliefs can influence an other-wise moral individual to engage in corruption. The redefining of corrupt behavior in a more favorable light can be accomplished through the application of tech-niques such as euphemistic labeling and rationalizations as described in chapter 2.6.1 (p. 87). Finally, another way of institutionalization of corruption is the socialization process in organizations. A newcomer's initial engagement in cor-ruption may represent an inconsiderate response to a superior's request or a delib-erate response to conformity pressure. Newcomers are forced, step by step, to accept corrupt practices, gradually altering their psychological situation. Once they have taken part in corrupt practices, individuals tend to develop self-justifi-cations, using socially constructed beliefs and values shared by the collective that are internalized and help to redefine the corrupt reality into something normal. When successfully introduced into a culture of corruption, the individual may have the capacity for autonomous evildoing, contributing to a culture that sup-ports ongoing corruption.

The Approach by Darley (2005)

Darley (2005) focuses on answering the question why once there have been initiating corrupt actions, other people in the organization take actions that amplify, extend, and continue these corrupt acts. He outlines two major reasons:

(1) Imperceptible differences: Others often accept the implied assumption that the initial corrupt actions are ethical in nature. If a committed corrupt act is neither punished nor labeled wrong, corruption becomes a standard procedure. Even if people may believe that the act is wrong but do not dare to say this publicly because the silence of others lets them think that corruption is ethical, this means, if a process of "pluralistic ignorance" (Darley, 2005, p. 1186) occurs, slightly more unethical actions are induced using past practices as the benchmark for evaluating new practices. Thus, if practices are similar, the distance between the first act and the next one that amplifies it are not easily recognizable, which makes following acts also acceptable. In small steps, in an organization acts are undertaken that are not seen as ethical first, as ethically grey in later stages, and finally as simply immoral. The continuous progression makes an organizational group never become aware of the moral wrongness of the final resulting proce-dures.

(2) Group loyalty and commitment: Even if other actors in the organization realize that a corrupt act is bad, they may allow or support the continuation of the actions because of loyalty to the group, loyalty to the corrupt actor, or a commitment to the course of action. Group loyalty or commitment leads to hiding corrupt actions from the public, which entails further corrupt actions. According to social identity theory, as a committed member of an organization, an individual's personality is altered. The person becomes a prototypic member of the group, imitating the group's engagement in corrupt action. So even actors who previously were careful to act morally now adopt the corrupt practice and become an independent origins of corruption.

2.6.3 Summary

Corruption seldom remains a single phenomenon within organizations. Rather, in an organization there are tendencies of a normalization of corruption. Two mechanisms appear to be important: rationalization and neutralization strategies combined with social influences. They both contribute to institutionalization and spread of corruption within organizations.

3 Conceptual Framework and Research Hypotheses

The previous chapter underlined the vast body of research on corruption. Nevertheless, the corrupt actors themselves are often neglected when examining the corruption phenomenon. My research tries to close one of the research gaps that exist in regard to the person-based determinants of corrupt action. In the following, I outline my research questions. To answer these research questions, I developed and proposed a theoretical model of corrupt action that provides the conceptual framework and was the base of my hypotheses.

3.1 Research Questions

As shown in the literature review in the previous chapter, there is only scarce research that takes into account the person who acts corruptly. While there are some data on sociodemographic factors, personality traits, values, and motives of corrupt actors, the interrelation of behavioral components making a person offer a return service in exchange for a norm violation or making a person accept or demand such a return service has only rarely been investigated. These behavioral components can be conceptualized as

- motivation, the "arousal, direction, intensity, and persistence of voluntary actions that are goal directed" (Mitchell, 1997, p. 20);

- volition, that is, processes that determine which motivational tendencies should be realized; they seek to initiate action and realize the formed intention (Heckhausen, 1989, p. 17);

- emotion, that is,

   a complex set of interactions among subjective and objective factors, mediated by neural-hormonal systems, which can (a) give rise to affective experiences such as feelings of arousal, pleasure/displeasure; (b) generate cognitive processes such as emotionally relevant perceptual effects, appraisals, labeling processes; (c) activate widespread physiological adjustments to the arousing conditions; and (d) lead to behavior that is often, but not always, expressive, goal-directed, and adaptive (Kleinginna & Kleinginna, 1981, p. 355);

- cognition, that is,

   all the processes by which the sensory input is transformed, reduced, elaborated, stored, recovered, and used. [...] Such terms as sensations, perception, imagery, retention, recall, problem-solving, and thinking, among many others, refer to hypothetical stages or aspects of cognition (Neisser, 1967, p. 4).

Because of the lack of research regarding the interrelation of these aspects, my study aimed at examining these person-based determinants of human behavior in interaction with a specific situational context, the business context. My concern was to answer the following research questions: What makes decision makers in companies act corruptly? Which motivational, volitional, emotional, and cognitive aspects play a role? How does their interplay finally lead to corrupt action?

3.2   Development of the Research Model

To answer these research questions, I developed a model of corrupt action. A first step in the model development process was to screen the literature on both action models and decision making models, also in regard to ethical and unethical behavior, to find models that include motivational, volitional, emotional, and/or cognitive aspects. I decided on basing the development of my model of corrupt action on aspects incorporated in the Rubicon model of action phases (Gollwitzer, 1990; Heckhausen, 1987a; Heckhausen, 1987b; Heckhausen, 1989, pp. 203 – 218), in the theory of planned behavior (Ajzen, 1991), as well as in the model of effortful decision making and enactment (Bagozzi, Dholakia, & Basuroy, 2003). In the following, I briefly review[33] the three relevant theoretical models. Then, I describe the reasons for my final decision, outlining why these theoretical models appeared suitable for an application to my research questions.

3.2.1 The Rubicon Model of Action Phases

The Rubicon model of action phases (Gollwitzer, 1990; Heckhausen, 1987a; Heckhausen, 1987b; Heckhausen, 1989, pp. 203 – 218) tackles both the motivational issue of goal choice and the volitional (willful) issue of goal striving in a theory that analyzes both concepts in relation to each other. It takes a comprehensive temporal perspective on the course of action, beginning with the awakening of an individual's wishes prior to goal setting and ending with an evaluation after the end of goal striving. The model posits four distinct phases that represent a sequence but may be overlapping (see figure 8):

---

[33] For a detailed discussion of the relevant theoretical models as well as a description of their theoretical development see the papers, books, and book chapters of the original authors.

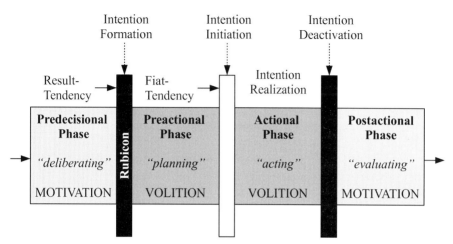

Figure 8:   The Rubicon Model of Action Phases (adopted from Heckhausen, 1989, p. 212)

(1) Predecisional phase ("deliberating"): The first phase aims at choosing the best of different action alternatives for later realization. This decision demands deliberating on the possible choices regarding the desirability, the expected value of the outcome, and the feasibility with which the outcome can be obtained by the actor's own activity. At the end of this deliberating process stands the choice of the action alternative with the greatest expected utility that is wished to be realized. This wish has to be transformed into an intention to achieve the goal (goal intention), a feeling of determination to fulfill the wish. A result-tendency arises. The transition is described by the metaphor of "crossing the Rubicon" (Heckhausen, 1987b, pp. 6 – 7) and marks the transition to the second phase.

(2) Preactional phase ("planning"): In the second phase, the feeling of obligation associated with the goal intention makes people plan how to realize their goal intention and how to achieve the chosen goal. They form behavioral intentions by planning where, when, how, and how long to act. These behavioral intentions promote the smooth initiation, execution, and termination of a relevant course of action. Whether a goal intention leads to the initiation of relevant actions depends on both its volitional strength and on how favorable the situation is for readily initiating the particular goal intention. The stronger the volitional strength and the more favorable the situation, the stronger is the fiat[34]-tendency to initiate action. In case of competing goal intentions, the one with the strongest fiat-tendency is executed. Action initiation marks the transition to the third phase.

---

[34] Latin: it may happen

(3) Actional phase ("acting"): In the third phase, the goal intention is transformed into action toward goal achievement. It has to be protected against competing intentions. A person's efforts to pursue the chosen goal intention depend on its volitional strength. The more hindrances are encountered in achieving the goal, the stronger the volitional strength becomes. This relationship is described in Ach-Hillgruber's difficulty law of motivation (Ach, 1935; Hillgruber, 1912). The last phase is entered when the goal is achieved or appears to be unachievable. The intention is deactivated and the action is terminated.

(4) Postactional phase ("evaluating"): In the fourth and last phase, people evaluate whether their goal striving has been successful by comparing the outcomes with the expectancies. This evaluation occurs both past oriented and future oriented. Past oriented, it addresses the questions: Has the intended outcome been achieved? Does the actual value of the goal striving match its expected value? Future oriented, it leads to conclusions for future planning and acting, influencing future expectations regarding the feasibility and desirability of action outcomes.

The Rubicon model of action phases (Gollwitzer, 1990; Heckhausen, 1987a; Heckhausen, 1987b; Heckhausen, 1989, pp. 203 – 218) considers both motivational as well as volitional processes. Accordingly, two distinct mind-sets were postulated: As in both the predecisional and the postactional phase, the desirability and feasibility of a goal are at issue; these action phases and the associated mind-sets are termed "motivational". Both the preactional and actional phase and the associated mindsets are termed "volitional" because they both address implementing the chosen goal. The motivational mind-set is characterized by "reality orientation' – that is, an orientation toward processing available information in a nonselective, unbiased manner" (Gollwitzer, 1990, p. 64). The volitional mind-set, in contrast, is characterized by "realization orientation' – that is, an orientation toward processing available information in a selective manner biased in favor of attaining the chosen goal" (Gollwitzer, 1990, p. 64).

3.2.2 The Theory of Planned Behavior

The theory of planned behavior (Ajzen, 1991) is an extension of the theory of reasoned action (Fishbein & Ajzen, 1975) and one of the most influential and most widespread attitude-behavior models. It is depicted in figure 9.

The theory suggests that the individual's intention to perform a given behavior directly determines an individual's behavior. But such a behavioral intention only is expressed in behavior if the behavior is under volitional control. This means that the individual can decide at will whether to perform or not perform the behavior. The behavioral intention is determined by three conceptually independent aspects:

- the attitude toward the behavior, "the degree to which a person has a favorable or unfavorable evaluation or appraisal of the behavior in question" (Ajzen, 1991, p. 188);

- the subjective norm, "the perceived social pressure to perform or not to perform the behavior" (Ajzen, 1991, p. 188);

- the perceived behavioral control, "the perceived ease or difficulty of performing the behavior" (Ajzen, 1991, p. 188), reflecting past experiences in addition to anticipated impediments and obstacles.

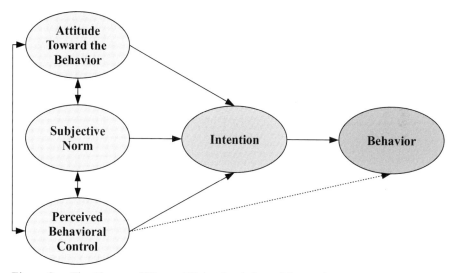

Figure 9: The Theory of Planned Behavior (adopted from Ajzen, 1991, p. 182)

The theory of planned behavior assumes: "The more favorable the attitude and subjective norm with respect to a behavior, and the greater the perceived behavioral control, the stronger should be an individual's intention to perform the behavior under consideration" (Ajzen, 1991, p. 188).

The theory traces attitudes, subjective norms, and perceived behavioral control to an underlying foundation of beliefs about the behavior:

- Behavioral beliefs are the foundation for attitudes toward the behavior. An individual's attitude is a function of the strength of the belief regarding the probability that the behavior will result in a certain outcome, in addition to the subjective evaluation of the behavior's consequences. Thus, the theory is also termed an expectancy-value model.

- Normative beliefs determine subjective norms. The subjective norm is a function of the normative belief regarding the likelihood that important referent individuals or groups approve or disapprove of performing a given behavior coupled with the individual's motivation to comply with the referent in question.

- Control beliefs are the base for perceptions of behavioral control. The perceived behavioral control is a function of the control belief regarding the available resources and opportunities and anticipated obstacles and impediments as well as the perceived power of the particular control factor to facilitate or inhibit performance of the behavior.

3.2.3 The Model of Effortful Decision Making and Enactment

The theoretical[35] model of effortful decision making and enactment (Bagozzi et al., 2003) with its proposed relationships is shown in figure 10. It incorporates aspects of the two models outlined above.

The model's focus is on decision making, which appears at two stages: at the stage of goal selection as well as at the stage of the selection of means needed to achieve the chosen goal. The three aspects important in the process by which goals and means are chosen include importance, effort investment, and confidence. Decision process importance refers to "the level of interest or drive aroused by the process of decision making itself" (Bagozzi et al., 2003, p. 278). Decision process effort investment reflects "the investment of resources in the decision process" (Bagozzi et al., 2003, p. 278). Decision process confidence addresses the "decision maker's perception of self-efficacy with regard to enacting his/her choice" (Bagozzi et al., 2003, p. 278). These three decision process characteristics "play a motivation-mustering role, mobilizing effort and facilitating persistence in the subsequent goal-striving process" (Bagozzi et al., 2003, p. 278) and are the starting point in the model.

They influence both goal desire and implementation desire, which are antecedents to goal intention and implementation intention respectively. While goal desire and intention refer to the goal that is sought, implementation desire and intention refer to the means to achieve the goal. Desire refers to the motivational state of mind of the decision maker, and intention addresses the volitional state of mind, a distinction that can also be found in the Rubicon model of action phases (Gollwitzer, 1990; Heckhausen, 1987a; Heckhausen, 1987b; Heckhausen, 1989, pp. 203 – 218). Goal feasibility, the perceived ease or difficulty of attaining the goal, is an antecedent to goal intention.

Based on existing literature, the authors posit the influence of emotional processes arising from the assessment of the prospects for success or failure in goal achievement. Positive anticipated emotions as emotional reactions to the prospect of successful decision enactment, and negative anticipated emotions as emotional reactions to the prospect of failing to enact the decision both positively influence goal desire.

---

[35] In their paper, Bagozzi et al. (2003) also tested their theoretical model empirically with good measures of fit but with some of the theoretically proposed paths being insignificant. Because of the different research context, I chose the original theoretical model as basis for the development of my model of corrupt action.

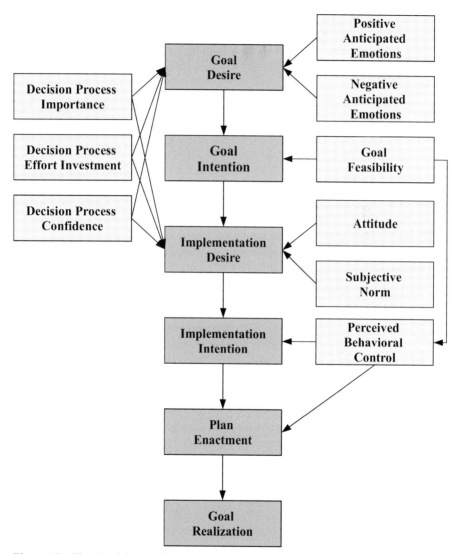

Figure 10: The Model of Effortful Decision Making and Enactment (adopted from Bagozzi et al., 2003, p. 276)

Two elements of the theory of planned behavior (Ajzen, 1991) influence implementation desires: Attitudes and subjective norms, which constitute reasons for acting. A further element of Ajzen's (1991) theory – perceived behavioral control – influences the implementation intention. As the authors assume that decision makers choose behaviors after considering their efficacy in decision enactment, higher goal feasibility is posited to be positively linked with perceived behavioral control. Furthermore, in the model perceived behavioral control is an antecedent to plan enactment.

The actions and outcome of the goal striving process are reflected in the concepts of plan enactment and goal realization. Plan enactment refers to "the degree of successful enactment of the chosen plan" (Bagozzi et al., 2003, p. 280), goal realization is "the attainment of the goal chosen by the decision maker on this account" (Bagozzi et al., 2003, p. 280).

3.2.4 Reasons for Model Selection

I decided on choosing the model of effortful decision making and enactment (Bagozzi et al., 2003) as a starting point for the development of a model of corrupt action. This comprehensive action model appeared suitable for my research intention because it integrates both aspects of the Rubicon model of action phases (Gollwitzer, 1990; Heckhausen, 1987a; Heckhausen, 1987b; Heckhausen, 1989, pp. 203 – 218), which covers the stages of motivated behavior from choice to evaluation, in addition to aspects of the theory of planned behavior (Ajzen, 1991), an attitude-behavior-model. This combination is necessary for several reasons:

- First, the theory of planned behavior (Ajzen, 1991) does not specify clearly the relationship between intention and behavior; rather the intention concept in Ajzen's (1991) theory remains underdeveloped (Eagly & Chaiken, 1993). This weakness has been tackled in the Rubicon model of action phases (Gollwitzer, 1990; Heckhausen, 1987a; Heckhausen, 1987b; Heckhausen, 1989, pp. 203 – 218) under the heading of the volition construct.

- Second, Ajzen's (1991) theory does not incorporate desires as a determinant of intentions to perform an action that have been found to improve explanation and prediction substantially (Perugini & Bagozzi, 2001; Perugini & Conner, 2000) and have been conceptualized in the Rubicon model (Gollwitzer, 1990; Heckhausen, 1987a; Heckhausen, 1987b; Heckhausen, 1989, pp. 203 – 218).

- Third, both the theory of planned behavior (Ajzen, 1991) as an expectancy-value model and the Rubicon model (Gollwitzer, 1990; Heckhausen, 1987a; Heckhausen, 1987b; Heckhausen, 1989, pp. 203 – 218) are based on rational choice, but do not consider emotional aspects. As the latter are included in Bagozzi et al.'s (2003) model in addition to motivational, volitional, and cognitive components, it qualifies for an application to my research intention.

For similar reasons, I did not build upon models explaining ethical decision making (e.g., Bommer, Gratto, Gravander, & Tuttle, 1987; Dubinsky & Loken, 1989; Ferrell & Gresham, 1985; Hunt & Vitell, 1986; Jones, 1991; Rest, 1986; Trevino, 1986). Each of these models includes different subsets of, for example, individual factors such as gender and cognitive moral development, organizational factors such as codes of ethics and ethical climate/culture, and moral intensity factors such as magnitude of consequences and social consensus. They do not examine the complex interplay of motivations, volitions, emotions, and cognitions that should be represented in my model.

In contrast, the model of effortful decision making and enactment (Bagozzi et al., 2003) is a comprehensive action model that is applicable to a variety of decision making domains like organizational, managerial, medical, consumer, or health decision making. It bases on the fact that conscious choices between at least two alternative actions (Brunsson, 1982) can initiate actions when they incorporate cognitive, motivational, volitional, and emotional aspects. As the model applies to decisions that are novel and of significance to the decision maker, where there is some gap between reaching the decision and implementing it, and where decision enactment is effortful, it seemed appropriate to apply it to corrupt action.

3.3   The Model of Corrupt Action

Although my model of corrupt action is based on the model of effortful decision making and enactment (Bagozzi et al., 2003), some modifications to the original model became necessary:

- The terminology was adapted to the context of corruption: The goal desire/intention in the case of corruption is the desire/intention to achieve a private or professional goal (e.g., Ashforth & Anand, 2003; Huntington, 1989; Khan, 1996; Nye, 1967; Pitt & Abratt, 1986). The implementation desire/intention is the desire/ intention to achieve the private or professional goal through corrupt action.

- I dropped the decision process as motivation-mustering component (Dholakia & Bagozzi, 2002) from the model due to two major reasons: First, regarding the goal that is wished to be achieved there is no decision to make because in the case of corruption the decision to achieve a certain private or professional goal is already made. Second, the components are not selective. Decision process effort investment and importance are already implied in the intention concept, whereas decision process confidence depends on attitude and subjective norms.

- I also removed the link between goal feasibility and perceived control over corrupt behavior. The fact how easy it is to achieve the private or professional goal does not have an influence on how much control one assumes to have over one's own corrupt behavior, that is, over the way to achieve the goal. Rather, perceived behavioral control is determined by the special situational circumstances of corrupt behavior set from outside (likelihood of detection, penalties).

- The link between perceived behavioral control and plan enactment can not be justified according to the theory of planned behavior (Ajzen, 1991), where perceived behavioral control only has an influence on behavior by the mediating behavioral intention. Moreover, the link has not been shown to be significant (Bagozzi et al., 2003). Thus, I removed it from the model.

Therefore, my proposed model of corrupt action, which is shown in figure 11, includes the following components and relationships (see Rabl & Kühlmann, 2006; Rabl & Kühlmann, 2006, November; Rabl & Kühlmann, 2007, September; Rabl & Kühlmann, 2008; Rabl & Kühlmann, 2008, August):

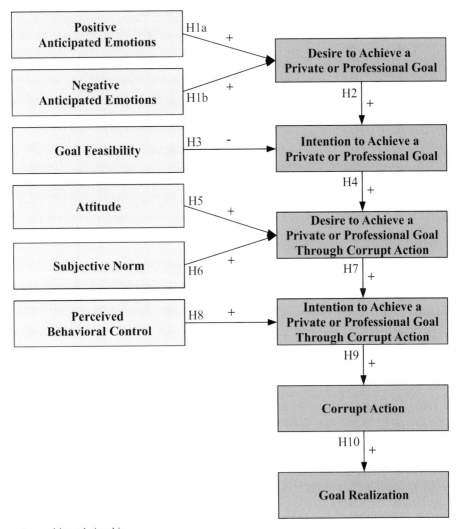

+ = positive relationship
- = negative relationship

Figure 11: The Proposed Model of Corrupt Action

The Desire to Achieve a Private or Professional Goal

Research trying to define corruption showed that corrupt action aims at achieving a private or professional goal (e.g., Ashforth & Anand, 2003; Huntington, 1989; Khan, 1996; Nye, 1967; Pitt & Abratt, 1986). Thus, starting point in the model is the desire to achieve a private or professional goal.

The Influence of Positive and Negative Anticipated Emotions

The strength of desire depends on the positive and negative emotions anticipated with regard to goal attainment. People, when deliberating to act or not, take into account the emotional consequences of both achieving and not achieving a sought-for goal (Bagozzi, Baumgartner, & Pieters, 1998). These emotions have motivating power (e.g., Bagozzi et al., 1998; Parker, Manstead, & Stradling, 1995; Perugini & Bagozzi, 2001; Sheeran & Orbell, 1999) and enact decisions as part of a general process of self-regulation (Bagozzi, 1992; Carver & Scheier, 1998, pp. 142 – 143). They are related to the concept of valences, which describes the goal's attractiveness in the predecisional phase of the Rubicon model of action phases (Gollwitzer, 1990; Heckhausen, 1987a; Heckhausen, 1987b; Heckhausen, 1989, pp. 203 – 218). Both the strength of anticipated emotions regarding attaining and failing the goal influence goal desire (Bagozzi et al., 2003; Perugini & Bagozzi, 2001). Thus,

> *Hypothesis 1a: The more positive emotions anticipated if the goal is achieved, the stronger the desire to achieve a private or professional goal.*

> *Hypothesis 1b: The more negative emotions anticipated if the goal is not achieved, the stronger the desire to achieve a private or professional goal.*

The Intention to Achieve a Private or Professional Goal

The desire to achieve the private or professional goal has to be transformed into an intention. This transition from the fluid state of deliberation to a firm sense of commitment is described by the metaphor of "crossing the Rubicon" (Heckhausen, 1987b, pp. 6 – 7) and takes place in the preactional phase of the Rubicon model of action phases (Gollwitzer, 1990; Heckhausen, 1987a; Heckhausen, 1987b; Heck-hausen, 1989, pp. 203 – 218). Compared to intentions, desires are perceived as less performable by the decision maker, are less connected to actions, and enacted over longer time frames (Perugini & Bagozzi, 2004).

Davis (1984) speaks of a "connection condition" (p. 53) for intentions. Desires have a particular kind of relationship to intentions in the sense that, once one is aware of and accepts one's desire to act, this will motivate one to make a decision or form an intention to act. Frankfurt (1988) has a similar view. For him, desires function as determinants of decisions when decision makers give self-reflective consideration to their desires and come to endorse them as motivators to act (pp. 11 – 16). Empirical work supports the hypothesis that desires mediate and transform the effects of reasons and motives for acting and influence intentions (e.g., Leone, Perugini, & Ercolani, 1999; Perugini & Conner, 2000). Desires are necessary antecedents to intentions and pertain to the intensity with which the goal is sought (Bagozzi & Dholakia, 1999). That is why my proposed model, like Bagozzi et al.'s (2003) model, incorporates desires as a main determinant of intentions to perform an action like other recent models of volitional decision making (Perugini & Bagozzi, 2001; Perugini & Conner, 2000) that have been found to improve explanation and prediction substantially over the theory of planned behavior (Ajzen, 1991). Thus,

> *Hypothesis 2: The stronger the desire to achieve a private or professional goal, the stronger the intention to achieve this goal.*

The Influence of Goal Feasibility

People consider how difficult it is to achieve the goal. They investigate whether they can obtain the goal through their own activity, whether the situational context they face is facilitating or impeding, and whether the necessary means or opportunities will be available (Gollwitzer, 1990). According to the Rubicon model of action phases (Gollwitzer, 1990; Heckhausen, 1987a; Heckhausen, 1987b; Heckhausen, 1989, pp. 203 – 218), the strength of the intention to achieve a private or professional goal depends on Ach-Hillgruber's difficulty law of motivation (Ach, 1935; Hillgruber, 1912): The lower the goal feasibility, the higher the strength of intention. This law also was the precursor of Locke and Latham's (1990, pp. 27 – 30) goal difficulty function in their theory of goal setting. Several empirical findings approved this linear function between goal difficulty and performance, which only levels off when subjects reach the limits of their ability at high goal difficulty levels[36]. Thus,

> *Hypothesis 3: The more difficult the achievement of a realistic private or professional goal, the stronger the intention to achieve it.*

The Desire to Achieve a Private or Professional Goal Through Corrupt Action

When a goal intention is formed, plans for how to achieve this goal develop. In my case, one of the ways is corrupt action. As desires are not only directed at ultimate goals, but also to means to these goals (Mele, 1995), in our model, as in the model of effortful decision making and enactment (Bagozzi et al., 2003), desire functions on the goal stage as well as on the implementation stage. Similar to the predecisional phase of the Rubicon model (Gollwitzer, 1990; Heckhausen, 1987a; Heckhausen, 1987b; Heckhausen, 1989, pp. 203 – 218), the desirability of corrupt action as a way to achieve the private or professional goal is considered. In the model of effortful decision making and enactment (Bagozzi et al., 2003), implementation desires are caused by goal intention. If there is a strong intention to achieve the private or

---

[36] In contrast, expectancy theory (Vroom, 1984) asserts a positive linear relationship between expectancy of success, that is, low goal difficulty, and the motivation for performance (pp. 192 – 196). Atkinson (1958) proposed a curvilinear relationship with the highest level of performance occurring at moderate levels of probability of success.

professional goal, it can be assumed that this may result in a certain desirability of corrupt action. Thus,

Hypothesis 4: The stronger the intention to achieve a private or professional goal, the stronger the desire to achieve this goal through corrupt action.

The Influence of Attitude and Subjective Norm

According to the theory of planned behavior (Ajzen, 1991), an individual's intention to perform the behavior under consideration is stronger, the more favorable the attitude and subjective norm with respect to a behavior are. While the attitude refers to the degree to which a person has a favorable or unfavorable evaluation of the behavior in question, the subjective norm refers to the perceived social pressure to perform or not to perform that behavior (Ajzen, 1991; Ajzen, 1996). Bagozzi et al. (2003) argue that the attitude and the subjective norm influence intentions only to the extent that they lead to a desire to act. Desires function as mediator variables between attitude and subjective norm on the one hand and intentions on the other hand (Perugini & Bagozzi, 2001; Perugini & Conner, 2000). Thus,

Hypothesis 5: The desire to achieve the private or professional goal through corrupt action is stronger if the actors have a positive attitude toward corruption.

Hypothesis 6: The desire to achieve the private or professional goal through corrupt action is stronger if people important to the actors accept corrupt action.

The Intention to Achieve a Private or Professional Goal Through Corrupt Action

For non-routine goals, important components of the Rubicon model of action phases (Gollwitzer, 1990; Heckhausen, 1987a; Heckhausen, 1987b; Heckhausen, 1989, pp. 203 – 218) are the goal intention and implementation intention. While the goal intention, the decision maker's self-commitment to achieve a chosen goal, is formed as a result of deliberative processes wherein available alternatives are each gauged for their desirability and feasibility, the implementation intention is the selection of an implementation plan, considering and finalizing details regarding when, where, how, and how long to perform goal-directed action in the service of decision enactment (Bagozzi et al., 2003; Gollwitzer, 1996; Gollwitzer, 1999).

Goal intentions refer to a certain outcome to which the person is committed, while implementation intentions commit the individual to the performance of a certain goal-directed behavior once a certain critical situation is encountered. This way, a mental link is created between a specific future situation and the intended goal-directed response. Implementation intentions are formed in the service of goal intentions (Gollwitzer, 1996; Gollwitzer, 1999).

Implementation intentions become necessary to solve problems that occur at the transition point between the preactional and actional phase. There may be conflict between various ways of acting on the goal intention, or good opportunities to act on one's goal may be missed. Thus, implementation intentions are a powerful self-regulatory strategy that alleviates such problems and promotes the initiation of goal-directed behaviors (Gollwitzer & Brandstätter, 1997).

Similar to the formation of goal intentions out of goal desires described above, implementation desires result in implementation intentions after crossing the Rubicon (see Heckhausen, 1989, p. 214) and pertain to the intensity and level to which the way of goal achievement is sought (Bagozzi & Dholakia, 1999). Thus,

> *Hypothesis 7: The stronger the desire to achieve a private or professional goal through corrupt action, the stronger the intention to achieve this goal through corrupt action.*

The Influence of Perceived Behavioral Control

Whether implementation intentions are actually formed depends on the anticipation of difficulties (Gollwitzer & Brandstätter, 1997). The theory of planned behavior (Ajzen, 1991) includes perceived behavioral control as the concept referring to the perceived ease or difficulty of performing the behavior and being assumed to reflect past experiences as well as anticipated impediments and obstacles (Ajzen, 1991; Ajzen, 1996). It is used in order to explain behavior over which people have incomplete volitional control.

For corrupt action, an incomplete degree of volitional control can be assumed because external factors like the likelihood of detection (Borner & Schwyzer, 1999; Carrillo, 1999; Goel & Rich, 1989) and the extent of penalties (Borner & Schwyzer, 1999; Goel & Rich, 1989) play a role. Moreover, perceived behavioral control depends on the transaction costs that occur before, during, and after the corrupt relationship (Lambsdorff, 2002; Lambsdorff & Teksoz, 2002). Big risk for disclosure, high expected penalties, and high transaction costs diminish perceived behavioral control. According to the theory of planned behavior (Ajzen, 1991), an individual's intention to perform the behavior under consideration is the stronger, the greater the perceived behavioral control is. Bagozzi et al. (2003) accordingly argued and showed that perceived behavioral control complemented implementation desires in influencing the implementation intention. Thus,

> *Hypothesis 8: The intention to achieve the private or professional goal through corrupt action is stronger if the actors think they have control over their corrupt action.*

The Corrupt Action

Whether the intention formed in the preactional phase of the Rubicon model of action phases (Gollwitzer, 1990; Heckhausen, 1987a; Heckhausen, 1987b; Heckhausen, 1989, pp. 203 – 218) is transformed into action in the actional phase depends on the volitional strength. The stronger the person is committed to a certain way of achieving a goal, the more likely it is that relevant actions are actually initiated (Gollwitzer, 1990). In the theory of planned behavior (Ajzen, 1991) the reason for an ineffective translation of an intention into behavior also lies in a weak intention. Studies of Brandstätter, Lengfelder, and Gollwitzer (2001) as well as Gollwitzer and Brandstätter (1997) showed that implementation intentions facilitated the immediate initiation of goal-directed behavior in the face of the specified situation or opportunities. Thus,

Hypothesis 9: The stronger the intention to achieve a private or professional goal through corrupt action, the more likely is corrupt action.

Goal Realization

For most effortful decisions, Bagozzi et al. (2003) show a strong positive relationship between plan enactment and goal realization. As the probability for the detection of corrupt behavior is low, corrupt actions are expected to be performed successfully. Thus,

Hypothesis 10: If a corrupt action is undertaken, the probability of achieving the private or professional goal is higher than if no corrupt action is undertaken.

4   Methods

The aim of my study was to empirically test the proposed model of corrupt action outlined in the previous chapter. Therefore, my research design had to fulfill three conditions: First, it had to allow for directly observing corrupt behavior. Second, it had to offer the possibility to measure the components relevant in the decision making process on corrupt action. Third, it had to focus on private corruption, this means, corruption in and between companies. The first point was obviously the most difficult to realize. It is a widely stated problem to get empirical data on corruption. I outline these difficulties in the following. Then, I describe the research instruments chosen for my research questions, the sample, the procedures, and the methods of analyses used in this study.

4.1   Problem of an Empirical Investigation of Corruption

It is difficult to investigate corruption empirically. Important reasons lie in the nature of the phenomenon itself (Wei, 1999): Corruption is an illegal act that happens in secrecy. All participants engaged in a corrupt transaction have good reasons to keep silent (Abbink et al., 2002; Ahlf, 1998; Arnim, 2003; Bannenberg & Schaupen-steiner, 2004, p. 37; Renner, 2004). There are few direct witnesses (Johnston, 2000, August) because there are no direct victims who are interested in making a report (Ahlf, 1998; Arnim, 2003; Bannenberg & Schaupensteiner, 2004, p. 37). In extreme cases, investigators are either compromised themselves or intimidated by violence (Johnston, 2000, August). Thus, there is a big dark field, which, for example, for Germany is estimated to be about 95% (Bannenberg & Schaupensteiner, 2004, p. 38). This explains why using the number of detected corruption cases as it can be found in crime statistics is a very noisy measure (see Pies et al., 2005, for a detailed discussion). An empirical investigation of corruption becomes even more complex because of the problem of defining corruption (see chap. 2.1, p. 23). As there is much dissent about what corruption is, which offenses count among corrupt offenses, and where the margins to non-corrupt behavior are, corruption means different things to different people so that measurement is critical (Johnston, 2000, August; Manandhar, 2005).

Despite these claims, Kaufmann (1997) argues that the presumption that corruption cannot be measured is incorrect. But the methodology that is suitable to study corruption depends on the research interest. It "will have to reflect the terms of refer-ence (the frame of understanding), the scope of the study (narrative, explorative, explanatory, hypothesizing), and the specific variety of corruption one is focusing on" (Amundsen, 1999, pp. 26 – 27). By now, a variety of different instruments for the research on corruption are available.

One school of thought argues that "what can be measured is percep-tion" (Manandhar, 2005, p. 26). There exist a number of indexes that are survey-based measures of corruption perception (Wei, 1999) and are used in many quantitative studies to assess the level of corruption in and across nations (Amundsen, 1999). The most well-known of these subjective estimates are:

- The Business International (BI) Index: This index is based on surveys conducted during 1980 to 1983 by Business International, which is now a subsidiary of the Economist Intelligence Unit. They asked their international network of correspondents – journalists, country specialists, and international business people – about whether and to what extent business transactions in the country in question involved corruption or questionable payments. The index ranks countries from one to ten according to the perceived degree of corruption (Amundsen, 1999; Andvig & Fjeldstad, 2001; Pies et al., 2005; Wei, 1999).

- The International Country Risk Guide (ICRG) Index: This index, which is produced every year since 1982 by Political Risk Services, a private international investment risk service, is based on the opinion of experts. It is supposed to capture the extent to which high government officials are likely to demand special payments and to which illegal payments are generally expected through lower levels of government in the form of bribes connected with import and export licenses, exchange controls, tax assessments, police protection, or loans (Amundsen, 1999; Pies et al., 2005; Wei, 1999).

- The Global Competitiveness Report (GCR) Index: In contrast to the two indexes mentioned above, the GCR Index is based on a 1996 survey of private firm managers in top and middle management, rather than of experts or consultants. Responding firms were asked about various aspects of competitiveness in the host countries where they invest. Regarding corruption, respondents had to rate the level of corruption on a one-to-seven scale according to the extent of irregular, additional payments connected with import and export permits, business licenses, exchange controls, tax assessments, police protection, or loan applications. The GCR corruption index for a particular country is the average of all respondents' ratings for that country (Amundsen, 1999; Wei, 1999).

- The Transparency International Corruption Perceptions Index (CPI)[37]: Transparency International is an international non-governmental organization incorporated under German law and dedicated to fighting corruption worldwide. Since 1995, the CPI has been a regularly generated and published index that is based on the perceptions of international business people, risk analysts, and business journalists. It is a "poll of polls" (Andvig & Fjeldstad, 2001, p. 27) based on a weighted average of several different surveys of varying coverage conducted by several reputable organizations. The CPI is the most comprehensive quantitative indicator of cross-country corruption available[38]. It ranks countries on a scale from ten to zero regarding the degree to which corruption is perceived to exist among public officials and politicians. A score of ten refers to a corruption-free

---

[37] For a detailed discussion of the index and its criticism see Andvig and Fjeldstad (2001) and Johnston (2000, August).

country; a score of zero refers to a country where most transactions or relations are tainted by corruption (Amundsen, 1999; Andvig & Fjeldstad, 2001; Eigen, 2003; Jayawickrama, 2001; Pies et al., 2005; Tanzi, 1998; Wei, 1999). The CPI is a demand side measure of corruption (Manandhar, 2005).

• The Transparency International Bribe Payers Index (BPI)[39]: Besides the CPI, Transparency International also developed the Bribe Payers Index, an index that ranks the leading exporting countries according to the propensity of their big companies to win business contracts through bribing senior public officials in foreign countries. The BPI is based on in-depth interviews conducted by Gallup International Association with senior executives of major foreign and national companies, chartered accountants, members of national chambers of commerce, commercial bankers, and commercial lawyers (Andvig & Fjeldstad, 2001; Eigen, 2003; Jayawickrama, 2001; Pies et al., 2005). It was a pioneering effort to measure the supply side of corruption (Jayawickrama, 2001; Manandhar, 2005).

All of these indexes are based on the personal judgments, perceptions, and opinion of a number of observers (Amundsen, 1999). They are often used at the macro level in cross-country analyses examining macroeconomic, political, or social correlates in order to better understand the causes and consequences of corruption (Kaufmann, Pradhan, & Ryterman, 1998; Lambsdorff, 1999). Perceptions of corruption appear as a suitable method for many questions, such as how corruption affects foreign direct investment, policy, aid, and lending decisions (Johnston, 2000, August; Wei, 1999). Nevertheless, they raise concerns about perception biases and causation (Reinikka & Svensson, 2006; Wei, 1999). Moreover, they provide no information on the within-country variation of corruption (Reinikka & Svensson, 2006). Therefore, there have been attempts to create more objective measures of corruption, developing instruments that are mostly used at the micro level or for case studies (Manandhar, 2005). The most famous examples are the following:

• The World Bank's Public Expenditure Tracking Survey (PETS): The PETS assesses the quality of public expenditure and determines the level of corruption in government public expenditure programs. On a sample survey basis, it tracks the flow of resources on their way through several layers of government bureaucracy to the service facilities that exercise the spending. It aims at determining how much of the originally allocated resources reach each level and therefore helps to shed light on corrupt acts. It combines information from different sources that are least contaminated by an incentive to misreport. A typical PETS consists of a survey of front line providers and local governments, complemented by central government financial and other data (Reinikka & Svensson, 2002; Reinikka & Svensson, 2003; Reinikka & Svensson, 2006).

---

[38] A similar, but broader index aiming at measuring governance is the World Bank's Control of Corruption Index, which also includes different sources of subjective data (Kaufmann, Kraay, & Mastruzzi, 2004; Manandhar, 2005; Pies et al., 2005).

[39] For a detailed discussion and criticism of the index see Johnston (2000, August).

- The World Bank's Quantitative Service Delivery Survey (QSDS): The QSDS is a variant of service provider surveys that examines the efficiency of public spending, incentives, corrupt behavior, and various other dimensions of service delivery in provider organizations, especially those on the front lines. The QSDS focuses on the front line service provider and emphasizes on systematic quantitative data on finance, inputs, outputs, pricing, quality, oversight, and other aspects of service provision. It can be applied to government and to private profit and non-profit providers. It provides information on both performance as well as corrupt practices in service delivery (Reinikka & Svensson, 2003; Reinikka & Svensson, 2006).

The researchers Reinikka and Svensson (2002, 2003, 2006) emphasize that, using surveys, it is possible to study corruption at the firm level. It is necessary that these surveys arouse the firm managers' willingness to cooperate and truly report their own experiences with corruption. The authors report one such survey study regarding corruption across firms in Uganda. They collected a data set (also used by a number of follow-up studies) that includes information on the firm's finances, the firm's structures, and the aggregate graft paid by the individual firm. Also, the cost information on the provision of public services was used to measure corruption indirectly.

Another possible instrument in corruption research is the analysis of court cases (Amundsen, 1999; Andvig & Fjeldstad, 2001). Such an analysis was, for example, undertaken by Bannenberg (2002) in Germany. The number of court cases cannot be used as an indicator for the frequency of corruption or for cross-country comparisons because of the large dark field mentioned above. But they provide information on the scope and characteristics of specific corrupt incidents and on the relevant institutional and motivational mechanisms. Problems may arise from the varying quality of this information, the high confidentiality of the data, and the resulting limited access to the data (Amundsen, 1999; Andvig & Fjeldstad, 2001; Tanzi, 1998).

Research may also obtain information on corruption from reports available in the media (e.g., newspapers, internet). These reports do not allow one to draw any conclusions on the prevalence of corruption in a country. There are evident biases caused by the selection of spectacular stories and the special kind of reporting due to journalistic professionalism. Nevertheless, media reports offer insights into the factors relevant for corruption (Andvig & Fjeldstad, 2001; Tanzi, 1998).

To examine ethical judgments of corrupt behavior, a number of survey studies on ethical decision making have used vignettes. Participants had to judge corrupt scenarios on whether they perceive them as unethical or ethical (e.g., Hoffman, 1998; Kidwell et al., 1987; Loo, 1996; Lund, 2000; Poorsoltan et al., 1991; Weeks et al., 1999). Frank and Schulze (2000) are skeptical about survey results because they contain a number of weaknesses. A major problem is people's tendency to give socially desirable, and therefore biased, answers. They report what they perceive as socially acceptable or normal rather their real opinion.

With the development of behavioral economics, an alternative approach to the empirical analysis of corruption has established itself. Laboratory experiments allow observance of behavior in simulated corruption scenarios directly. It is possible to systematically investigate human decision making behavior. In contrast to the real world, the environment for decision situations can be implemented and controlled. The systematic variation of parameters enables an isolation of causes by reducing the real world's complexity (Abbink et al., 2002; Renner, 2004). There are several studies that investigate decision making in corrupt situations with experimental designs[40] (e.g., Abbink, 2002; Abbink, 2004; Abbink & Hennig-Schmidt, 2006; Abbink et al., 2002; Frank & Schulze, 2000; Hegarty & Sims, 1978, Schulze & Frank, 2003).

4.2   Research Design

Due to the secrecy of corrupt transactions and the resulting difficulty to gain empirical data, the empirical test of the proposed theoretical model of corrupt action was a great challenge. The section above shows that there are a number of possibilities to investigate corruption despite several problems each method brings along. Depending on the research interest and the research subject, different methods may be the most suitable. As already outlined at the beginning of the chapter for my research questions, an instrument was needed that allowed me to directly observe corrupt behavior, to investigate the decision making process on corrupt behavior, and to focus on private corruption. Possible research approaches are a qualitative analysis of court cases (see e.g., Bannenberg, 2002) or qualitative interviews conducted with detected corrupt actors. Because of legal restrictions and availability problems, these research approaches are difficult to realize. Moreover, there might be biases in the results on person-based components. The small number of detected actors may have certain personal characteristics not applicable to non-detected corrupt actors.

Therefore, I decided on an experimental simulation design combining a business game with a standardized questionnaire on the components of the model of corrupt action. This research design appeared suitable because of the following reasons: First, to adequately test the model of corrupt action, the circumstances of private corruption had to be taken into account. A business game simulating a cut-out of the real business world with participants slipping into the roles of decision makers in companies (Kriz, 2005) offers a realistic environment for studying corrupt action. Certain conditions and restrictions have to be set concerning standardization, controlled variable variation, and randomized subject allocation to the test conditions, which result in an experimental setting contributing to internal validity, but limiting external validity (Kriz, 2005). Second, business games allow one to incorporate specially created ethical dilemmas – in my case dilemmas concerning corrup-

---

[40] Some of the bribery games used model a bribery relationship as a trust game where reciprocal behavior is socially undesirable and punished (Abbink & Hennig-Schmidt, 2006). For a detailed description of trust games see Camerer (2003, pp. 83 – 100).

tion –, which do not allow participants to make an easy decision that is both ethical and profitable (Schumann, Scott, & Anderson, 2006). Third, to avoid biases by socially desirable responses, the research intention had to remain hidden. Due to the complexity of a business game where several different decisions under changing conditions have to be taken, offers or possibilities for corruption should not become obvious as such. Fourth, information had to be gained on all relevant person-based components of the model of corrupt action. This could be realized by a standardized questionnaire measuring the different model components.

In the following, I briefly review the business game as a general research method. After that, I describe the business game and the standardized questionnaire used in my study as well as the sample, procedures, and the quality criteria of my research design.

4.2.1 Business Game as Experimental Simulation Method

Originally, business games were developed as teaching devices. In recent years, business games also have been applied as a research instrument (Babb & Eisgruber, 1966, p. 15). They have been used as tools of experimental research in psychological, economic, and management research to investigate a variety of behavioral and organizational issues (Fripp, 1984b; Kern, 2003, p. 96). Primarily – and that's also the reason why I chose a business game for my research design –, business games provide an ideal environment for observing and analyzing individual behavior and decision making under conditions of stress as well as its influencing situational and personal factors (Adamowsky, 1964; Atthill, 1978; Bowen, 1978, pp. 11 – 14; Carson, 1969; Nanus, 1969). As research objects are not investigated in their natural environment, business games represent a kind of laboratory experiment (Eisenführ, 1974). The complexity of the reality simulated in the business game is much higher than in the classical laboratory experiment (Kühl, 2005). The laboratory, thereby, is no contrast to reality, but a reality itself (Eisenführ, 1974). But similar to the laboratory experiment, a social situation is forced on the participants, conditions are systematically manipulated under controlled conditions, and the effects are observed (Kühl, 2005). Therefore, business games can be applied to gain empirical data to generate or test hypotheses and therefore to build theory (Böhret & Wordelmann, 1975, pp. 33 – 34; Kern, 2003, p. 96). But a careful design of business games according to the research purpose is necessary (Bowen, 1978, pp. 11 – 14).

Business games can be defined as

> simulations, that is simplified working representations of reality, in which participants, in competition with each other and in a compressed time-scale, make decisions in the light of their interpretation of that reality, and receive feedback on the outcomes of their decisions (Atthill, 1978, p. viii).

As participants go through a number of decision periods on which they get feedback, they acquire more knowledge about their decisions, their competitors, and the model on which the business game is based (Lloyd, 1978). Participants' actions in the business game are geared to four aspects: first, to the formal rules of the business game; second, to the legal conditions and social norms of the simulated environment; third, to the own interests, goals, and action principles; fourth, to the supposed positions of the competitors (Geuting, 2000).

The business game is a hybrid form of different methods (Capaul & Ulrich, 2003, pp. 18 – 20; Kriz, 2005):

- Simulation: A business game is a highly formalized kind of simulation (Babb & Eisgruber, 1966, p. 15; Böhret & Wordelmann, 1975, pp. 24, 27 – 29; Strina & Haferkamp, 2003). A simulation refers to models of real world situations (Babb & Eisgruber, 1966, p. 15; Geuting, 2000; Kriz, 2005), to models that represent a simplified snapshot of reality (Heidack, 1980, p. 35; Schmidt, 1988, pp. 47 – 48). This is achieved by using precise terminology as well as taking facts, figures, and situations from real world (Lloyd, 1978). The model reflects the structure of the economic environment in which participants make decisions (Geuting, 2000; Heidack, 1980, p. 35; Schmidt, 1988, pp. 47 – 48) and therefore provides the business game's framework (Heidack, 1980, p. 35; Weitz, 2000, p. 4). It mathematically characterizes the basics of companies, the interrelations of inputs and outputs, as well as the interactions of functional sectors and the economic environment (Carson, 1969, p. 39; Geuting, 2000; Schmidt, 1988, pp. 47 – 48).

- Game: As business games are a kind of game, the simulated economic situations become dynamic (Heidack, 1980, pp. 35 – 36; Schmidt, 1988, p. 49; Weitz, 2000, p. 4). There are several dynamic elements: First, business games are arranged in time units or game periods (Capaul & Ulrich, 2003, p. 19; Geuting, 2000; Weitz, 2000, p. 4), mostly quarter years (Carson, 1969). Second, by simulated time restraints, decisions have to be taken under time pressure (Geuting, 2000; Weitz, 2000, p. 4). Third, business games integrate a competitive factor (Geuting, 2000). Decisions by single participants affect the outcome of their own firms as well as the results of other firms, and vice versa (Babb & Eisgruber, 1966, p. 16). Fourth, participants have to face changing conditions. Their decisions cause changes in certain parameters (Weitz, 2000, p. 4) and result in certain environmental states (Eisenführ, 1974). Business games also integrate the concepts of rules and strategies characterizing games (Babb & Eisgruber, 1966, p. 16; Gardner, 2003, p. 3). Despite the similarities to games, business games should not be confused with gambling (Kriz, 2005). Their primary purpose is not entertainment and fun, but serious teaching and research (Babb & Eisgruber, 1966, p. 16).

- Role play: By the role-playing component, a human aspect is integrated into the simulated environment in business games (Geuting, 2000). Participants act directly and actively by taking over certain roles and perceiving situations from a different perspective (Arbeitsgruppe Planspiel, 1995; Capaul & Ulrich, 2003, p. 19; Geuting, 2000; Weitz, 2000, p. 4). They assume the role of managing the simulated operation – either the whole firm or an aspect of it – by making business decisions for successive periods (Carson, 1969, p. 39). Business games are role playing studies "because the participants [...] are behaving as if they are in a certain situation, but realize, of course, that their actions have no real impact" (Greenberg & Eskew, 1993, p. 229). Nevertheless, the game may be so involving that it elicits highly realistic responses (Greenberg & Eskew, 1993).

- Case study: Business games are a more complex and more dynamic realization of case studies (Kriz, 2005). In a simple way, they are often defined as "case studies with feedback and a time dimension added" (Carson, 1969, p. 39; Lloyd, 1978, p. 13). In a case study, participants are confronted with a concrete situation from business life for which they have to develop solutions on certain questions (Capaul & Ulrich, 2003, p. 20).

Heidack (1980, p. 37) contrasts the method of the business simulation game with case study and role play (see table 3):

Table 3:   Comparison of Case Study, Role Play, and Simulation Game (adopted
            from Heidack, 1980, p. 37)

Case study	Role play	Simulation game
Static	Dynamic	Combines static model and dynamic game
Shows principles	Shows processes	Combines concepts and processes
Focus on the object	Focus on the subject	The subject has to prove oneself in dealing with the object
Decision among several solutions; their consequences and results cannot be made visible	Regarding the solutions and their evaluations there is opinion versus opinion; no possibility for decision making	The results and consequences of the decisions are exactly identified; it is possible to establish value relations between the decision making groups
Only one decision, although in alternatives, is possible	Only one decision, although in alternatives, is possible	A chain of decisions is possible, which build on each other; each decision set is starting point for the next decision set.
No feedback for the next decision level possible	No feedback for the next decision level possible	Feedback absolutely necessary for keeping the decision making process going
No trend of decisions is visible	No trend of decisions is visible	Trend as necessary result of the decision chain
No cumulation effect of good and bad decisions	No cumulation effect of good and bad decisions	Exact cumulation effect of good and bad decisions
Repetition of decisions useless because different decisions can be juxtaposed as alternatives	Repetition of decisions useless because different decisions can be juxtaposed as alternatives	Decision can be repeated with completely new results
No competition effect because different solutions are only alternatives, no results	No competition effect because different solutions are only alternatives, no results	When modeled: Real competition that allows the comparison of results and optimization to a certain degree

There exist different types of business games, which can be distinguished according to the following criteria:

- Decision scope and level of the decision making process: Total management games are representations of a firm as a whole and include all its main functions. Participants take over the role of top management and take decisions for the whole company. Functional business games concentrate on industrial functions of a firm such as production, finance, or marketing. Participants take over the roles of lower management levels and take decisions for certain functional areas (Atthill, 1978; Carson, 1969; Ebert, 1992; Fripp, 1984a; Kern, 2003, p. 86; Lloyd, 1978; Schmidt, 1988, pp. 45 – 46; Weitz, 2000, p. 7).

- Industrial sector: General management games refer to medium-sized, not closer defined companies. They are based on economic insights independent of certain industrial sectors. Special management games refer to the special circumstances and problems of companies of certain industrial sectors (Ebert, 1992; Kern, 2003, p. 85; Schmidt, 1988, p. 45; Weitz, 2000, p. 7).

- Degree of freedom regarding decision making: Rigid games are based on rigid rules to evaluate decisions. They are based on a mathematical simulation model that calculates the results objectively. In free games, there is no rule system. Decisions are evaluated by the game administrator (Ebert, 1992; Kern, 2003, p. 89; Weitz, 2000, p. 7). A new development are free-form games. They offer participants themselves the possibility to determine the game progress (Kern, 2003, p. 90).

- Influences of chances: In deterministic games, results only depend on the participants' decisions. In stochastic games, there are elements of chance so that the results are not clearly determined by the participants' decisions (Ebert, 1992; Kern, 2003, p. 88; Weitz, 2000, p. 7).

- Degree of competition: In competitive business games, the decisions of each group influence the decisions of the other groups. Thus, each group should consider the others' activities in their decisions. In non-competitive business games, the decisions of one group have no influence on the decisions of the other group. Each group is isolated. There is no relationship between the decisions and the results of the different teams (Atthill, 1978; Carson, 1969; Ebert, 1992; Kern, 2003, pp. 87 – 88; 92; Schmidt, 1988, p. 47; Weitz, 2000, p. 7).

- Openness of games: Open games allow participants to get in contact with each other. Closed games isolate teams from each other. Interaction and information is mediated by the game administrator (Ebert, 1992; Weitz, 2000, p. 7).

- Complexity of the model: In simple games, the model has a simple structure and the amount of information that has to be processed is low. In complex games, there is a large amount of information to process and many and difficult decisions to take in each period (Carson, 1969; Ebert, 1992; Kern, 2003, pp. 93 – 94; Weitz, 2000, p. 7).

- Way of analysis: In manual games, the analysis is done by the instructor manually using paper, pencil, and calculator. In computer-based games, the model is programmed into the computer, which allows an automatic analysis of results (Atthill, 1978; Ebert, 1992; Kern, 2003, pp. 91 – 92; Lloyd, 1978; Schmidt, 1988, p. 46; Weitz, 2000, p. 7).

- Degree of distribution of participants: In local games, participants and game administrator are in the same place. In long-distance games, the different teams and the game administrator act in different places (Ebert, 1992; Kern, 2003, pp. 94 – 95; Weitz, 2000, p. 7).

The methodology of business games as a research tool offers a useful compromise between field and laboratory research. It combines some of the best features of both (Fripp, 1984b): Like laboratory experiments, business games aim at high internal validity, but like field research, they also try to achieve external validity. Internal validity is defined as "the basic minimum without which any experiment is uninterpretable. Did in fact the experimental treatments make a difference in this specific experimental instance" (Campbell & Stanley, 1963, p. 175). External validity "asks the question of generalizability: To what populations, settings, treatment variables, and measurement variables can this effect be generalized" (Campbell & Stanley, 1963, p. 175).

A major factor contributing to the internal validity of business games is control (Fripp, 1984b): Business games – like laboratory experiments (see Kühl, 2005) – provide controlled research conditions. Researchers are able to create the conditions they are interested in and want to test for (Fripp, 1984b). By a controlled variation of independent variables, it is possible to exactly determine what is cause and what is effect (see Kühl, 2005). In case of teams operating in business games, social processes in the interaction of groups may occur. These do not contribute to exactly standardized conditions, but cause uncontrolled interactions and effects (Kriz, 2005). The controlled research conditions also provide the possibility for a replication over a number of participants to test for the general applicability of results (Fripp, 1984b).

Despite their similarities to laboratory experiments, the simulation of realistic conditions may contribute to a higher external validity of business games than "pure" laboratory experiments (Atthill, 1978; Fripp, 1984b; Hägg, Johanson, & Ramström, 1974). But external validity does not necessarily increase when elements – persons, tasks, environmental attributes – are more and more approximated to reality (Eisenführ, 1974). For example, it is unclear whether "real" managers show more typical manager behavior in a business game than students (Eisenführ, 1974). When using students as participants, an approximation of too many attributes to reality brings along the danger that the students are confused and unable to analyze the problem (Atthill, 1978) or that they behave as they believe that managers behave (Eisenführ, 1974). Therefore, Zelditch and Evan (1962) emphasize the "rule of genotypic similarity" (p. 53): "The properties of a simulate need not look like the properties they represent; what is required is that the obey the same laws" (Zelditch & Evan, 1962,

p. 53). So the possibility to transfer the results of the business game to real companies depends on the extent to which the conditions in the game also apply to real
companies (Hägg et al., 1974). For example, one frequent criticism is that decision
making in business games and in companies is different because problems in real
companies are more complex. But decisions in companies are taken under "bounded
rationality" (Hägg et al., 1974; p. 259). Managers in reality base their decisions on a
simplified definition of the situation. Thus, not the complexity as such has to be
similar, but rather the degree of complexity perceived by the participants in the game
and the members of an organization (Hägg et al., 1974). Another aspect reducing the
artificiality of the situation (see Kühl, 2005) is the high degree of involvement and
motivation of participants in business games (Atthill, 1978). Participants are highly
motivated because of their will to use the chance to win as well as the possibility to
actively take part and to take over responsibility (Heidack, 1980, p. 39). As for laboratory experiments, there is evidence that people take them very seriously (Dawes,
1980) and Frank and Schulze (2000) therefore conclude that the results may be a
good approximation for real-world behavior; for business games with controlled
conditions the same may be assumed.

Thus, it becomes apparent that business games face the dilemma of high experimental control and the need of a realistic research environment (Fripp, 1984b).
Despite attempts of business games to achieve external validity, one should be
cautious with drawing generalizations (Atthill, 1978). Nevertheless, the great advantage of business games is their high face validity (Schriesheim & Yaney, 1975).
Moreover, besides the research interest, there is also a learning effect: On the one
hand, participants learn functional knowledge and techniques, develop specific abilities, and improve their decision making (Atthill, 1978). On the other hand, when the
research intention is uncovered, they have Eureka moments, reflect their behavior,
and get new insights (Eisenführ, 1974). In summary, when using business games as a
research tool, one may follow the advise by Fripp (1984b): "The guiding principle
[...] is that the game design must be appropriate to the aims of the research" (p. 20).

4.2.2 Simulating the Business Environment: The Used Business Game

To simulate a competitive business environment, I used the competitive business
game WiN-ABSATZ (Nagel, 2005), which I adapted to the purpose of my study. As
a functional business game, it focuses on the marketing sector. Although in my case,
a company that sells bicycles was chosen, WiN-ABSATZ represents a general
management game that is not bound to special problems of a certain industrial sector
or company. While the original form allows for teams, in my case, each participant
played by oneself. As no interaction between participants is allowed, it is a closed
business game. So in my research, participants were sales and marketing chiefs of a
company over four periods and competed with two to five other companies. Their
aim was to achieve a profit as high as possible after the expiration of the four
periods. In each period, they had to decide on price, expenses for advertisement,
product improvement, sales promotion, customer service, and market research. This

shows the medium complexity of the business game that was necessary to meet the premises of my sample (see chap. 4.2.4, p. 124). WiN-ABSATZ is rigid with an underlying mathematical model to evaluate decisions, deterministic without influences of chance, and computer-based for the analysis of results. So after each period, the participants reported their decisions to the business game conductor using a paper-pencil sheet. Their decisions were then fed into a computer and analyzed. Before starting the next period, they received a printed report of their performance. The business game was conducted in a computer lab of the Faculty of Law, Economics, and Business Administration of the University of Bayreuth, Germany. So, WiN-ABSATZ is a local business game with both instructors and participants being at the same place.

Two experimental elements were added: First, an ethical dilemma regarding corruption was incorporated in the business game according to the recommendations given by Schumann et al. (2006). Once, during the business game, participants had to decide whether they accepted a corrupt offer (condition 1) or whether they submitted a corrupt offer (condition 2). For both conditions, the size of the bribe was varied (50,000 euros versus 100,000 euros). The different corrupt offers can be found in Appendix D (p. 224) and Appendix E (p. 228). The four key elements of ethical dilemmas were ensured:

> (1) There should be a violation of an ethical principle in the dilemma [...]. (2) The dilemma should force a choice, or at least appear to force a choice, between ethical behavior and improved financial performance. (3) The potential loss in profits from taking an ethical course of action should be significant so that students must reconcile their desire to beat the competition with their desire to behave ethically. (4) The dilemma should reflect the students' readiness to manage the issues involved in the situation presented (Schumann et al., 2006, pp. 202 – 203).

As "game comprehension involves the students' ability to understand the software, the rules of the game, and how the game is played" (Schumann et al., 2006, p. 201), these ethical dilemmas were introduced as a handout in either period two, three, or four. This variation of the time when participants got the opportunity of accepting or submitting a corrupt offer provided the possibility to check whether the performance feedback of lower/higher scores than the competitors towards the end of the game influenced the decision on corrupt action. The corrupt offers were not explicitly labeled as corrupt but as offers by a large customer. So it was possible to avoid signaling the participants that these offers involved corruption (see Schumann et al., 2006). It has to be noted that the participants' decision on accepting or making a corrupt offer or not had no influence on the business game results in period two or three, only on the overall performance indicated by the finally accumulated profit at the end of the business game. Furthermore, to get hints on the reasons for corrupt action, I used an open question on the decision paper-pencil sheet asking for the participants' statement on their decision regarding corruption (see Appendix C,

p. 222). This question was asked at the time when the participants had to make their decision, not being told that they were deciding on a corrupt offer.

Second, participants represented companies with slightly differing business codes. A business code is a policy document that defines the responsibilities of the corporation towards its stakeholders and/or the conduct the corporation expects of employees. A code clarifies the objectives the company pursues, the norms and values it upholds, and what it can be held accountable for (Kaptein, 2004, p. 13).

The business code in the company was either formulated at high abstraction level demanding integrity (business code 1) or at low abstraction level explicitly not tolerating corrupt action (business code 2) (see Appendix B, p. 205).

A central aim in designing the business game was to keep the real research intention hidden. Participants should not be aware that they are dealing with corrupt offers to avoid biases in their responses. Thus, I also abandoned an introduction of penalties into the business game. This procedure also seemed to be appropriate for another reason: In real business life, employees are not permanently made aware of the consequences of their behavior because the enforcement of sanctions is not permanently communicated. This means, that in times where there is no high sensitization to corruption because of a great number of detected cases, an especially high enforcement of sanctions will not be present. Although this may be the desired state to prevent corruption, lacking or inappropriate communication of sanctions is the actual situation in most companies. So employees themselves have to gain an awareness of the consequences of their behavior without being permanently hinted at them. Thus, my business game also tried to test for the participants' awareness without special enforcements of sanctions by the business game instructor. To assess the participants' calculation of risk, they should be left unaware of whether there would be any sanctions and what they might be.

4.2.3 Operationalizing the Model Components: The Used Standardized Questionnaire

To measure the motivational, volitional, cognitive, and emotional components of the model of corrupt action, I constructed a standardized questionnaire, which was provided online. I used five-point Likert-scaled items for which the participants were asked to indicate their level of agreement or disagreement (1 = "does not apply at all" to 5 = "fully applies"). As recommended, I tried to specify at least three items for the operationalization of each model component (Bühner, 2004, p. 209; see Appendix F, p. 236). I adopted and selected most of these items from Bagozzi et al. (2003) and from Perugini and Conner (2000). I additionally took items from Perugini and Bagozzi (2001) to operationalize positive and negative emotions in addition to items from various studies using the theory of planned behavior (e.g., Taylor & Todd, 1995) to measure the intention to achieve a private or professional goal as well as the subjective norm. As I explain in the Results section (see chap. 5.1, p. 141), items not considered for the data analysis because of small factor loadings are marked by an asterisk (*).

Desire to Achieve a Private or Professional Goal

As measures for the goal desire, I used the items "I have a strong wish to achieve a higher profit than my competitors in the business game," "For me other goals are more important in the business game than achieving a higher profit than my competitors" (reverse-coded), and "I regard it desirable to perform better in the business game than my competitors." Low scores indicate a weak goal desire, high scores a strong one.

Positive and Negative Anticipated Emotions

Regarding the positive anticipated emotions, participants were asked to indicate their level of agreement with the item "If I achieve a higher profit in the business game than my competitors, I will feel ..." with the response options "happy," "proud" (*), "surprised" (*), and "relieved." Regarding the negative anticipated emotions, I used the item "If I achieve a lower profit in the business game than my competitors, I will feel ..." with the response options "angry," "ashamed" (*), "disappointed" (*), and "depressed." Low scores indicate a lower intensity of anticipated emotions, higher scores a higher intensity.

Goal Feasibility

Items used as indicators for this construct included "I hardly see any possibility of achieving a higher profit in the business game than my competitors" (reverse-coded), "I am convinced I am able to perform better in the business game than my competitors," and "I regard it difficult to be more successful in the business game than my competitors" (reverse-coded). Low scores indicate high difficulty to achieve the goal, high scores low difficulty.

Intention to Achieve a Private or Professional Goal

My items measuring the goal intention were "I am very serious in being more successful in the business game than my competitors," "I will do everything possible to perform better in the business game than my competitors," and "I do not care whether I achieve a higher profit in the business game than my competitors or not" (reverse-coded). Low scores indicate a weak goal intention, high scores a strong one.

Desire to Achieve a Private or Professional Goal Through Corrupt Action

I operationalized the desire to act corruptly by the items "My desire to accept the customer's offer/to make the customer an offer was strong," "The customer's offer/The possibility to make the customer an offer left me cold" (reverse-coded), and "I considered it attractive to accept the customer's offer/to make the customer an offer." Low scores indicate a weak desire to act corruptly, high scores a strong desire.

Attitude

The participants' attitude toward corruption was measured by nine seven-point semantic differential items. We asked the participants to respond to the item "I think accepting the customer's offer/making the customer an offer is ..." with the adjective pairs "bad – good" (*), "wrong – right," "foolish – wise," "useless – useful," "disadvantageous – advantageous," "boring – exciting," "unpleasant – pleasant," "unattractive – attractive," and "dissatisfying – satisfying." Low scores indicate a negative attitude toward corruption, high scores indicate a positive attitude.

Subjective Norm

As indicators for the subjective norm served the items "Most people important to me in my life think that I should have accepted the customer's offer/that I should have made the customer an offer," "My family would bear me out in the decision to accept the customer's offer/to make the customer an offer," and "My friends would have rejected the customer's offer/would not have made the customer an offer" (reverse-coded). Low scores indicate a corruption-aversive subjective norm, high scores indicate a corruption-friendly subjective norm.

Intention to Achieve a Private or Professional Goal Through Corrupt Action

To measure the intention to act corruptly, I used the items "For me, it was out of question to accept the customer's offer/to make the customer an offer" (reverse-coded), "I was sure that I would accept the customer's offer/would make the customer an offer," and "My intention to accept the customer's offer/to make the customer an offer was strong." Low scores indicate a weak intention to act corruptly, high scores indicate a strong intention.

Perceived Behavioral Control

To come up with items relevant for corruption to operationalize perceived behavioral control, I referred to the research findings that big risk for disclosure, high expected penalties, and high transaction costs diminish perceived behavioral control (see chap. 3.3, p. 106). So, items included "I anticipated negative consequences if I accepted the customer's offer/if I made the customer an offer" (reverse-coded), "I was convinced to be able to conduct the transaction with the customer without any risk," and "I assessed the likelihood that the transaction with the customer will be kept secret in front of my competitors to be high" (*). Low scores indicate low perceived behavioral control, high scores indicate high perceived behavioral control.

Corrupt Action

As a dichotomous measure for corrupt action served the participants' decision on whether they finally accept respectively make the corrupt offer or not.

Goal Realization

The items used to measure goal realization included "In the business game, I performed better than my competitors," "My decisions during the business game led to success," "I failed my goal to achieve a higher profit than my competitors" (reverse-coded). Low scores indicate a low level of goal realization, high scores a high level.

Rationalization Strategies

In my study, I additionally was interested in the rationalization strategies used by participants who acted corruptly. I tried to cover the rationalization strategies identified by Ashforth and Anand (2003; see chap. 2.6.1, p. 87). I formulated rationalizations that appeared suitable from the background of my business game. For both conditions – active and passive corruption – the bribe was to get an order in exchange for a private favor. At the end of the questionnaire, the participants were confronted with the following situation: "You accepted the customer's offer. One of your colleagues has heard about it and says: 'But that's not okay!' What would you answer him/her?" They then were asked to check the three of the following alternatives that were most obvious for rationalizing their corrupt action: "It's not written anywhere that this is not allowed" (legality), "It was the only chance to increase our profit" (denial of responsibility), "Everybody does it" (denial of responsibility), "It didn't harm anybody. It paid off for everybody" (denial of injury), "It was only about relatively small amounts" (denial of injury), "Because of the competitors? It doesn't matter that they once also get the short end of the stick" (denial of victim), "Why? Because of the competitors who miss out? That's business" (denial of victim), "To get orders, others are doing things that are even worse" (social weighting), "I only did everything to increase the order situation and the income of our company" (appeal to higher loyalties), "I only tried to maintain the good business relationship with a good customer" (appeal to higher loyalties), "Why shouldn't I take advantage of the good business relationship I developed over several years" (metaphor of the ledger), "After all I got the order for our business" (refocusing attention). The answer to each item was dummy-coded (1 = yes; 0 = no). Participants also had the possibility to indicate other rationalization strategies than those outlined above by choosing the "Others" option.

4.2.4 Sample

The sample of my study included 196 native German participants in the research project. 97 participants were students at the University of Bayreuth, Germany, and came from different disciplines (see table 4). University students at the beginning, in the middle, and at the end of their studies were covered.

Table 4:   Fields of Study of the 97 University Students

Subjects	Frequency
Business Administration	58
Business Administration Studies for the High School Teaching Profession	2
Economics	6
Engineering	3
Health Management	12
Law (with additional courses in business administration and economics)	4
Philosophy and Economics	3
Sports Management	9

99 participants were students from the final classes preparing for the general higher education entrance qualification of a high school (*German:* Gymnasium) in Bayreuth, Germany, who attended business courses. I intended to acquire both high school and university students with an interest to take over the position of a decision maker in a company in their later professional life. 171 participants clearly indicated this intention.

90 participants were female, 106 were male. The participants had a median age of 20.91 years (*SD* = 3.37).

4.2.5 Procedures

To optimize procedures and to check for clarity and comprehensibility, both business game and standardized questionnaire were pretested with two samples of nine and twelve university students. In the pretest, no major problems occurred. Thus, after minor revisions, I started the main study.

How participants were acquired, how the business game and the standardized questionnaire were integrated, and which procedures were followed, I describe in the following:

To acquire participants without communicating the research intention, the research project was announced as a business game competition on the "decision making behavior in a competitive business environment" (see Appendix A, p. 201). To increase the number of volunteers, prizes[41] for the ten best participants in the business game competition were advertised as incentives. Rewards are a common motivational method when business games are experimentally used (Babb & Eisgruber,

---

[41] Prizes for the the the best participants in the business game competition were sponsored by the foundation "Wertevolle Zukunft", the Business Keeper AG, the Telekom AG, and the ABB AG.

1966, p. 38). Nevertheless, in the announcement it was additionally pointed out that everybody would benefit from the experience gained in the business game (see Babb & Eisgruber, 1966, p. 38).

To acquire a subsample of university students, I used the e-mail newsletters of the relevant chairs and student councils as well as announcements in lectures. To get a subsample of high school students, I contacted teachers of business courses in the final classes at local high schools (*German:* Gymnasien) and informed them about the business game competition. Interested teachers with their classes and interested university students contacted me to agree on date and time of the business game session they would like to take part in. The business game competition was conducted between April and July 2006.

When the participants came into the computer lab, they were welcomed, assigned a seat, and handed their confirmation of participation with their anonymous participant code. This confirmation remained with the participants. It was the only means for them to identify themselves as potential winners as soon as the winners of the business game competition were announced. During the whole research process, the participants acted under their anonymous code so that all their decisions and results in the business game were kept anonymous.

As soon as all participants in one session[42] had arrived, the research session started. At the beginning, the participants were encouraged to read the business game instructions provided online (see Appendix B, p. 205). If there were no questions on the instructions, participants followed the provided link to the first part of the standardized online questionnaire (see Appendix G, p. 247), which included questions regarding their goal desire, their goal intention, the goal feasibility, and their positive and negative anticipated emotions. After that, they were given the paper-pencil sheets on which they had to note down the decisions they had to make in each period of the business game (see Appendix C, p. 222). Then, the business game as described in chapter 4.2.2 (p. 119) started. For each period, participants had about 20 minutes time to make the required decisions. The instructor fed the results into the computer for analyzing and gave feedback. At the end of the game, participants also received their final results regarding the overall profit and the rank achieved compared to their direct competitors in the business game. Then, they were asked to follow the link to the second part of the standardized online questionnaire (see Appendix H, p. 251), which included questions on whether they accepted or submitted the offer to the large customer[43], their desire and intention to do this, their attitude, their subjective norm, the perceived behavioral control, the goal realization, and – in case they acted corruptly – on their rationalization strategies[44]. Finally, they were informed about the

---

[42] As the computer lab had 24 seats, it was possible to simultaneously test four groups of six competing participants each.

[43] In the questionnaire, only "the offer of a large customer" was used to indicate the corrupt offer.

[44] Here participants received hints that their behavior might have been wrong. But again, the term "corruption" was never mentioned.

procedures on the proclamation of the winners and thanked for their participation. At this stage, they were not informed about the research intention; this was in order to avoid biases in the results that might have arisen if the research intention were communicated to others. Together with the proclamation of winners[45] at the end of the data-gathering phase of the project and the business game competition, participants were debriefed on the research intention and the ethical dilemma.

The central aspects of the research design are summarized in table 5 (see Rabl, 2006, May):

---

[45] The winners were identified according to their "real" results in the business game without considering potential corrupt gains. As the prizes should be an incentive for participation, I intended to achieve a learning effect and an ethical sensibility by the business game rather than sanctioning behavior shown in the business game.

Table 5:   Research Design

Phase	Task	Participants
1	**Reading of business game instructions (1 or 2)**	1 – 6
2	**Standardized questionnaire, part I**	1 – 6
3	**Business game, period 1** – Marketing decisions	1 – 6
	Feedback: Results of period 1	1 – 6

	Business game, period 2
	– Marketing decisions
	and
	– Decision on accepting (condition 1) or
	  making (condition 2) a corrupt offer:
	  50,000 euros bribe or
	  150,000 euros bribe
		1 – 6
		
		1
		4

	Feedback: Results of period 2	1 – 6

	Business game, period 3
	– Marketing decisions
	and
	– Decision on accepting (condition 1) or
	  making (condition 2) a corrupt offer:
	  50,000 euros bribe or
	  150,000 euros bribe
		1 – 6
		
		2
		5

	Feedback: Results of period 3	1 – 6

	Business game, period 4
	– Marketing decisions
	and
	– Decision on accepting (condition 1) or
	  making (condition 2) a corrupt offer:
	  50,000 euros bribe or
	  150,000 euros bribe
		1 – 6
		
		3
		6

	Feedback: Results of period 4 and final result of the whole business game	1 – 6
4	**Standardized questionnaire, part II**	1 – 6

4.2.6 Quality Criteria

The quality of the research instruments can be evaluated according to three criteria: objectivity, reliability, and validity (Lienert & Raatz, 1994, p. 7).

The *objectivity* of a research instrument is the degree to which the results are independent from the conductor of the research (Bortz & Döring, 1995, p. 180; Lienert & Raatz, 1994, p. 7).

Procedure objectivity is the degree to which the results are independent from variations in the researcher's behavior (Lienert & Raatz, 1994, p. 8). High procedure objectivity is achieved by clear, standardized instructions for participants and a minimum of social interaction between participant and researcher (Bortz & Döring, 1995, p. 180; Lienert & Raatz, 1994, p. 8). In the case of my business game, a high procedure objectivity could be realized by standardized game instructions and standardized responses to potential queries on the game instructions. The same applies for the standardized questionnaire.

Assessment objectivity refers to the degree to which the assessment of certain test behavior follows certain rules and is independent from the researcher who assesses the results (Bortz & Döring, 1995, p. 180; Lienert & Raatz, 1994, p. 8). In the case of my business game, high assessment objectivity can be assumed because the analysis of the game results followed the mathematical model incorporated into the business game. The same applies for the standardized questionnaire because there were predominantly standardized response options and only a low number of open response possibilities (Lienert & Raatz, 1994, p. 8).

Interpretation objectivity refers to the degree to which the interpretation of results is independent from the researcher and oriented to certain reference values and norms (Bortz & Döring, 1995, p. 180; Lienert & Raatz, 1994, p. 8). In the case of my business game, a high interpretation objectivity could be achieved because the interpretation of the results was clearly determined by the comparison with the competitors. Regarding the standardized questionnaire, responses resulted in a numerical value, which clearly determined the participant's position on the test scale. This contributes to high interpretation objectivity (Lienert & Raatz, 1994, p. 8).

Reliability refers to the degree of measurement accuracy of a research instrument regardless whether it measures what it is intended to measure (Bortz & Döring, 1995, p. 181; Lienert & Raatz, 1994, p. 9). The instrument used to measure decision making behavior on corrupt action was the standardized questionnaire. The relevant reliability measures are reported in the Results section (see chap. 5.1, p. 139) because they are calculated within the data analysis procedure used to test the theoretical model.

Validity is the most important quality criterion and refers to the degree to which the research instrument measures what it intends to measure (Bortz & Döring, 1995, p. 185; Lienert & Raatz, 1994, p. 10).

Content validity is achieved when the construct that is intended to be measured is exhaustively or representatively represented in its most important aspects (Bortz & Döring, 1995, p. 181; Lienert & Raatz, 1994, p. 10). For the standardized questionnaire used as measurement instrument in my study, content validity can be assumed because the operationalization of the model components tries to cover each construct's aspects and is based on the items used by experts (Lienert & Raatz, 1994, p. 11), in this case, by other authors who examined these constructs, like, for example, Bagozzi et al. (2003). Although the business game in my case was not used as a measurement instrument but rather as a simulation instrument so that its content validity does not need to be evaluated, it can be noted that high face validity – which is similar to content validity (Bortz & Döring, 1995, p. 185) – is highlighted as a great advantage of business games (Schriesheim & Yaney, 1975).

Criterion validity is given when assessments of a construct correspond with an external criterion. It is the correlation of the results of the measurement instrument with the criterion (Bortz & Döring, 1995, p. 185; Lienert & Raatz, 1994, p. 11). To test for the criterion validity of my measurement instrument, the standardized questionnaire, no external criterion was available.

Construct validity refers to the degree of correspondence of the tested construct with the theoretical construct. A research instrument is valid regarding its construct if hypotheses can be derived for the construct that can be confirmed by the test results (Bortz & Döring, 1995, p. 186; Lienert & Raatz, 1994, p. 11). My theoretical model is based on the model by Bagozzi et al. (2003), which was successfully tested by the authors. Thus, there are hints for construct validity. One aspect of construct validity is discriminant validity, which demands that the construct to be measured is different from other constructs (Bortz & Döring, 1995, p. 187). The measures for this quality criterion are reported in the Results section (see chap. 5.1, p. 143) because they are calculated within the data analysis procedure used to test the theoretical model.

Another aspect of validity – which is relevant for the business game used in my study – is the distinction between *internal and external validity* (for a detailed discussion see chap. 4.2.1, p. 118). As I used the business game as kind of laboratory experiment (Eisenführ, 1974), high internal validity can be assumed because of standardization, controlled variable variation, and randomization (Kriz, 2005; Kühl, 2005). This reduces external validity although a cut-out of the real world is simulated (Kriz, 2005; Kühl, 2005). There are two major reasons why the sample of high school and university students may not be seen as a limiting factor to external validity: On the one hand, it is argued that demands of the business game and the abilities of the sample should match (e.g., Atthill, 1978; Eisenführ, 1974), which was the case. On the other hand, a number of studies found business students' propensity to ethical behavior similar to those of practitioners and managers (see e.g., O'Fallon & Butterfield, 2005).

4.3   Analyses

My study used two approaches to analyze the gathered data: To test the theoretical model of corrupt action and the corresponding hypotheses, the Partial Least Squares (PLS) structural equation modeling procedure was used. Furthermore, some explorative analyses were conducted to examine selected issues that are discussed in the corruption literature or seem to be an interesting contribution to the corruption litera-ture. In the following, I describe the various procedures used for the data analysis.

4.3.1 Hypothesis Testing with Partial Least Squares Structural Equation Modeling

In social sciences, structural equation modeling (SEM) – also called causal analysis – is a widely used method for representing, estimating, and empirically testing a theo-retical network of linear causal relationships between variables (Henseler, 2005; Rigdon, 1998). Belonging to "a second generation of multivariate analysis" (Fornell, 1985, p. 1), it enables the researcher to:

- construct latent, not directly observable variables (Backhaus, Erichson, Plinke, & Weiber, 2003, p. 334; Chin, 1998a; Chin, 1998b);

- investigate relationships among latent variables (Chin, 1998a; Chin, 1998b; Henseler, 2005);

- perform confirmatory analysis, that is, to statistically test whether the a priori theoretical assumptions match the empirical data (Backhaus et al., 2003, p. 334; Byrne, 2001, p. 3; Chin, 1998a; Chin, 1998b; Ringle, 2004b);

- model errors in measurement for observed variables (Chin, 1998a; Chin, 1998b);

- investigate the quality of construct measurement regarding reliability and validity (Henseler, 2005).

The general SEM model can be decomposed into two submodels: the measurement model and the structural model.

The measurement model (also called outer model) contains observable manifest vari-ables as empirical indicators reflecting the not directly observable latent variables. It indicates how the latent variables relate to these manifest variables (Backhaus et al., 2003, p. 337; Byrne, 2001, p. 12; Chatelin, Vinzi, & Tenenhaus, 2002; Henseler, 2005; Sellin, 1995; Tenenhaus, Vinzi, Chatelin, & Lauro, 2005). There are two important ways to relate the manifest variables to their latent variables: the reflective way and the formative way. A summary of differences[46] between these two types of measurement models is given in table 6:

---

[46] For a detailed discussion of differences see e.g., Chin (1998b); Diamantopoulos and Winklhofer (2001); Fassott and Eggert (2005); Jarvis, MacKenzie, & Podsakoff (2003); Zinnbauer and Eberl (2004).

Table 6:   Summary of Differences Between Types of Measurement Models
(adopted from Jarvis et al., 2003, p. 2001)

Reflective (principal factor) model	Formative (composite latent variable) model
Direction of causality is from construct to measure	Direction of causality is from measure to construct
Measures expected to be correlated (Measures should possess internal consistency reliability)	No reason to expect the measures are correlated (Internal consistency is not implied)
Dropping an indicator from the measurement model does not alter the meaning of the construct	Dropping an indicator from the measurement model may alter the meaning of the construct
Takes measurement error into account at the item level	Takes measurement error into account at the construct level
Construct possesses "surplus" meaning; they refer to processes that are not directly observed	Construct possesses "surplus" meaning; they refer to processes that are not directly observed
Summed scale score does not adequately represent the construct	Summed scale score does not adequately represent the construct

Eberl (2004) recommends the application of the following questions to decide on the specification of the measurement model: (1) Is the construct causally for the indicators? (2) Do all indicators change their direction if one indicator changes direction? (3) Are all indicators of a construct exchangeable? If all questions are answered "yes", a reflective specification should be used.

The structural model (also called the inner model) describes the linear relationships between the latent variables (Backhaus et al., 2003, p. 336; Byrne, 2001, p. 12; Chatelin et al., 2002; Sellin, 1995; Tenenhaus et al., 2005). A latent variable that never appears as a dependent variable is called an exogenous variable; otherwise, it is called an endogenous variable (Chatelin et al., 2002; Henseler, 2005; Ringle, Boysen, Wende, & Will, 2006; Tenenhaus et al., 2005). The causality model must be recursive, this means, it must be a causal chain without any loop (Chatelin et al., 2002; Henseler, 2005; Ringle et al., 2006; Tenenhaus et al., 2005).

SEM is a multivariate method that combines both regression and factor analytic approaches (Rigdon, 1998; Ringle, 2004a; Ringle, 2004b). To determine causal models, there are two competing procedures: on the one hand, the covariance structure analysis, which was mainly advanced by Jöreskog and Sörbom (e.g., Jöreskog, 1970; Jöreskog, 1979) and called LISREL ("Linear Structural Relations", Magidson, 1979, p. 103); on the other hand, the Partial Least Squares (PLS) analysis developed by Wold (e.g., Wold, 1966; Wold, 1982; Wold, 1985). Both have similar formal assumptions regarding the structural model and allow the modeling of measurement errors. The differences are found in the estimation methods (partial least squares versus maximum likelihood) and the measurement models that can be applied for latent variables (Chin, 1998b; Ringle, 2004a; Ringle, 2004b). An overview[47] on the major differences between covariance structure analysis and PLS analysis is given in table 7:

---

[47] For a detailed discussion see e.g., Bliemel, Eggert, Fassott, and Henseler (2005); Chin and Newsted (1999); Fornell and Bookstein (1982); Lohmöller (1989, pp. 199 – 226); Schneeweiß (1991).

Table 7:   A Comparison of Structural Equation Modeling using PLS and
           Covariance-Based Structural Equation Modeling (adopted from Chin &
           Newsted, 1999, p. 314; Ringle, 2004b, p. 34; Hansmann & Ringle, 2005,
           p. 225)

Criterion	Structural equation modeling with Partial Least Squares	Covariance-based structural equation modeling
Objective	Prediction oriented	Parameter oriented
Approach	Variance based	Covariance based
Assumptions	Predictor specification (nonparametric)	Typically multivariate normal distribution and independent observations (parametric)
Parameter estimates	Consistent as indicators and sample size increase (i.e., consistency at large)	Consistent
Latent variable scores	Explicitly estimated	Indeterminate
Epistemic relationship between a latent variable and its measures	Can be modeled in either formative or reflective mode	Typically only with reflective indicators
Implications	Optimal for prediction accuracy	Optimal for parameter accuracy
Model complexity	Large complexity (e.g., 100 constructs and 1000 indicators)	Small to moderate complexity (e.g., less than 100 indicators)
Sample size	Power analysis based on the portion of the model with the largest number of predictors; minimal recommendations range from 30 to 100 cases	Ideally based on power analysis of specific model; minimal recommendations range from 200 to 800

A great advantage of PLS analysis is that it ensures against improper solutions and
factor indeterminacy (Fornell & Bookstein, 1982) because it has less restrictive
demands than covariance-based approaches. It is a distribution-free procedure and
therefore able to model latent constructs under conditions of non-normality. It also

requires a relatively small sample size[48]. Furthermore, there are no assumptions about the scales of measurement so that nominal, ordinal, and interval-scaled variables are permissible in PLS (Chin, 1998b; Chin & Newsted, 1999; Fornell & Bookstein, 1982; Ringle et al., 2006; Sellin, 1995). Wold (1982) therefore refers to PLS as a "soft modeling" (p. 1; Tenenhaus et al., 2005, p. 160) approach in contrast to the "hard modeling" (Tenenhaus et al., 2005, p. 160) approach of covariance-based SEM. Because of the high complexity of my model and the therefore low sample size for an application of covariance-based structural equation modeling (see table 7) and the inclusion of one nominal-scaled variable (corrupt action), I chose the PLS approach, which is able to handle these restrictions. According to the central limit theorem[49] (Bortz, 1999, pp. 93 – 94), the normal distribution of my variables can be assumed.

As there are a number of very good overviews on the PLS approach (Chin, 1998b; Henseler, 2005, Ringle, 2004a; Ringle, 2004b; Ringle et al., 2006; for a theory-oriented description see Tenenhaus et al., 2005), I do not outline it in detail here. I only sketch the most important aspects. When the PLS approach offers more alternatives, I briefly describe them to underline the decision I have taken.

PLS is a components-based SEM technique and therefore similar to regression (Chin, 1998a). It is characterized by an iterative, successive approximation of estimates. Subset by subset is estimated by using ordinary multiple regressions that involve the values of parameters in other subsets (Fornell & Bookstein, 1982). As each step minimizes a residual variance with respect to a subset of the parameters being esti-mated, the procedure is partial in a least square sense (Chin, 1998b). The PLS algo-rithm does not assume equal weights for all indicators of a latent variable, but considers weightings according to the strength of the indicators' relationships with the latent variable in the estimation (Chin, 1998a). The PLS algorithm can be summarized as follows:

> The PLS procedure is [...] used to estimate the latent variables as an exact linear combination of its indicators with the goal of maximizing the explained variance for the indicators and latent variables. Following a series of ordinary least squares analyses, PLS optimally weights the indicators such that a resulting latent variable estimate can be obtained. The weights provide an exact linear combination of the indicators for forming the latent variable score, which is not only maximally correlated with its own set of indicators, as in components analysis, but also correlated with other latent variables according

---

[48] The necessary sample size is determined by the most complex (in regard to the number of regres-sors) multiple regression in the model (Chin, 1998b; Henseler, 2005). Barclay, Higgins, and Thompson (1995, p. 292) demand as a rule of thumb ten data sets multiplied with the number of regressors in the most complex regression.

[49] The central limit theorem states that as the sample size n increases ($n \geq 30$), the distribution of the sample average approaches the normal distribution (Bortz, 1999, pp. 93 – 94).

to the structural, or theoretical, model (Chin, Marcolin, & Newsted, 2003, p. 199).

To obtain the weights and subsequent loading and path estimates, the PLS approach uses a three-stage estimation algorithm (for a detailed description see Chin, 1998b, pp. 302 – 303). At one stage in this algorithm, the researcher has to make a decision. There are three inside approximation weighting schemes to combine neighboring latent variables to obtain a proxy for a specific latent variable: centroid weighting, factor weighting, and path weighting. The centroid weighting scheme equates the inner weights with the signs of the correlation. The factor weighting scheme uses the correlation itself rather than the correlation's sign. The path weighting scheme equates the inner weights with the regression coefficients for all independent variables impacting the target latent variable. The regression coefficients are provisional path coefficients of the structural model. All dependent latent variables are weighted by the correlation coefficients (Chin, 1998b, Henseler, 2005; Ringle et al., 2006). Although the path-weighting scheme is most often used for models with hypothesized causal relations because it takes into account the directionality of the structural model (Chin, 1998b), I decided on the factor weighting scheme. While the path weighting is oriented to the latent variable that is intended to be explained and therefore maximizes R^2 for endogenous variables, the factor weighting scheme treats all constructs equally and therefore is recommended for well-balanced models: "It may be possible to obtain stable estimates for weights and loadings of each component independent of the final estimates for the structural model" (Chin, 1998b, p. 311). No matter which weighting scheme has been chosen, it has little influence on the results (Ringle et al., 2006): .005 or less for structural paths and .05 or less for measurement paths (Noonan & Wold, 1982).

In contrast to covariance-based SEM, there is no global quality index like the Goodness of Fit Index for the total PLS model (Ringle, 2004a). Therefore, a PLS model is usually analyzed and interpreted sequentially in two stages: First, the reliability and validity of the measurement model are assessed. Second, the structural model is assessed (Henseler, 2005; Hulland, 1999; Tenenhaus et al., 2005). "This sequence ensures that the researcher has reliable and valid measures of constructs before attempting to draw conclusions about the nature of the construct relationships" (Hulland, 1999, p. 198). A detailed description of the quality criteria relevant for the evaluation of PLS models is given in Chin (1998b; for an overview see also Hansmann & Ringle, 2005, p. 230, and Ringle et al., 2006, p. 87). As I discuss them in the Results section (see chap. 5.1, p. 139), I do not outline them here. For obtaining a good PLS model, the different quality criteria should be fulfilled as well as possible. Otherwise, the model has to be modified to at least obtain significant results for some parts or some explorative model modifications (Ringle, 2004a).

The statistical software program I used to conduct the PLS analysis for my model of corrupt action was SmartPLS (Ringle, Wende, & Will, 2005), which was developed at the Institute for Industrial Management and Organization at the University of Hamburg, Germany.

4.3.2 Quantitative and Qualitative Explorative Analyses

In addition to the core of my analysis – the empirical test of the theoretical model of corrupt action – I exploratively examined how certain sociodemographic and situational factors influence the strengths of relationships in the model of corrupt action, how they relate to single model components, and whether their variation results in differences in the single model components.

All these additional analyses were conducted on the assumption of the normal distribution of the variables following the central limit theorem (Bortz, 1999, pp. 93 – 94).

To compare differences in the path coefficients in the model of corrupt action between the values of the independent variable, I followed the procedure recommended by Chin (2000). I ran bootstrap re-samplings for the respective groups, treated the standard error estimates from each re-sampling in a parametric sense, and calculated pairwise two-sided t-tests.

To investigate how sociodemographic and situational factors relate to the model components, correlation coefficients were calculated according to the scale level of the respective variables.

To analyze the data on whether there are any differences regarding the values of the independent variable in the model components, I conducted multivariate variance analyses (MANOVAs) using Wilks' lamda. As it is neither in my research intention to determine the relative contribution of specific model components to possible differences in the whole model nor to prioritize certain constructs in the model, I abandoned post-hoc discriminant or step-down analyses, which are among the recommended follow-up procedures in case of a significant MANOVA (Bray & Maxwell, 1982; Huberty & Morris, 1989). Instead, if the MANOVA revealed significant results, I additionally report the results of the significant univariate variance analyses (ANOVAs), only to get further insights of what the differences in the whole model are like. According to Bray and Maxwell (1982) this is an appropriate procedure when – as in my case – the MANOVA is conducted to control the experiment-wise error rate and intercorrelations between the single variates are not of interest (in my case, the intercorrelations are examined by the PLS procedure). Although the MANOVA – like the ANOVA – is relatively robust to violations of its assumptions (Bortz, 1999, p. 276; Bray & Maxwell, 1985, p. 33), all premises for this statistical procedure were met: The independence of error components may be assumed to the degree that subjects have been randomly assigned to the groups; following the central limit theorem for each single dependent variable univariate normality may exist, which is necessary for a multivariate normal distribution; because of non-significant F-tests, the homogeneity of variances is given; and as indicated by the non-significant box tests, the homogeneity of variance-covariance-matrices is fulfilled (Bortz, 1999, pp. 576, 578; Bray & Maxwell, 1985, pp. 32 – 33).

Furthermore, to examine the reasons given for corrupt and non-corrupt behavior, I conducted a quantitative content analysis (Mayring, 2000) deducing categories out of the verbal material provided by the participants and counting the frequency with which they were mentioned. Two independent researchers coded the responses to determine the inter-coder reliability using Cohen's kappa ($\kappa = .96$). To test for differences in the frequencies of reasons given for passive and active corruption, I used a binomial test. A quantitative content analysis was also carried out for the responses mentioned in the "Others" option of the rationalization strategies.

All quantitative analyses, apart from the PLS procedure, were conducted using SPSS 14.

5 Results

In the following chapter, I report the results of my data analyses. The core of this chapter is the model of corrupt action finally resulting from the PLS analyses. Following sections deal with sociodemographic and situational influence factors, the reasons given for corrupt versus non-corrupt behavior, and the rationalization strategies used by corrupt actors.

5.1 The Model of Corrupt Action

In chapter 3.3 (p. 101), I proposed a theoretical model of corrupt action and set up a number of hypotheses regarding the relationships between the single model components. The results of the PLS analyses are the following (see Rabl & Kühlmann, 2007, September; Rabl & Kühlmann, 2008; Rabl & Kühlmann, 2008, August):

5.1.1 Evaluation of the Proposed Model

The descriptive statistics with means and standard deviations are presented in table 8, the correlations among all latent variables in table 9. I computed these correlations via a fully saturated PLS model.

Table 8:   Descriptive Statistics

Variable	Mean	*SD*
GD	3.87	0.73
PAE	4.15	0.81
NAE	2.31	0.91
GI	3.50	0.84
GF	3.03	0.79
ID	3.80	0.95
AT	4.88	1.17
SN	3.28	0.76
II	3.64	1.08
PBC	3.48	1.11
CA	_[1]	_[1]
GR	2.77	1.26

GD = Desire to achieve a private or professional goal; PAE = Positive anticipated emotions; NAE = Negative anticipated emotions; GI = Intention to achieve a private or professional goal; GF = Goal feasibility; ID = Desire to achieve a private or professional goal through corrupt action; AT = Attitude; SN = Subjective norm; II = Intention to achieve a private or professional goal through corrupt action; PBC = Perceived behavioral control; CA = Corrupt action; GR = Goal realization
-    $N = 196$
[1]   dichotomous, nominal-scaled variable

Table 9: Correlations

Variable	GD	PAE	NAE	GI	GF	ID	AT	SN	II	PBC	CA
PAE	.38**										
NAE	.26**	.38**									
GI	.70**	.35**	.35**								
GF	.42**	.05	.05	.47**							
ID	.13	.08	.01	.15*	-.01						
AT	.09	-.01	.01	.11	.10	.65**					
SN	.09	.11	-.04	.07	-.01	.54**	.58**				
II	.08	.03	.01	.11	-.07	.82**	.73**	.58*			
PBC	.01	.01	-.08	.00	.03	.59**	.62**	.51**	.71**		
CA	-.06	-.07	.02	.00	-.13	.78**	.66**	.49**	.78**	.72**	
GR	-.11	-.09	-.08	-.05	-.02	.07	.18*	-.02	.07	.02	.13*

GD = Desire to achieve a private or professional goal; PAE = Positive anticipated emotions; NAE = Negative anticipated emotions; GI = Intention to achieve a private or professional goal; GF = Goal feasibility; ID = Desire to achieve a private or professional goal through corrupt action; AT = Attitude; SN = Subjective norm; II = Intention to achieve a private or professional goal through corrupt action; PBC = Perceived behavioral control; CA = Corrupt action; GR = Goal realization
- $N = 196$
- Pearson correlations for the relationships among interval-scaled variables, point-biserial correlations for he relationship between the interval-scaled variables and the dichotomous variable "corrupt action"
- one-tailed significance test for relationships proposed in the model, two-tailed significance test for all other relationships
* $p < .05$
** $p < .01$

To evaluate causal models estimated by PLS procedures, I refer to Chin's (1998b) catalogue of non-parametric quality criteria. As in contrast to covariance-based SEM no global quality index exists, the structural model and the measurement model of the latent variables have to be evaluated separately (Hansmann & Ringle, 2005).

Evaluation of the Reflective Measurement Models

I only used reflective measurement models, assuming that the indicators measure the same underlying phenomenon (Chin, 1998b; see chap. 4.3.1, p. 131). In PLS, individual item reliability is assessed by examining the loadings of the measures with their respective construct (Hulland, 1999). To assure that each indicator shares more variance with the component score than with error variance, I only chose indicators with loadings of at least .70 (Chin, 1998b; Hansmann & Ringle, 2005; Hulland, 1999). I also accepted loadings of .60 in the case that there were additional comparable indicators in the block (Chin, 1998b; Hansmann & Ringle, 2005). Indicators I therefore eliminated are marked by an asterisk (*) in the Methods section (see chap. 4.2.3, p. 121).

To examine the scales' internal consistency, I used three measures. One is Cronbach's alpha, where according to Nunnally (1978, p. 245) in basic research a value of .70 is acceptable. A second one is the composite reliability assessed by Dillon-Goldstein's rho (Tenenhaus et al., 2005), which corresponds with the measure developed by Werts, Linn, and Jöreskog (1974). As Cronbach's alpha assumes tau equivalence, which means that all items have to measure the construct equally well and may only differ in the measurement error, the rho as a measure for the composite reliability is applicable if there is no tau-equivalence. It considers the real factor loadings in contrast to the equal weighting conducted in computing Cronbach's alpha and is therefore a closer approximation under the assumption that the parameter estimates are accurate (Chin, 1998b; Ringle et al., 2006). Rho can be interpreted like Cronbach's alpha and should be higher than .70 (Ringle et al., 2006). Fornell and Larcker's (1981) average variance extracted (AVE) measures the amount of variance that a latent variable component captures from its indicators relative to the amount due to measurement error. It can be interpreted as a measure of reliability for the latent variable component score and is more conservative than the composite reliability rho. The AVE should be greater than .50 (Chin, 1998b). Results for these three measures are shown in table 10. Only for the desire to achieve a goal and positive as well as negative anticipated emotions, Cronbach's alpha fell below the recommended level. But both the rho taking into account the indicators' different weighting and the conservative AVE were acceptable for all latent variables.

Table 10:   Reliability Measures

Scales	α[1]	ρ[2]	AVE[3]
GD	.67	.81	.60
PAE	.64	.84	.73
NAE	.59	.82	.70
GI	.73	.85	.65
GF	.76	.85	.66
ID	.83	.90	.75
AT	.93	.94	.67
SN	.72	.84	.64
II	.87	.92	.79
PBC	.80	.91	.84
CA	_[4]	_[4]	_[4]
GR	.91	.94	.85

GD = Desire to achieve a private or professional goal; PAE = Positive anticipated emotions; NAE = Negative anticipated emotions; GI = Intention to achieve a private or professional goal; GF = Goal feasibility; ID = Desire to achieve a private or professional goal through corrupt action; AT = Attitude; SN = Subjective norm; II = Intention to achieve a private or professional goal through corrupt action; PBC = Perceived behavioral control; CA = Corrupt action; GR = Goal realization
[1]   Cronbach's alpha
[2]   Dillon-Goldstein's rho (composite reliability)
[3]   Average variance extracted
[4]   The construct was measured by a single item.

As a means of evaluating discriminant validity, "the extent to which measures of a given construct differ from measures of other constructs in the same model" (Hulland, 1999, p. 199), there are two measures: First, the *AVEs* of the latent variables according to Fornell and Larcker (1981) should be greater than the square of the correlations among the latent variables (Chin, 1998b; Hulland, 1999). Second, when calculating the cross-loadings between latent variable component scores and other indicators outside its own block, an indicator should not load higher with other latent variables than the one it is intended to measure (Chin, 1998b). As both these conditions were fulfilled (see tables 11 and 12), I assume the discriminant validity of my latent variables.

Table 11:   Discriminant Validity Following the Fornell-Larcker-Criterion for the Model of Corrupt Action

Var-iable	GD	PAE	NAE	GI	GF	ID	AT	SN	II	PBC	CA	GR
GD	**.60**											
PAE	.15	**.73**										
NAE	.07	.14	**.70**									
GI	.49	.13	.12	**.65**								
GF	.18	.00	.00	.22	**.66**							
ID	.02	.01	.00	.02	.00	**.75**						
AT	.01	.00	.00	.01	.01	.42	**.67**					
SN	.01	.01	.00	.00	.00	.29	.34	**.64**				
II	.01	.00	.00	.01	.00	.66	.53	.34	**.79**			
PBC	.00	.00	.01	.00	.00	.35	.39	.25	.51	**.84**		
CA	.00	.00	.00	.00	.02	.43	.44	.24	.61	.51	**1.00**	
GR	.01	.01	.01	.00	.00	.01	.03	.00	.00	.00	.02	**.85**

GD = Desire to achieve a private or professional goal; PAE = Positive anticipated emotions; NAE = Negative anticipated emotions; GI = Intention to achieve a private or professional goal; GF = Goal feasibility; ID = Desire to achieve a private or professional goal through corrupt action; AT = Attitude; SN = Subjective norm; II = Intention to achieve a private or professional goal through corrupt action; PBC = Perceived behavioral control; Corrupt action; GR = Goal realization
- $N = 196$
- The grey-shaded inner cells contain the results also relevant for the revised model of corrupt action (see chap. 5.1.2, p. 150).
- Diagonal elements: AVE; Non-diagonal elements: squared correlations

Table 12:   Crossloadings for the Model of Corrupt Action

Item[1]	GD	PAE	NAE	GI	GF	ID	AT	SN	II	PBC	CA	GR
GD1	**.83**	.28	.16	.60	.41	.09	.06	.09	.07	.00	-.05	-.02
r_GD2	**.64**	.09	.13	.43	.23	.12	.14	.13	.10	.07	.01	-.04
GD3	**.84**	.44	.28	.58	.32	.10	.04	.01	.03	-.01	-.08	-.18
r_GF1	.39	.09	.03	.36	**.82**	-.02	.08	.06	-.08	.00	-.14	-.01
GF2	.42	.09	.11	.48	**.87**	.02	.09	-.01	-.02	.05	-.08	-.04
r_GF3	.13	.13	.00	.24	**.75**	-.04	.07	-.09	-.07	.01	-.09	.02
PAE1	.38	**.91**	.32	.33	.10	.00	-.05	.09	.05	-.02	-.12	-.11
PAE4	.26	**.80**	.34	.27	-.03	.17	.05	.09	.12	.06	.03	-.03
NAE1	.26	.37	**.91**	.34	.01	-.01	-.04	-.12	.04	-.13	-.01	-.05
NAE4	.16	.24	**.75**	.23	.09	.04	.10	.10	.10	.04	.06	-.09
GI1	.56	.35	.34	**.83**	.40	.02	.02	-.06	.00	-.05	-.07	-.04
GI2	.56	.24	.25	**.81**	.33	.13	.05	.10	.07	.04	-.02	-.01
r_GI3	.56	.27	.25	**.78**	.41	.19	.20	.12	.18	.02	-.08	-.07
ID1	.17	.10	.06	.18	-.01	**.89**	.56	.47	.75	.50	.52	.03
r_ID2	.05	.10	.03	.07	-.03	**.81**	.48	.34	.58	.45	.59	.10
ID3	.10	.02	-.05	.12	.01	**.90**	.63	.56	.76	.58	.59	.07
r_II1	-.03	.01	-.05	-.03	-.15	.71	.66	.51	**.87**	.66	.76	.06
II2	.08	.01	.00	.13	-.02	.70	.64	.52	**.89**	.64	.67	.06
II3	.16	.07	.10	.19	.00	.76	.64	.52	**.90**	.60	.63	.06
AT2	.11	.08	.02	.09	.08	.54	**.76**	.33	.53	.36	.49	.13
AT3	.09	.04	-.05	.11	.16	.58	**.88**	.47	.60	.53	.56	.15
AT4	.01	.04	.01	.08	.07	.45	**.71**	.36	.49	.38	.41	.15
AT5	.00	.03	.01	-.01	-.03	.44	**.67**	.42	.47	.49	.43	.14
AT6	.07	.01	.01	.09	.05	.58	**.87**	.62	.71	.63	.64	.11
AT7	.09	.06	.05	.12	.05	.59	**.90**	.58	.70	.61	.64	.16
AT8	.07	.00	.01	.11	.10	.56	**.91**	.59	.70	.63	.65	.13
AT9	.10	-.05	.01	.14	.14	.48	**.81**	.37	.53	.40	.46	.21
SN1	.01	-.01	-.07	.00	-.04	.47	.55	**.85**	.52	.45	.48	-.04
SN2	.08	.10	-.01	.05	.00	.48	.47	**.84**	.50	.43	.41	.04
r_SN3	.13	.21	-.01	.14	.04	.33	.36	**.70**	.36	.28	.25	-.08

Item[1]	GD	PAE	NAE	GI	GF	ID	AT	SN	II	PBC	CA	GR
r_PBC1	-.01	-.07	-.10	-.03	-.01	.58	.61	.48	.68	**.92**	.70	.05
PBC2	.04	.10	-.04	.03	.08	.50	.53	.43	.62	**.91**	.60	-.02
GR1	-.08	-.08	-.04	-.01	-.02	.12	.19	.02	.09	.05	.14	**.95**
GR2	-.10	-.08	-.10	-.09	-.03	.03	.16	-.06	.05	.03	.09	**.88**
r_GR3	-.14	-.09	-.09	-.06	-.01	.04	.14	-.05	.05	-.01	.13	**.93**
CA1	-.06	-.06	.02	.00	-.13	.65	.66	.49	.78	.72	**1.00**	.13

GD = Desire to achieve a private or professional goal; PAE = Positive anticipated emotions; NAE = Negative anticipated emotions; GI = Intention to achieve a private or professional goal; GF = Goal feasibility; ID = Desire to achieve a private or professional goal through corrupt action; AT = Attitude; SN = Subjective norm; II = Intention to achieve a private or professional goal through corrupt action; PBC = Perceived behavioral control; CA = Corrupt action; GR = Goal realization

[1]   The item abbreviations consist of the code for the construct they represent as well as the item number. Items named with r_ were recoded. The items in their complete wording are listed in Appendix F (p. 236).

-   $N = 196$

-   The grey-shaded inner cells contain the results also relevant for the revised model of corrupt action (see chap. 5.1.2, p. 150).

Evaluation of the Structural Model

My proposed structural model including the parameters estimated by the PLS analysis is shown in figure 12. The weights of the relationship between the latent exogenous and latent endogenous variables in figure 12 indicate the strength of the relationship of these variables. To assess the significance of the path estimates (see figure 12), I used a bootstrapping procedure[50] calculating *t*-values with 500 resamples[51], which allows an evaluation of the stability and precision of the PLS results. All path coefficients were significant – except one. This was one essential path in the model, the path between the intention to achieve a private or professional goal and the desire to achieve the goal through corrupt action. All significant paths were in the proposed direction except the relationship between goal feasibility and the intention to achieve a private or professional goal. Contrary to my hypothesis, the relationship was positive, indicating that the more difficult it is to achieve the goal, the lower the intention to achieve it. This finding contradicts Ach-Hillgruber's difficulty law of motivation (Ach, 1935; Hillgruber, 1912) as well as Locke and Latham's (1990, pp. 27 – 30) goal difficulty function, but supports Vroom's (1984, pp. 192 –

---

[50] Bootstrap samples are built by re-sampling with replacement from the original sample (Chin, 1998b; Tenenhaus et al., 2005).

[51] Higher numbers than the default of 100 lead to more reasonable standard error estimates (Tenenhaus et al., 2005). Following Chin (1998b, p. 323), I chose 500 re-samples.

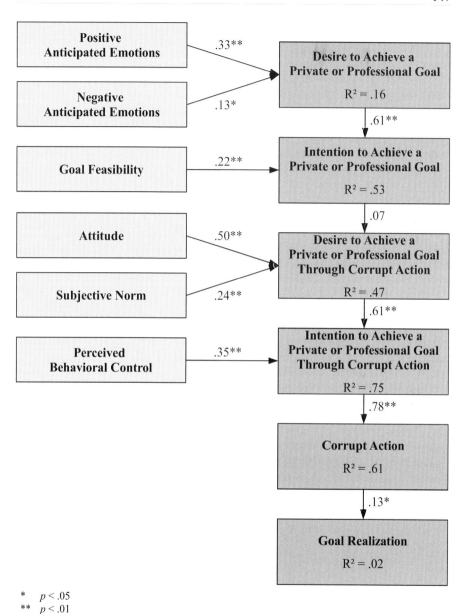

*   *p* < .05
** *p* < .01

Figure 12: The Proposed Model of Corrupt Action – Results of the PLS Analysis

196) proposition (see chap. 3.3, p. 104). Thus, hypotheses 3 and 4 have to be rejected, while hypotheses 1a, 1b, 2, 5, 6, 7, 8, 9 and 10 can be accepted.

The central evaluation criterion of the structural model is the R-Square (R^2) whose interpretation is identical to that of traditional regression. For each multiple regression, it represents the variance of each dependent variable, which is explained by the corresponding independent variables. The R^2 of the latent dependent variables are also shown in figure 12. According to Chin's (1998b) classification[52], the R^2 of the intention to act corruptly was substantial, while the model showed a more moderate level for the intention to achieve a private or professional goal, the desire to act corruptly and corrupt action. The desire to achieve a private or professional goal as well as goal realization had a weak R^2.

The effect size f^2 represents changes in the R^2 and indicates whether a predictor latent variable has substantive impact on a dependent latent variable. An effect size of 0.02, 0.15, and 0.35 can be viewed as a gauge for whether a predictor latent variable has a small, medium, or large effect at the structural level (Chin, 1998b). Results for the f^2 measures are presented in table 13. Confirming the non-significance of the corresponding path coefficient, the intention to achieve a private or professional goal had no effect on the desire to act corruptly. Furthermore, the negative anticipated emotions had no influence on the desire to achieve a private or professional goal. Corrupt action also had no effect on goal realization.

Another measure underlining these results is the predictive relevance. The predictive relevance of the latent predictor variable for the explanation of latent dependent variables is indicated by Stone-Geisser's Q^2 of redundancy (Geisser, 1975; Stone, 1974; see also Fornell & Bookstein, 1982), which is calculated by a blindfolding procedure[53] delivering cross-validated measures. As this measure was greater than zero (Chin, 1998b) for the desire to achieve a private or professional goal $(Q^2 = .11)$, the intention to achieve a private or professional goal $(Q^2 = .34)$, the desire to act corruptly $(Q^2 = .34)$, the intention to act corruptly $(Q^2 = .59)$, and corrupt action $(Q^2 = .60)$, these latent variables had a reliable predictive relevance. Scarcely above the critical threshold of zero was the predictive relevance of goal realization $(Q^2 = .01)$. As in the case of the effect size f^2, changes in the Q^2 can be used for a block-wise evaluation of the predictive relevance of the latent predictor variables. Results of the corresponding q^2 measures are shown in table 13. A q^2 of 0.02, 0.15, and 0.35 indicates whether a latent predictor variable has a small, medium, or large predictive relevance (Chin, 1998b). The intention to achieve a private or professional goal had no predictive relevance for the desire to act corruptly and the negative anticipated

---

[52] In his example, Chin (1998b, p. 323) termed an R^2 of .67 as substantial, an R^2 of .33 as moderate, and an R^2 of .19 as weak.

[53] The blindfolding procedure "omits a part of the data for a particular block of indicators during parameter estimations and then attempts to estimate the omitted part using the estimated parameters. This procedure is repeated until every data point has been omitted and estimated" (Chin, 1998b, p. 317).

emotions were not a relevant predictor of the desire to achieve a private or professional goal. Corrupt action also appeared to be not relevant for a prediction of goal realization.

Table 13:   Evaluation of the Proposed Model of Corrupt Action

Latent dependent variable	Latent predictor variable	f^{2} [1]	q^{2} [2]
GD	PAE	0.12	0.11
	NAE	0.01	0.00
GI	GD	0.64	0.36
	GF	0.08	0.05
ID	GI	0.01	0.01
	AT	0.31	0.28
	SN	0.08	0.06
II	ID	0.93	0.69
	PBC	0.32	0.24
CA	II	1.53	1.50
GR	CA	0.01	0.01

GD = Desire to achieve a private or professional goal; PAE = Positive anticipated emotions; NAE = Negative anticipated emotions; GI = Intention to achieve a private or professional goal; GF = Goal feasibility; ID = Desire to achieve a private or professional goal through corrupt action; AT = Attitude; SN = Subjective norm; II = Intention to achieve a private or professional goal through corrupt action; PBC = Perceived behavioral control; CA = Corrupt action; GR = Goal realization
[1]   Effect size: 0.02 – small effect, 0.15 – medium effect, 0.35 – large effect
[2]   Predictive relevance: 0.02 – small predictive relevance, 0.15 – medium predictive relevance, 0.35 – large predictive relevance

As the evaluation of the structural model showed, the link between the first part of the model concerning the goal one would like to achieve and the way to achieve this goal, namely corrupt action, was not significant. This indicates that my model was not appropriate. Thus, I revised[54] it and conducted another PLS analysis. The revised model is described below.

5.1.2 Evaluation of the Revised Model

For the revised model, again the structural model and the measurement model of the latent variables are evaluated separately (Hansmann & Ringle, 2005).

---

[54] Further analyses showed that there were no significant paths between constructs of the first part and constructs of the second part of the model either.

Evaluation of the Reflective Measurement Models

The measures for Cronbach's alpha, the composite reliability rho, and the *AVE* are presented in table 10 (p. 143). For all latent variables, both Cronbach's alpha and rho were greater than .70 (Ringle et al., 2006) and the *AVE* greater than .50 (Chin, 1998b).

Furthermore, the discriminant validity of the latent variables in my revised model can be assumed because both the conditions set by Chin (1998b) were fulfilled (see grey-shaded inner cells in table 11 and 12): The *AVE*s of the latent variables were greater than the square of the correlations among the latent variables. When calculating the cross-loadings, no indicator loaded higher with other latent variables than the one it was intended to measure.

Evaluation of the Structural Model

The R^2 of the latent dependent variables as presented in figure 13 were substantial for the intention to act corruptly and moderate for the desire to act corruptly as well as corrupt action, but weak for goal realization. Results for the effect size f^2 are shown in table 14. They indicate that the attitude toward corruption had a medium effect on the desire to act corruptly, while the subjective norm had a small influence. While the intention to act corruptly was strongly influenced by the desire to act corruptly, perceived behavioral control only had a medium effect. The intention to act corruptly had a strong effect on corrupt action. Corrupt action, in contrast, had no effect on goal realization.

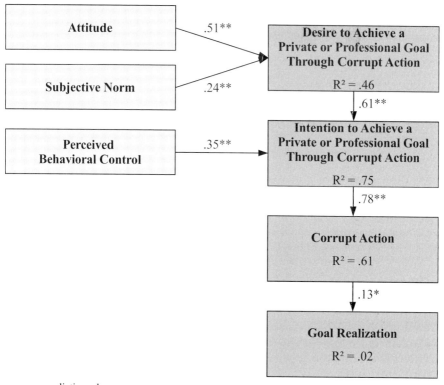

--- no predictive relevance
* $p < .05$
** $p < .01$

Figure 13: The Revised Model of Corrupt Action – Results of the PLS Analysis

As in my first model, all latent predictor variables had a reliable predictive relevance (desire to act corruptly: $Q^2 = .34$; intention to act corruptly: $Q^2 = .59$; corrupt action: $Q^2 = .60$), except goal realization ($Q^2 = .01$) that just passed the threshold of zero. Results of q^2 measures indicating the relative impact of each latent predictor variable are presented in table 14. While attitude had a medium predictive relevance for the desire to act corruptly, the impact of the subjective norm was small. The desire to act corruptly had a high predictive relevance for the intention to act corruptly, while perceived behavioral control only had medium impact. The intention to act corruptly was a strong predictor of corrupt action. Corrupt action was not relevant for a prediction of goal realization.

Table 14:   Evaluation of the Revised Model of Corrupt Action

Latent dependent variable	Latent predictor variable	$f^{2\,1}$	$q^{2\,2}$
ID	AT	0.32	0.29
	SN	0.08	0.06
II	ID	0.93	0.69
	PBC	0.32	0.24
CA	II	1.53	1.50
GR	CA	0.02	0.01

ID = Desire to achieve a private or professional goal through corrupt action; AT = Attitude; SN = Subjective norm; II = Intention to achieve a private or professional goal through corrupt action; PBC = Perceived behavioral control; CA = Corrupt action; GR = Goal realization
1   Effect size: 0.02 – small effect, 0.15 – medium effect, 0.35 – large effect
2   Predictive relevance: 0.02 – small predictive relevance, 0.15 – medium predictive relevance, 0.35 – large predictive relevance

Thus, when referring to the final model of corrupt action in the following (see figure 14), I do not consider the path between corrupt action and goal realization.

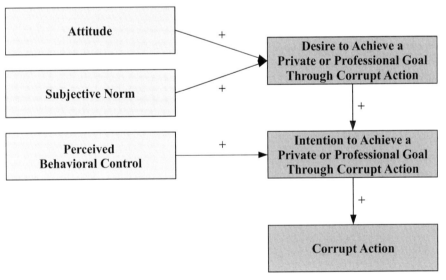

+ = positive relationship

Figure 14: The Final Model of Corrupt Action

5.2   Sociodemographic Factors

How do sociodemographic factors like age and sex influence corrupt action and its determinants? This question is answered in the following. I omitted a comparison of business and non-business students (see chap. 2.2.3, p. 51) because my sample did not allow for a selective distinction.

5.2.1   Age

To investigate how age relates to the single components of the final model of corrupt action, I conducted two-tailed Pearson correlations for the relationships with the interval-scaled model components and a point-biserial correlation for the relationship with the dichotomous variable "corrupt action". As the correlation coefficients displayed in table 15 show, age was not significantly related to any of the model components.

Table 15:   Correlations Between Age and the Components of the Model of Corrupt Action

Model component[1]	Age	
	r	*p*
ID	-.07	.32
AT	-.12	.11
SN	-.04	.62
II	.12	.11
PBC	.01	.94
CA	-.01	.94

ID = Desire to achieve a private or professional goal through corrupt action; AT = Attitude; SN = Subjective norm; II = Intention to achieve a private or professional goal through corrupt action; PBC = Perceived behavioral control, CA = Corrupt action
1    $N = 196$
* $p < .05$
** $p < .01$

In my case, age corresponded with the distinction between high school and university students. Therefore, I investigated whether there are differences between these two groups in the model components. The MANOVA revealed no significant differences (*Wilks' lamda* = 0.97, $F_{5,190}$ = 1.71, p = .33, *partial* η^2 = 0.03) as did the univariate ANOVAS. The results of the latter are displayed in table 16.

Table 16:   Differences in the Components of the Model of Corrupt Action between
High School and University Students (Univariate ANOVAs)

Model components	High school students[1]		University students[2]		F^3	p	Partial η^2
	Mean	SD	Mean	SD			
ID	3.83	0.95	3.77	0.95	0.17	.68	0.00
AT	4.98	1.19	4.79	1.16	1.30	.26	0.01
SN	3.32	0.68	3.24	0.84	0.59	.44	0.00
II	3.73	1.04	3.56	1.11	1.32	.25	0.01
PBC	3.45	1.14	3.51	1.09	0.14	.71	0.00

ID = Desire to achieve a private or professional goal through corrupt action; AT = Attitude; SN = Subjective norm; II = Intention to achieve a private or professional goal through corrupt action; PBC = Perceived behavioral control
[1] $n = 99$
[2] $n = 97$
[3] $df = 1$
* $p < .05$
** $p < .01$

80 (80.81%) high school students and 80 (82.47%) university students acted corruptly. A chi-square test revealed no statistically significant relationship between the type of student and corrupt action ($\chi^2_1 = 0.09, p = .85$).

Furthermore, I examined whether the path coefficients in the final model of corrupt action are different for the two groups of students. As table 17 shows, t-tests revealed no significant results.

Table 17: Differences in the Path Coefficients of the Model of Corrupt Action Between High School and University Students (t-Tests)

Model paths	High school students[1] Path coefficient	University students[2] Path coefficient	t[3]
AT → ID	.45	.61	-1.31
SN → ID	.34	.13	1.54
ID → II	.61	.59	0.17
PBC → II	.38	.34	0.39
II → CA	.79	.78	0.19

ID = Desire to achieve a private or professional goal through corrupt action; AT = Attitude; SN = Subjective norm; II = Intention to achieve a private or professional goal through corrupt action; PBC = Perceived behavioral control; CA = Corrupt action

[1] $n = 99$
[2] $n = 97$
[3]   The exact p-values could not be reported because for determining the significance of the t-values the empirically found t-values had to be compared with the t-values displayed in statistical tables for the t-distribution. The values for a two-tailed t-test are reported.
* $p < .05$
** $p < .01$

5.2.2 Sex

A second sociodemographic factor often discussed in the corruption literature is sex. Thus, my aim was to examine my data for sex differences. A first step was to test for differences between female and male participants in the components of the model of corrupt action. The MANOVA revealed no significant differences (*Wilks' lamda* = 0.99, $F_{5,190} = 0.58$, $p = .71$, *partial η^2* = 0.02) as did the univariate ANOVAS. The results of the latter are displayed in table 18.

Table 18:   Differences in the Components of the Model of Corrupt Action Between
            Female and Male Participants (Univariate ANOVAs)

Model components	Females[1]		Males[2]				
	Mean	SD	Mean	SD	F[3]	p	Partial η^2
ID	3.82	0.92	3.78	0.98	0.11	.74	0.00
AT	4.82	1.06	4.95	1.26	0.57	.45	0.00
SN	3.24	0.75	3.31	0.77	0.48	.49	0.00
II	3.60	1.04	3.68	1.12	0.27	.61	0.00
PBC	3.41	1.05	3.54	1.17	0.72	.40	0.00

ID = Desire to achieve a private or professional goal through corrupt action; AT = Attitude; SN = Subjective norm; II = Intention to achieve a private or professional goal through corrupt action; PBC = Perceived behavioral control

[1] $n = 90$
[2] $n = 106$
[3] $df = 1$
* $p < .05$
** $p < .01$

75 (83.33%) female participants and 80 (80.19%) male participants acted corruptly. A chi-square test revealed no statistically significant relationship between sex and corrupt action ($\chi^2_1 = 0.32$, $p = .59$).

Furthermore, I examined whether the path coefficients in the final model of corrupt action are different for females and males. As table 19 shows, t-tests revealed no significant results.

Table 19:   Differences in the Path Coefficients of the Model of Corrupt Action
            Between Female and Male Participants (t-Tests)

Model paths	Females[1] Path coefficient	Males[2] Path coefficient	t[3]
AT → ID	.49	.52	0.27
SN → ID	.31	.21	-0.73
ID → II	.61	.60	-0.16
PBC → II	.35	.36	0.09
II → CA	.77	.79	0.42

ID = Desire to achieve a private or professional goal through corrupt action; AT = Attitude; SN = Subjective norm; II = Intention to achieve a private or professional goal through corrupt action; PBC = Perceived behavioral control; CA = Corrupt action

[1] $n = 90$
[2] $n = 106$
[3]   The exact p-values could not be reported because for determining the significance of the t-values the empirically found t-values had to be compared with the t-values displayed in statistical tables for the t-distribution. The values for a two-tailed t-test are reported.
* $p < .05$
** $p < .01$

I also investigated whether there is a relationship between the share of women in a group and the single components of the model of corrupt action. I conducted two-tailed Pearson correlations for all interval-scaled model components. For the dichotomous variable "corrupt action" I calculated a point-biserial correlation. The results presented in table 20 show no significant correlation coefficients.

Table 20:   Correlations Between the Share of Women in a Group and the Compo-
            nents of the Model of Corrupt Action

Model component[1]	Share of women in a group	
	r	*p*
ID	.02	.77
AT	.02	.92
SN	-.00	.96
II	.03	.65
PBC	-.08	.26
CA	.00	.95

ID = Desire to achieve a private or professional goal through corrupt action; AT = Attitude; SN =
Subjective norm; II = Intention to achieve a private or professional goal through corrupt action;
PBC = Perceived behavioral control; CA = Corrupt action
[1] $N = 196$
* $p < .05$
** $p < .01$

5.3   Situational Factors

Not only did characteristics of my sample allow for an investigation of sociodemographic factors. My experimental simulation design also included the variation of
selected situational factors. How they influence corrupt action and its determinants is
described in the following.

5.3.1 Opportunity for Passive or Active Corruption

Participants in the business game either had the opportunity for passive corruption,
that is, to accept a corrupt offer, or the opportunity for active corruption, that is, to
submit a corrupt offer. Thus, in a first step, I investigated whether there are differences between these two conditions in regard to the components of the model of
corrupt action. The MANOVA revealed significant differences (*Wilks' lamda* = 0.94,
$F_{5,190}$ = 2.69, p = .02, *partial* η^2 = 0.07). As the results of the univariate ANOVAs
show (see table 21), in the case of passive corruption the desire to achieve a private
or professional goal through corrupt action was significantly stronger than in the
case of active corruption.

Table 21: Differences in the Components of the Model of Corrupt Action Between the Conditions of Passive and Active Corruption (Univariate ANOVAs)

Model components	Passive corruption[1]		Active corruption[2]		F[3]	p	Partial η^2
	Mean	SD	Mean	SD			
ID	3.95	0.84	3.65	1.03	5.15*	.02	0.03
AT	4.92	1.16	4.85	1.19	0.18	.67	0.00
SN	3.25	0.76	3.30	0.77	0.18	.67	0.00
II	3.68	1.03	3.61	1.12	0.17	.69	0.00
PBC	3.54	1.08	3.42	1.15	0.60	.44	0.00

ID = Desire to achieve a private or professional goal through corrupt action; AT = Attitude; SN = Subjective norm; II = Intention to achieve a private or professional goal through corrupt action; PBC = Perceived behavioral control
[1] $n = 99$
[2] $n = 97$
[3] $df = 1$
* $p < .05$
** $p < .01$

83 (83.84%) participants who had the opportunity to passive corruption and 77 (79.38%) participants who had the opportunity to active corruption acted corruptly. A chi-square test revealed no statistically significant relationship between the respective condition and corrupt action ($\chi^2_1 = 0.65, p = .46$).

Furthermore, I examined whether the path coefficients in the final model of corrupt action are different for the conditions of passive and active corruption. As table 22 shows, t-tests revealed no significant results.

Table 22: Differences in the Path Coefficients of the Model of Corrupt Action
Between the Conditions of Passive and Active Corruption (*t*-Tests)

Model paths	Passive corruption[1] Path coefficient	Active corruption[2] Path coefficient	t^3
AT → ID	.47	.53	-0.46
SN → ID	.29	.24	0.43
ID → II	.63	.60	0.35
PBC → II	.30	.39	-0.85
II → CA	.73	.82	-1.33

ID = Desire to achieve a private or professional goal through corrupt action; AT = Attitude; SN = Subjective norm; II = Intention to achieve a private or professional goal through corrupt action; PBC = Perceived behavioral control; CA = Corrupt action

[1] $n = 99$
[2] $n = 97$
[3]   The exact *p*-values could not be reported because for determining the significance of the *t*-values the empirically found *t*-values had to be compared with the *t*-values displayed in statistical tables for the *t*-distribution. The values for a two-tailed *t*-test are reported.
* $p < .05$
** $p < .01$

5.3.2 Size of the Bribe

Another variable in the experimental design was the size of the bribe, which was either 50,000 or 150,000 euros. Does the size of the bribe make a difference? The MANOVA revealed significant differences (*Wilks' lamda* = 0.92, $F_{5,190}$ = 3.51, p = .01, *partial* η^2 = 0.09). As the results of the univariate ANOVAs show (see table 23), in the case of a high bribe of 150,000 euros, the desire and the intention to achieve a private or professional goal through corrupt action and a corruption favoring attitude and subjective norm were significantly stronger than in the case of a low bribe of 50,000 euros.

Table 23: Differences in the Components of the Model of Corrupt Action Between a Low Bribe and a High Bribe (Univariate ANOVAs)

Model components	Low bribe[1]		High bribe[2]				
	Mean	SD	Mean	SD	F[3]	p	Partial η^2
ID	3.67	1.01	3.95	0.86	4.26*	.04	0.02
AT	4.63	1.18	5.17	1.11	10.64**	.00	0.05
SN	3.11	0.79	3.46	0.68	10.79**	.00	0.05
II	3.45	1.17	3.86	0.92	7.25**	.01	0.04
PBC	3.40	1.14	3.57	1.08	1.04	.31	0.01

ID = Desire to achieve a private or professional goal through corrupt action; AT = Attitude; SN = Subjective norm; II = Intention to achieve a private or professional goal through corrupt action; PBC = Perceived behavioral control; CA = Corrupt action

[1] $n = 103$
[2] $n = 93$
[3] $df = 1$
* $p < .05$
** $p < .01$

79 (76.70%) participants who had the opportunity to get a low bribe and 81 (87.10%) participants who had the opportunity to get a high bribe acted corruptly. A chi-square test revealed no statistically significant relationship between the size of the bribe and corrupt action ($\chi^2_1 = 3.52, p = .07$).

Furthermore, I examined whether the path coefficients in the final model of corrupt action are different for the conditions of a low bribe and a high bribe. As table 24 shows, t-tests revealed no significant results.

Table 24:   Differences in the Path Coefficients of the Model of Corrupt Action
            Between a Low Bribe and a High Bribe (*t*-Tests)

Model paths	Low bribe[1] *Path coefficient*	High bribe[2] *Path coefficient*	*t*[3]
AT → ID	.48	.54	-0.39
SN → ID	.28	.20	0.65
ID → II	.57	.62	-0.43
PBC → II	.39	.34	0.43
II → CA	.78	.76	0.40

ID = Desire to achieve a private or professional goal through corrupt action; AT = Attitude; SN = Subjective norm; II = Intention to achieve a private or professional goal through corrupt action; PBC = Perceived behavioral control; CA = Corrupt action

[1] $n = 103$
[2] $n = 93$
[3]   The exact *p*-values could not be reported because for determining the significance of the *t*-values the empirically found *t*-values had to be compared with the *t*-values displayed in statistical tables for the *t*-distribution. The values for a two-tailed *t*-test are reported.
* $p < .05$
** $p < .01$

5.3.3 Time of the Opportunity to Act Corruptly

Participants in the business game had the opportunity to act corruptly in period two, three, or four. Thus, I investigated whether the participants' propensity to act corruptly was higher towards the end of the business game. The MANOVA revealed no significant differences (*Wilks' lamda* = 0.96, $F_{5,190}$ = 0.86, $p = .60$, *partial η^2* = 0.02). As the results of the univariate ANOVAs show (see table 25), there were no differences between the points of time.

Table 25: Differences in the Components of the Model of Corrupt Action Between the Points of Time of the Opportunity to Act Corruptly (Univariate ANOVAs)

Model components	Period 2[1]		Period 3[2]		Period 4[3]		F^4	p	Partial η^2
	Mean	SD	Mean	SD	Mean	SD			
ID	3.68	1.00	3.91	0.88	3.80	0.97	0.89	.41	0.01
AT	4.69	1.28	5.15	0.93	4.80	1.25	2.81	.06	0.03
SN	3.26	0.80	3.31	0.74	3.26	0.76	0.09	.91	0.00
II	3.48	1.14	3.81	0.98	3.64	1.10	1.48	.23	0.02
PBC	3.43	1.23	3.61	1.05	3.40	1.07	0.73	.48	0.01

ID = Desire to achieve a private or professional goal through corrupt action; AT = Attitude; SN = Subjective norm; II = Intention to achieve a private or professional goal through corrupt action; PBC = Perceived behavioral control

[1] $n = 63$
[2] $n = 67$
[3] $n = 66$
[4] $df = 1$
* $p < .05$
** $p < .01$

47 (74.60%) participants who had the opportunity to corruption in period two, 60 (89.55%) participants who had the opportunity to corruption in period three, and 53 (80.30%) participants who had the opportunity to corruption in period four acted corruptly. A chi-square test revealed no statistically significant relationship between the point of time of the opportunity to act corruptly and corrupt action ($\chi^2_1 = 4.96$, $p = .08$).

Furthermore, I examined whether the path coefficients in the final model of corrupt action were different for the different points of time. As table 26 shows, the subjective norm had a significantly stronger influence on the desire to act corruptly in period four than in period two and three.

Table 26:   Differences in the Path Coefficients of the Model of Corrupt Action for the Different Points of Times of the Opportunity to Act Corruptly (*t*-Tests)

Model paths	Period 2[1] Path coefficient	Period 3[2] Path coefficient	Period 4[3] Path coefficient	Period 2 vs. Period 3 t[4]	Period 2 vs. Period 4 t[4]	Period 3 vs. Period 4 t[4]
AT → ID	.63	.54	.41	0.59	1.56	0.93
SN → ID	.12	.11	.45	0.08	-2.13*	-2.52*
ID → II	.61	.59	.59	0.18	0.15	-0.05
PBC → II	.35	.35	.39	-0.02	-0.35	-0.39
II → CA	.77	.72	.82	0.46	-0.69	-1.00

ID = Desire to achieve a private or professional goal through corrupt action; AT = Attitude; SN = Subjective norm; II = Intention to achieve a private or professional goal through corrupt action; PBC = Perceived behavioral control; CA = Corrupt action

[1] $n = 63$
[2] $n = 67$
[3] $n = 66$
[4]   The exact *p*-values could not be reported because for determining the significance of the *t*-values the empirically found *t*-values had to be compared with the *t*-values displayed in statistical tables for the *t*-distribution. The values for a two-tailed *t*-test are reported.
* $p < .05$
** $p < .01$

5.3.4 Game Score at the Point of Time of the Opportunity to Act Corruptly

In a next step, I examined the influence of the game score at the point of time of the opportunity to corrupt action. As measures I used the profit achieved in the period before the opportunity to act corruptly, the group position regarding the profit achieved in the period before the opportunity to act corruptly, the accumulated profit achieved up to the point of time of the opportunity to act corruptly, and the group position regarding the accumulated profit achieved up to the point of time of the opportunity to act corruptly. To account for the affiliation to different groups playing against each other in the business game and the resulting influence on the achieved results, all profit values were *z*-standardized. To account for different group sizes, the group position scores were standardized in regard to the group size. I conducted Pearson correlations for the relationships of the ratio-scaled profit variables and the interval-scaled model components, point-biserial correlations for the relationship of the ratio-scaled profit variables and the dichotomous variable "corrupt action", Spearman rank correlations for the relationships of the ordinal-scaled group position variables and the interval-scaled model components, and biserial rank correlations for the relationships of the ordinal-scaled group position variables and the dichotomous variable "corrupt action." The results presented in table 27 revealed no significant relationships of the game scores with the components of the final model of corrupt action.

Table 27:   Correlations Between the Game Score at the Point of Time of the Opportunity to Act Corruptly and the Components of the Model of Corrupt Action

Model components[1]	Profit achieved in the period before the opportunity to act corruptly		Group position regarding the profit achieved in the period before the opportunity to act corruptly		Accumulated profit achieved up to the point of time of the opportunity to act corruptly		Group position regarding the accumulated profit achieved up to the point of time of the opportunity to act corruptly	
	r	*p*	*r*	*p*	*r*	*p*	*r*	*p*
ID	.05	.51	-.02	.75	.02	.76	-.04	.62
AT	.11	.12	-.12	.09	.07	.31	-.08	.26
SN	-.01	.88	-.02	.78	-.04	.63	.04	.62
II	.01	.85	-.02	.76	-.02	.75	.02	.75
PBC	.05	.51	-.08	.27	.01	.88	.00	.99
CA	.09	.21	-.12	.09	.03	.64	-.02	.82

ID = Desire to achieve a private or professional goal through corrupt action; AT = Attitude; SN = Subjective norm; II = Intention to achieve a private or professional goal through corrupt action; PBC = Perceived behavioral control; CA = Corrupt action
[1] $N = 196$
* $p < .05$
** $p < .01$

5.3.5 Degree of Abstractness of the Business Code

Another situational factor varied in the experimental design was the degree of the abstractness of the business code. Does it make a difference whether the business code is formulated at a high or low abstraction level, that is, whether integrity in general is demanded or corruption is explicitly not tolerated? The MANOVA revealed no significant differences (*Wilks' lamda* = 0.96, $F_{5,190}$ = 1.54, p = .18, *partial* η^2 = 0.04). The univariate ANOVAs also showed no significant results (see table 28).

Table 28:   Differences in the Components of the Model of Corrupt Action Between
a Business Code of Low Abstractness and a Business Code of High
Abstractness (Univariate ANOVAs)

Model components	Business code of low abstractness[1]		Business code of high abstractness[2]		F[3]	p	Partial η^2
	Mean	SD	Mean	SD			
ID	3.71	0.95	3.92	0.95	2.25	.14	0.01
AT	4.92	1.17	4.84	1.19	0.26	.61	0.00
SN	3.26	0.74	3.30	0.79	0.14	.71	0.00
II	3.57	1.09	3.75	1.06	1.43	.23	0.01
PBC	3.40	1.16	3.59	1.05	1.27	.26	0.01

ID = Desire to achieve a private or professional goal through corrupt action; AT = Attitude; SN =
Subjective norm; II = Intention to achieve a private or professional goal through corrupt action;
PBC = Perceived behavioral control
[1] $n = 112$
[2] $n = 84$
[3] $df = 1$
* $p < .05$
** $p < .01$

74 (88.10%) of the participants who received the business code formulated at a high
abstraction level and 86 (76.79%) participants who received the business code
formulated at a low abstraction level acted corruptly. A chi-square test revealed no
statistically significant relationship between the degree of abstractness of the business code and corrupt action ($\chi^2_1 = 4.10, p = .06$).

Furthermore, I examined whether the path coefficients in the final model of corrupt
action are different for the different business codes. As table 29 shows, t-tests
revealed a significantly stronger influence of the desire to act corruptly on the intention to act corruptly for the business code formulated at a high abstraction level and a
significantly stronger influence of the perceived behavioral control on the intention
to act corruptly for the business code formulated at a low abstraction level.

Table 29: Differences in the Path Coefficients of the Model of Corrupt Action Between the Business Code of Low Abstractness and the Business Code of High Abstractness (t-Tests)

Model paths	Business code of low abstractness[1] Path coefficient	Business code of high abstractness[2] Path coefficient	t[3]
AT → ID	.46	.60	1.07
SN→ ID	.25	.21	-0.28
ID → II	.52	.74	2.19*
PBC → II	.45	.21	-2.26*
II → CA	.79	.78	-0.17

ID = Desire to achieve a private or professional goal through corrupt action; AT = Attitude; SN = Subjective norm; II = Intention to achieve a private or professional goal through corrupt action; PBC = Perceived behavioral control; CA = Corrupt action

[1] $n = 112$
[2] $n = 84$
[3]   The exact p-values could not be reported because for determining the significance of the t-values the empirically found t-values had to be compared with the t-values displayed in statistical tables for the t-distribution. The values for a two-tailed t-test are reported.
* $p < .05$
** $p < .01$

5.3.6 Degree of Competition

Another situational factor discussed in the corruption literature is the degree of competition. Thus, I examined whether the number of competing companies in the business game is related to the single components of the final model of corrupt action. I conducted two-tailed Pearson correlations for the relationships with the interval-scaled model components and a point-biserial correlation for the relationship with the dichotomous variable "corrupt action". As table 30 shows, no correlation coefficient was significant.

Table 30:   Correlations Between the Number of Competing Companies and the
            Components of the Model of Corrupt Action

Model component[1]	Number of competing companies	
	r	p
ID	.08	.27
AT	.07	.34
SN	.03	.63
II	.09	.22
PBC	.09	.20
CA	.02	.74

ID = Desire to achieve a private or professional goal through corrupt action; AT = Attitude; SN =
Subjective norm; II = Intention to achieve a private or professional goal through corrupt action;
PBC = Perceived behavioral control; CA = Corrupt action
[1] $N = 196$
* $p < .05$
** $p < .01$

5.4   Reasons Given for Corrupt and Non-Corrupt Behavior

In my study, 160 participants (81.63%) acted corruptly, 83 (83.84%) accepted the
corrupt offer, 77 (79.38%) submitted the corrupt offer. A chi-square test revealed no
significant result ($\chi^2_1 = 0.65$, $p = .46$). Thus, there were similar frequencies for active
and passive corruption. The question arises why participants acted corruptly or why
they rejected corrupt behavior.

5.4.1 Reasons Given for Corrupt Behavior

In a first step, I aimed at answering the question what reasons were given for corrupt
behavior. To examine whether the reasons given for active and passive corruption
differ from each other, I compared the corresponding frequencies of reasons. As one
participant with the opportunity for active corruption and one participant with the
opportunity for passive corruption did not answer the question, 82 participants who
accepted the corrupt offer and 76 participants who submitted the corrupt offer
entered the final analysis. Some participants also mentioned more than one reason
for their behavior. Results are presented in table 31.

Table 31:   Reasons Given for Corrupt Behavior

Reasons	Corrupt behavior[1] %	Passive corruption[2] %	Active corruption[3] %	Passive vs. active corruption p^4
Additional profit	51.90	56.10	47.37	.43
Assurance of orders/ Maintenance of business connections	27.22	25.61	28.95	.79
Improvement of a bad economic situation	14.56	15.85	13.16	.71
Correspondence with price strategy	6.33	3.66	9.21	.27
Favor	5.06	6.10	5.26	1.00
No expectancy of negative consequences	5.06	3.66	6.58	.55
Savings regarding expenses for advertisement and sales promotion	5.06	4.88	5.26	1.00
Justification	3.80	3.66	3.95	1.00
Additional market share	3.80	3.66	3.95	1.00
Free capacities	3.16	3.66	2.63	1.00
Trust	1.90	1.22	2.63	.63
Economies of scale	1.90	2.44	1.32	1.00
Innovation and investment	1.27	1.22	1.32	1.00
Quality leadership	0.63	1.22	0.00	1.00

[1] $n = 158$
[2] $n = 82$
[3] $n = 76$
[4]   binomial test
* $p < .05$
** $p < .01$

For both active and passive corruption, participants gave very similar reasons. There were no statistically significant differences. For corruption in general as well as

passive and active corruption, additional profit, the assurance of orders and maintenance of business connections, and the improvement of a bad economic situation
were among the most frequently mentioned reasons.

An interesting finding besides was that only 4% of the participants who acted
corruptly indicated that they were aware of their corrupt action as an illegal and
immoral behavior. This share might be a little higher when taking into account that
not every participant might have indicated his or her awareness of corrupt action to
maybe later use the "not knowing" as a justification.

5.4.2 Reasons Given for Non-Corrupt Behavior

In a second step, I tried to answer the question what reasons were given for non-
corrupt behavior, this means, for a denial of the acceptance (passive corruption) or
submission (active corruption) of a corrupt offer. I again compared the frequencies of
reasons given for passive and active corruption. All participants who did not act
corruptly entered the final analysis because they all gave reasons for their behavior;
some even mentioned more than one reason. Results are presented in table 32.

Table 32:   Reasons Given for Non-Corrupt Behavior

Reasons	Corrupt behavior[1] %	Passive corruption[2] %	Active corruption[3] %	Passive vs. active corruption p[4]
Rejection of corruption	38.89	25.00**	50.00**	.01
Economic inefficiency	27.78	37.50*	20.00*	.03
Damage to the company's image	16.67	18.75	15.00	.61
Immorality	13.89	25.00**	5.00**	.00
Dependency	11.11	12.50	10.00	.68
Illegality	8.33	12.50	5.00	.10
Unfairness	8.33	0.00**	15.00**	.00
High risk	5.56	0.00**	10.00**	.00
Injury of the company's business code	2.78	6.25*	0.00*	.03
No necessity	2.78	0.00	5.00	.06

[1] $n = 36$
[2] $n = 16$
[3] $n = 20$
[4]   binomial test
* $p < .05$
** $p < .01$

The most frequent reasons given for a denial of corrupt behavior were that corruption in general was rejected, that – especially in a long-term perspective – corrupt behavior was seen as economically unprofitable, and that the company's image was feared for. The reasons given for a rejection of passive and active corruption differed. Active corruption was significantly more frequently denied because corruption was rejected in general, because such an act was considered as unfair against the competitors, and because high risks were expected. In contrast, passive corruption was significantly more frequently denied because of economic inefficiency (e.g., losses in a long-term perspective), immorality, and because otherwise the company's business code would be injured. The most frequent reasons given for a denial of passive corruption were economic inefficiency, a general rejection of corruption, immorality, and the fear that the company's image might be damaged. The most frequent reasons given for a denial of active corruption were a general rejection of corruption, economic inefficiency, unfairness, and the fear for the company's image.

5.5   Rationalization Strategies

In a next step, I examined the rationalization strategies given by the participants when they received hints that their behavior might have been wrong. The following results are based on the group of 160 participants who acted corruptly in the business game. Regarding the standardized response options, for both active and passive corruption there were nine missing values in total each. Thus, 142 participants, 74 who accepted the corrupt offer and 68 who submitted the corrupt offer, entered the final analyses. 15 participants chose the "Others" option and gave free comments. The frequencies of the rationalization strategies used are shown in table 33.

Table 33:   Rationalization Strategies for Corrupt Behavior

Rationalization strategy	Corrupt behavior[1] %	Passive corruption[2] %	Active corruption[3] %	Passive vs. active corruption p^4
"Why shouldn't I take advantage of the good business relationship I developed over several years?" *(metaphor of the ledger)*	53.50	54.10	52.90	1.00
"I only tried to maintain the good business relationship with a good customer." *(appeal to higher loyalties)*	47.20	52.70	41.20	.26
"I only did everything to increase the order situation and the income of our company." *(appeal to higher loyalties)*	45.10	45.90	44.10	.92
"It was the only chance to increase our profit." *(denial of responsibility)*	23.90	23.00	25.00	.89

Rationalization strategy	Corrupt behavior[1] %	Passive corruption[2] %	Active corruption[3] %	Passive vs. active corruption p[4]
"It didn't harm anybody. It paid off for everybody." *(denial of injury)*	18.30	17.60	19.10	1.00
"It's not written anywhere that this is not allowed." *(legality)*	16.90	14.90	19.10	.61
"After all I got the order for our business." *(refocusing attention)*	16.90	20.30	13.20	.30
"To get orders, others are doing things that are even worse." *(social weighting)*	16.20	16.20	16.20	1.00
"Why? Because of the competitors who miss out? That's business." *(denial of victim)*	15.50	10.80	20.60	.11
"Because of the competitors? It doesn't matter that they once also get the short end of the stick." *(denial of victim)*	6.30	9.50	2.90	.09
"Everybody does it." *(denial of responsibility)*	4.90	9.50**	0.00**	.00
"It was only about relatively small amounts." *(denial of injury)*	4.90	4.10	5.90	.75

[1] $n = 142$
[2] $n = 74$
[3] $n = 68$
[4]   binomial test
* $p < .05$
** $p < .01$

Corrupt actors predominantly justified their behavior using the metaphor of the ledger, arguing that they only used the credit earned by good work in the past, or the appeal to higher loyalties, arguing that the organizational goals like orders, profit, and good customer relationships were more important than universalistic ethical norms. The denial of responsibility, arguing that everybody does it, the denial of injury by minimizing the relevant amounts, and the denial of victim as a kind of revenge were the least popular strategies. The only significant difference found was that no participant used "Everybody does it" for justifying active corruption, but seven participants used it for justifying passive corruption. All other rationalization strategies did not differ in the frequency of usage between passive and active corruption.

The results of the analysis of the free response options are presented in table 34. The free comments of the participants also showed similar rationalizations for both active and passive corruption.

Table 34:   Free Rationalizations Given for Corrupt Behavior

Free rationalizations given for passive corruption	Type of rationalization strategy
"If it pays off, I like offering special conditions to a friend."	Appeal to higher loyalties
"As the success of my business was related to a maximization of profit, I've done what was advantageous."	Appeal to higher loyalties
"Not only the company, but also its employees, will benefit from the achieved profit."	Appeal to higher loyalties
"The competitors would have done the same. To accept the offer was for the purpose of the company's future and of the aim to maximize profit."	Denial of responsibility Appeal to higher loyalties
"Those were only marketing expenses."	Denial of injury
"I don't see the bicycle as a return service. It's no corruption."	Legality
"I'm positive about my product. Even under competition, I would have got the order."	Refocusing attention
"Don't make a mountain out of a molehill."	Social weighting
Free rationalizations given for active corruption	**Type of rationalization strategy**
"I only tried to maintain the business connections and to achieve the customers' commitment."	Appeal to higher loyalties
"Because of such high losses, I tried everything to reduce the losses."	Denial of responsibility
"Get rich or die trying!"	Denial of responsibility
"It's the customers' responsibility whether he accepts my offer. He has the choice to check all other offers."	Denial of victim
"There's nothing condemnable about it."	Legality
"Why is it problem? It's a neutral favor."	Legality
"I'm working on my own authority and have to take the blame for my decisions by myself. I can account for my actions and therefore do not justify to anybody."	Social weighting (condemnation of the condemner)

6 Discussion

The various data gained in my study allow further insights into the corruption phenomenon – into the person-based components leading to corrupt action, into sociodemographic and situational influence factors, into the reasons given for corrupt and non-corrupt behavior, and into the rationalization strategies of corrupt actors. In the following, I first summarize the results, then discuss their managerial implications, and finally outline the study's limitations and implications for future research.

6.1 Summary of Results

The focus of my research was on the development and empirical validation of a model of corrupt action that tries to explain the subjective decision making processes of corrupt actors. Based on the finally resulting model of corrupt action, I analyzed sociodemographic and situational influence factors. Furthermore, because of its importance for future corrupt behavior, I examined how corrupt behavior was reasoned and justified.

6.1.1 The Model of Corrupt Action

The aim of my study was to investigate the interrelation of behavioral components leading to corrupt action. Thus, I proposed and empirically tested a model of corrupt action. The results show that all those components concerning the achievement of a certain private or professional goal (anticipated emotions, goal feasibility, goal desire, and goal intention) do not allow for a prediction of corrupt action. This finding contradicts criminological research (e.g., Bannenberg, 2002) that suggests a high achievement motive of corrupt actors. An explanation for the missing predictive relevance of general goals may be deduced from attitude-behavior research. It suggests that the degree of specificity of the behavior to predict and the predictors have to correspond (Ajzen & Fishbein, 1977). Thus, corrupt action as a very specific behavior can only be predicted by components measured with the same specificity; this means by all those components in the model directly addressing corrupt action, but not relating to a general professional or private goal. In contrast, Bagozzi et al. (2003) were able to predict specific behavior using generally formulated goals. While in their study participants were also asked to indicate their plans for how to achieve a goal they have set themselves, in my case, the ways chosen for goal achievement were not planned together with the goal setting in advance. Participants in my study were not sensitized to possible ways of goal achievement. Thus, corruption does not appear to be implemented in an overarching action plan. Rather, it seems that if the situation offers the opportunity, an individual decision on whether to act corruptly or not is evoked. While in my design the anteceding situation – namely, to achieve a profit as high as possible – was the same for all participants, the individual decision for each participant turned out differently either pro or contra corruption. This underlines the importance of person-based components for the prediction of corrupt action.

The resulting model is a modified extension of Ajzen's (1991) theory of planned behavior. In addition to his model, the desire component as proposed by Bagozzi et al. (2003) represented an important antecedent of the intention component. This also reflects my assumption that Heckhausen's (1989, pp. 203 – 218) distinction between desire and intention, between motivation and volition, is relevant to explain corrupt action. Furthermore, the transformation of the intention to act corruptly in real corrupt action is not considered in Ajzen's (1991) model, but in the Rubicon model of action phases (Gollwitzer, 1990; Heckhausen, 1987a; Heckhausen, 1987b; Heckhausen, 1989, pp. 203 – 218) and in the model of effortful decision making and enactment (Bagozzi et al., 2003) and therefore also in my model.

The intention to act corruptly was a very strong predictor of corrupt action, explaining more than 60% of its variance. This R^2 indicates that a great portion of the variance in corrupt action is determined by the person-based components included in the model. The remaining variance may be due to other person-based factors like, for example, sociodemographics and situational factors like, for example, organizational culture and climate, codes of conduct, rewards and sanctions, organizational size and level, and industry type and business competitiveness (e.g., Ford & Richardson, 1994; Loe et al., 2000), which were not considered in my model because of my research intention to cover behavioral components leading to corrupt action.

The attitude toward corrupt action had the main impact on the desire to act corruptly. This is consistent with Powpaka's (2002) finding in his survey study using scenarios where the attitude had the strongest impact on the intention to bribe compared to the subjective norm and perceived choice. The subjective norm in my model also had a substantial, but lower impact. Together, the cognitive model components attitude and subjective norm explained nearly half of the variance in the desire to act corruptly. Perceived behavioral control and the desire to act corruptly explained 75% of the variance in the intention to act corruptly with the desire to act corruptly having a stronger impact than the perceived behavioral control. Thus, my results show that in the case of an opportunity, an interplay of motivational, volitional, and cognitive – but not emotional – components within a situational context lead to corrupt action. While criminological research on corruption (e.g., Bannenberg, 2002) focuses on personal characteristics of corrupt actors, my research stresses the process of action choice and underlines the usefulness of an interactionist perspective of person and situation.

6.1.2 Sociodemographic Factors

Based on the final model of corrupt action, I analyzed the influence of selected sociodemographic factors – age and sex.

As outlined in chapter 2.2.3 (p. 50), there are hints that age relates to corrupt action in that older individuals are more averse to corruption (e.g., Deshpande, 1997; Gatti et al., 2003; Lund, 2000). My sample did not cover the whole range of age but focused on young high school and university students, who were mainly from 16 to 28 years old. Therefore, it is not surprising that no significant correlations could be found between age and corrupt action and age and the other model components. Neither the model components nor the strength of the model paths differed between high school and university students. Thus, there are no hints of high school students showing a greater impartiality than university students regarding ethical dilemmas. At first glance, the high share of corrupt actors among both high school and university students (more than 80% each) seems to support the notion of a high willingness of students to engage in corrupt behavior (e.g., Kohut & Corriher, 1994; Wood et al., 1988). Nevertheless, one has to be cautious when drawing such a conclusion: In my study, participants were not explicitly told that they were dealing with a corrupt offer, while in previous studies on unethical dilemmas (e.g., Kohut & Corriher, 1994; Wood et al., 1988), participants knew that they were to judge the ethicality of corrupt behavior. Thus, it is likely that students do refuse corrupt action when directly asked (see e.g., Chen & Tang, 2006; Poorsoltan et al., 1991), but may have difficulties in recognizing corrupt offers. This suggestion is supported by the finding that only 4% of the participants who acted corruptly reported awareness of their corrupt action. Most of the participants did not recognize that they dealt with an ethical dilemma including corruption.

There is a broad discussion in the academic literature whether there are sex differences in regard to corrupt behavior (see chap. 2.2.3, p. 49). The great advantage of my study was the ability to investigate behavior in a similar situational context for both men and women. This allows for conclusions about their corruptibility that are not impaired by the different life and work environments of men and women. Findings of previous studies on differences between the two sexes both regarding unethical behavior and corrupt behavior are inconsistent. Regarding corruption, there were strong hints from the few studies examining behavior actually shown outside the laboratory (e.g., Bannenberg, 2002) that men are more likely to act corruptly than women. Like Frank and Schulze's (2000) and Hegarty and Sims' (1978) laboratory studies, my study using a business simulation game did not find any sex differences regarding the propensity to corrupt action. This indicates that in a standardized situational context, men's and women's corruptibility is similar. A larger share of women in the group also had no influence. Thus, a female environment does not lead to lower corruption as some economic studies (Dollar et al., 2001; Swamy et al., 2001) might suggest. These findings are consistent with the structural or occupational socialization theory (e.g., Betz, O'Connell, & Shepard, 1989; Dawson, 1997; Mason & Mudrack, 1996; Smith & Rogers, 2000), according to which women and men were already socialized consistently from early adulthood on, both in college and university, and later in business life, too. In regard to the other model components, I also did not find any sex differences or relationships with the share of women in a group[55].

6.1.3 Situational Factors

Besides sociodemographic factors, I also investigated the influence of selected situational factors on the model of corrupt action: the opportunity for passive or active corruption, the size of the bribe, the point of time of the opportunity to act corruptly, the game score at the point of time of the opportunity to act corruptly, the degree of abstractness of the business code, and the degree of competition.

Up to now, there is no empirical documentation on whether the propensity to act corruptly differs in dependence on whether there is the opportunity to passive or active corruption. My results did not show any differences in regard to corrupt action nor in regard to the strength of the model paths. Thus, similar mechanisms seem to underlie passive and active corruption. Even the propensity to accept a corrupt offer appears to be similar to the propensity to submit a corrupt offer, although one might have expected that the threshold to corrupt action is lower for passive than for active corruption. The only difference found in regard to the model components was a stronger desire to act corruptly in the case of passive corruption than in the case of active corruption.

Some authors (e.g., Borner & Schwyzer, 1999; Carrillo, 1999; Carrillo, 2000) argue that the higher the size of the bribe, the more likely is corrupt action. This is not supported by my findings, which showed no relationship between the size of the bribe and corrupt action, although the critical significance level of 5% was only slightly missed. Nevertheless, high bribes seem to lead to a positive evaluation of corrupt action. In case of a high bribe, participants had a more positive attitude toward corruption, a more corruption-favoring subjective norm, and both a stronger desire and intention to act corruptly. These components are important determinants of corrupt behavior. Thus, despite the lacking differences in the propensity to corrupt action and the path coefficients, the differences in important model components hint at the critical influence of the size of the bribe. Further research may deliver further evidence.

I also examined whether corrupt action was more likely towards the end of the business game. The point of time of the opportunity to act corruptly obviously did not result in any differences in the model components. Differences were found in only one model path: The relationship between the subjective norm and the desire to act corruptly was stronger in the later phase of the business game than in the earlier periods. This shows that the influence of people's subjective norm changes with the circumstances. An assumption of a high tolerance of corrupt behavior by people important to the actor is more strongly related to a strong desire to act corruptly

---

[55] For a further discussion of sex differences in regard to corrupt behavior and rationalization strategies see Rabl and Kühlmann (2007, April).

when there is a high time pressure to achieve the set goals. Thus, in case of time pressure in their job, the attitudes, values, and practices of others seem to gain in importance in an individual's decision making.

Furthermore, I investigated the influence of the game score at the point of time of the opportunity to corrupt action. No significant correlations were found between the single model components and the profit achieved in the period before the opportunity to act corruptly, the accumulated profit achieved up to the point of time of the opportunity to act corruptly, and the corresponding group positions. This contradicts Schweitzer et al. (2004) who found a high propensity of people with unmet goals to behave unethically. Therefore, it might be questionable whether the frustration of needs is an important motive for corruption, although the measures used in this study may at best be seen as indicators for this psychological concept. Martin et al.'s (2007) study also delivered a contrary result: Financial constraints increased a firm's propensity to corruption. Looking at my findings, financial pressure appears to have no influence on the individual decision making process, although the improvement of a bad economic situation was among the most frequently mentioned reasons indicated by 15% of the participants. Further research, using the best possible measures for these concepts, may shed further light on the motivating function of financial pressure and frustration.

To prevent corruption, many companies internally use anti-corruption commitments (Gordon & Miyake, 2001) in the form of business codes. Kaptein (2004) distinguishes three clusters of codes: the stakeholder statute/business principles, the values statement, and the code of conduct. A number of companies integrate two, or even three, approaches in their codes. The types of corporate codes also differ, especially in the level of abstraction (Kaptein, 2004). Therefore, I tried to answer the question whether a business code of more or less abstraction concerning the non-tolerance of corruption is of different efficiency in preventing corruption. My results showed no differences in the single model components. Regarding the propensity to corrupt action, the critical significance level of 5% was slightly missed. Participants who acted for companies with a business code explicitly not tolerating corruption more often refused corruption than participants acting for companies with a more abstract business code simply demanding integrity. The degree of abstractness also had an influence on the strength of two model paths: In the case of a business code of low abstractness, the relationship between the perceived behavioral control and the intention to act corruptly was stronger. Thus, in the case of an explicitly communicated non-tolerance of corruption, a higher perceived behavioral control seems to be more strongly related to the intention to act corruptly. In the case of a business code of high abstractness simply demanding integrity, the relationship between the desire to act corruptly and the intention to act corruptly was stronger. Thus, in the case that generally integrity is demanded, the desire to act corruptly appears to have a stronger influence on the intention to act corruptly. In reverse, this also shows that in case of a business code of high abstractness, perceived behavioral control is of less importance than anteceding model components like, for example, attitude or subjective norm. It has to be noted that my design used two business codes that both represented a statement of general business principles and values rather than very detailed codes of conduct. This may explain why only very few differences were found.

Research on corruption assumes a relationship between the extent of economic competition and corruption (see chap. 2.2.1, p. 39), although results are inconsistent. While empirical economic studies showed lower levels of corruption in case of higher competition (Ades & Di Tella, 1999; Clarke & Xu, 2002, Emerson, 2006), both Hegarty and Sims (1978) and Martin et al. (2007) found higher levels of corruption under increased (perceived) competition. In contrast, my study did not reveal any significant correlations between any of the model components and the number of competing companies. Thus, my study adds to the number of inconsistent findings of previous research. How may the lacking relationship be explained? I did not assess how participants perceived the competitive situation in the business game. Maybe participants based their evaluation of the competitive situation on the whole business game competition where the number of about 200 participants was fixed rather than on the single business game where they acted within a group of competitors whose number was varied.

6.1.4 Reasons Given for Corrupt and Non-Corrupt Behavior

One further research interest was to analyze the reasons given for corrupt and non-corrupt behavior in a situation where participants were not explicitly told that they were dealing with corrupt offers.

A very surprising finding was the high share of corrupt actors. The reasons given for the behavior regarding the corrupt offer provide an explanation: Most participants obviously did not recognize that they were dealing with corruption. Only 4% of the corrupt actors indicated their awareness, while all participants refusing the corrupt offer seemed to recognize the corrupt character of the offer. Why was the sensitization to corruption at such a low level? One might argue that students only participated in a game where they did not have to fear any "real" consequences. But previous research on business games and laboratory experiments delivers contradictory arguments: Participants are highly motivated (Heidack, 1980, p. 39) and take the situation very seriously (Dawes, 1980). Additionally, none of the participants acting corruptly in the business game provided as an argument "It was just a game". Another explanation may be that in the high school and university context, students have not yet got in touch with corruption directly, but only heard about corruption cases in the media. Moreover, in their courses at high school and even at university, business ethics – at the point of time of the study – played no, or only a subordinate, role.

As the participants' aim in the business game was to achieve a profit as high as possible, a great number of corrupt actors used the arguments of additional profit and the improvement of a bad economic situation for their behavior. But besides these short-term oriented reasons for acting corruptly, a high percentage of corrupt actors also took a long-term perspective in arguing that they would like to assure orders and the maintenance of business connections.

A consideration of future perspectives can also be noticed for the participants who refused the corrupt offers. For both passive and active corruption, corrupt behavior was denied because of economic inefficiency in a long-term perspective and a fear for the company's image. Moreover, a general rejection of corrupt behavior predominated. Nevertheless, differences appeared in the frequencies with which participants gave certain reasons for rejecting corrupt behavior. For a denial of active corruption, the normative aspect of a general rejection, the altruistic motive to stay fair in the business competition, and the egoistic motive to avoid the high risks associated with corruption were important. In contrast, relevant arguments for a denial of passive corruption were normative aspects like immorality and a violation of the company's business code besides the economic aspect of inefficiency. Despite the differences in the concrete formulation of reasons, they were very similar in regard to their content.

6.1.5 Rationalization Strategies

I also intended to identify the rationalization strategies that were most frequently used as post hoc justifications of corrupt behavior. While for the assessment of the reasons given for corrupt action participants were not explicitly told about the potential wrongness of their behavior, when investigating rationalization strategies, participants received hints of their potential misbehavior.

In this study, the appeal to higher loyalties and the metaphor of the ledger appeared as the most popular strategies for both active and passive corruption. Both strategies reflect a reference to the organization and the individual's work. While the metaphor of the ledger focuses on the credits earned in the job, the appeal to higher loyalties focuses on the organizational goals that are to be achieved. The denial of responsibility, injury, and victim were important but played a subordinate role. This shows that rationalizations do not primarily address a denial of the negative implications of corrupt action, but rather highlight the "positive" intention lying behind the corrupt action. What is eye-catching in the free responses is the redefinition of the corrupt act regarding its legality. The corrupt offer is seen as something neutral and nothing condemnable, and the corrupt character is denied.

The type of post hoc rationalization strongly depends on the kind of bribes exchanged in the corrupt relationship. In my design, both the active corrupter and the passive corrupter were offered the possibility to achieve a business advantage by acting corruptly. The bribe was to get an order in exchange for a private favor. This explains the similarities of rationalization strategies given for both passive and active corruption.

6.2   Managerial Implications

This research intended to get hints for the prevention of and fight against corruption in and between companies. Because of the psychological focus of the model of corrupt action, I especially aim at giving recommendations in the area of human resource management. Nevertheless, managerial implications have to be drawn carefully because – as will be discussed later (see chap. 6.3, p. 193) – our experimental design with a sample of high school and university students allows only limited extrapolation of results to managerial positions in companies.

In the study, three major factors were identified as important influence factors in the decision making process: the individual's attitude toward corruption, the subjective norm, and the perceived behavioral control. The question that arises is which measures can be undertaken to influence these factors to reduce corruption in organizations. Figure 15 shows a summary of potential measures. They cannot be assigned to the distinct constructs uniquely so that there are overlaps. All measures may be expected to influence the subjective norm in order to establish a corruption-aversive organizational climate. Some measures may be specifically used to check for or to create a corruption-aversive attitude; some measures may be specifically suitable to reduce the perceived behavioral control.

Subjective Norm

• **Creating a corruption-aversive organizational culture:**
  ➤ Anti-corruption policy as part of the business strategy
  ➤ Introduction of a code of conduct/code of ethics
  ➤ Ethical leadership:
    · Managers as role models
    · Communication and support of the anti-corruption policy from top-down
  ➤ Cooperation with other companies, governments, employers' organizations
    and NGOs in the fight against corruption
  ➤ Ethic committees/Anti-corruption committees

Attitude Toward Corruption

• **Personnel selection:**
  ➤ Use of specific corruption-relevant attitude measures
  ➤ Background investigations
  ➤ Inclusion of the code of conduct in the recruiting material
  ➤ Self-commitment of applicants to the company's anti-corruption policy

• **Personnel development:**
  ➤ Anti-corruption trainings and workshops
  ➤ Train-the-trainer procedure
  ➤ Anti-corruption circles

• **Reinforcement system:**
  ➤ Rewarding ethical behavior
  ➤ Punishing corrupt behavior

• **Performance appraisal tied to ethical behavior**

Perceived Behavioral Control

• **Maximizing the likelihood of detection and transparency in job design:**
  ➤ Clearly defined responsibilities
  ➤ Separation of functions
  ➤ More-eyes-principle
  ➤ Job rotation
  ➤ Effective documentation and records management

• **Maximizing the likelihood of detection and transparency by institutional control and support tools:**
  ➤ Anti-corruption officer or ombudsperson
  ➤ Internal audits and revisions
  ➤ Effective reporting mechanisms for whistle-blowing
  ➤ Regular performance reviews and employee interviews

• **Maximizing risk awareness by a clear communication of sanctions**

Figure 15: Measures for Corruption Prevention in Organizations

To create a corruption-aversive subjective norm, employees should be shown in various ways that corruption is not tolerated in a company and that the integrity of employees is absolutely demanded. This demands the investment of time, financial, and human resources (Kubal, Baker, & Coleman, 2006).

Proactive efforts have to be made to stem a normalization of corruption in organizations often mediated by rationalization strategies (Ashforth & Anand, 2003; Brief et al., 2001), especially those appealing to higher loyalties. The company should aim at establishing an ethical organizational climate (Jones & Kavanagh, 1996) and adopt an attitude of permanent rejection of corruption, even if it appears that corruption would benefit the company (Argandoña, 2003). A non-tolerance of corruption has to be seen as high priority value for the company and all its operations. It should be clear that ethical values are ranked higher than business values (Stoner, 1989). This is especially important because my results show the great influence of the subjective norm, especially in situations of time pressure. An anti-corruption policy should be part of the business strategy in the way that it is tied to the business plan and to the organizational vision (Argandoña, 2003; see also Kubal et al., 2006).

One possibility to institutionally condemn corrupt behavior is the introduction of a code of conduct or code of ethics by the top management (Ahlf, 1998, p. 48; Argandoña, 2003; Pies et al., 2005; Schilling, 2004; Schwitzgebel, 2003; Then, 1997; Van Duyne, 1999). This code may also become part of each employee's labor contract (BDI, 1997; Wieland & Grüninger, 2000). It is the most visible sign of a company's ethical principles (Stead, Worrell, & Stead, 1990). My results show the importance of concreteness, especially from the background of a generally low awareness for corruption. Thus, in contrast to a much more general business code only focusing on general business principles, a code of conduct or code of ethics should formulate the motivation and the reasons to prevent corruption (Argandoña, 2003; Schwitzgebel, 2003). To be meaningful, it needs to clearly outline the organization's standards, principles, and expectations, which apply to all members of the organization, in a written form (Brien, 2001; Gellerman, 1989; Schwitzgebel, 2003; Stead et al., 1990), also including the disciplinary consequences of violation (McDonald, 2000). It should be written in simple terms (McDonald, 2000). The code should provide decision making criteria for dealing with corruption problems (Argandoña, 2003). It should focus on the potential corrupt dilemmas employees may face (McDonald, 2000; Stead et al., 1990) and integrate concrete instructions and solutions referring to specific job situations (Ahlf, 1998, p. 48; Argandoña, 2003; McDonald, 2000; Schwitzgebel, 2003). The code needs to be communicated to all employees so that it is assured that everybody is aware of the guidelines (Gellerman, 1989; Kohut & Corriher, 1994; Stead et al., 1990). The code has to be made a "living document[...]" (Carroll, 1978, p. 9), in that it is accepted and internalized (Stead et al., 1990) and not only affects what employees say, but also what they actually do (Gellerman, 1989). Case studies, role plays, business games, and simulations of corruption scenarios may serve as measures to deepen the knowledge of the code of conduct and its application, for example, in anti-corruption training (Göbel, 2006, p. 231; Stead et al., 1990). The studies by Weeks and Nantel (1992) and Wotruba et al. (2001) provide evidence for the codes' impact when they are well communicated and employees are familiar with them. Codes have to be institutionally assured to be effective. Thus, they should include concrete hints on control instances, which individuals can appeal to in the case of conflict or in case of code violation (Ahlf, 1998, p. 48; Göbel, 2006, p. 192; McDonald, 2000). In developing the code, employees of all sectors and levels should participate (Ahlf, 1998, p. 49; Schwitzgebel, 2003; Stead et al., 1990).

In creating a corruption-aversive climate, ethical leadership[56] by the (top) management plays an important role. The constitutive definition of ethical leadership by Brown, Trevino, and Harrison (2005) covers the aspects that seem to be appropriate measures in regard to influencing the subjective norm: Ethical leadership is "the demonstration of normatively appropriate conduct through personal actions and interpersonal relationships, and the promotion of such conduct to followers through two-way communication, reinforcement, and decision making" (Brown et al., 2005, p. 120). The first aspect that can be derived from this definition is the recommendation that (top) management should serve as an example, as a role model for their employees (Ahlf, 1998, p. 47; Anand et al., 2005; BDI, 1997; Cole & Smith, 1996; Gellerman, 1989; McDonald, 2000; McKendall et al., 2002; Schmidt, 2004; Trevino, Brown, & Hartman, 2003; Vickers, 2005). "Managers are the most significant role models in the organizational setting; thus they have a major socializing influence on lower level employees" (Stead et al., 1990, p. 238). The same values apply to them as for all other employees at lower levels (Stoner, 1989; Van Duyne, 1999). It should become obvious that management as "the first servant" (Van Duyne, 1999, p. 56) of the company back up its words with deeds, acting strictly in accordance with its stated aims in all its actions and decisions (Argandoña, 2003; Boardman & Klum, 2001; Trevino et al., 2003), therefore demonstrating consistency between ethical philosophy and ethical behavior (Stead et al., 1990). The second aspect that can be deduced from the definition above is the importance of a clear communication and support of the anti-corruption policy and of anti-corrupt conduct from the top down (Argandoña, 2003; Homann, 1997; McDonald, 2000; McKendall et al., 2002; Stead et al., 1990). It is the management's task to be actively involved in promoting and maintaining an anti-corruption climate in the organization by institutionalizing ethical norms and practices at all organizational levels (Boardman & Klum, 2001; Sims, 1992; Stead et al., 1990). This is one method for a company's management to declare its intent to comply with all legislation and to make anti-corruption policy a top priority (Argandoña, 2003; Cole & Smith, 1996; Schmidt, 2004; Schwitzgebel, 2003). All institutionalized measures should be combined with the management's self-commitment against corruption, which is communicated in open letters to employees, public speeches, company newsletters, wall posters, or wallet cards (Argan-

---

[56] For a review on the concept of ethical leadership see Brown and Trevino (2006).

doña, 2003; Kubal et al., 2006; McDonald, 2000; Then, 1997; Wieland & Grüninger, 2000). Clear decisions by top managers against corruption, despite conventional practices and temptations should be disseminated widely (Anand et al., 2005).

A positive signal, which may also contribute to a corruption-aversive subjective norm, is the cooperation with other companies, governments, employers' organizations, NGOs, etc. in the fight against corruption by, for example, supporting their work, volunteering information, or offering help (Argandoña, 2003). Guidelines provided by government or material provided by NGOs should be customized to the specific risks the company confronts (Vickers, 2005).

Not only (top) management but all company members should be included in establishing a corruption-aversive organizational culture. Thus, companies should establish ethics or anti-corruption committees. These consist of employees from different sectors and levels and membership is rotated. Such committees discuss ethical dilemmas, especially those including corruption, and support the realization of anti-corruption measures. Their function is orientated to policy making, underlining the importance of corruption prevention, and contributing to the acceptance of the undertaken measures (McDonald, 2000; Schwitzgebel, 2003).

Attitude

In this study, attitude was found to be an important determinant of the desire to act corruptly. So how can a company, on the one hand, assure a corruption-aversive attitude of its employees and on the other hand, undertake measures for changing their employees' attitudes?

One possibility is to check for potential employees' attitude toward corruption during the recruitment and hiring process (Argandoña, 2003; Cole & Smith, 1996; Göbel, 2006, p. 203; McDonald, 2000; Then, 1997; Vickers, 2005). To allow for a choice of candidates who will resist corruption, selection procedures should not only include general integrity tests[57] like, for example, the three major integrity tests used in Germany, the Personality Inventory for Integrity ("Persönlichkeitsinventar zur Integritätsabschätzung" (PIA)[58], Mussel, 2003), the Psychological Integrity Test ("Psychologischer Integritätstest" (PIT)[59], Hoffmann, Mokros, & Wilmer, 2008), and the Inventory of Job-Related Attitudes and Self-Assessments ("Inventar berufsbezogener Einstellungen und Selbsteinschätzungen" (IBES)[60], Marcus, 2006). Rather, as my study shows, it is absolutely necessary to use specific corruption-relevant attitude measures. Additionally, background investigations including, for example, the call-

---

[57] For a review on integrity tests and their problems see, for example, Berry, Sackett, and Wiemann (2007) and Sackett and Wanek (1996).

[58] The PIA was developed by Heinz Schuler at the University of Hohenheim, Germany, in 2000.

[59] The PIT was developed by researchers of the Technical University of Darmstadt, Germany, and the University of Regensburg, Germany, in cooperation with the Team Psychologie & Sicherheit in 2005.

[60] The IBES was developed by Bernd Marcus in 2006.

ing of references (Cole & Smith, 1996; Stead et al., 1990) can be valuable tools in screening employees for their propensity to act corruptly. Moreover, companies may allow their potential employees to check their personal attitude with the company's attitude toward corruption by including the code of conduct in all recruiting material and addressing it in the job interview (Schwitzgebel, 2003; Stead et al., 1990). Furthermore, companies may require their candidates to read the anti-corruption policy and to commit themselves to these standards by signing an obligatory statement during the application process (Stead et al., 1990).

As soon as employees are members of the company, the organization may undertake efforts to shape their attitude toward corruption. According to social psychological research, one possibility – based on cognitive theories on attitude change – is persuasive communication (Bohner, 2001). This can be realized in training and workshops for all employees (Ahlf, 1998, p. 48; Argandoña, 2003; Gellerman, 1989; Kubal et al., 2006; Sims, 1992; Stead et al., 1990). This may already start as part of the employee orientation program for new hires (Kubal et al., 2006; McDonald, 2000; Stoner, 1989). Again, specificity is necessary. Thus, general ethics training does not suffice. As my study showed a low sensitivity of participants to the corruption phenomenon, employees have to be sensitized to the corruption problem, in that they understand what corruption is, why it should be rejected, and what consequences it may have (Argandoña, 2003; BDI, 1997; Gellerman, 1989; McDonald, 2000; Pies et al., 2005; Schwitzgebel, 2003; Then, 1997). Training should serve to increase employees' awareness of corruption and therefore their ability to identify corrupt behavior. They should explain the ethical and legal principles underlying corruption (Sims, 1992). The knowledge of common rationalization strategies of corrupt actors as identified in my study can help to underline that the goals do not justify the means. Thus, an identification of the rationalization strategies frequently used for corrupt behavior and a familiarization with these tactics should represent a part of the anti-corruption training (Anand et al., 2005; McDonald, 2000). As empirical results show (e.g., Callan, 1992), the employees need to be taught how to confront ethical dilemmas including corruption (McDonald, 2000; Veiga, Golden, & Dechant, 2004) and how to carry out the company's code of conduct (Gellerman, 1989; McDonald, 2000; Pies et al., 2005; Sims, 1992; Schwitzgebel, 2003). Here, corruption cases from daily business as, for example, reported in the media or dilemmas directly experienced by the participants[61] can be used for discussion and a demonstration of the practical consequences of corruption (Gellerman, 1989; McDonald, 2000; Schwitzgebel, 2003; Stead et al., 1990; Wieland & Grüninger, 2000). Besides case studies, role plays, business games, and simulations of corruption scenarios may be elements in the anti-corruption training (Göbel, 2006, p. 231; Stead et al., 1990). The development of rules of thumb and methodical instructions may provide guidelines for solving corruption dilemmas (McDonald, 2000; Schwitzgebel, 2003; Stead

---

[61] Delaney and Sockell's (1992) study showed that individuals are more likely to refuse unethical behavior when confronted with their most serious ethical dilemma.

et al., 1990; Wieland & Grüninger, 2000). Gellerman's (1989) general advice here is: "When in doubt, don't" (p. 78). Sims (1992) reviews a useful seven-step checklist that may help employees in dealing with ethical dilemmas:

> (1) Recognize and clarify the dilemma. (2) Get all the possible facts. (3) List your options – all of them. (4) Test each option by asking: Is it legal? Is it right? Is it beneficial? (5) Make your decision. (6) Double check your decision by asking: How would I feel if my family found out about this? How would I feel if my decision was printed in the local newspaper?[62] (7) Take action (pp. 511 – 512).

By following a train-the-trainer procedure, employees and managers who have undergone anti-corruption training themselves start conducting training session themselves (McDonald, 2000). This also appears a very suitable measure to shape a corruption-aversive attitude. Besides training off-the-job, anti-corruption circles following the example of quality circles may be used as training method near-the-job (Göbel, 2006, p. 232). In these regular circles, the discussion of corruption dilemmas faced in the job may provide guidance for managing such conflicts (Göbel, 2006, p. 232; Stoner, 1989) and may be useful in questioning any rationalizations used (Anand et al., 2005). Another possibility is informal training including coaching and mentoring (Göbel, 2006, p. 232; McDonald, 2000). Mentors may provide a real-life example of how to handle corruption dilemmas (Vickers, 2005).

As the sample in this study consisted of students who will be the managers in the future, it is necessary to start early to sensitize students to the phenomenon of corruption in business ethics courses. In Germany, the accreditation of the newly introduced bachelor and master studies (e.g., AACSB, EQUIS) may contribute to an introduction of business ethics education in studies of business administration and management at universities (AACSB International, 2008; European Foundation for Management Development (EFMD), 2008). Nevertheless, they should be integrated in all studies whose alumni will be the future decision makers in companies, regardless of the subject.

This approach using persuasive communication to change the employees' attitude toward corruption may be seen as an engendering mechanism that is based upon persuasion, discussion, affirmation, and demonstration (Brien, 2001). Following social psychological research, another possibility to change attitudes is the use of rewards and sanctions (Bohner, 2001). This resembles an enforcement mechanism based upon surveillance, coercion, threats, and sanctions, finally leading to deterrence (Brien, 2001). To create a corruption-aversive attitude, it is necessary that ethical behavior is reinforced and corrupt behavior is punished. On the one hand, a company should aim at identifying and publicizing examples of good ethical and anti-corrupt behavior in business and establish a practice of seeking out and

---

[62] This is called the "headline test" (Anand et al., 2005, p. 18), the "flashlight/newspaper test" , or the "golden rule" (Trevino et al., 2003, p. 19).

rewarding employees' ethical behavior (Cole & Smith, 1996; Homann, 1997; McDonald, 2000; Stead et al., 1990; Stoner, 1989), for example, by introducing reporting or audit systems (Stead et al., 1990). On the other hand, corrupt conduct must not be tolerated at all, has to be identified by, for example, effective reporting, auditing, and whistle-blowing systems (see p. 192) and followed by discipline (Cole & Smith, 1996; Gellerman, 1989; Jones & Kavanagh, 1996; McDonald, 2000; Stead et al., 1990; Trevino et al., 2003). Guilty employees may be fired, prosecuted, and required to make restitution (Cole & Smith, 1996; Stead et al., 1990) so that there is, for example, the threat of dismissal and financial losses (Pies et al., 2005; Renner, 2004; Then, 1997). The question of how sanctions have to appear to be effective arises (see chap. 2.2.1, p. 37; chap. 2.2.2, p. 44). The predominant view is that high penalties lower corruption (e.g., Abbink et al., 2002; Goel & Rich, 1989). But it is especially important that sanctions follow corrupt behavior immediately (Stein-rücken, 2004). It should be clear to all employees what counts as corruption and violation of the code of conduct, and what will happen in case they act corruptly (Argandoña, 2003; Cederblom & Dougherty, 1990, p. 194). Thus, there should be guidelines on the procedure in case of the suspicion of corruption (Bussmann, 2004). Sanctioning corrupt behavior is not enough. Punishment should be followed up by immediately spreading the news of the offense and the punishment through the company's grapevine (Kubal et al., 2006; Stead et al., 1990) to foster the employees' awareness for the consequences of corrupt behavior.

Based upon this enforcement mechanism is the demand for an integration of ethical decision making into the performance appraisal. Performance evaluations and the associated rewards have to be tied to ethical behavior (Göbel, 2006, p. 208; Kubal et al., 2006; Sims, 1992; Stoner, 1989). They should go beyond numeric outcomes. A performance appraisal that not only considers whether the numbers are met, but also how they are met prevents the onset of rationalizations justifying corrupt behavior (Anand et al., 2005) and discourages corrupt practices (McDonald, 2000).

Perceived Behavioral Control

The results of this study showed that high perceived behavioral control had a positive impact on the intention to act corruptly. Thus, it is important to establish effective control mechanisms to maximize the risk for corrupt actors by increasing the likelihood of detection and punishment. As control alone reduces corruption but also destroys the intrinsic motivation for honesty (Schulze & Frank, 2003), it it necessary to assure high transparency, which not only assures control but also creates trust (Heuskel, 2004). This may be realized by different measures.

Job design offers a number of possibilities to contribute to high transparency and a high likelihood of detection:

• First, the responsibilities of each employee should be clearly defined so that at all times it is clear who can be made accountable in case of corrupt action (Argandoña, 2003; Schmidt, 2004).

- Second, the risk of corruption may be reduced by avoiding a combination of certain functions and decision competencies within one person or position. Thus, a division of work and functional separation, for example, between action and control, can contribute to a detection of corrupt behavior (BDI, 1997; Bussmann, 2004; Göbel, 2006, pp. 234 – 237; Schilling, 2004; Schmidt, 2004).

- Third, the more-eyes-principle should be followed in important decisions and negotiations. At least two employees from one party should be involved to avoid an abuse of decision-scope and corrupt action (BDI, 1997; Bussmann, 2004; Pies et al., 2005; Schilling, 2004; Schmidt, 2004; Then, 1997).

- Fourth, where possible and especially in endangered sectors of a company, job rotation may increase the risk of detection and prevent the establishment of long-term relationships on which corruption is often based (BDI, 1997; Pies et al., 2005; Renner, 2004; Then, 1997), a fact that is also shown in Abbink's (2004) experimental study. Nevertheless, this measure causes costs because employees have to be familiarized to a new field and know-how might get lost (Renner, 2004; Schmidt, 2004).

- Fifth, an effective documentation and records management should be part of the job design. All transactions and decisions – especially those that involve receipts or payments of money – must be faithfully, accurately, promptly, and completely recorded. Besides documentation in the company's accounts and books, this may be realized by a confidential file recording all transactions including the names of the involved business partners, the subjects of matter, as well as the dates of negotiation (Argandoña, 2003; BDI, 1997; Cain, Doig, Flanary, & Barata, 2001; Schmidt, 2004).

These measures addressing job design should be complemented by institutional control and support tools that help in spotting corruption conflicts in the workplace (Göbel, 2006, p. 237 – 239; Vickers, 2005):

- First, an internal anti-corruption officer or an external ombudsperson may be appointed (McDonald, 2000). While an anti-corruption officer belongs to the organization and is directly subordinated to top management, an ombudsperson is recruited from outside the organization (Pies et al., 2005; Schwitzgebel, 2003). The anti-corruption officer functions as problem solver, primarily dealing with the establishment of effective anti-corruption programs to create a corruption-aversive organizational climate (McDonald, 2000). In contrast, an ombudsperson acts as a third party resolver of conflicts. An ombudsperson's functions include investigation, counseling, and advice. Employees can give hints on violations of the company's code of conduct, corrupt offenses, and on suspicious cases. More-over, they have the possibility of discussing corrupt dilemmas with the ombudsperson without fearing retribution as names are kept anonymously. The ombudsperson gives advice and assists in finding an appropriate solution for the problem (Anand et al., 2005; McDonald, 2000).

- Second, internal audits and revisions should be undertaken to monitor the company's activities for evidence of corruption (Ahlf, 1998, p. 50; Argandoña, 2003; Boardman & Klum, 2001; BDI, 1997; Stead et al., 1990; Then, 1997). Such audits may help to identify factors or pressures that encourage corrupt behavior or serve as incentives (McDonald, 2000).

- Third, effective reporting mechanisms for whistle-blowing should be established (Boardman & Klum, 2001; Gellerman, 1989; Pies et al., 2005; Schilling, 2004; Sims, 1992). Whistle-blowing is "the disclosure by organization members (former or current) of illegal, immoral, or illegitimate practices under the control of their employers, to persons or organizations that may be able to effect action" (Near & Miceli, 1985, p. 4). Employees should be offered communication channels to voice their concerns (Argandoña, 2003; Barnett, Cochran, & Taylor, 1993; McDonald, 2000). Besides the appointment of an ombudsperson as mentioned above, the must common means is the use of anonymous ethics and whistle-blowing phone hotlines (Kubal et al., 2006; Lambsdorff & Nell, 2005; McDonald, 2000). These mechanisms also provide the means by which corruption dilemmas can be reviewed, discussed, and resolved (McDonald, 2000), as well as the procedures to assess the validity of employees' concerns regarding corrupt acts, to protect whistle-blowers (Barnett et al., 1993; Gellerman, 1989), and to inform about legal means and consequences (Lambsdorff & Nell, 2005).

- Fourth, regular performance reviews and employee interviews may also help to detect corrupt tendencies and to establish the employees' trust to announce corrupt offers to the supervisor.

In addition to efforts in increasing the likelihood of detection, companies should also aim at clearly communicating the sanctions that impend in the case of detection to create the employees' awareness for the risks of corrupt action. It is not sufficient to set high penalties, as outlined in the section on influencing the attitude toward corruption (see p. 189), but the consequences of corrupt action for the individual have to be clearly stressed in speeches, guidelines, newsletters, anti-corruption campaigns, training, and seminars (Amundsen, 1999).

Additional Managerial Implications

Further results on sociodemographic and situational factors raise some additional managerial implications.

As both women and men were found as likely to act corruptly and a greater share of women in the group did not reduce corruption, demands to select more women for management positions (e.g., Beltramini, Peterson, & Kozmetsky, 1984) to make business more ethical are not justified. That Bannenberg's (2002) study examining court cases found more men accused may be due to the higher rate of males in management positions (Holtfreter, 2005), or due to a higher skillfulness of women to keep corrupt transactions secret, or due to the fact that women are less likely to be asked for a bribe (Mocan, 2004).

Situational influences contributing to corruption – as, for example, a highly competitive environment, time pressures, and high incentives by high bribes – hardly can be influenced by companies themselves. Thus, besides making use of the measures already mentioned above, companies should aim at an exemplary conduct in regard to corruption and should support any initiatives undertaken to establish an anti-corruption commitment in the whole business environment. If every company begins in itself to consequently prevent and combat corruption, this is the most effective starting point to achieve fair and ethical business conditions.

6.3   Limitations and Implications for Future Research

The model of corrupt action proposed and validated in this study is a starting point to map corrupt action among business partners and to get insights in what makes decision makers in companies act corruptly. As the theoretical development and discussion of the model shows, corrupt action is the result of a network of complex relationships. While existing research mainly focuses on either the inputs or the outputs of corruption, I aimed at investigating the complex interplay of behavioral components leading to corrupt action. Thereby, I also considered their interaction with the situational context.

Because of the complexity of the corruption phenomenon, not every single aspect could be covered in the model. So, some restrictions concerning the applicability of my model of corrupt action have to be made. The action model outlined in this study deals with the simple case of a corrupt relationship between only two single actors. Groups of actors and resulting group influences are not considered. Furthermore, corruption often takes place in an international context, which means it occurs between actors from different socio-cultural backgrounds. These external influences also are not covered by the model. Moreover, the model focuses on the case of a first initiation of a corrupt relationship. Thus, the model intends to describe the relevant person-based components for a first-time corrupt action between two single partners in a mono-national context. Dynamics of a longer-lasting corrupt relationship will have to be included in the model. In this case, corruption already may have been experienced as an effective way of goal achievement. Therefore, it may be regarded as an option from the beginning. Thus, in the case of longer-lasting relationships the link between the model part concerning the goal and the part concerning corrupt action may become significant. My focus was on private corruption, that is, corruption in and between companies. As corruption also occurs in other sectors like politics and administration, it will require further research to find out whether one general action model for corruption can be identified or whether there are differences in the person-based components of corrupt action according to the sector in which it takes place. Therefore, it will be a great challenge for future research to model aspects of international corrupt relationships, group influences, and the development of the relationship between corrupt actors in different settings.

A business game simulating a cut-out of the real business world with participants slipping into the roles of decision makers in companies (Kriz, 2005) offers a realistic environment for studying corrupt action (see chap. 4.2.1, p. 113), a phenomenon that is hardly empirically researchable in a real world context. Nevertheless, when generalizing my results, some restrictions have to be made, especially because of the standardization of the initial situation and the corrupt offers as well as the controlled variation of selected experimental conditions in the business game. For future research, it is advisable to cross-check the model using different research approaches, such as qualitative interviews with real-life corrupters and corruptees that will also allow researchers to capture the varieties and different kinds of corrupt action.

Furthermore, this study used a sample of high school and university students. Although they are the future leaders of and in companies and O'Fallon and Butterfield's (2005) review found students less ethical than practitioners in only three out of seven studies, I recommend a validation of my model with a sample of managers, especially from the background of the mixed results on differences (see chap. 2.2.3, p. 50).

The sample for the empirical test of the model of corrupt action in my study was German. Thus, to test for possible differences in the model of corrupt action for corrupt relationships within one single country, a similar study may be conducted using samples of a variety of different countries, especially of countries with strongly different attitudes and policies toward corruption.

As I created a strong incentive structure by the size of the bribes chosen, it also will be interesting to see whether the findings will hold true for weaker incentive structures as they may occur in the case of small-scale corruption. Moreover, I did not provide explicit deterrents. Thus, future research may also examine situations where corrupt behavior is penalized.

This study also examined the use of rationalization strategies by corrupt actors. Thus, I assessed the rationalization strategies used by corrupt actors post hoc. It might be an interesting subject of future research to also get hints for the potential of rationalization strategies as ex ante determinants of corrupt action (see Rabl & Kühlmann, 2008, May) asking participants in advance for their internalized and learned rationalization strategies for corrupt action. This would offer the possibility to examine the direct relationship between rationalization strategies and corrupt behavior in addition to causal effects. In my design, such an attempt may have caused distortions because participants may be primed to the fact that the business game is on and about corruption, which I clearly intended to avoid. The best way to examine the function of rationalization strategies may be a business game as used in my study. Qualitative interviews with real-life corrupters and corruptees would be difficult because on the one hand, an ex ante assessment of rationalization strategies will not be possible, and because on the other hand, determinants of corrupt behavior are assessed post hoc, therefore including tendencies to give socially desirable self-descriptions.

The type of post hoc rationalization strongly depends on the kind of bribes exchanged in the corrupt relationship. In my design, both the active corrupter and the passive corruptee were offered the possibility to achieve a business advantage by acting corruptly. Other scenarios – also including private advantages – should be included in future studies on corruption and their rationalization. Furthermore, one might aim at examining pairs, or even networks, of interacting corrupt business partners, which the design of my business game did not allow for.

In addition to the aspects covered in my model of corrupt action, it seems desirable to assess the role of additional factors that may influence corrupt behavior. For example, regarding further person-based factors one may investigate whether certain personality traits, in addition to certain moral or ethical ideologies, help or hinder corrupt behavior. Moreover, there is a lack of research in regard to the motives for corrupt action. Future studies may use scales for assessing motives and other possibly relevant psychological constructs like, for example, achievement motivation or frustration. Aiming at a comprehensive model of corrupt action, another further step may be the inclusion of the various situational factors determining corrupt behavior and also important in investigating the function of rationalization strategies.

Taking all these aspects into account and using different methodical approaches, research will be able to deliver further contributions to an effective prevention of and fight corruption in and between companies. The model of corrupt action developed in this study offers a promising attempt to fill the research gap in regard to the person-based components of corrupt action.

7   Conclusion

Do you remember the case of David Molton and Brian West at the beginning of this work? If not, take a brief look again at the introduction of this book (see chap. 1, p. 16). This case clearly describes scenario of corrupt action.

The central aim of this study was to examine the subjective decision making processes of corrupt actors to get insights in what makes them act corruptly. Therefore, a theoretical action model was deduced from existing models on decision making, motivation, volition, emotion, and cognition. This theoretical model mainly grounded on Bagozzi et al.'s (2003) model of effortful decision making and enactment incorporating aspects of the Rubicon model of action phases (Gollwitzer, 1990; Heckhausen, 1987a; Heckhausen, 1987b; Heckhausen, 1989, pp. 203 – 218) as well as Ajzen's (1991) theory of planned behavior. It was adopted for corrupt action from the background of the existing knowledge on the corruption phenomenon. To test the theoretical model, an experimental simulation design combining a business game with a standardized questionnaire was used and conducted with a sample of high school and university students who will be the future decision makers in companies. The result of the PLS structural equation modeling procedure was a model of corrupt action that reflects the interplay of the motivational, volitional, and cognitive person-based components that lead to corruption. Emotional aspects did not seem to be relevant. Three person-based components appeared to be important determinants of corruption, three components that are also present in the case of David Molton and Brian West:

• A corruption-friendly attitude: Corruption is seen as right, as wise, as useful, as advantageous, as attractive. Both David and Brian judge corruption to be beneficial. David gets provisions derived from advertising efforts ("Why not get some additional income for my efforts?"), Brian may overcome the bad situation of his company in the way that he gets additional orders ("You would get provisions if you conveyed some further sponsoring contracts to my firm").

• A corruption-friendly subjective norm: People in the professional surrounding of the actor (e.g., colleagues, supervisors, the company's top management) tolerate or even encourage corrupt behavior, creating a corruption-friendly organizational climate. In the case, David is convinced that his company tolerates corrupt action ("And why should my company have a problem – it's an investment in our good business relationship. [....] And maintaining good business relationships with our partners is even one of the top priorities in our mission statement"). And Brian here makes a persuasive contribution: "Your company will profit, too."

• A high perceived behavioral control: The corrupt actor estimates the risks of his behavior; this means, for example, the probability of detection, punishment, and negative consequences to be low. Considering the risks that might threaten him, David comes to the conclusion: "I don't see any risk." Possible reasons that can be identified in the case are a lacking more-eyes principle ("Negotiating with you was always my responsibility") and a lacking effective recording system ("And your provisions will be paid to your private account, so that they will not occur in any of your company's documentation").

These three main pillars in the subjective decision making process of corrupt actors influence the desire and the intention to act corruptly, which finally lead to corrupt action.

Further explorative analyses additionally showed the following:

- The sociodemographic factors examined in this study – sex and age/educational level (high school versus university students) – did not make any difference in the model components and relationships.

- For both active and passive corruption, similar processes in decision making occurred and most of the model components did not differ either. Only the desire to act corruptly was stronger in the case of passive corruption than in the case of active corruption. Referring to the case again, for both David's and Brian's corrupt behavior the same determinants in a similar interrelation are relevant.

- The size of the bribe did not affect the relationships in the model, but single model components. High bribes contributed to a corruption-friendly attitude and subjective norm as well as to a stronger desire and intention to act corruptly.

- Time pressure only affected the strength of the path between the subjective norm and the desire to act corruptly. In case of high time pressure, the positive relationship between the subjective norm and the desire to act corruptly was stronger.

- Financial pressure was not related to the model components.

- The degree of economic competition was also not related to the model components.

- The way business codes were formulated made a difference. In the case of an explicit non-tolerance of corruption, perceived behavioral control appeared to be stronger related to the intention to act corruptly than in the case of a general demand for integrity. Moreover, the relationship between the desire and the intention to act corruptly was weaker.

A supporting mechanism for the occurrence of corruption are rationalization strategies. These also become obvious in the case of David and Brian. David justifies his behavior predominantly by an appeal to higher loyalties, one of the most frequently used rationalization strategies as this study showed: "[...] why should my company have a problem – it's an investment in our good business relationship. You always offered very good service on good terms." He was supported by Brian: "[...] there is no better advertisement for [the] company than that". A denial of injury also may be heard: "So, why not? Where's the problem?"

An important finding of this study was the low sensitivity to the corruption phenomenon, which shows how important it is to inform, to inform early and continuously, starting in high school and university education and continuing throughout professional life.

In providing a model of corrupt action, this study is a first attempt to fill the gap that exists in corruption research regarding the corrupt actor and the corrupt actor's decision making. It not only enriches the body of theoretical research on corruption, but also offers a useful tool for companies to derive suitable measures to prevent and combat corruption. This study gives some hints as to which measures may be used to influence the critical person-based determinants of corruption. A further validation of the model and extensions in regard to, for example, different situational contexts, different countries, or international relationships are promising avenues for future research.

This work also reviews and summarizes the vast body of interdisciplinary theoretical and empirical corruption literature – but from the perspective of private corruption, a perspective that often has been neglected up to now. Lots of findings and arguments referring to public and partly also political corruption may be transferred; nevertheless, an empirical foundation for the case of private corruption is absolutely necessary. The literature review will give rise to a number of research questions in relation to private corruption, which may be addressed in future empirical research.

The present study advances the knowledge and the understanding of the problem of private corruption. The model of corrupt action may serve as a guide for solving the corruption problem in companies. This work also underlines the great need for further research on this topic and outlines ideas for a promising advancement of corruption research. Corruption must not be considered a side issue, neither in research nor in practice. Both academics and practitioners should combine efforts and pool resources to collaboratively address the issue. This will be the best way to achieve effective mechanisms of preventing corruption in and between companies, to establish a commitment to integrity in the economic competition, and to arrive at a corruption-free business environment. So my hope for the future is that cases like David's and Brian's will become singular and isolated ones, that all Davids will arrive at overcoming the temptation of corruption and responding to the Brians:

> *"No, Brian, I won't accept your offer. Corruption is illegal, immoral, and unethical. My company does not tolerate corruption and I personally also absolutely deny it. There are other ways for you – legal ones, moral ones, ethical ones – that may help you to achieve your goal."*

APPENDIX

APPENDIX

Appendix A: Invitation to the Mini Business Game Contest

Appendix A1: English Version

Who can realize the highest profit?

Invitation to a mini business game contest concerning "the decision making behavior of companies in competition"

Dear student,

Have you ever wished to be in the position of a manager who is – due to the decisions he takes – solely responsible for the success of a whole company?

In the context of a series of studies concerning "the decision making behavior of companies in competition" conducted by our chair BWL IV, you will get the chance! You can match with your fellow students and gain the live experience of empirical research!

You will take the **role of the sales and marketing chief of a company** selling bicycles and bicycle equipment. Over the period of four quarters, you will be solely responsible for the selling of bicycles for children. In the business game, the market for bicycles for children will be an oligopoly market and you will compete with up to five other companies.

Your goal should be to achieve the **highest possible profit** after the expiration of the four quarters. The winner of each mini business game is going to be the representative of the company that achieved the highest profit at the end of the game.

The sales and marketing chief who will be performing best out of all the **approximately 200 participants**, that means, the sales and marketing chief who will achieve the highest profit compared to the competitors, **will be named at the end of our studies.**

You have the chance to win the following **attractive prizes**:

1st place:	250 euros
2nd place:	200 euros
3rd place:	150 euros
4th to 6th place:	50 euros
7th to 10th place:	25 euros

Take this chance to test and train your decision making competence in this mini business game, match with your fellow students, and win attractive prizes. Please support our series of studies with your participation!

The mini business game will take place in **building B IX, room 24** at different dates and will last about approximately 1.5 hours up to a maximum of 2.5 hours. The length of time will depend on the number of participants.

The **scheduled dates** are: ...

If you are interested in participating, please let me know as soon as possible what date you prefer. I appreciate it very much! Please also contact me if you want to participate but cannot make one of the scheduled dates. I will keep you posted about extra dates! Of course, you can inform your fellow students and friends if they are interested – I would be pleased!

Many thanks for your participation in our business game! We need every single one of you! It will be worthwhile for you!

If you have any questions, please do not hesitate to contact me!

Yours sincerely,

Tanja Rabl
University of Bayreuth
Chair of Human Resource Management (BWL IV)

Appendix A2: German Version

Wer erzielt den höchsten Gewinn?

Einladung zum Mini-Planspiel-Wettbewerb zum „Entscheidungsverhalten im Unternehmenswettbewerb"

Liebe Studentin, lieber Student,

wollten Sie nicht schon immer einmal in die Rolle eines Managers schlüpfen, der allein durch seine Entscheidungen steuert, wie erfolgreich sein Unternehmen ist?

Im Rahmen der Untersuchungsreihe unseres Lehrstuhls BWL IV zum „Entscheidungsverhalten im Unternehmenswettbewerb" haben Sie die Möglichkeit dazu! Messen Sie sich mit Ihren Kommilitoninnen und Kommilitonen und erleben Sie empirische Forschung „live"!

Schlüpfen Sie in die **Rolle des Marketing- und Vertriebsleiters eines Unternehmens**, das Fahrräder und Fahrradzubehör vertreibt. Über vier Quartale hinweg sind Sie allein für den Verkauf von Kinderfahrrädern zuständig. Der Markt für Kinderfahrräder stellt dabei ein Oligopol dar, d.h. Sie konkurrieren mit bis zu fünf anderen Unternehmen.

Ihr Ziel sollte es sein, einen **möglichst hohen Gewinn** über vier Perioden hinweg zu erzielen. Gewinner jedes Mini-Planspiels ist daher das Unternehmen, das zum Schluss die höchste Gewinnsumme aus allen vier Runden erreicht hat.

Der beste Marketing- und Vertriebsleiter aus allen im Rahmen unserer Untersuchungsreihe durchgeführten Planspielen **(ca. 200 Teilnehmer)**, d.h. der- oder diejenige, die den höchsten relativen Gewinn im Vergleich zu den jeweiligen Konkurrenten erzielt hat, **wird zum Ende der Untersuchungsreihe gekürt.**

Es können folgende **attraktive Preise** gewonnen werden:

1. Preis:	**250 Euro**
2. Preis:	**200 Euro**
3. Preis:	**150 Euro**
4. – 6. Preis:	**50 Euro**
7. – 10. Preis:	**25 Euro**

Nutzen Sie diese Chance, beim Mini-Planspiel Ihre Entscheidungskompetenz zu testen und zu trainieren, sich mit Ihren Kommilitoninnen und Kommilitonen zu messen und einen attraktiven Preis zu bekommen. Unterstützen Sie unsere Untersuchungsreihe mit Ihrer Teilnahme!

Das Mini-Planspiel findet zu verschiedenen Zeitpunkten im **B IX Raum 24** statt und dauert je nach Teilnehmerzahl ca. 1,5 bis max. 2,5 Stunden.

Folgende **Termine** sind vorerst vorgesehen: ...

Bitte geben Sie mir bei Interesse baldmöglichst Rückmeldung, ob und zu welchem Termin Sie teilnehmen können und wollen. Danke! Bitte melden Sie sich auch, wenn

Sie teilnehmen möchten, aber keiner der Termine bei Ihnen zeitlich passt. Ich halte Sie gerne über weitere Termine auf dem Laufenden! Selbstverständlich können Sie diese Informationen auch an Kommilitonen und Freunde weitergeben, die Interesse haben – das würde mich sehr freuen!

Schon jetzt vielen herzlichen Dank für Ihre Teilnahme! Wir brauchen jede und jeden von Ihnen! Es wird sich für Sie lohnen!

Bei Rückfragen stehe ich Ihnen selbstverständlich jederzeit zur Verfügung!

Mit freundlichen Grüßen

Tanja Rabl
Universität Bayreuth
Lehrstuhl BWL IV – Personalwesen und Führungslehre

Appendix B: Business Game Instructions

Appendix B1.1: High Abstract Level – English Version

Dear student,

Many thanks that you decided to take part in our business game.

Our goal is to learn more about the decision making behavior of companies in competition. With your participation, you make an important contribution to the success of our research! Thank you!

Before you start, please read the following business game instructions carefully!

Your role in the business game

You are the sales and marketing chief of a company selling bicycles and bicycle equipment. Over the next four quarters, you are responsible for the sale of bicycles for children.

The business code of your company

Customer:

The central focus of our work is to offer our customers products and services that are one-of-a-kind. To achieve this, we always direct our actions towards our customers' wishes and needs.

Strategy:

We cooperate with our suppliers and customers in a fair and constructive way. We want to learn from them and tend to be one of the leading companies in our sector.

Leadership:

We emphasize the employee's personal responsibility. We lead by communication, objectives, and performance review.

Employees:

Our goal is well-trained, motivated, and dedicated employees. Everybody contributes to achieving outstanding results by his/her knowledge and his/her initiative. Therefore, everybody gets the necessary freedom of action. We attach great importance to the absolute integrity of all actors.

Communication:

We communicate with each other in an open and honest way and treat everybody with respect and confidence.

Success:

We approve of profit and see it as an essential force in assuring the success of the company. We aim at long-term and profitable growth and at a positive image in the market.

Type of market

The market for bicycles for children is an oligopoly market. You compete with up to five other companies. All of your business activities directly affect the result of the whole market. Therefore, it is not without risk to try to obtain an advantage by price-cutting. There is the danger that the other companies follow your strategy so that you may end up having a price war with very low prices harming all companies. That's why it is not surprising that for companies in "real" oligopoly markets price competition plays a subordinate role. Rather they try to be successful in the competition by creating a certain product image. They take great efforts to make their product unique in the customers' eyes. Advertisement supports these efforts.

The decisions you have to make

In each of the four periods – each representing a quarter of the year –, you have to take the following decisions:

- **Selling price:** You can only choose a price between 150 and 380 euros.
- **Expenses for advertisement:** By undertaking advertising efforts like, for example, posters or television and radio commercials, you aim at making your product attractive for your customers.
- **Expenses for product improvement:** By improving the quality of your products, you try to be better than your competitors.
- **Expenses for customer service:** These expenses serve to satisfy your customers by quick and low-priced service.
- **Expenses for sales promotion:** These shall offer the customers incentives to decide on buying the product, for example, gift certificates, presents, raffles, guarantee items, or promotional gifts.

These expenses are summarized as "sales expenses."

Furthermore, in each period you are asked whether you desire market research or not. Paying 3,000 euros, you get information on the prices of your competitors and can compare their sales expenses with yours.

Your goal

Your goal should be to achieve the highest possible profit after the expiration of the four periods. Thus, it is not the profit achieved in each single period that is important, but rather the profit achieved in sum at the end of the business game. Therefore, the winner of the business game is the company that achieved the highest profit at the end of the business game.

The sales and marketing chief who is performing best out of all approximately 200 participants, that means, the sales and marketing chief who achieves the highest profit compared to the competitors, will be named at the end of our studies.

You can win the following prizes:

1st place:	250 euros
2nd place:	200 euros
3rd place:	150 euros
4th to 6th place:	50 euros
7th to 10th place:	25 euros

How to calculate the profit

The profit is calculated as follows:

Revenue (= selling price x sales volume)

- variable costs (production costs = costs per unit x quantity; basic value for the costs per unit: 150 euros; increase of 5 euros every quarter)

- fixed costs (sales expenses + 12,000 euros general costs of administration + if so: 3000 euros market research)

= profit

The business game has one simplification: Your company is selling as many units as it produces. You do not have a stock that causes extra costs. Furthermore, you do not have to decide each quarter on the number of units you produce.

Market demand

The expected values for the total market demand in each quarter of the business game are:

1st quarter: 13,000 units
2nd quarter: 14,000 units
3st quarter: 12,000 units
4th quarter: 9,000 units

How these values develop, depends on a seasonal trend regarding the product "bicycles for children"; this means, it depends on good weather. Thus, the market demand in spring and summer, in the first and second quarter, is the highest. Please keep this in mind when making your decisions.

The total market demand increases or decreases depending on the selling prices of all companies. In the extreme case that all companies have high selling prices, the total market demand is getting close to zero. The customers are holding off on their buying decision or are buying a different product.

Moreover, the total market demand is affected by the expenses for advertisement of all companies. Although expenses for advertisement tend to increase the market demand, this only applies to a certain point. Too much advertisement does not have a positive effect on sales anymore, but has no effect at all.

Your market share based on price and sales expenses

For the company you are representing, just having a high market demand is not enough. It is important which share of this market demand you can gain. On the one hand, this share depends on how much your price differs from those of your competitors. This market share, which is due to the selling price, will equal zero in one period if your selling price differs more than 100 euros from the lowest of all selling prices. Thus, an extremely high selling price will be punished.

But the share of the market demand your company can achieve does not only depend on the selling price. Your expenses for advertisement, product improvement, customer service, and sales promotion play an important role as well. To simplify the game, it is assumed that the sales expenses always have the same effect. The problem in deciding on the sum of expenses is that there only will be a positive effect in favor of your bicycles for children if your competitors do not make the same decision. When calculating your market share for each period based on the sales expenses, the single activities are not considered equally but with decreasing weight: advertisement, product improvement, sales promotion, customer service. Thus, when spending the same amount, expenses for advertisement have the biggest effect, expenses for customer service the lowest effect. If your selling price is more than 100 euros higher than the lowest of all selling prices, the calculated market share of your company is cut down to one quarter. So it is not possible to get an extremely high selling price accepted by spending a large amount of sales expenses.

The quantity of sales is calculated considering the market share based on the price and the market share based on the sales expenses. The market share based on the price is considered with double weight than the market share based on sales expenses.

The revenue is the result of multiplying the selling price with the sales volume.

And now you can start!

Now you know what you are in for in this business game. If there are any questions, please ask the instructor of the business game now. We wish you good luck in making your decisions and a lot of fun and success in the business game!

Appendix B1.2: High Abstract Level – German Version

Liebe Studentin, lieber Student,

vielen herzlichen Dank, dass Sie sich für die Teilnahme an unserem Planspiel entschieden haben.

Unser Anliegen ist es, mit diesem Planspiel das Entscheidungsverhalten im Unternehmenswettbewerb näher zu untersuchen. Sie leisten mit Ihrer Teilnahme einen entscheidenden Beitrag! Danke!

Bitte lesen Sie sich zunächst die folgenden Planspielinstruktionen sorgfältig durch!

Ihre Rolle im Planspiel

Im Planspiel sind Sie Marketing- und Vertriebsleiter eines Unternehmens, das Fahrräder und Fahrradzubehör vertreibt. In den nächsten vier Quartalen sind Sie für den Verkauf von Kinderfahrrädern zuständig.

Das Leitbild Ihres Unternehmens

Kunde:

Im Mittelpunkt unserer Arbeit steht das Streben, unseren Kunden Produkte und Dienstleistungen mit einzigartigen Vorteilen anzubieten. Dazu richten wir unser Denken und Handeln an den Wünschen und Bedürfnissen unserer Kunden aus.

Strategie:

Wir arbeiten konstruktiv, fair und partnerschaftlich mit unseren Lieferanten und Kunden zusammen. Wir wollen von Ihnen lernen und in der Bewertung zu den Besten im Wettbewerbsvergleich gehören.

Führung:

Wir betonen die Eigenverantwortlichkeit des Mitarbeiters. Wir führen mittels Gespräch, Zielvereinbarung und Erfolgskontrolle.

Mitarbeiter:

Wir wollen gut ausgebildete, motivierte und engagierte Mitarbeiter. Jeder von uns trägt mit seinem Wissen und seiner Initiative eigenverantwortlich zu einem hochwertigen Ergebnis bei und erhält den dafür erforderlichen Handlungsrahmen. Dabei legen wir Wert auf die absolute Integrität aller handelnden Personen.

Kommunikation:

Wir sprechen offen und ehrlich miteinander und gehen vertrauensvoll und verantwortungsbewusst miteinander um.

Erfolg:

Wir bejahen den Gewinn und sehen in ihm die treibende Kraft zur Unternehmenssicherung. Wir streben ein langfristiges und profitables Wachstum und eine positive Wahrnehmung unseres Unternehmens im Markt an.

Die Marktform

Der Markt für Kinderfahrräder stellt ein Oligopol dar. Sie konkurrieren mit bis zu fünf anderen Unternehmen. Alle Handlungen Ihres Unternehmens wirken sich unmittelbar auf das Marktergebnis aus. Alle Versuche, durch Preissenkungen einen Vorteil zu erzielen, sind daher etwas riskant. Es besteht nämlich die Gefahr, dass die anderen Unternehmen nachziehen, vielleicht sogar übermäßig reagieren, so dass es zu einem Preiskampf mit übermäßig niedrigen Preisen kommt, der allen Unternehmen schadet. Daher ist es nicht überraschend, dass bei „echten" Oligopolen der Preiswettbewerb nicht dominiert. Vielmehr versucht man sich durch ein entsprechendes Produktimage von der Konkurrenz abzusetzen. Die Unternehmen machen daher große Anstrengungen, um ihr Produkt in den Augen der Nachfrager zu einer Besonderheit zu machen. Eine wichtige Unterstützungsfunktion kommt dabei der Werbung zu.

Die von Ihnen zu treffenden Entscheidungen

In jeder der vier Perioden, die Sie als Vierteljahre eines Geschäftsjahres verstehen können, haben Sie folgende Entscheidungen zu treffen:

- **Preis:** Dieser darf nur einen Wert zwischen 150 und 380 Euro annehmen.

- **Ausgaben für Werbung:** Über Werbemaßnahmen soll Ihr Produkt für den Kunden attraktiv gemacht werden, z.B. über Plakate, Werbespots in Radio und Fernsehen.

- **Ausgaben für Produktverbesserung:** Dies sind Aufwendungen Ihres Unternehmens, um sich durch höhere Qualität von der Konkurrenz abzuheben.

- **Ausgaben für Kundendienst:** Diese dienen dazu, durch schnelle und kostengünstige Betreuung die Kunden zufrieden zu stellen.

- **Ausgaben für Verkaufsförderung:** Diese sollen Kunden Anreize bieten, sich für den Kauf eines Produkts zu entschließen, z.B. Gutscheine, Geschenke, Gewinnspiele, Garantieleistungen oder Werbegeschenke.

Diese Ausgaben werden unter dem Namen „Vertriebsausgaben" zusammengefasst.

Außerdem werden Sie in jeder Periode gefragt, ob Sie Marktforschung wünschen. Für ein Entgelt von 3.000 Euro erhalten Sie dabei Informationen über die Preise der anderen Unternehmen und können deren Vertriebsausgaben mit Ihren eigenen vergleichen.

Ihr Ziel

Ihr Ziel sollte es sein, einen möglichst hohen Gewinn über die vier Perioden zu erzielen. Es kommt also nicht auf den Gewinn in der jeweiligen Runde an, sondern auf die Gewinnsumme aus allen vier Perioden. Gewinner dieses Planspiels ist daher das Unternehmen, das zum Schluss die höchste Gewinnsumme aus allen vier Runden erreicht hat.

Der beste Marketing- und Vertriebsleiter aus allen im Rahmen der Untersuchungsreihe durchgeführten Planspielen (ca. 200 Teilnehmer), d.h. der- oder diejenige, die den höchsten relativen Gewinn im Vergleich zu den jeweiligen Konkurrenten erzielt hat, wird zum Ende der Untersuchungsreihe gekürt.

Es können folgende Preise gewonnen werden:

1. Preis:	250 Euro
2. Preis:	200 Euro
3. Preis:	150 Euro
4. – 6. Preis:	50 Euro
7. – 10. Preis:	25 Euro

Die Berechnung des Gewinns

Der Gewinn errechnet sich dabei folgendermaßen:

Erlös (= Verkaufspreis x Absatzmenge)

- variable Kosten (Herstellungskosten = Kosten je Stück x Menge; Ausgangswert für Kosten je Stück: 150 Euro; Anstieg um je 5 Euro pro Periode)

- fixe Kosten (Vertriebsausgaben + allgemeine Verwaltungskosten von 12.000 Euro + ggf. Marktforschung für 3.000 Euro)

= Gewinn

Eine Vereinfachung sieht das Planspiel dadurch vor, dass Ihr Unternehmen genau so viel herstellt, wie es auch absetzt. Es gibt daher kein Lager mit entsprechenden Kosten. Außerdem müssen Sie nicht in jeder Periode über die Fertigungsmenge entscheiden.

Die Marktnachfrage

Für jede Periode im Planspiel liegen Erfahrungswerte über die Gesamtnachfrage vor:

Periode 1:	13.000 Stück
Periode 2:	14.000 Stück
Periode 3:	12.000 Stück
Periode 4:	9.000 Stück

Den Verlauf dieser Werte kann man als Saison-Entwicklung auffassen, die für das Produkt „Kinderfahrrad" gilt, bei dem es auf schönes Wetter ankommt. Daher ist im Frühjahr und Sommer, d.h. in den Quartalen 1 und 2, die Nachfrage am höchsten. Dies muss bei den Entscheidungen berücksichtigt werden.

Diese Gesamtnachfrage wird jedoch erhöht oder vermindert, je nach den Produktpreisen aller Unternehmen. Im Extremfall hoher Preise aller Unternehmen wird sich die Nachfrage sogar dem Wert Null nähern, da Verbraucher den Kauf verschieben oder auf ein anderes Produkt ausweichen.

Die gesamte Marktnachfrage wird darüber hinaus von den Ausgaben für Werbung aller Unternehmen beeinflusst. Wenn die Ausgaben für Werbung auch tendenziell die Marktnachfrage erhöhen, so gilt dies dennoch nur bis zu einem gewissen Sättigungsniveau. Übermäßig viel Werbung beeinflusst ab einer bestimmten Größenordnung den Absatz nicht mehr positiv, sondern verpufft wirkungslos.

Ihr Marktanteil aufgrund von Preis und Vertriebsausgaben

Für das Unternehmen, das Sie vertreten, ist mit einer hohen Marktnachfrage noch nicht viel gewonnen. Entscheidend ist nämlich, welchen Anteil der Marktnachfrage Sie an sich ziehen. Dieser Anteil ist zum einen vom Abstand Ihres Preises zu den Preisen aller konkurrierenden Unternehmen abhängig. Dieser Marktanteil aufgrund des Preises wird bei der Periodenabrechnung auf Null gesetzt, wenn Ihr Unternehmen mehr als 100 Euro vom niedrigsten Preis aller Unternehmen abweicht. Somit wird ein exotisch hoher Preis massiv bestraft.

Der Anteil Ihrer Unternehmung an der Nachfrage ist allerdings nicht nur vom Preis abhängig. Auch Ihre Ausgaben für Werbung, Produktverbesserung, Kundendienst und Verkaufsförderung spielen eine große Rolle. Zur Vereinfachung wird hier angenommen, dass auf Grund der Vertriebsausgaben immer der gleiche Effekt erreicht wird. Das Problem bei Ihrer Entscheidung über die Höhe dieser Ausgaben besteht darin, dass ein Einfluss zugunsten Ihrer Kinderfahrräder nur dann entsteht, wenn die Konkurrenz nicht dasselbe tut. Die einzelnen Aktivitäten werden bei der Periodenberechnung Ihres Marktanteils aufgrund der Vertriebsausgaben unterschiedlich stark berücksichtigt, und zwar in folgender Reihenfolge bei abnehmendem Gewicht: Werbung, Produktverbesserung, Verkaufsförderung, Kundendienst. Demnach wirken sich bei gleichem Betrag die Ausgaben für Werbung am meisten und die Ausgaben für Kundendienst am wenigsten aus. Sollte Ihr Preis den niedrigsten Preis aller Unternehmen um mehr als 100 Euro überschreiten, wird der errechnete Anteil Ihres Unternehmens auf ein Viertel des ursprünglichen Werts gekürzt. Damit wird erreicht, dass ein übermäßig hoher Preis nicht durch massiven Einsatz der Vertriebsausgaben durchgesetzt werden kann.

Aus den beiden Anteilen an der Marktnachfrage aufgrund des Preises und aufgrund der Vertriebsausgaben jedes Unternehmens wird die Absatzmenge errechnet. Dabei wird jedoch der Anteil wegen der Preisdifferenz etwa doppelt so stark berücksichtigt wie der Anteil an den Vertriebskosten.

Der Erlös ergibt sich schließlich aus der abgesetzten Menge, multipliziert mit dem jeweiligen Preis.

Und jetzt geht's los!

Sie wissen jetzt, was Sie im Planspiel erwartet. Sollten Sie noch Fragen haben, so wenden Sie sich bitte jetzt an die Spielleitung. Wir wünschen Ihnen gute Entscheidungen sowie viel Spaß und Erfolg beim Planspiel!

Appendix B2.1: Low Abstract Level – English Version

Dear student,

Many thanks that you decided to take part in our business game.

Our goal is to learn more about the decision making behavior of companies in competition. With your participation, you make an important contribution to the success of our research! Thank you!

Before you start, please read the following business game instructions carefully!

Your role in the business game

You are the sales and marketing chief of a company selling bicycles and bicycle equipment. Over the next four quarters, you are responsible for the sale of bicycles for children.

The business code of your company

Customer:

The central focus of our work is to offer our customers products and services that are one-of-a-kind. To achieve this, we always direct our actions towards our customers' wishes and needs.

Strategy:

We cooperate with our suppliers and customers in a fair and constructive way. We want to learn from them and tend to be one of the leading companies in our sector.

Leadership:

We emphasize the employee's personal responsibility. We lead by communication, objectives, and performance review.

Employees:

Our goal is well-trained, motivated, and dedicated employees. Everybody contributes to achieving outstanding results by his/her knowledge and his/her initiative. There-fore, everybody gets the necessary freedom of action. We attach great importance to the absolute integrity of all actors (that means, for example, mutual respect and honesty, law-abiding behavior, no corruption, secrecy in dealing with company inter-nals, data protection and data security).

Communication:

We communicate with each other in an open and honest way and treat everybody with respect and confidence.

Success:

We approve of profit and see it as an essential force in assuring the success of the company. We aim at long-term and profitable growth and at a positive image in the market.

Type of market

The market for bicycles for children is an oligopoly market. You compete with up to five other companies. All of your business activities directly affect the result of the whole market. Therefore, it is not without risk to try to obtain an advantage by price-cutting. There is the danger that the other companies follow your strategy so that you may end up having a price war with very low prices harming all companies. That's why it is not surprising that for companies in "real" oligopoly markets price competition plays a subordinate role. Rather they try to be successful in the competition by creating a certain product image. They take great efforts to make their product unique in the customers' eyes. Advertisement supports these efforts.

The decisions you have to make

In each of the four periods – each representing a quarter of the year –, you have to take the following decisions:

- **Selling price:** You can only choose a price between 150 and 380 euros.

- **Expenses for advertisement:** By undertaking advertising efforts like, for example, posters or television and radio commercials, you aim at making your product attractive for your customers.

- **Expenses for product improvement:** By improving the quality of your products, you try to be better than your competitors.

- **Expenses for customer service:** These expenses serve to satisfy your customers by quick and low-priced service.

- **Expenses for sales promotion:** These shall offer the customers incentives to decide on buying the product, for example, gift certificates, presents, raffles, guarantee items, or promotional gifts.

These expenses are summarized as "sales expenses."

Furthermore, in each period you are asked whether you desire market research or not. Paying 3,000 euros, you get information on the prices of your competitors and can compare their sales expenses with yours.

Your goal

Your goal should be to achieve the highest possible profit after the expiration of the four periods. Thus, it is not the profit achieved in each single period that is important, but rather the profit achieved in sum at the end of the business game. Therefore, the winner of the business game is the company that achieved the highest profit at the end of the business game.

The sales and marketing chief who is performing best out of all approximately 200 participants, that means, the sales and marketing chief who achieves the highest profit compared to the competitors, will be named at the end of our studies.

You can win the following prizes:

1st place:	250 euros
2nd place:	200 euros
3rd place:	150 euros
4th to 6th place:	50 euros
7th to 10th place:	25 euros

How to calculate the profit

The profit is calculated as follows:

Revenue (= selling price x sales volume)

-   variable costs (production costs = costs per unit x quantity; basic value for the costs per unit: 150 euros; increase of 5 euros every quarter)

-   fixed costs (sales expenses + 12,000 euros general costs of administration + if so: 3,000 euros market research)

= profit

The business game has one simplification: Your company is selling as many units as it produces. You do not have a stock that causes extra costs. Furthermore, you do not have to decide each quarter on the number of units you produce.

Market demand

The expected values for the total market demand in each quarter of the business game are:

1st quarter: 13,000 units
2nd quarter: 14,000 units
3st quarter: 12,000 units
4th quarter: 9,000 units

How these values develop, depends on a seasonal trend regarding the product "bicycles for children"; this means, it depends on good weather. Thus, the market demand in spring and summer, in the first and second quarter, is the highest. Please keep this in mind when making your decisions.

The total market demand increases or decreases depending on the selling prices of all companies. In the extreme case that all companies have high selling prices, the total market demand is getting close to zero. The customers are holding off on their buying decision or are buying a different product.

Moreover, the total market demand is affected by the expenses for advertisement of all companies. Although expenses for advertisement tend to increase the market demand, this only applies to a certain point. Too much advertisement does not have a positive effect on sales anymore, but has no effect at all.

Your market share based on price and sales expenses

For the company you are representing, just having a high market demand is not enough. It is important which share of this market demand you can gain. On the one hand, this share depends on how much your price differs from those of your competitors. This market share, which is due to the selling price, will equal zero in one period if your selling price differs more than 100 euros from the lowest of all selling prices. Thus, an extremely high selling price will be punished.

But the share of the market demand your company can achieve does not only depend on the selling price. Your expenses for advertisement, product improvement, customer service, and sales promotion play an important role as well. To simplify the game, it is assumed that the sales expenses always have the same effect. The problem in deciding on the sum of expenses is that there only will be a positive effect in favor of your bicycles for children if your competitors do not make the same decision. When calculating your market share for each period based on the sales expenses, the single activities are not considered equally but with decreasing weight: advertisement, product improvement, sales promotion, customer service. Thus, when spending the same amount, expenses for advertisement have the biggest effect, expenses for customer service the lowest effect. If your selling price is more than 100 euros higher than the lowest of all selling prices, the calculated market share of your company is cut down to one quarter. So it is not possible to get an extremely high selling price accepted by spending a large amount of sales expenses.

The quantity of sales is calculated considering the market share based on the price and the market share based on the sales expenses. The market share based on the price is considered with double weight than the market share based on sales expenses.

The revenue is the result of multiplying the selling price with the sales volume.

And now you can start!

Now you know what you are in for in this business game. If there are any questions,please ask the instructor of the business game now. We wish you good luck in making your decisions and a lot of fun and success in the business game!

Appendix B2.2: Low Abstract Level – German Version

Liebe Studentin, lieber Student,

vielen herzlichen Dank, dass Sie sich für die Teilnahme an unserem Planspiel entschieden haben.

Unser Anliegen ist es, mit diesem Planspiel das Entscheidungsverhalten im Unternehmenswettbewerb näher zu untersuchen. Sie leisten mit Ihrer Teilnahme einen entscheidenden Beitrag! Danke!

Bitte lesen Sie sich zunächst die folgenden Planspielinstruktionen sorgfältig durch!

Ihre Rolle im Planspiel

Im Planspiel sind Sie Marketing- und Vertriebsleiter eines Unternehmens, das Fahrräder und Fahrradzubehör vertreibt. In den nächsten vier Quartalen sind Sie für den Verkauf von Kinderfahrrädern zuständig.

Das Leitbild Ihres Unternehmens

Kunde:

Im Mittelpunkt unserer Arbeit steht das Streben, unseren Kunden Produkte und Dienstleistungen mit einzigartigen Vorteilen anzubieten. Dazu richten wir unser Denken und Handeln an den Wünschen und Bedürfnissen unserer Kunden aus.

Strategie:

Wir arbeiten konstruktiv, fair und partnerschaftlich mit unseren Lieferanten und Kunden zusammen. Wir wollen von Ihnen lernen und in der Bewertung zu den Besten im Wettbewerbsvergleich gehören.

Führung:

Wir betonen die Eigenverantwortlichkeit des Mitarbeiters. Wir führen mittels Gespräch, Zielvereinbarung und Erfolgskontrolle.

Mitarbeiter:

Wir wollen gut ausgebildete, motivierte und engagierte Mitarbeiter. Jeder von uns trägt mit seinem Wissen und seiner Initiative eigenverantwortlich zu einem hochwertigen Ergebnis bei und erhält den dafür erforderlichen Handlungsrahmen. Dabei legen wir Wert auf die absolute Integrität aller handelnden Personen (d.h. z.B. gegenseitiger Respekt und Ehrlichkeit, gesetzestreues Verhalten, keine Korruption, verschwiegener Umgang mit Firmeninterna, Datenschutz und Datensicherheit).

Kommunikation:

Wir sprechen offen und ehrlich miteinander und gehen vertrauensvoll und verantwortungsbewusst miteinander um.

Erfolg:

Wir bejahen den Gewinn und sehen in ihm die treibende Kraft zur Unternehmenssicherung. Wir streben ein langfristiges und profitables Wachstum und eine positive Wahrnehmung unseres Unternehmens im Markt an.

Die Marktform

Der Markt für Kinderfahrräder stellt ein Oligopol dar. Sie konkurrieren mit bis zu fünf anderen Unternehmen. Alle Handlungen Ihres Unternehmens wirken sich unmittelbar auf das Marktergebnis aus. Alle Versuche, durch Preissenkungen einen Vorteil zu erzielen, sind daher etwas riskant. Es besteht nämlich die Gefahr, dass die anderen Unternehmen nachziehen, vielleicht sogar übermäßig reagieren, so dass es zu einem Preiskampf mit übermäßig niedrigen Preisen kommt, der allen Unternehmen schadet. Daher ist es nicht überraschend, dass bei „echten" Oligopolen der Preiswettbewerb nicht dominiert. Vielmehr versucht man sich durch ein entsprechendes Produktimage von der Konkurrenz abzusetzen. Die Unternehmen machen daher große Anstrengungen, um ihr Produkt in den Augen der Nachfrager zu einer Besonderheit zu machen. Eine wichtige Unterstützungsfunktion kommt dabei der Werbung zu.

Die von Ihnen zu treffenden Entscheidungen

In jeder der vier Perioden, die Sie als Vierteljahre eines Geschäftsjahres verstehen können, haben Sie folgende Entscheidungen zu treffen:

- **Preis:** Dieser darf nur einen Wert zwischen 150 und 380 Euro annehmen.

- **Ausgaben für Werbung:** Über Werbemaßnahmen soll Ihr Produkt für den Kunden attraktiv gemacht werden, z.B. über Plakate, Werbespots in Radio und Fernsehen.

- **Ausgaben für Produktverbesserung:** Dies sind Aufwendungen Ihres Unternehmens, um sich durch höhere Qualität von der Konkurrenz abzuheben.

- **Ausgaben für Kundendienst:** Diese dienen dazu, durch schnelle und kostengünstige Betreuung die Kunden zufrieden zu stellen.

- **Ausgaben für Verkaufsförderung:** Diese sollen Kunden Anreize bieten, sich für den Kauf eines Produkts zu entschließen, z.B. Gutscheine, Geschenke, Gewinnspiele, Garantieleistungen oder Werbegeschenke.

Diese Ausgaben werden unter dem Namen „Vertriebsausgaben" zusammengefasst.

Außerdem werden Sie in jeder Periode gefragt, ob Sie Marktforschung wünschen. Für ein Entgelt von 3.000 Euro erhalten Sie dabei Informationen über die Preise der anderen Unternehmen und können deren Vertriebsausgaben mit Ihren eigenen vergleichen.

Ihr Ziel

Ihr Ziel sollte es sein, einen möglichst hohen Gewinn über die vier Perioden zu erzielen. Es kommt also nicht auf den Gewinn in der jeweiligen Runde an, sondern auf die Gewinnsumme aus allen vier Perioden. Gewinner dieses Planspiels ist daher das Unternehmen, das zum Schluss die höchste Gewinnsumme aus allen vier Runden erreicht hat.

Der beste Marketing- und Vertriebsleiter aus allen im Rahmen der Untersuchungsreihe durchgeführten Planspielen (ca. 200 Teilnehmer), d.h. der- oder diejenige, die den höchsten relativen Gewinn im Vergleich zu den jeweiligen Konkurrenten erzielt hat, wird zum Ende der Untersuchungsreihe gekürt.

Es können folgende Preise gewonnen werden:

1. Preis:	250 Euro
2. Preis:	200 Euro
3. Preis:	150 Euro
4. – 6. Preis:	50 Euro
7. – 10. Preis:	25 Euro

Die Berechnung des Gewinns

Der Gewinn errechnet sich dabei folgendermaßen:

Erlös (= Verkaufspreis x Absatzmenge)

– variable Kosten (Herstellungskosten = Kosten je Stück x Menge; Ausgangswert für Kosten je Stück: 150 Euro; Anstieg um je 5 Euro pro Periode)

– fixe Kosten (Vertriebsausgaben + allgemeine Verwaltungskosten von 12.000 Euro + ggf. Marktforschung für 3.000 Euro)

= Gewinn

Eine Vereinfachung sieht das Planspiel dadurch vor, dass Ihr Unternehmen genau so viel herstellt, wie es auch absetzt. Es gibt daher kein Lager mit entsprechenden Kosten. Außerdem müssen Sie nicht in jeder Periode über die Fertigungsmenge entscheiden.

Die Marktnachfrage

Für jede Periode im Planspiel liegen Erfahrungswerte über die Gesamtnachfrage vor:

Periode 1: 13.000 Stück
Periode 2: 14.000 Stück
Periode 3: 12.000 Stück
Periode 4:   9.000 Stück

Den Verlauf dieser Werte kann man als Saison-Entwicklung auffassen, die für das Produkt „Kinderfahrrad" gilt, bei dem es auf schönes Wetter ankommt. Daher ist im

Frühjahr und Sommer, d.h. in den Quartalen 1 und 2, die Nachfrage am höchsten. Dies muss bei den Entscheidungen berücksichtigt werden.

Diese Gesamtnachfrage wird jedoch erhöht oder vermindert, je nach den Produktpreisen aller Unternehmen. Im Extremfall hoher Preise aller Unternehmen wird sich die Nachfrage sogar dem Wert Null nähern, da Verbraucher den Kauf verschieben oder auf ein anderes Produkt ausweichen.

Die gesamte Marktnachfrage wird darüber hinaus von den Ausgaben für Werbung aller Unternehmen beeinflusst. Wenn die Ausgaben für Werbung auch tendenziell die Marktnachfrage erhöhen, so gilt dies dennoch nur bis zu einem gewissen Sättigungsniveau. Übermäßig viel Werbung beeinflusst ab einer bestimmten Größenordnung den Absatz nicht mehr positiv, sondern verpufft wirkungslos.

Ihr Marktanteil aufgrund von Preis und Vertriebsausgaben

Für das Unternehmen, das Sie vertreten, ist mit einer hohen Marktnachfrage noch nicht viel gewonnen. Entscheidend ist nämlich, welchen Anteil der Marktnachfrage Sie an sich ziehen. Dieser Anteil ist zum einen vom Abstand Ihres Preises zu den Preisen aller konkurrierenden Unternehmen abhängig. Dieser Marktanteil aufgrund des Preises wird bei der Periodenabrechnung auf Null gesetzt, wenn Ihr Unternehmen mehr als 100 Euro vom niedrigsten Preis aller Unternehmen abweicht. Somit wird ein exotisch hoher Preis massiv bestraft.

Der Anteil Ihrer Unternehmung an der Nachfrage ist allerdings nicht nur vom Preis abhängig. Auch Ihre Ausgaben für Werbung, Produktverbesserung, Kundendienst und Verkaufsförderung spielen eine große Rolle. Zur Vereinfachung wird hier angenommen, dass auf Grund der Vertriebsausgaben immer der gleiche Effekt erreicht wird. Das Problem bei Ihrer Entscheidung über die Höhe dieser Ausgaben besteht darin, dass ein Einfluss zugunsten Ihrer Kinderfahrräder nur dann entsteht, wenn die Konkurrenz nicht dasselbe tut. Die einzelnen Aktivitäten werden bei der Periodenberechnung Ihres Marktanteils aufgrund der Vertriebsausgaben unterschiedlich stark berücksichtigt, und zwar in folgender Reihenfolge bei abnehmendem Gewicht: Werbung, Produktverbesserung, Verkaufsförderung, Kundendienst. Demnach wirken sich bei gleichem Betrag die Ausgaben für Werbung am meisten und die Ausgaben für Kundendienst am wenigsten aus. Sollte Ihr Preis den niedrigsten Preis aller Unternehmen um mehr als 100 Euro überschreiten, wird der errechnete Anteil Ihres Unternehmens auf ein Viertel des ursprünglichen Werts gekürzt. Damit wird erreicht, dass ein übermäßig hoher Preis nicht durch massiven Einsatz der Vertriebsausgaben durchgesetzt werden kann.

Aus den beiden Anteilen an der Marktnachfrage aufgrund des Preises und aufgrund der Vertriebsausgaben jedes Unternehmens wird die Absatzmenge errechnet. Dabei wird jedoch der Anteil wegen der Preisdifferenz etwa doppelt so stark berücksichtigt wie der Anteil an den Vertriebskosten.

Der Erlös ergibt sich schließlich aus der abgesetzten Menge, multipliziert mit dem jeweiligen Preis.

Und jetzt geht's los!

Sie wissen jetzt, was Sie im Planspiel erwartet. Sollten Sie noch Fragen haben, so wenden Sie sich bitte jetzt an die Spielleitung. Wir wünschen Ihnen gute Entscheidungen sowie viel Spaß und Erfolg beim Planspiel!

Appendix C: Decision Making Sheet

Appendix C1: English Version

Dear sales and marketing chief of the company ....
(Please insert here your participation code for the business game!)!

Please write down *legibly* in the table below the decisions you make in each quarter.

First, make your decisions for the first quarter and then pass the decision making sheet to the instructor of the business game. She will feed the decisions of all companies into the computer, which calculates the result for the first quarter. After that, you get back your decision making sheet. ***Please pay attention if there are any enclosures!*** Then, make your decisions for the second quarter, pass the decision making sheet to the instructor, and so on. For the following quarters, the same procedure applies.

	1st quarter	2nd quarter	3rd quarter	4th quarter
Selling price *(Please insert an amount between 150 and 380 euros!)*				
Expenses for advertisement *(Please insert an amount!)*				
Expenses for product improvement *(Please insert an amount!)*				
Expenses for sales promotion *(Please insert an amount!)*				
Expenses for customer service *(Please insert an amount!)*				
Market research *(Please tick the box if desired!)*				
Other *(Please **give information here only when asked** during the business game; **tick the box if** your decision is "yes"; please write down your reasons for your decision, no matter what it looks like.)*	☐ Reason:	☐ Reason:	☐ Reason:	☐ Reason:

Appendix C2: German Version

Liebe/r Marketing- und Vertriebsleiter/in des Unternehmens ....
(Bitte geben Sie hier Ihren Planspiel-Teilnehmercode an!)!

Bitte tragen Sie in der unten stehenden Tabelle *leserlich* für jedes Quartal die von Ihnen getroffenen Entscheidungen ein.

Treffen Sie zunächst Ihre Entscheidungen für das erste Quartal und geben Sie dann Ihren Entscheidungsbogen an die Spielleitung. Diese gibt die Entscheidungen aller Unternehmen in den Computer ein und lässt die Ergebnisse des ersten Quartals berechnen. Sie bekommen dann Ihren Entscheidungsbogen zurück. ***Bitte beachten Sie etwaige Anlagen!*** Treffen Sie dann Ihre Entscheidung für das zweite Quartal, geben Sie Ihren Entscheidungsbogen an die Spielleitung usw. Für die folgenden Quartale gilt jeweils dasselbe Vorgehen.

	1. Quartal	2. Quartal	3. Quartal	4. Quartal
Verkaufspreis *(Bitte Betrag zwischen 150 und 380 Euro angeben!)*				
Ausgaben für Werbung *(Bitte Betrag angeben!)*				
Ausgaben für Produktverbesserung *(Bitte Betrag angeben!)*				
Ausgaben für Verkaufsförderung *(Bitte Betrag angeben!)*				
Ausgaben für Produktverbesserung *(Bitte Betrag angeben!)*				
Marktforschung *(Bitte ankreuzen, wenn gewünscht!)*				
Sonstiges *(Bitte **hier nur Angaben** machen, **wenn** Sie im Laufe des Planspiels dazu **aufgefordert** werden; **Kreuzen Sie das Kästchen an, wenn** Ihre Entscheidung "ja" ist; **begründen Sie Ihre Entscheidung, egal wie Sie** ausfällt!)*	☐ Begründung:	☐ Begründung:	☐ Begründung:	☐ Begründung:

Appendix D: The Corrupt Offer (Passive Corruption)

Appendix D1.1: Condition 1, Low Bribe – English Version

An offer of a large customer

Dear sales and marketing chief,

While you are trying to make your decisions for the upcoming quarter, the phone rings:

It's Andreas Renner. He is the chief buyer of a large customer in the sector. You successfully collaborated with him a couple of times before. Meanwhile, a good private acquaintanceship developed from this business relationship: You share the passion of cycling. Several times you jointly went in for a tour, which you both always enjoyed a lot. You start talking with each other about the last bicycle tours and the new developments in the market of racing bicycles. Andreas Renner tells you about his wish to buy a new racing bicycle. As this is no cheap undertaking, he asks for your advice. Of course, you can give him a recommendation: The latest version is perfect for him and regarding the equipment, there are also some nice, but expensive, pieces.

After this little conversation among you hobby racing cyclists, Andreas Renner comes to business: Once again, his company wants to place an order, which is always strongly desired by all companies. This time, he wants to buy 1,000 bicycles for children, paying a selling price that would result in a profit of 50,000 euros after the deduction of production costs. As he had been collaborating with you many times, as he was convinced of the quality of your bicycles, and as to boot, he knew you very well, he first would like to make this offer to you. If you accepted, you could return the favor with a racing bicycle of the latest version and new equipment. The profit probably would be booked after the expiration of the fourth quarter.

You tell Andreas Renner that you are going to think about his offer and that you will give him a call after you make your decision.

Now it's your turn to decide. Do you want to accept the offer and give him a racing bicycle worth 5,000 euros in return? **If so, please check the box "other"** on the decision making sheet below the quarter you are planning right now. **If not, don't check the box. But in any case, please briefly give the reasons for your decision!**

The additional profit of 50,000 euros will not appear in the next period settlement, but in the final settlement after the fourth quarter.

Appendix D1.2: Condition 1, Low Bribe – German Version

Angebot eines Großabnehmers

Liebe/r Marketing- und Vertriebsleiter/in,

Sie sind gerade dabei, Ihre Entscheidungen für das nächste Quartal zu treffen, da klingelt das Telefon:

Andreas Renner, Einkaufsleiter eines Großabnehmers in der Branche, ist am Apparat. Sie haben schon des Öfteren mit ihm erfolgreich zusammen gearbeitet. Aus dieser Geschäftsbeziehung ist mittlerweile auch eine gute private Bekanntschaft erwachsen: Sie teilen die Liebe für den Fahrradrennsport und haben schon einige Male gemeinsame Touren unternommen, was Ihnen beiden immer großen Spaß gemacht hat. Sie tauschen sich zunächst über Ihre letzten Touren und die neusten Entwicklungen auf dem Rennrad-Markt aus. Andreas Renner will sich nämlich ein neues Rennrad zulegen und da dies kein ganz billiges Unterfangen ist, fragt er Sie um Rat. Selbstverständlich können Sie ihm da eine Empfehlung geben: Das neuste Modell ist geradezu passend für ihn, und auch bei der Rennausrüstung gibt es schöne, aber nicht ganz billige Sachen.

Nach diesem kleinen Austausch unter Ihnen Hobby-Rennfahrern kommt Andreas Renner schließlich zum Geschäftlichen: Wieder einmal habe sein Unternehmen einen Auftrag zu vergeben, der von allen Unternehmen stets heiß begehrt sei. Diesmal handele es sich um 1.000 Kinderfahrräder, die er zu einem Verkaufspreis abnehmen würde, bei dem nach Abzug der Herstellkosten 50.000 Euro Gewinn bleiben würden. Da er mit Ihnen schon öfter zusammen gearbeitet habe, von der Qualität Ihrer Fahrräder überzeugt sei und Sie noch dazu gut kenne, wende er sich mit diesem einmaligen Angebot zuerst an Sie. Wenn Sie annähmen, könnten Sie sich ja mit einem Rennrad des neusten Modelltyps und einer neuen Rennausrüstung bei ihm bedanken. Der Gewinn werde allerdings wohl erst nach Ende des vierten Quartals verbucht werden können.

Sie wollen sich dieses Angebot durch den Kopf gehen lassen und verbleiben mit Andreas Renner so, dass Sie ihn telefonisch kontaktieren, wenn Sie Ihre Entscheidung getroffen haben.

Nun ist es an Ihnen, Ihre Entscheidung zu treffen. Wollen Sie dieses Angebot des Auftrages gegen ein Rennrad (5.000 Euro) annehmen? **Wenn ja**, so **kreuzen** Sie bitte auf dem Entscheidungsbogen unter dem Quartal, das Sie gerade planen, das **Kästchen bei „Sonstiges" an. Wenn nein, lassen Sie das Kästchen frei. Begründen Sie aber bitte in jedem Falle kurz Ihre Entscheidung!**

Ihr zusätzlicher Gewinn von 50.000 Euro wird bei der nächsten Periodenabrechnung noch nicht erscheinen, sondern erst bei der Endabrechnung nach dem vierten Quartal.

Appendix D2.1: Condition 2, High Bribe – English Version

An offer of a large customer

Dear sales and marketing chief,

While you are trying to make your decisions for the upcoming quarter, the phone rings:

It's Andreas Renner. He is the chief buyer of a large customer in the sector. You successfully collaborated with him a couple of times before. Meanwhile, a good private acquaintanceship developed from this business relationship: You share the passion of cycling. Several times you jointly went in for a tour, which you both always enjoyed a lot. You start talking with each other about the last bicycle tours and the new developments in the market of racing bicycles. Andreas Renner tells you about his wish to buy a new racing bicycle. As this is no cheap undertaking, he asks for your advice. Of course, you can give him a recommendation: The latest version is perfect for him and regarding the equipment, there are also some nice, but expensive, pieces.

After this little conversation among you hobby racing cyclists, Andreas Renner comes to business: Once again, his company wants to place an order, which is always strongly desired by all companies. This time, he wants to buy 3,000 bicycles for children, paying a selling price that would result in a profit of 150,000 euros after the deduction of production costs. As he had been collaborating with you many times, as he was convinced of the quality of your bicycles, and as to boot, he knew you very well, he first would like to make this offer to you. If you accepted, you could return the favor with a racing bicycle of the latest version and new equipment. The profit probably would be booked after the expiration of the fourth quarter.

You tell Andreas Renner that you are going to think about his offer and that you will give him a call after you make your decision.

Now it's your turn to decide. Do you want to accept the offer and give him a racing bicycle worth 5,000 euros in return? **If so, please check the box "other"** on the decision making sheet below the quarter you are planning right now. **If not, don't check the box. But in any case, please briefly give the reasons for your decision!**

The additional profit of 150,000 euros will not appear in the next period settlement, but in the final settlement after the fourth quarter.

Appendix D2.2: Condition 2, High Bribe – German Version

Angebot eines Großabnehmers

Liebe/r Marketing- und Vertriebsleiter/in,

Sie sind gerade dabei, Ihre Entscheidungen für das nächste Quartal zu treffen, da klingelt das Telefon:

Andreas Renner, Einkaufsleiter eines Großabnehmers in der Branche, ist am Apparat. Sie haben schon des Öfteren mit ihm erfolgreich zusammen gearbeitet. Aus dieser Geschäftsbeziehung ist mittlerweile auch eine gute private Bekanntschaft erwachsen: Sie teilen die Liebe für den Fahrradrennsport und haben schon einige Male gemeinsame Touren unternommen, was Ihnen beiden immer großen Spaß gemacht hat. Sie tauschen sich zunächst über Ihre letzten Touren und die neusten Entwicklungen auf dem Rennrad-Markt aus. Andreas Renner will sich nämlich ein neues Rennrad zulegen und da dies kein ganz billiges Unterfangen ist, fragt er Sie um Rat. Selbstverständlich können Sie ihm da eine Empfehlung geben: Das neuste Modell ist geradezu passend für ihn, und auch bei der Rennausrüstung gibt es schöne, aber nicht ganz billige Sachen.

Nach diesem kleinen Austausch unter Ihnen Hobby-Rennfahrern kommt Andreas Renner schließlich zum Geschäftlichen: Wieder einmal habe sein Unternehmen einen Auftrag zu vergeben, der von allen Unternehmen stets heiß begehrt sei. Diesmal handele es sich um 3.000 Kinderfahrräder, die er zu einem Verkaufspreis abnehmen würde, bei dem nach Abzug der Herstellkosten 150.000 Euro Gewinn bleiben würden. Da er mit Ihnen schon öfter zusammen gearbeitet habe, von der Qualität Ihrer Fahrräder überzeugt sei und Sie noch dazu gut kenne, wende er sich mit diesem einmaligen Angebot zuerst an Sie. Wenn Sie annähmen, könnten Sie sich ja mit einem Rennrad des neusten Modelltyps und einer neuen Rennausrüstung bei ihm bedanken. Der Gewinn werde allerdings wohl erst nach Ende des vierten Quartals verbucht werden können.

Sie wollen sich dieses Angebot durch den Kopf gehen lassen und verbleiben mit Andreas Renner so, dass Sie ihn telefonisch kontaktieren, wenn Sie Ihre Entscheidung getroffen haben.

Nun ist es an Ihnen, Ihre Entscheidung zu treffen. Wollen Sie dieses Angebot des Auftrages gegen ein Rennrad (5.000 Euro) annehmen? **Wenn ja**, so **kreuzen** Sie bitte auf dem Entscheidungsbogen unter dem Quartal, das Sie gerade planen, das **Kästchen bei „Sonstiges"** an. **Wenn nein, lassen Sie das Kästchen frei. Begründen Sie aber bitte in jedem Falle kurz Ihre Entscheidung!**

Ihr zusätzlicher Gewinn von 150.000 Euro wird bei der nächsten Periodenabrechnung noch nicht erscheinen, sondern erst bei der Endabrechnung nach dem vierten Quartal.

Appendix E: The Corrupt Offer (Active Corruption)

Appendix E1.1: Condition 1, Low Bribe – English Version

The call for bids of a large customer

Dear sales and marketing chief,

While you are trying to make your decisions for the upcoming quarter, the phone rings:

It's Andreas Renner. He is the chief buyer of a large customer in the sector. You successfully collaborated with him a couple of times before. Meanwhile, a good private acquaintanceship developed from this business relationship: You share the passion of cycling. Several times you jointly went in for a tour, which you both always enjoyed a lot. You start talking with each other about the last bicycle tours and the new developments in the market of racing bicycles. Andreas Renner tells you about his wish to buy a new racing bicycle. As this is no cheap undertaking, he asks for your advice. Of course, you can give him a recommendation: The latest version is perfect for him. Your friend totally agrees, but right now he unfortunately cannot afford it because all of his financial resources are invested in the house he is building. And even for a renewal of his equipment, he hasn't any cash left at the moment, so that the fulfillment of his wish will have to wait.

After this little conversation among you hobby racing cyclists, Andreas Renner comes to business: Once again, his company is calling for bids and wants to place an order, which is always strongly desired by all companies. This time he would buy 1,000 bicycles for children from the company offering the lowest selling price. The profit probably would be booked after the expiration of the fourth quarter. As he knew you very well, he wanted to take the chance to call you. And of course, you, like your competitors, will get a written version of the call for bids. He would be very happy if your company made him a lucrative offer because he had been collaborating with you many times, because he was convinced of the quality of your bicycles, and as to boot, he knew you very well. You tell him that you are soon going to make him an offer.

Now you are thinking about what offer you can make Andreas Renner to win the bid. If you got the order, it would be an enormous advantage compared to your competitors. Given a selling price of 205 euros in the second period, a selling price of 210 euros in the third period, and a selling price of 215 euros in the fourth period, the deal would result in a profit of 50,000 euros after the deduction of production costs. Besides this low selling price, you are deliberating on whether you pitch your offer to him by giving a racing bicycle of the latest version worth 5,000 euros to him, which he cannot afford himself at the moment.

Now it's your turn to decide. Do you want to submit the offer with the low price and the racing bicycle as additional incentive? **If so, please check the box "other"** on the decision making sheet below the quarter you are planning right now. **If not, don't check the box. But in any case, please briefly give the reasons for your decision!**

The additional profit of 50,000 euros will not appear in the next period settlement, but in the final settlement after the fourth quarter.

Appendix E1.2: Condition 1, Low Bribe – German Version

Ausschreibung eines Großabnehmers

Liebe/r Marketing- und Vertriebsleiter/in,

Sie sind gerade dabei, Ihre Entscheidungen für das nächste Quartal zu treffen, da klingelt das Telefon.

Andreas Renner, Einkaufsleiter eines Großabnehmers in der Branche, ist am Apparat. Sie haben schon des Öfteren mit ihm erfolgreich zusammen gearbeitet. Aus dieser Geschäftsbeziehung ist mittlerweile auch eine gute private Bekanntschaft erwachsen: Sie teilen die Liebe für den Fahrradrennsport und haben schon einige Male gemeinsame Touren unternommen, was Ihnen beiden immer großen Spaß gemacht hat. Sie tauschen sich zunächst über Ihre letzten Touren und die neusten Entwicklungen auf dem Rennrad-Markt aus. Andreas Renner will sich nämlich ein neues Rennrad zulegen und da dies kein ganz billiges Unterfangen ist, fragt er Sie um Rat. Selbstverständlich können Sie ihm da eine Empfehlung geben: Das neuste Modell ist geradezu passend für ihn. Dem stimmt Ihr Bekannter durchweg zu, nur übersteigt es momentan leider seine finanziellen Ressourcen, die momentan komplett in den Hausbau fließen. Auch für die Erneuerung seiner Rennausrüstung habe er momentan kein Geld, sodass dies wohl oder übel erstmal warten müsse.

Nach diesem kleinen Austausch unter Ihnen Hobby-Rennfahrern kommt Andreas Renner schließlich zum Geschäftlichen: Wieder einmal habe sein Unternehmen eine Ausschreibung laufen und einen Auftrag zu vergeben, der von allen Unternehmen stets heiß begehrt sei. Diesmal handele es sich um 1.000 Kinderfahrräder, die er dem Unternehmen abnehmen würde, das den günstigen Verkaufspreis biete. Der Gewinn werde allerdings wohl erst nach Ende des vierten Quartals verbucht werden können. Da er Sie persönlich gut kenne, wollte er die Gelegenheit nutzen, Sie mal wieder anzurufen. Selbstverständlich ginge Ihnen genau wie den Konkurrenzunternehmen sein Angebot noch schriftlich zu. Er würde sich aber freuen, wenn Ihr Unternehmen ihm ein attraktives Angebot unterbreiten würde, zumal Sie ja schon öfter zusammen gearbeitet haben, er von der Qualität Ihrer Kinderfahrräder überzeugt ist und Sie noch dazu gut kenne. Sie verbleiben mit Ihm so, dass Sie ihm in Kürze auf seine Ausschreibung ein Angebot unterbreiten.

Sie überlegen nun, welches Angebot Sie Andreas Renner unterbreiten könnten, um den Kampf um die Ausschreibung zu gewinnen. Wenn Sie den Auftrag bekämen, wäre dies im Vergleich zu den Konkurrenzunternehmen ein enormer Vorteil. Bei einem Verkaufspreis von 205 Euro in Periode 2, 210 Euro in Periode 3 und 215 Euro in Periode 4 würde dies nach Abzug der Herstellkosten einen Gewinn für Ihr Unternehmen von 50.000 Euro bedeuten. Zusätzlich zu diesem günstigen Verkaufspreis überlegen Sie, ihm Ihr Angebot noch durch die Überlassung eines Rennrads des neusten Modelltyps im Wert von 5.000 Euro schmackhaft zu machen, das er sich momentan finanziell nicht leisten kann.

Nun ist es an Ihnen, Ihre Entscheidung zu treffen. Wollen Sie Ihm dieses Angebot mit dem günstigen Verkaufspreis und dem Rennrad als zusätzlichen Anreiz unterbreiten? Wenn ja, so kreuzen Sie bitte auf dem Entscheidungsbogen unter dem Quartal, das Sie gerade planen, das Kästchen bei „Sonstiges" an. Wenn nein, lassen Sie das Kästchen frei. Begründen Sie aber bitte in jedem Falle kurz Ihre Entscheidung!

Ihr zusätzlicher Gewinn von 50.000 Euro wird bei der nächsten Periodenabrechnung noch nicht erscheinen, sondern erst bei der Endabrechnung nach dem vierten Quartal.

Appendix E2.1: Condition 2, High Bribe – English Version

The call for bids of a large customer

Dear sales and marketing chief,

While you are trying to make your decisions for the upcoming quarter, the phone rings:

It's Andreas Renner. He is the chief buyer of a large customer in the sector. You successfully collaborated with him a couple of times before. Meanwhile, a good private acquaintanceship developed from this business relationship: You share the passion of cycling. Several times you jointly went in for a tour, which you both always enjoyed a lot. You start talking with each other about the last bicycle tours and the new developments in the market of racing bicycles. Andreas Renner tells you about his wish to buy a new racing bicycle. As this is no cheap undertaking, he asks for your advice. Of course, you can give him a recommendation: The latest version is perfect for him. Your friend totally agrees, but right now he unfortunately cannot afford it because all of his financial resources are invested in the house he is building. And even for a renewal of his equipment, he hasn't any cash left at the moment, so that the fulfillment of his wish will have to wait.

After this little conversation among you hobby racing cyclists, Andreas Renner comes to business: Once again, his company is calling for bids and wants to place an order, which is always strongly desired by all companies. This time he would buy 3,000 bicycles for children from the company offering the lowest selling price. The profit probably would be booked after the expiration of the fourth quarter. As he knew you very well, he wanted to take the chance to call you. And of course, you, like your competitors, will get a written version of the call for bids. He would be very happy if your company made him a lucrative offer because he had been collaborating with you many times, because he was convinced of the quality of your bicycles, and as to boot, he knew you very well. You tell him that you are soon going to make him an offer.

Now you are thinking about what offer you can make Andreas Renner to win the bid. If you got the order, it would be an enormous advantage compared to your competitors. Given a selling price of 205 euros in the second period, a selling price of 210 euros in the third period, and a selling price of 215 euros in the fourth period, the deal would result in a profit of 150,000 euros after the deduction of production costs. Besides this low selling price, you are deliberating on whether you pitch your offer to him by giving a racing bicycle of the latest version worth 5,000 euros to him, which he cannot afford himself at the moment.

Now it's your turn to decide. Do you want to submit the offer with the low price and the racing bicycle as additional incentive? **If so**, **please check the box "other"** on the decision making sheet below the quarter you are planning right now. **If not,**

don't check the box. But in any case, please briefly give the reasons for your decision!

The additional profit of 150,000 euros will not appear in the next period settlement, but in the final settlement after the fourth quarter.

Appendix E2.2: Condition 1, High Bribe – German Version

Ausschreibung eines Großabnehmers

Liebe/r Marketing- und Vertriebsleiter/in,

Sie sind gerade dabei, Ihre Entscheidungen für das nächste Quartal zu treffen, da klingelt das Telefon.

Andreas Renner, Einkaufsleiter eines Großabnehmers in der Branche, ist am Apparat. Sie haben schon des Öfteren mit ihm erfolgreich zusammen gearbeitet. Aus dieser Geschäftsbeziehung ist mittlerweile auch eine gute private Bekanntschaft erwachsen: Sie teilen die Liebe für den Fahrradrennsport und haben schon einige Male gemeinsame Touren unternommen, was Ihnen beiden immer großen Spaß gemacht hat. Sie tauschen sich zunächst über Ihre letzten Touren und die neusten Entwicklungen auf dem Rennrad-Markt aus. Andreas Renner will sich nämlich ein neues Rennrad zulegen und da dies kein ganz billiges Unterfangen ist, fragt er Sie um Rat. Selbstverständlich können Sie ihm da eine Empfehlung geben: Das neuste Modell ist geradezu passend für ihn. Dem stimmt Ihr Bekannter durchweg zu, nur übersteigt es momentan leider seine finanziellen Ressourcen, die momentan komplett in den Hausbau fließen. Auch für die Erneuerung seiner Rennausrüstung habe er momentan kein Geld, sodass dies wohl oder übel erstmal warten müsse.

Nach diesem kleinen Austausch unter Ihnen Hobby-Rennfahrern kommt Andreas Renner schließlich zum Geschäftlichen: Wieder einmal habe sein Unternehmen eine Ausschreibung laufen und einen Auftrag zu vergeben, der von allen Unternehmen stets heiß begehrt sei. Diesmal handele es sich um 3.000 Kinderfahrräder, die er dem Unternehmen abnehmen würde, das den günstigen Verkaufspreis biete. Der Gewinn werde allerdings wohl erst nach Ende des vierten Quartals verbucht werden können. Da er Sie persönlich gut kenne, wollte er die Gelegenheit nutzen, Sie mal wieder anzurufen. Selbstverständlich ginge Ihnen genau wie den Konkurrenzunternehmen sein Angebot noch schriftlich zu. Er würde sich aber freuen, wenn Ihr Unternehmen ihm ein attraktives Angebot unterbreiten würde, zumal Sie ja schon öfter zusammen gearbeitet haben, er von der Qualität Ihrer Kinderfahrräder überzeugt ist und Sie noch dazu gut kenne. Sie verbleiben mit Ihm so, dass Sie ihm in Kürze auf seine Ausschreibung ein Angebot unterbreiten.

Sie überlegen nun, welches Angebot Sie Andreas Renner unterbreiten könnten, um den Kampf um die Ausschreibung zu gewinnen. Wenn Sie den Auftrag bekämen, wäre dies im Vergleich zu den Konkurrenzunternehmen ein enormer Vorteil. Bei einem Verkaufspreis von 205 Euro in Periode 2, 210 Euro in Periode 3 und 215 Euro in Periode 4 würde dies nach Abzug der Herstellkosten einen Gewinn für Ihr Unternehmen von 150.000 Euro bedeuten. Zusätzlich zu diesem günstigen Verkaufspreis überlegen Sie, ihm Ihr Angebot noch durch die Überlassung eines Rennrads des neusten Modelltyps im Wert von 5.000 Euro schmackhaft zu machen, das er sich momentan finanziell nicht leisten kann.

Nun ist es an Ihnen, Ihre Entscheidung zu treffen. Wollen Sie Ihm dieses Angebot mit dem günstigen Verkaufspreis und dem Rennrad als zusätzlichen Anreiz unterbreiten? Wenn ja, so kreuzen Sie bitte auf dem Entscheidungsbogen unter dem Quartal, das Sie gerade planen, das Kästchen bei „Sonstiges" an. Wenn nein, lassen Sie das Kästchen frei. Begründen Sie aber bitte in jedem Falle kurz Ihre Entscheidung!

Ihr zusätzlicher Gewinn von 150.000 Euro wird bei der nächsten Periodenabrechnung noch nicht erscheinen, sondern erst bei der Endabrechnung nach dem vierten Quartal.

Appendix F: List of Items in the Standardized Questionnaire

Appendix F1: English Version

No.	Item
Desire to achieve a private or professional goal	
GD1	I have a strong wish to achieve a higher profit than my competitors in the business game.
r_GD2	For me other goals are more important in the business game than achieving a higher profit than my competitors.
GD3	I regard it desirable to perform better in the business game than my competitors.
Goal feasibility	
r_GF1	I hardly see any possibility of achieving a higher profit in the business game than my competitors.
GF2	I am convinced I am able to perform better in the business game than my competitors.
r_GF3	I regard it difficult to be more successful in the business game than my competitors.
Positive anticipated emotions	
PAE...	If I achieve a higher profit in the business game than my competitors, I will feel ...
PAE1	... happy.
PAE2	... proud.
PAE3	... surprised.
PAE4	... relieved.
Negative anticipated emotions	
NAE...	If I achieve a lower profit in the business game than my competitors, I will feel ...
NAE1	... angry.
NAE2	... ashamed.
NAE3	... disappointed.
NAE4	... depressed.

No.	Item
Intention to achieve a private or professional goal	
GI1	I am very serious in being more successful in the business game than my competitors.
GI2	I will do everything possible to perform better in the business game than my competitors.
r_GI3	I do not care whether I achieve a higher profit in the business game than my competitors or not.
Desire to achieve a private or professional goal through corrupt action	
ID1	*Passive corruption:* My desire to accept the customer's offer was strong. *Active corruption:* My desire to make the customer an offer was strong.
r_ID2	*Passive corruption:* The customer's offer left me cold. *Active corruption:* The possibility to make the customer an offer left me cold.
ID3	*Passive corruption:* I considered it attractive to accept the customer's offer. *Active corruption:* I considered it attractive to make the customer an offer.
Intention to achieve a private or professional goal through corrupt action	
r_II1	*Passive corruption:* For me, it was out of question to accept the customer's offer. *Active corruption:* For me, it was out of question to make the customer an offer.
II2	*Passive corruption:* I was sure that I would accept the customer's offer. *Active corruption:* I was sure that I would make the customer an offer.
II3	*Passive corruption:* My intention to accept the customer's offer was strong. *Active corruption:* My intention to make the customer an offer was strong

No.	Item
Attitude[1]	
AT...	*Passive corruption:* I think accepting the customer's offer is … *Active corruption:* I think making the customer an offer is …
AT1	… bad/good.
AT2	… wrong/right.
AT3	… foolish/wise.
AT4	… useless/useful.
AT5	… disadvantageous/advantageous.
AT6	… boring/exciting.
AT7	… unpleasant/pleasant.
AT8	… unattractive/attractive.
AT9	… dissatisfying/satisfying.
Subjective norm	
SN1	*Passive corruption:* Most people important to me in my life think that I should have accepted the customer's offer. *Active corruption:* Most people important to me in my life think that I should have made the customer an offer.
SN2	*Passive corruption:* My family would bear me out in the decision to accept the customer's offer. *Active corruption:* My family would bear me out in the decision to make the customer an offer.
r_SN3	*Passive corruption:* My friends would have rejected the customer's offer. *Active corruption:* My friends would not have made the customer an offer.
Perceived behavioral control	
r_PBC1	*Passive corruption:* I anticipated negative consequences if I accepted the customer's offer. *Active corruption:* I anticipated negative consequences if I made the customer an offer.
PBC2	*Passive/active corruption:* I was convinced to be able to conduct the transaction with the customer without any risk.
PBC3	*Passive/active corruption:* I assessed the likelihood that the transaction with the customer will be kept secret in front of my competitors to be high.

No.	Item
Goal realization	
GR1	In the business game, I performed better than my competitors.
GR2	My decisions during the business game led to success.
r_GR3	I failed my goal to achieve a higher profit than my competitors.
Corrupt action	
CA1	*Passive corruption:* Did you accept the offer made by your friend working at the large customer that you will get the order if you give him a racing bicycle of the latest version in return? – No/Yes *Active corruption:* Did you submit the offer to your friend working at the large customer that you will give the bicycles for children to him at a low price as well as a racing bicycle of the latest version? – No/Yes
Rationalization strategies[2]	
RS...	*Passive corruption:* You accepted the customer's offer. One of your colleagues has heard about it and says: "But that's not okay!" What would you answer him? *Active corruption:* You made the customer an offer. One of your colleagues has heard about it and says: "But that's not okay!" What would you answer him?
RS1	"It's not written anywhere that this is not allowed."
RS2	"It was the only chance to increase our profit."
RS3	"Everybody does it."
RS4	"It didn't harm anybody. It paid off for everybody."
RS5	"It was only about relatively small amounts."
RS6	"Because of the competitors? It doesn't matter that they once also get the short end of the stick."
RS7	"Why? Because of the competitors who miss out? That's business."
RS8	"To get orders, others are doing things that are even worse."
RS9	"I only did everything to increase the order situation and the income of our company."
RS10	"I only tried to maintain the good business relationship with a good customer."
RS11	"Why shouldn't I take advantage of the good business relationship I developed over several years?"
RS12	"After all I got the order for our business."
RS13	Others: ...

No.	Item
Sociodemographic data	
S1/S7	Your participation code: ...
S2	Your age: ...
S3	Your sex: Female/Male
S4	Your subject *(only asked in the case of university students)*: Business Administration/Business Administration Studies for the High School Teaching Profession/Economics/Engineering/Health Management/ Law (with additional courses in business administration and economics)/Philosophy & Economics/ Sports Management
S5	Your number of semesters *(only asked in the case of university students)*: ...
S6	Do you aim at a function as a decision maker in your future professional life? – No/Yes

Items named with r_... were recoded.
Response formats:
- Unless indicated otherwise, five-point Likert scales: 1 = does not apply at all, 2 = does predominantly not apply, 3 = partly applies, 4 = predominantly applies, 5 = fully applies
- [1] Measurement of attitude by using a semantic differential with seven-point bipolar scale each: -3 = very ... (-), -2 = quite ... (-), -1 = rather ... (-), 0 = neither ... (-) nor ... (+), 1 = rather ...(+), 2 = quite ...(+), 3 = very ... (+)
- [2] Rationalization strategies: "Please tick the three alternatives that are the most obvious to you."

APPENDIX 241

Appendix F2: German Version

Nr.	Item
Wunsch, ein privates oder berufliches Ziel zu erreichen	
GD1	Mein Wunsch, im Planspiel einen höheren Gewinn als die Konkurrenz zu erzielen, ist stark ausgeprägt.
r_GD2	Für mich sind andere Ziele im Planspiel wichtiger, als einen höheren Gewinn als die Konkurrenz zu erzielen.
GD3	Ich halte es für erstrebenswert, im Planspiel besser abzuschneiden als die Konkurrenz.
Leichtigkeit der Zielerreichung	
r_GF1	Ich sehe kaum Möglichkeiten, im Planspiel einen höheren Gewinn als die Konkurrenz erzielen zu können.
GF2	Ich bin überzeugt, im Planspiel besser als die Konkurrenz abschneiden zu können.
r_GF3	Ich halte es für schwierig, im Planspiel erfolgreicher zu sein als meine Konkurrenten.
Antizipierte positive Emotionen	
PAE...	Wenn ich im Planspiel einen höheren Gewinn als die Konkurrenz erziele, fühle ich mich ...
PAE1	... erfreut.
PAE2	... stolz.
PAE3	... überrascht.
PAE4	... erleichtert.
Antizipierte negative Emotionen	
NAE...	Wenn ich im Planspiel weniger Gewinn als die Konkurrenz erziele, fühle ich mich ...
NAE1	... verärgert.
NAE2	... beschämt.
NAE3	... enttäuscht.
NAE4	... niedergeschlagen.

Nr.	Item
Absicht, ein privates oder berufliches Ziel zu erreichen	
GI1	Ich nehme es sehr ernst, im Planspiel erfolgreicher zu sein als meine Konkurrenten.
GI2	Ich werde alles dafür tun, um im Planspiel besser abzuschneiden als die Konkurrenz.
r_GI3	Es ist mir egal, ob ich einen höheren Gewinn als die Konkurrenz erziele oder nicht.
Wunsch, ein privates oder berufliches Ziel durch korruptes Handeln zu erreichen	
ID1	*Passive Korruption:* Mein Wunsch, auf das Angebot des Großabnehmers einzugehen, war stark ausgeprägt. *Aktive Korruption:* Mein Wunsch, dem Großabnehmer ein Angebot zu unterbreiten, war stark ausgeprägt.
r_ID2	*Passive Korruption:* Das Angebot des Großabnehmers hat mich völlig kalt gelassen. *Aktive Korruption:* Die Möglichkeit, dem Großabnehmer ein Angebot zu unterbreiten, hat mich völlig kalt gelassen.
ID3	*Passive Korruption:* Ich hielt es für reizvoll, auf das Angebot des Großabnehmers einzugehen. *Aktive Korruption:* Ich hielt es für reizvoll, dem Großabnehmer ein Angebot zu unterbreiten.
Absicht, ein privates oder berufliches Ziel durch korruptes Handeln zu erreichen	
r_II1	*Passive Korruption:* Es kam für mich nicht in Frage, auf das Angebot des Großabnehmers einzugehen. *Aktive Korruption:* Es kam für mich nicht in Frage, dem Großabnehmer ein Angebot zu unterbreiten.
II2	*Passive Korruption:* Ich war mir sicher, dass ich auf das Angebot des Großabnehmers eingehe. *Aktive Korruption:* Ich war mich sicher, dass ich dem Großabnehmer ein Angebot unterbreite.
II3	*Passive Korruption:* Meine Absicht, auf das Angebot des Großabnehmers einzugehen, war stark ausgeprägt. *Aktive Korruption:* Meine Absicht, dem Großabnehmer ein Angebot zu unterbreiten, war stark ausgeprägt.

Nr.	Item
Einstellung[1]	
AT...	*Passive Korruption:* Ich denke, auf das Angebot des Großabnehmers einzugehen, ist ... *Aktive Korruption:* Ich denke, dem Großabnehmer ein Angebot zu unterbreiten, ist ...
AT1	... schlecht/gut.
AT2	... falsch/richtig.
AT3	... unklug/klug.
AT4	... nutzlos/nützlich.
AT5	... nachteilig/vorteilhaft.
AT6	... langweilig/aufregend.
AT7	... unangenehm/angenehm.
AT8	... unattraktiv/attraktiv.
AT9	... unbefriedigend/befriedigend.
Subjektive Norm	
SN1	*Passive Korruption:* Die meisten Personen, die mir in meinem Leben wichtig sind, denken, dass ich auf das Angebot des Großabnehmers eingehen hätte sollen. *Aktive Korruption:* Die meisten Personen, die mir in meinem Leben wichtig sind, denken, dass ich dem Großabnehmer ein Angebot unterbreiten hätte sollen.
SN2	*Passive Korruption:* Meine Familie würde mich in der Entscheidung, auf das Angebot des Großabnehmers einzugehen, bestätigen. *Aktive Korruption:* Meine Familie würde mich in der Entscheidung, dem Großabnehmer ein Angebot zu unterbreiten, bestätigen.
r_SN3	*Passive Korruption:* Meine Freunde hätten das Angebot des Großabnehmers abgelehnt. *Aktive Korruption:* Meine Freunde hätten dem Großabnehmer kein Angebot unterbreitet.

Nr.	Item
Wahrgenommene Verhaltenskontrolle	
r_PBC1	*Passive Korruption:* Ich rechnete mit negativen Konsequenzen, wenn ich auf das Angebot des Großabnehmers eingehe. *Aktive Korruption:* Ich rechnete mit negativen Konsequenzen, wenn ich dem Großabnehmer ein Angebot unterbreite.
PBC2	*Passive/Aktive Korruption:* Ich war überzeugt, die Transaktion mit dem Großabnehmer risikolos abwickeln zu können.
PBC3	*Passive/Aktive Korruption:* Ich schätzte die Wahrscheinlichkeit, dass die Transaktion mit dem Großabnehmer meinen Konkurrenten gegenüber geheim bleibt, hoch ein.
Zielerreichung	
GR1	Ich habe im Planspiel besser als die Konkurrenz abgeschnitten.
GR2	Meine Entscheidungen während des Planspiels führten zum Erfolg.
r_GR3	Ich habe mein Ziel, einen höheren Gewinn als die Konkurrenz zu erzielen, verfehlt.
Korruptes Handeln	
CA	*Passive Korruption:* Haben Sie das Angebot des Ihnen gut bekannten Mitarbeiters eines Großabnehmers angenommen, dass Sie den Auftrag bekommen, wenn Sie ihm ein Rennrad des neusten Modelltyps überlassen? – Nein/Ja *Aktive Korruption:* Haben Sie dem beim Großabnehmer arbeitenden guten Bekannten das Angebot unterbreitet, ihm die Kinderfahrräder zu einem günstigen Preis und zusätzlich ein Rennrad des neusten Modell-Typs zu überlassen? – Nein/Ja

Nr.	Item
Rechtfertigungsstrategien[2]	
RS…	*Passive Korruption:* Sie haben das Angebot des Großabnehmers angenommen. Ein Kollege von Ihnen erfährt davon und meint: „Ja aber das geht doch nicht!" Was würden Sie ihm antworten? *Aktive Korruption:* Sie haben dem Großabnehmer ein Angebot unterbreitet. Ein Kollege von Ihnen erfährt davon und meint: „Ja aber das geht doch nicht!" Was würden Sie ihm antworten?
RS1	„Aber es steht doch nirgends geschrieben, dass ich das nicht darf."
RS2	„Es war die einzige Möglichkeit, unseren Gewinn zu steigern."
RS3	„Das macht doch jeder so!"
RS4	„Das hat doch niemandem geschadet. Es hatten doch alle etwas davon."
RS5	„Es ging doch nur um verhältnismäßig kleine Beträge."
RS6	„Sie meinen wegen der Konkurrenz? Die können ruhig auch mal den Kürzeren ziehen."
RS7	„Warum denn? Weil die Mitbewerber leer ausgehen? Tja, so ist das Geschäft!"
RS8	„Andere machen da noch ganz andere Sachen, um an Aufträge zu kommen."
RS9	„Ich habe nur alles getan, um die Auftragslage und den Gewinn unseres Unternehmens zu steigern."
RS10	„Ich habe nur versucht, die gute Geschäftsbeziehung zu einem guten Kunden zu erhalten."
RS11	„Wieso soll ich die guten Beziehungen, die ich über Jahre hinweg mühsam aufgebaut habe, nicht auch nutzen?"
RS12	„Immerhin habe ich den Auftrag für unser Unternehmen an Land gezogen."
RS13	Sonstige Antwort: …

Nr.	Item
Soziodemographische Angaben	
S1/S7	Ihr Planspiel-Teilnehmercode: ...
S2	Ihr Alter ...
S3	Ihr Geschlecht: männlich/weiblich
S4	Ihr Studienfach *(nur im Falle der Studenten)*: Betriebswirtschaftslehre/Gesundheitsökonomie/Ingenieurwissenschaft/ Jura (mit wirtschaftswissenschaftlicher Zusatzausbildung)/Lehramt Wirtschaft Gymnasium/Philosophy & Economics/Sportökonomie/ Volkswirtschaftslehre
S5	Ihre Semesterzahl *(nur im Falle der Studenten)*: ...
S6	Streben Sie in Ihrem späteren Berufsleben eine Funktion als Entscheidungsträger an? – Nein/Ja

Mit r_... benannte Items wurden rekodiert.
Antwortformate:
- Sofern nicht anders angegeben fünfstufige Likertskala: 1 = trifft überhaupt nicht zu, 2 = trifft überwiegend nicht zu, 3 = trifft teilweise zu, 4 = trifft überwiegend zu, 5 = trifft vollkommen zu
[1] Messung der Einstellung über Semantisches Differential mit jeweils siebenstufiger bipolarer Skala:
-3 = sehr ... (-), -2 = ziemlich ... (-), - 1 = eher ... (-), 0 = weder ... (-) noch ... (+),
1 = eher ... (+), 2 = ziemlich ... (+) , 3 = sehr ... (+)
[2] Rechtfertigungsstrategien: „Bitte kreuzen Sie die 3 für Sie nahe liegenden Alternativen an!"

Appendix G: Standardized Questionnaire – Part 1

Appendix G1: English Version[63]

Dear student,

Many thanks for your readiness to take part in our mini business game.

You already read the business game instructions so that you know what you are in for. Before starting the business game, we would like to ask you to give estimations regarding the goal you would like to achieve in the business game on the basis of the following questions.

Please consider for each of the following statements – even if some of them seem to be similar to you – to what extent they apply or not. Then tick the adequate answer.

Please answer all questions honestly and without deliberating too long; please do not skip any question!

There is no wrong or right. We are only interested in knowing which statements apply best to you.

Your answers will be kept absolutely confidential. We are not going to make an individual related data analysis. You can only be identified through your participation code as the sales and marketing chief of a special company.

Many thanks for answering the following questions!

A. The goal

It is your goal in the business game to achieve the highest possible profit after the expiration of the four periods and to perform better than your competitors.

A1

(GD1)   I have a strong wish to achieve a higher profit than my competitors in the business game.

(r_GF3)   I regard it difficult to be more successful in the business game than my competitors.

(r_GI3)   I do not care whether I achieve a higher profit in the business game than my competitors or not.

(GI1)   I am very serious in being more successful in the business game than my competitors.

(GF2)   I am convinced I am able to perform better in the business game than my competitors.

---

[63] The questionnaire was provided online. Here you find the relevant text passages and questions following the sequence in which they were asked and the blocks in which the questions were grouped.

A2

(r_GD2) For me other goals are more important in the business game than achieving a higher profit than my competitors.

(GI2) I will do everything possible to perform better in the business game than my competitors.

(r_GF1) I hardly see any possibility of achieving a higher profit in the business game than my competitors.

(GD3) I regard it desirable to perform better in the business game than my competitors.

A3

(PAE...) If I achieve a higher profit in the business game than my competitors, I will feel ...

(PAE1)   ... happy.
(PAE2)   ... proud.
(PAE3)   ... surprised.
(PAE4)   ... relieved.

(NAE...) If I achieve a lower profit in the business game than my competitors, I will feel ...

(NAE1)   ... angry.
(NAE2)   ... ashamed.
(NAE3)   ... disappointed.
(NAE4)   ... depressed.

(S1) Finally, we ask you to indicate your participation code for the business game: ...

Many thanks for answering the questions!

Used response formats:

If not indicated otherwise, five-point Likert scale (1 – 5):

☐ does not apply at all
☐ does predominantly not apply
☐ partly applies
☐ predominantly applies
☐ fully applies

Appendix G2: German Version[64]

Liebe Studentin, lieber Student,

vielen herzlichen Dank für Ihre Bereitschaft, an unserem Mini-Planspiel teilzunehmen.

Sie haben die Planspiel-Instruktion gelesen und wissen, was Sie erwartet. Vor Beginn des Planspiels bitten wir Sie nun zunächst, anhand der nachfolgenden Fragen Einschätzungen hinsichtlich des von Ihnen zu erreichenden Ziels abzugeben.

Bitte überlegen Sie für jede der Aussagen – auch wenn Ihnen manche davon ähnlich erscheinen mögen –, in welchem Ausmaß diese zutreffen oder nicht. Kreuzen Sie dann die entsprechend passende Antwort an.

Bitte beantworten Sie alle Fragen aufrichtig und ohne lange zu überlegen; lassen Sie bitte keine Fragen aus!

Es gibt weder falsche noch richtige Antworten. Uns interessiert ausschließlich, welche Aussagen für Sie am besten zutreffen.

Ihre Antworten werden absolut vertraulich behandelt. Eine personenbezogene Auswertung findet nicht statt. Sie sind allein über Ihren Planspiel-Teilnehmercode als Marketing- und Vertriebsleiter eines Unternehmens zu identifizieren.

Vielen herzlichen Dank für die Beantwortung der folgenden Fragen!

A. Ziel

Ihr Ziel im Planspiel ist es, einen möglichst hohen Gewinn nach den vier Perioden zu erzielen und besser als die Konkurrenz abzuschneiden.

A1

(GD1)   Mein Wunsch, im Planspiel einen höheren Gewinn als die Konkurrenz zu erzielen, ist stark ausgeprägt.

(r_GF3)   Ich halte es für schwierig, im Planspiel erfolgreicher zu sein als meine Konkurrenten.

(r_GI3)   Es ist mir egal, ob ich einen höheren Gewinn als die Konkurrenz erziele oder nicht.

(GI1)   Ich nehme es sehr ernst, im Planspiel erfolgreicher zu sein als meine Konkurrenten.

(GF2)   Ich bin überzeugt, im Planspiel besser als die Konkurrenz abschneiden zu können.

---

[64] The questionnaire was provided online. Here you find the relevant text passages and questions following the sequence in which they were asked and the blocks in which the questions were grouped.

A2

(r_GD2)   Für mich sind andere Ziele im Planspiel wichtiger, als einen höheren Gewinn als die Konkurrenz zu erzielen.

(GI2)   Ich werde alles dafür tun, um im Planspiel besser abzuschneiden als die Konkurrenz.

(r_GF1)   Ich sehe kaum Möglichkeiten, im Planspiel einen höheren Gewinn als die Konkurrenz erzielen zu können.

(GD3)   Ich halte es für erstrebenswert, im Planspiel besser abzuschneiden als die Konkurrenz.

A3

(PAE...)   Wenn ich im Planspiel einen höheren Gewinn als die Konkurrenz erziele, fühle ich mich:

(PAE1)   ... erfreut.
(PAE2)   ... stolz.
(PAE3)   ... überrascht.
(PAE4)   ... erleichtert.

(NAE...)   Wenn ich im Planspiel einen höheren Gewinn als die Konkurrenz erziele, fühle ich mich:

(NAE1)   ... verärgert.
(NAE2)   ... beschämt.
(NAE3)   ... enttäuscht.
(NAE4)   ... niedergeschlagen.

(S1)   Zum Abschluss bitten wir Sie noch, Ihren Planspiel-Teilnehmercode anzugeben: ...

Vielen herzlichen Dank für die Beantwortung der Fragen!

Verwendete Antwortformate:

Sofern nicht anders angegeben, fünfstufige Likertskalen (1 – 5):

☐ trifft überhaupt nicht zu
☐ trifft eher nicht zu
☐ trifft teilweise zu
☐ trifft eher zu
☐ trifft vollkommen zu

Appendix H: Standardized Questionnaire – Part 2

Appendix H1: English Version[65]

Dear student,

Now you have finished the mini business game. Many thanks for your participation!

How successful you were and how you performed compared to the competitors is shown in the feedback of results you got.

During the business game you had to make many decisions. We are interested in taking a closer look at these decisions. That's why we ask you to reflect your decision making behavior during the business game as well as the reasons for your decisions on the basis of the following questions.

Please consider for each of the following statements – even if some of them seem to be similar to you – to what extent they apply or not. Then tick the adequate answer.

Please answer all questions honestly and without deliberating too long; please do not skip any question!

There is no wrong or right. We are only interested in knowing which statements best reflect your decision making behavior during the business game.

Your answers will be kept absolutely confidential. We are not going to make an individual related data analysis. You can only be identified through your participation code as the sales and marketing chief of a special company.

Many thanks for answering the following questions!

B. (Passive corruption) **The offer of a large customer**
   (Active corruption) **The call for bids of a large customer**

Passive corruption: In one of the last three periods, you got the offer from a friend working at a large customer that you get his order if you give him a racing bicycle of the latest version. You now had to decide whether you accept this offer or not.

Active corruption: During the mini business game you had the opportunity to make your friend working at the large customer the offer that you give the bicycles for children to him at a low price as well as a racing bicycle of the latest version to win the call for bids.

---

[65] The questionnaire was provided online. Here you find the relevant text passages and questions following the sequence in which they were asked and the blocks in which the questions were grouped. For the second part, there were two versions – one for passive corruption, one for active corruption. Participants did not know which condition they belonged to. In the following, all not-bold passages in italics give explanations that were not part of the original questionnaires.

B1

(r_ID2)   *Passive corruption:* The customer's offer left me cold.
            Active corruption: The possibility to make the customer an offer left me cold.

(r_II1)   *Passive corruption:* For me, it was out of question to accept the customer's offer.
            Active corruption: For me, it was out of question to make the customer an offer.

(r_PBC1)   *Passive corruption:* I anticipated negative consequences if I accepted the customer's offer.
            Active corruption: I anticipated negative consequences if I made the customer an offer.

(GR2)   My decisions during the business game led to success.

(PBC3)   *Passive/active corruption:* I assessed the likelihood that the transaction with the customer will be kept secret in front of my competitors to be high.

B2

(AT...)   *Passive corruption:* I think accepting the customer's offer is ...
            Active corruption: I think making the customer an offer is ...

(AT1)   ... bad/good.
(AT2)   ... wrong/right.
(AT3)   ... foolish/wise.
(AT4)   ... useless/useful.
(AT5)   ... disadvantageous/advantageous.
(AT6)   ... boring/exciting.
(AT7)   ... unpleasant/pleasant.
(AT8)   ... unattractive/attractive.
(AT9)   ... dissatisfying/satisfying.

B3

(ID1)   *Passive corruption:* My desire to accept the customer's offer was strong.
            Active corruption: My desire to make the customer an offer was strong.

(SN2)   *Passive corruption:* My family would bear me out in the decision to accept the customer's offer.
            Active corruption: My family would bear me out in the decision to make the customer an offer.

(GR1)   In the business game, I performed better than my competitors.

(ID3)   *Passive corruption:* I considered it attractive to accept the customer's offer.
            Active corruption: I considered it attractive to make the customer an offer.

(II2)   *Passive corruption:* I was sure that I would accept the customer's offer.
         Active corruption: I was sure that I would make the customer an offer.

B4

(r_GR3) I failed my goal to achieve a higher profit than my competitors.

(r_SN3) *Passive corruption:* My friends would have rejected the customer's offer.
         Active corruption: My friends would not have made the customer an offer.

(PBC2)   *Passive/active corruption:* I was convinced to be able to conduct the trans-
         action with the customer without any risk.

(II3)   *Passive corruption:* My intention to accept the customer's offer was strong.
         Active corruption: My intention to make the customer an offer was strong.

(SN1)   *Passive corruption:* Most people important to me in my life think that I
         should have accepted the customer's offer.
         Active corruption: Most people important to me in my life think that I
         should have made the customer an offer.

B5

(CA1)   *Passive corruption:* Did you accept the offer made by your friend working
         at the large customer that you will get the order if you give him a racing
         bicycle of the latest version in return?
         ☐ No   ☐ Yes
         Active corruption: Did you submit the offer to your friend working at the
         large customer that you will give the bicycles for children to him at a low
         price as well as a racing bicycle of the latest version?
         ☐ No   ☐ Yes

(RS...) *Passive corruption:* You accepted the customer's offer. One of your
         colleagues has heard about it and says: "But that's not okay!" What would
         you answer him?
         Active corruption: You made the customer an offer. One of your
         colleagues has heard about it and says: "But that's not okay!" What would
         you answer him?
         (Please tick the three alternatives that are the most obvious to you.)

(RS1)   ☐ "It's not written anywhere that this is not allowed."
(RS2)   ☐ "It was the only chance to increase our profit."
(RS3)   ☐ "Everybody does it."
(RS4)   ☐ "It didn't harm anybody. It paid off for everybody."
(RS5)   ☐ "It was only about relatively small amounts."
(RS6)   ☐ "Because of the competitors? It doesn't matter that they once also get
           the short end of the stick."
(RS7)   ☐ "Why? Because of the competitors who miss out? That's business?"
(RS8)   ☐ "To get orders, others are doing things that are even worse."

(RS9)   ☐ "I only did everything to increase the order situation and the income of our company."

(RS10)   ☐ "I only tried to maintain the good business relationship with a good customer."

(RS11)   ☐ "Why shouldn't I take advantage of the good business relationship I developed over several years?"

(RS12)   ☐ "After all I got the order for our business."

(RS13)   ☐ Others: ...

C. Sociodemographic Data

Finally, we ask you for some statistics:

(S7)   Your participation code: ... (This information is essential!)

(S2)   Your age: ...

(S3)   Your sex: ☐ Female   ☐ Male

(S4)   Your subject *(only asked in the case of university students)*:
         ☐ Business Administration
         ☐ Business Administration Studies for the High School Teaching Profession
         ☐ Economics
         ☐ Engineering
         ☐ Health Management
         ☐ Law (with additional courses in business administration and economics)
         ☐ Philosophy & Economics
         ☐ Sports Management

(S5)   Your number of semesters *(only asked in the case of university students)*: ...

(S6)   Do you aim at at function as a decision maker in your future professional life?
         ☐ No   ☐ Yes

Many thanks again for your participation in the business game and for filling out the questionnaire!

As soon as the study is finished, we will inform you whether you have won a prize with the result you achieved. Please keep the certificate of identification safe because otherwise no match of the company representatives with the names is possible. Thank you!

Used response formats:

If not indicated otherwise, five-point Likert scale (1 – 5):

    ☐ does not apply at all
    ☐ does predominantly not apply
    ☐ partly applies
    ☐ predominantly applies
    ☐ fully applies

Measurement of attitude (k19a – k19i) by using a semantic differential with seven-point bipolar scale each (-3, -2, -1, 0, 1, 2, 3):

    ☐ very ... (-)
    ☐ quite ... (-)
    ☐ rather ... (-)
    ☐ neither ... (-) nor ... (+)
    ☐ rather ... (+)
    ☐ quite ... (+)
    ☐ very ... (+)

Appendix H2: German Version[66]

Liebe Studentin, lieber Student,

Sie haben nun das Mini-Planspiel hinter sich gebracht. Vielen herzlichen Dank für Ihre Teilnahme!

Wie erfolgreich Sie waren und wie Sie im Vergleich zu den konkurrierenden Unternehmen abgeschnitten haben, können Sie der Ergebnisrückmeldung, die Sie erhalten haben, entnehmen.

Während des Planspiels hatten Sie eine Vielzahl von Entscheidungen zu treffen. Diese interessieren uns näher. Daher bitten wir Sie nun abschließend, anhand der nachfolgenden Fragen Ihr Entscheidungsverhalten während des Planspiels und Ihre Gründe dafür nochmals zu reflektieren.

Bitte überlegen Sie für jede der Aussagen – auch wenn Ihnen manche davon ähnlich erscheinen mögen –, in welchem Ausmaß diese zutreffen oder nicht. Kreuzen Sie dann die entsprechend passende Antwort an.

Bitte beantworten Sie alle Fragen aufrichtig und ohne lange zu überlegen; lassen Sie bitte keine Fragen aus!

Es gibt weder falsche noch richtige Antworten. Uns interessiert ausschließlich, welche Aussagen Ihr Entscheidungsverhalten während des Mini-Planspiels am besten kennzeichnen.

Ihre Antworten werden absolut vertraulich behandelt. Eine personenbezogene Auswertung findet nicht statt. Sie sind allein über Ihren Planspiel-Teilnehmercode als Marketing- und Vertriebsleiter eines Unternehmens zu identifizieren.

Vielen herzlichen Dank für die Beantwortung der folgenden Fragen!

B. *(Passive Korruption)* ***Angebot eines Großabnehmers***
   (Aktive Korruption) ***Ausschreibung eines Großabnehmers***

Passive Korruption: In einer der letzten drei Perioden haben Sie von einem Ihnen gut bekannten Mitarbeiter eines Großabnehmers das Angebot erhalten, seinen Auftrag zu bekommen, wenn Sie ihm ein Rennrad des neusten Modelltyps überlassen. Sie hatten nun zu entscheiden, ob Sie dieses Angebot annehmen oder nicht.

Aktive Korruption: Während des Mini-Planspiels hatten Sie die Möglichkeit, im Kampf um die Ausschreibung eines Großabnehmers einem dort arbeitenden guten Bekannten das Angebot zu unterbreiten, ihm die Kinderfahrräder zu einem günstigen Preis und zusätzlich ein Rennrad des neusten Modell-Typs zu überlassen.

---

[66] The questionnaire was provided online. Here you find the relevant text passages and questions following the sequence in which they were asked and the blocks in which the questions were grouped. For the second part, there were two versions – one for passive corruption, one for active corruption. Participants did not know which condition they belonged to. In the following, all not-bold passages in italics give explanations that were not part of the original questionnaire.

B1

(r_ID2)   *Passive Korruption:* Das Angebot des Großabnehmers hat mich völlig kalt gelassen.
Aktive Korruption: Die Möglichkeit, dem Großabnehmer ein Angebot zu unterbreiten, hat mich völlig kalt gelassen.

(r_II1)   *Passive Korruption:* Es kam für mich nicht in Frage, auf das Angebot des Großabnehmers einzugehen.
Aktive Korruption: Es kam für mich nicht in Frage, dem Großabnehmer ein Angebot zu unterbreiten

(r_PBC1) *Passive Korruption:* Ich rechnete mit negativen Konsequenzen, wenn ich auf das Angebot des Großabnehmers eingehe.
Aktive Korruption: Ich rechnete mit negativen Konsequenzen, wenn ich dem Großabnehmer ein Angebot unterbreite.

(GR2)   Meine Entscheidungen während des Planspiels führten zum Erfolg.

(PBC3)   *Passive/aktive Korruption:* Ich schätzte die Wahrscheinlichkeit, dass die Transaktion mit dem Großabnehmer meinen Konkurrenten gegenüber geheim bleibt, hoch ein.

B2

(AT...) *Passive Korruption:* Ich denke, auf das Angebot des Großabnehmers einzugehen, ist ...
Aktive Korruption: Ich denke, dem Großabnehmer ein Angebot zu unterbreiten, ist ...

(AT1)   ... schlecht/gut.
(AT2)   ... falsch/richtig.
(AT3)   ... unklug/klug.
(AT4)   ... nutzlos/nützlich.
(AT5)   ... nachteilig/vorteilhaft.
(AT6)   ... langweilig/aufregend.
(AT7)   ... unangenehm/angenehm.
(AT8)   ... unattraktiv/attraktiv.
(AT9)   ... unbefriedigend/befriedigend.

B3

(ID1)   *Passive Korruption:* Mein Wunsch, auf das Angebot des Großabnehmers einzugehen, war stark ausgeprägt.
Aktive Korruption: Mein Wunsch, dem Großabnehmer ein Angebot zu unterbreiten, war stark ausgeprägt.

(SN2)   *Passive Korruption:* Meine Familie würde mich in der Entscheidung, auf das Angebot des Großabnehmers einzugehen, bestätigen.

Aktive Korruption: Meine Familie würde mich in der Entscheidung, dem Großabnehmer ein Angebot zu unterbreiten, bestätigen.

(GR1)   Ich habe im Planspiel besser als die Konkurrenz abgeschnitten.

(ID3)   *Passive Korruption:* Ich hielt es für reizvoll, auf das Angebot des Großabnehmers einzugehen.
         Aktive Korruption: Ich hielt es für reizvoll, dem Großabnehmer ein Angebot zu unterbreiten.

(II2)   *Passive Korruption:* Ich war mir sicher, dass ich auf das Angebot des Großabnehmers eingehe.
         Aktive Korruption: Ich war mich sicher, dass ich dem Großabnehmer ein Angebot unterbreite.

B4

(r_GR3) Ich habe mein Ziel, einen höheren Gewinn als die Konkurrenz zu erzielen, verfehlt.

(r_SN3) *Passive Korruption:* Meine Freunde hätten das Angebot des Großabnehmers abgelehnt.
         Aktive Korruption: Meine Freunde hätten dem Großabnehmer kein Angebot unterbreitet.

(PBC2)   *Passive/aktive Korruption:* Ich war überzeugt, die Transaktion mit dem Großabnehmer risikolos abwickeln zu können.

(II3)   *Passive Korruption:* Meine Absicht, auf das Angebot des Großabnehmers einzugehen, war stark ausgeprägt.
         Aktive Korruption: Meine Absicht, dem Großabnehmer ein Angebot zu unterbreiten, war stark ausgeprägt.

(SN1)   *Passive Korruption:* Die meisten Personen, die mir in meinem Leben wichtig sind, denken, dass ich auf das Angebot des Großabnehmers eingehen hätte sollen.
         Aktive Korruption: Die meisten Personen, die mir in meinem Leben wichtig sind, denken, dass ich dem Großabnehmer ein Angebot unterbreiten hätte sollen.

B5

(CA1)   *Passive Korruption:* Haben Sie das Angebot des Ihnen gut bekannten Mitarbeiters eines Großabnehmers angenommen, dass Sie den Auftrag bekommen, wenn Sie ihm ein Rennrad des neusten Modelltyps überlassen?
         ☐ Nein   ☐ Ja

Aktive Korruption: Haben Sie dem beim Großabnehmer arbeitenden guten Bekannten das Angebot unterbreitet, ihm die Kinderfahrräder zu einem günstigen Preis und zusätzlich ein Rennrad des neusten Modell-Typs zu überlassen?

☐ Nein   ☐ Ja

(RS...)   *Passive Korruption:* Sie haben das Angebot des Großabnehmers angenommen. Ein Kollege von Ihnen erfährt davon und meint: „Ja aber das geht doch nicht!" Was würden Sie ihm antworten?
Aktive Korruption: Sie haben dem Großabnehmer ein Angebot unterbreitet. Ein Kollege von Ihnen erfährt davon und meint: „Ja aber das geht doch nicht!" Was würden Sie ihm antworten?
(Bitte kreuzen Sie die 3 für Sie nahe liegenden Alternativen an!)

(RS1)   ☐ „Aber es steht doch nirgends geschrieben, dass ich das nicht darf."
(RS2)   ☐ „Es war die einzige Möglichkeit, unseren Gewinn zu steigern."
(RS3)   ☐ „Das macht doch jeder so!"
(RS4)   ☐ „Das hat doch niemandem geschadet. Es hatten doch alle etwas davon."
(RS5)   ☐ „Es ging doch nur um verhältnismäßig kleine Beträge."
(RS6)   ☐ „Sie meinen wegen der Konkurrenz? Die können ruhig auch mal den Kürzeren ziehen."
(RS7)   ☐ „Warum denn? Weil die Mitbewerber leer ausgehen? Tja, so ist das Geschäft!"
(RS8)   ☐ „Andere machen da noch ganz andere Sachen, um an Aufträge zu kommen."
(RS9)   ☐ „Ich habe nur alles getan, um die Auftragslage und den Gewinn unseres Unternehmens zu steigern."
(RS10)   ☐ „Ich habe nur versucht, die gute Geschäftsbeziehung zu einem guten Kunden zu erhalten."
(RS11)   ☐ „Wieso soll ich die guten Beziehungen, die ich über Jahre hinweg aufgebaut habe, nicht auch nutzen?"
(RS12)   ☐ „Immerhin habe ich den Auftrag für unser Unternehmen an Land gezogen."
(RS13)   ☐ Sonstige Antwort: ...

C. Soziodemographische Angaben

Zum Abschluss bitten wir Sie noch um einige statistische Angaben:

(S7)   Ihr Planspiel-Teilnehmercode: ... (Bitte unbedingt angeben!)

(S2)   Ihr Alter: ....

(S3)   Ihr Geschlecht: ☐ Weiblich   ☐ Männlich

(S4)   Ihr Studienfach *(nur im Falle der Studenten)*:
    ☐ Betriebswirtschaftslehre
    ☐ Gesundheitsökonomie
    ☐ Ingenieurwissenschaft
    ☐ Jura (mit wirtschaftswissenschaftlicher Zusatzausbildung)
    ☐ Lehramt Wirtschaft Gymnasium
    ☐ Philosophy & Economics
    ☐ Sportökonomie
    ☐ Volkswirtschaftslehre

(S5)   Ihre Semesterzahl *(nur im Falle der Studenten)*: ...

(S6)   Streben Sie in Ihrem späteren Berufsleben eine Funktion als Entschei-
    dungsträger an?
    ☐ Nein   ☐ Ja

Nochmals vielen herzlichen Dank für Ihre Teilnahme am Planspiel und das
Ausfüllen des Fragebogens!

Nach Abschluss der Untersuchung informieren wir Sie, ob Sie mit dem von Ihnen
erzielten Ergebnis einen Preis erringen konnten. Bitte bewahren Sie dazu sorgfältig
Ihren Identifikationsnachweis auf, da wir sonst keinerlei Zuordnung der Unterneh-
mensvertreter zu den Namen vornehmen können. Vielen Dank!

Verwendete Antwortformate:

Sofern nicht anders angegeben, fünfstufige Likertskala (1 – 5):

    ☐ trifft überhaupt nicht zu
    ☐ trifft eher nicht zu
    ☐ trifft teilweise zu
    ☐ trifft eher zu
    ☐ trifft vollkommen zu

Messung der Einstellung (k19a – k19i) über Semantisches Differential mit jeweils
siebenstufiger bipolarer Skala (-3, -2, -1, 0, 1, 2, 3):

    ☐ sehr ... (-)
    ☐ ziemlich ... (-)
    ☐ eher ... (-)
    ☐ weder ... (-) noch ... (+)
    ☐ eher ... (+)
    ☐ ziemlich ... (+)
    ☐ sehr ... (+)

REFERENCES

AACSB International (2008). *Eligibility procedures and accreditation standards for business accreditation.* Tampa, FL: AACSB International. Retrieved April 30, 2008, from http://www.aacsb.edu/accreditation/process/documents/AACSB_STA NDARDS_Revised_Jan08.pdf

Abbink, K. (2002). *Fair salaries and the moral costs of corruption.* (CeDEx Working Paper No. 2002-5). Nottingham: University of Nottingham, School of Economics. Retrieved February 5, 2008, from http://www.nottingham.ac.uk/economics/cedex/papers/2002-05.pdf

Abbink, K. (2004). Staff rotation as an anti-corruption policy: An experimental study. *European Journal of Political Economy, 20*(4), 887 – 906.

Abbink, K., & Hennig-Schmidt, H. (2006). Neutral versus loaded instructions in a bribery experiment. *Experimental Economics, 9*(2), 103 – 121.

Abbink, K., Irlenbusch, B., & Renner, E. (2002). An experimental bribery game. *Journal of Law Economics & Organization, 18*(2), 428 – 454.

Acemoglu, D., & Verdier, T. (1998). Property rights, corruption and the allocation of talent: A general equilibrium approach. *The Economic Journal, 108*(450), 1381 – 1403.

Ach, N. (1935). *Analyse des Willens.* Berlin: Urban und Schwarzenberg.

Adamoli, S. (1999). Combatting corruption. In M. Joutsen (Ed.), *Five issues in European criminal justice: Corruption, women in the criminal justice system, criminal policy indicators, community crime prevention, and computer crime* (pp. 61 – 73). Helsinki: European Institute for Crime Prevention and Control.

Adamowsky, S. (1964). *Das Planspiel. Methode zur Aus- und Weiterbildung betrieblicher Führungskräfte.* Frankfurt/Main: Agenor-Verlag.

Ades, A., & Di Tella, R. (1996). The causes and consequences of corruption: A review of recent empirical contributions. *IDS Bulletin, 27*(2), 6 – 11.

Ades, A., & Di Tella, R. (1997). National champions and corruption: Some unpleasant interventionist arithmetic. *The Economic Journal, 107*(443), 1023 – 1042.

Ades, A., & Di Tella, R. (1999). Rents, competition, and corruption. *The American Economic Review, 89*(4), 982 – 993.

Aguilera, R. V., & Vadera, A. (2005, August). *A multi-level theory of organizational deviance: Corruption and corporate governance in a comparative perspective.* Paper presented at the Annual Meeting of the American Sociological Association, Philadelphia. Retrieved January 19, 2007, from http://search.ebscohost.com/login. aspx?direct=true&db=sih&AN=18614335& site=ehost-live

Ahlf, E. (1998). *Korruption.* Hilden: Verlag Deutsche Polizeiliteratur.

Ahrend, R. (2002). *Press freedom, human capital, and corruption*. (Working Paper No. 2002-11). Paris: DELTA. Retrieved September 24, 2007, from http://www.delta.ens.fr/abstracts/wp200211.pdf

Ajzen, I. (1991). The theory of planned behavior. *Organizational Behavior and Human Decision Processes, 50*(2), 179 – 211.

Ajzen, I. (1996). The directive influence of attitudes on behavior. In P. M. Gollwitzer, & J. A. Bargh (Eds.), *The psychology of action. Linking cognition and motivation to behavior* (pp. 385 – 403). New York: Guilford Press.

Ajzen, I., & Fishbein, M. (1977). Attitude-behavior relations: A theoretical analysis and review of empirical research. *Psychological Bulletin, 84*(5), 888 – 918.

Akaah, I. P. (1996). The influence of organizational rank and role on marketing professionals' ethical judgments. *Journal of Business Ethics, 15*(6), 605 – 613.

Akers, R. L. (2000). *Criminological theories: Introduction, evaluation, and application* (3rd ed.). Los Angeles, CA: Roxbury.

Alam, M. S. (1990). Some economic costs of corruption in LDCs. *Journal of Development Studies, 27*(4), 89 – 97.

Albrecht, W. S., McDermott, E. A., & Williams, T. L. (1994). Reducing the cost of fraud. *The Internal Auditor, 51*(1), 28 – 34.

Alemann, U. V. (2004). The unknown depths of political theory: The case for a multidimensional concept of corruption. *Crime, Law and Social Change, 42*(1), 25 – 34.

Alesina, A., Devleeschauwer, A., Easterly, W., Kurlat, S., & Wacziarg, R. (2003). Fractionalization. *Journal of Economic Growth, 8*(2), 155 – 194.

Ali, A. M., & Isse, H. S. (2003). Determinants of economic corruption: A cross-country comparison. *Cato Journal, 22*(3), 449 – 466.

Amundsen, I. (1999). *Political corruption: An introduction to the issues*. (Working Paper 99(7)). Bergen: Chr. Michelsen Institute. Retrieved November, 25, 2005, from http://www.cmi.no/publications/1999/wp/wp1999-7.pdf

Anand, V., Ashforth, B. E., & Joshi, M. (2005). Business as usual: The acceptance and perception of corruption in organizations. *The Academy of Management Executive, 19*(4), 9 – 23.

Andvig, J. C., & Fjeldstad, O. (2001). *Corruption: A review of contemporary research*. (CMI Report R 2001:7). Bergen: Chr. Michelsen Institute. Retrieved November 11, 2005, from http://cmi.no/publications/publication.cfm?pubid=861

Andvig, J. C., & Moene, K. O. (1990). How corruption may corrupt. *Journal of Economic Behavior and Organization, 13*(1), 63 -76.

Appelbaum, S. H., Deguire, K. J., & Lay, M. (2005). The relationship of ethical climate to deviant workplace behaviour. *Corporate Governance, 5*(4), 43 – 55.

Appelbaum, S. H., & Shapiro, B. T. (2006). Diagnosis and remedies for deviant workplace behaviors. *Journal of American Academy of Business*, *9*(2), 14 – 20.

Aquino, K., Lewis, M. U., & Bradfield, M. (1999). Justice constructs, negative affectivity, and employee deviance: A proposed model and empirical test. *Journal of Organizational Behavior*, *20*(7), 1073 – 1091.

Arbeitsgruppe Planspiel (1995). *Leitfaden Planspiel: Anleitung für eine alternative Lehr- und Lernform*. Berlin: Technische Universität, Universitätsbibliothek, Abteilung Publikationen.

Argandoña, A. (2003). Private-to-private corruption. *Journal of Business Ethics*, *47*(3), 253 – 267.

Argandoña, A. (2005). Corruption and companies: The use of facilitating payments. *Journal of Business Ethics*, *60*(3), 251 – 264.

Arlow, P. (1991). Personal characteristics in college students' evaluations of business ethics and corporate social responsibility. *Journal of Business Ethics*, *10*(1), 63 – 69.

Arnim, H. H. V. (2003). Korruption in Politik und Verwaltung. In H. H. V. Arnim (Ed.), *Korruption. Netzwerke in Politik, Ämtern und Wirtschaft* (pp. 16 – 30). München: Knaur.

Ashforth, B. E., & Anand, V. (2003). The normalization of corruption in organizations. *Research in Organizational Behavior*, *25*, 1 – 25.

Ashforth, B. E., & Kreiner, G. E. (1999). "How can you do it?": Dirty work and the challenge of constructing a positive identity. *The Academy of Management Review*, *24*(3), 413 – 434.

Ashforth, B. E., & Kreiner, G. E. (2002). Normalizing emotion in organizations: Making the extraordinary seem ordinary. *Human Resource Management Review*, *12*(2), 215 – 235.

Atkinson, J. W. (1958). Towards experimental analysis of human motivation in terms of motives, expectancies, and incentives. In J. W. Atkinson (Ed.), *Motives in fantasy, action, and society* (pp. 228 – 305). Princeton, NJ: Van Nostrand.

Atthill, C. (1978). The serious business of playing games. *Journal of European Industrial Training*, *2*(3), VIII – XII.

Aultman, M. G. (1976). A social psychological approach to the study of police corruption. *Journal of Criminal Justice*, *4*(4), 323 – 332.

Azfar, O., Lee, Y., & Swamy, A. (2001). The causes and consequences of corruption. *The Annals of the American Academy of Political and Social Science*, *573*(1), 42 – 56.

Babb, E. M., & Eisgruber, L. M. (1966). *Management games for teaching and research*. Chicago: Educational Methods.

Backhaus, K., Erichson, B., Plinke, W., & Weiber, R. (2003). *Multivariate Analyse-methoden: Eine anwendungsorientierte Einführung* (10ᵗʰ ed.). Berlin: Springer.

Bagozzi, R. P. (1992). The self-regulation of attitudes, intentions, and behavior. *Social Psychology Quarterly*, *55*(2), 178 – 204.

Bagozzi, R. P., Baumgartner, H., & Pieters, R. (1998). Goal-directed emotions. *Cognition and Emotion*, *12*(1), 1 – 26.

Bagozzi, R. P., & Dholakia, U. M. (1999). Goal setting and goal striving in consumer behavior. *Journal of Marketing*, *63*(Special issue), 19 – 32.

Bagozzi, R. P., Dholakia, U. M., & Basuroy, S. (2003). How effortful decisions get enacted: The motivating role of decision processes, desires, and anticipated emotions. *Journal of Behavioral Decision Making*, *16*(4), 273 – 295.

Bandura, A. (1977). *Social learning theory*. Englewood Cliffs, NJ: Prentice Hall.

Banfield, E. C. (1975). Corruption as a feature of governmental organization. *Journal of Law & Economics*, *18*(3), 587 – 605.

Bannenberg, B. (2002). *Korruption in Deutschland und ihre strafrechtliche Kontrolle*. Neuwied: Luchterhand.

Bannenberg, B. (2003a). Korruption in Deutschland. Befunde und Konsequenzen. In V. V. Nell, G. Schwitzgebel, & M. Vollet (Eds.), *Korruption. Interdisziplinäre Zugänge zu einem komplexen Phänomen* (pp. 119 – 136). Wiesbaden: Deutscher Universitäts-Verlag.

Bannenberg, B. (2003b). Korruption in Deutschland. Ergebnisse einer kriminolo-gisch-strafrechtlichen Untersuchung. In H. H. V. Arnim (Ed.), *Korruption. Netzwerke in Politik, Ämtern und Wirtschaft* (pp. 204 – 234). München: Knaur.

Bannenberg, B., & Schaupensteiner, W. (2004). *Korruption in Deutschland*. München: Beck.

Barclay, D., Higgins, C., & Thompson, R. (1995). The partial least squares (PLS) approach to causal modeling: Personal computer adoption and use as an illus-tration. *Technology Studies*, *2*(2), 285 – 309.

Bardhan, P. (1997). Corruption and development: A review of issues. *Journal of Economic Literature*, *35*(3), 1320 – 1346.

Barnett, T., Cochran, D. S., & Taylor, G. S. (1993). The internal disclosure policies of private-sector employers: An initial look at their relationship to employee whistleblowing. *Journal of Business Ethics*, *12*(2), 127 – 136.

Baucus, M. S. (1994). Pressure, opportunity and predisposition: A multivariate model of corporate illegality. *Journal of Management*, *20*(4), 699 – 721.

Baucus, M. S., & Near, J. P. (1991). Can illegal corporate behavior be predicted? An event history analysis. *Academy of Management Journal*, *34*(1), 9 – 36.

Baumol, W. J. (1996). Entrepreneurship: Productive, unproductive, and destructive. *Journal of Business Venturing*, *11*(1), 3 – 22.

Bausch, T. (2004). Korruption und Ethik. Reflexionen eines Unternehmers. In A. Brink, & O. Karitzki (Eds.), *Unternehmensethik in turbulenten Zeiten. Wirtschaftsführer über Ethik im Management* (pp. 129 – 150). Bern: Haupt.

Bayar, G. (2005). The role of intermediaries in corruption. *Public Choice*, *122*(3-4), 277 – 298.

Beck, P. J., & Maher, M. W. (1986). A comparison of bribery and bidding in thin markets. *Economics Letters*, *20*(1), 1 – 5.

Beets, S. D. (2005). Understanding the demand-side issues of international corruption. *Journal of Business Ethics*, *57*(1), 65 – 81.

Beltramini, R. F., Peterson, R. A., & Kozmetsky, G. (1984). Concerns of college students regarding business ethics. *Journal of Business Ethics*, *3*(3), 195 – 200.

Berg, W. (1997). *Bananenrepublik Deutschland. Korruption – Der ganz alltägliche Skandal*. Landsberg am Lech: mvg-Verlag.

Berry, C. M., Sackett, P. R., & Wiemann, S. (2007). A review of recent developments in integrity test research. *Personnel Psychology*, *60*(2), 271 – 301.

Betz, M., O'Connell, L., & Shepard, J. M. (1989). Gender differences in proclivity for unethical behavior. *Journal of Business Ethics*, *8*(5), 321 – 324.

Bilitza, K., & Lück, H. E. (1977). Sozialpsychologische Thesen zur Korruption. *Psychologie Heute*, *9*, 19 – 21.

Blau, P. M. (1964). *Exchange and power in social life*. New York: Wiley.

Bliemel, F., Eggert, A., Fassott, G., & Henseler, J. (2005). PLS und Kovarianzstrukturanalyse im Vergleich. In F. Bliemel, A. Eggert, G. Fassott, & J. Henseler (Eds.), *Handbuch PLS-Pfadmodellierung* (pp. 9 – 16). Stuttgart: Schäffer-Poeschel.

Boardman, C., & Klum, V. (2001). Building organisational integrity. In P. Larmour, & N. Wolanin (Eds.), *Corruption and anti-corruption* (pp. 82 – 96). Canberra: Asia Pacific Press.

Bobek, D. D., & Hatfield, R. C. (2003). An investigation of the theory of planned behavior and the role of moral obligation in tax compliance. *Behavioral Research in Accounting*, *15*, 13 – 38.

Bohner, G. (2001). Attitudes. In M. Hewstone, & W. Stroebe (Eds.), *Introduction to social psychology* (3rd ed.) (pp. 239 – 282). Oxford, UK: Blackwell.

Böhret, C., & Wordelmann, P. (1975). *Das Planspiel als Methode der Fortbildung. Zur allgemeinen und speziellen Verwendung der Simulationsmethode in der öffentlichen Verwaltung*. Köln: Carl Heymanns.

Bommer, M., Gratto, C., Gravander, J., & Tuttle, M. (1987). A behavioral model of ethical and unethical decision making. *Journal of Business Ethics*, *6*(4), 265 – 280.

Borner, S., & Schwyzer, C. (1999). Bekämpfung der Bestechung im Lichte der Neuen Politischen Ökonomie. In M. Pieth, & P. Eigen (Eds.), *Korruption im internationalen Geschäftsverkehr: Bestandsaufnahme, Bekämpfung, Prävention* (pp. 17 – 39). Neuwied: Luchterhand.

Bortz, J. (1999). *Statistik für Sozialwissenschaftler* (5th ed.). Berlin: Springer.

Bortz, J., & Döring, N. (1995). *Forschungsmethoden und Evaluation* (2nd ed.). Berlin: Springer.

Bowen, K. C. (1978). *Research games: An approach to the study of decision processes*. London: Taylor & Francis.

Bowman, J. S. (1976). Managerial ethics in business and government. *Business Horizons*, *19*(5), 48 – 54.

Bowyer, J. B. (1982). *Cheating. Deception in war & magic, games & sports, sex & religion, business & con games, politics & expionage, art & science*. New York: St. Martin's Press.

Brandstätter, V., Lengfelder, A., & Gollwitzer, P. M. (2001). Implementation intentions and efficient action initiation. *Journal of Personality and Social Psychology*, *81*(5), 946 – 960.

Brasz, H. A. (1970). Sociology of corruption. In A. J. Heidenheimer (Ed.), *Political corruption: Readings in comparative analysis* (pp. 41 – 45). New York: Holt, Rinehart & Winston.

Bray, J. H., & Maxwell, S. E. (1982). Analyzing and interpreting significant MANOVAs. *Review of Educational Research*, *52*(3), 340 – 367.

Bray, J. H., & Maxwell, S. E. (1985). *Multivariate analysis of variance*. Beverly Hills, CA: Sage.

Brief, A. P., Buttram, R. T., & Dukerich, J. M. (2001). Collective corruption in the corporate world: Toward a process model. In M. E. Turner (Ed.), *Groups at work: Theory and research* (pp. 471 – 499). Mahwah, NJ: Lawrence Erlbaum.

Brien, A. (2001). Regulating virtue: Formulating, engendering and enforcing corporate ethical codes. In P. Larmour, & N. Wolanin (Eds.), *Corruption and anti-corruption* (pp. 62 – 81). Canberra: Asia Pacific Press.

Brost, M., & Storn, A. (30/2005). Willkommen in der Backschischrepublik. *Die Zeit*. Retrieved July 21, 2005, from http://www.zeit.de/2005/30/Korruption

Brown, M. E., & Trevino, L. K. (2006). Ethical leadership: A review and future directions. *The Leadership Quarterly*, *17*(6), 595 – 616.

Brown, M. E., Trevino, L. K., & Harrison, D. A. (2005). Ethical leadership: A social learning perspective for construct development and testing. *Organizational Behavior and Human Decision Processes*, *97*(2), 117 – 134.

Browning, J., & Zabriskie, N. B. (1983). How ethical are industrial buyers? *Industrial Marketing Management*, *12*(4), 219 – 224.

Brünner, C. (Ed.) (1981a). *Korruption und Kontrolle*. Wien: Böhlau.

Brünner, C. (1981b). Zur Analyse individueller und sozialer Bedingungen von Korruption. In C. Brünner (Ed.), *Korruption und Kontrolle* (pp. 677 – 705). Wien: Böhlau.

Brunetti, A., Kisunko, G., & Weder, B. (1998). Credibility of rules and economic growth: Evidence from a worldwide survey of the private sector. *The World Bank Economic Review*, *12*(3), 353 – 384.

Brunetti, A., & Weder, B. (1997). *Investment and institutional uncertainty: A comparative study of different uncertainty measures*. (Technical Paper No. 4). Washington, DC: World Bank. Retrieved October 19, 2007, from http://www2. ifc.org/economics/pubs/techpap4/tp4.pdf

Brunetti, A., & Weder, B. (2003). A free press is bad news for corruption. *Journal of Public Economics*, *87*(7), 1801 – 1824.

Brunsson, N. (1982). The irrationality of action and action rationality: Decisions, ideologies and organizational actions. *The Journal of Management Studies*, *19*(1), 29 – 44.

Buchhorn, E. (10/2005). Korruption – Spirale der Versuchung. *Manager-Magazin*. Retrieved November 7, 2005, from http://www.manager-magazin.de/magazin/ artikel/0,2828,375808,00.html

Buckley, M. R., Wiese, D. S., & Harvey, M. G. (1998). An investigation into the dimensions of unethical behavior. *Journal of Education for Business*, *73*(5), 284 – 290.

Bühner, M. (2004). *Einführung in die Test- und Fragebogenkonstruktion*. München: Pearson Studium.

Bundesverband der Deutschen Industrie e.V. (1997). Empfehlungen für die gewerbliche Wirtschaft zur Bekämpfung der Korruption in Deutschland. In H. Reichmann, W. Schlaffke, & W. Then (Eds.), *Korruption in Staat und Wirtschaft* (pp. 110 – 117). Köln: Deutscher Instituts-Verlag.

Bunz, A. (2005). *Das Führungsverständnis der deutschen Spitzenmanager*. Frankfurt am Main: Lang.

Burguet, R., & Che, Y. (2004). Competitive procurement with corruption. *The Rand Journal of Economics*, *35*(1), 50 – 68.

Bussmann, K. (2004). Kriminalprävention durch Business Ethics: Ursachen von Wirtschaftskriminalität und die besondere Bedeutung von Werten. *Zeitschrift für Wirtschafts- und Unternehmensethik, 5*(1), 35 – 50.

Byrne, B. M. (2001). *Structural equation modeling with AMOS: Basic concepts, applications, and programming.* Mahwah, NJ: Erlbaum.

Cabelkova, I., & Hanousek, J. (2004). The power of negative thinking: corruption, perception and willingness to bribe in Ukraine. *Applied Economics, 36*(4), 383 – 397.

Cadot, O. (1987). Corruption as a gamble. *Journal of Public Economics, 33*(2), 223 – 244.

Caiden, G. E. (2001). Corruption and governance. In G. E. Caiden, O. P. Dwivedi, & J. Jabbra (Eds.), *Where corruption lives* (pp. 15 – 37). Bloomfield, CT: Kumarian Press.

Cain, P., Doig, A., Flanary, R., & Barata, K. (2001). Filing for corruption: Transparency, openness and record-keeping. *Crime, Law and Social Change, 36*(4), 409 – 425.

Callan, V. J. (1992). Predicting ethical values and training needs in ethics. *Journal of Business Ethics, 11*(10), 761 – 769.

Camerer, C. (2003). *Behavioral game theory. Experiments in strategic interaction.* New York: Russell Sage Foundation.

Cameron, K. (2006). Good or not bad: Standards and ethics in managing change. *Academy of Management Learning & Education, 5*(3), 317 – 323.

Campbell, D., & Stanley, J. (1963). Experimental and quasi-experimental designs for research on teaching. In N. L. Gage (Ed.), *Handbook of research on teaching* (pp. 171 – 246). Chicago: Rand McNally.

Campos, J. E., Lien, D., & Pradhan, S. (1999). The impact of corruption on investment: Predictability matters. *World Development, 27*(6), 1059 – 1067.

Capaul, R., & Ulrich, M. (2003). *Planspiele. Simulationsspiele für Unterricht und Training.* Altstätten: Toble.

Carnes, G. A., & Englebrecht, T. D. (1995). An investigation of the effect of detection risk perceptions, penalty sanctions, and income visibility on tax compliance. *The Journal of the American Taxation Association, 17*(1), 26 – 41.

Carrillo, J. D. (1999). Corruption in hierarchies. *Annales d'Economie et de Statistique, 59.* Retrieved January 21, 2005, from www.adres.prd.fr/annales/anciens numeros/resumes/n59/03.pdf

Carrillo, J. D. (2000). Grafts, bribes, and the practice of corruption. *Journal of Economics and Management Strategy, 9*(2), 257 – 286.

Carroll, A. B. (1975). Managerial ethics – A post-Watergate view. *Business Horizons*, *18*(2), 75 – 80.

Carroll, A. B. (1978). Linking business ethics to behavior in organizations. *SAM Advanced Management Journal*, *43*(3), 4 – 11.

Carson, J. R. (1969). Business games: A technique for teaching decision making. In R. G. Graham, & C. F. Gray (Eds.), *Business games handbook* (pp. 39 – 46). New York: American Management Association.

Carter, J. R., & Irons, M. D. (1991). Are economists different, and if so, why? *The Journal of Economic Perspectives*, *5*(2), 171 – 177.

Carver, C. S., & Scheier, M. F. (1998). *On the self-regulation of behavior*. Cambridge: Cambridge University Press.

Cederblom, J., & Dougherty, C. J. (1990). *Ethics at work*. Belmont, CA: Wadsworth.

Chan, R. Y. K., Cheng, L. T. W., & Szeto, R. W. F. (2002). The dynamics of guanxi and ethics for Chinese executives. *Journal of Business Ethics*, *41*(4), 327 – 336.

Chang, M. K. (1998). Predicting unethical behavior: A comparison of the theory of reasoned action on the theory of planned behavior. *Journal of Business Ethics*, *17*(16), 1825 – 1834.

Chatelin, Y. M., Vinzi, V. E., & Tenenhaus, M. (2002). *State-of-art on PLS path modeling through the available software*. (Les Cahiers de Recherche from Groupe HEC, No. 764). Retrieved September 26, 2005, from http://www.hec.fr/hec/fr/professeurs_recherche/upload/cahiers/CR764.pdf

Chen, Y., & Tang, T. L. (2006). Attitude toward and propensity to engage in unethical behavior: Measurement invariance across major among university students. *Journal of Business Ethics*, *69*(1), 77 – 93.

Cherry, J. (2006). The impact of normative influence and locus of control on ethical judgments and intentions: A cross-cultural comparison. *Journal of Business Ethics*, *68*(2), 113 – 132.

Cherry, J., & Fraedrich, J. (2000). An empirical investigation of locus of control and the structure of moral reasoning: Examining the ethical decision-making processes of sales managers. *The Journal of Personal Selling & Sales Management*, *20*(3), 173 – 188.

Chin, W. W. (1998a). Issues and opinion on structural equation modeling. *MIS Quarterly*, *22*(1), VII – XVI.

Chin, W. W. (1998b). The partial least squares approach to structural equation modeling. In G. A. Marcoulides (Ed.), *Modern methods for business research* (pp. 295 – 336). Mahwah, NJ: Lawrence Erlbaum.

Chin, W. W. (2000). *Frequently asked questions – Partial Least Squares & PLS-Graph*. Retrieved February 13, 2008, from http://disc-nt.cba.uh.edu/chin/plsfaq.htm

Chin, W. W., Marcolin, B. L., & Newsted, P. R. (2003). A partial least squares latent variable modeling approach for measuring interaction effects: Results from a Monte Carlo simulation study and an electronic-mail emotion/adoption study. *Information Systems Research*, *14*(2), 189 – 217.

Chin, W. W., & Newsted, P. R. (1999). Structural equation modeling analysis with small samples using partial least squares. In R. H. Hoyle (Ed.), *Statistical strategies for small sample research* (pp. 307 – 342). Thousand Oaks: Sage.

Christie, R., & Geis, F. L. (1970). *Studies in machiavellianism*. New York: Academic Press.

Clarke, G. R. G., & Xu, L. C. (2002). *Ownership, competition, and corruption: Bribe takers versus bribe payers*. (World Bank Policy Research Working Paper No. 2783). Washington, DC: World Bank. Retrieved December 23, 2004, from http://www1.worldbank.orf/publicsector/anticorrupt/readings.htm

Clinard, M. B. (1990). *Corporate corruption. The abuse of power*. New York: Praeger.

Clinard, M. B., & Quinney, R. (1973). *Criminal behavior systems: A typology* (2nd ed.). New York: Holt, Rinehart and Winston.

Clinard, M. B., & Yeager, P. C. (1980). *Corporate crime*. New York: Free Press.

Clinard, M. B., Yeager, P. C., Brissette, J., Petrasehk, K., & Harries, E. (1979). *Illegal corporate behavior*. Washington, DC: US Department for Justice.

Cloward, R. A., & Ohlin, L. E. (1960). *Delinquency and opportunity: A theory of delinquent gangs*. New York: Free Press.

Cole, B. C., & Smith, D. L. (1996). Perceptions of business ethics: Students vs. business people. *Journal of Business Ethics*, *15*(8), 889 – 896.

Coleman, J. W. (1998). *The criminal elite. Understanding white-collar crime* (4th ed.). New York: St. Martin's Press.

Collier, M. W. (2002). Explaining corruption: An institutional choice approach. *Crime, Law and Social Change*, *38*(1), 1 – 32.

Collins, J. M., & Schmidt, F. L. (1993). Personality, integrity, and white collar crime: A construct validity study. *Personnel Psychology*, *46*(2), 295 – 311.

Compte, O., Lambert-Mogiliansky, A., & Verdier, T. (2005). Corruption and competition in procurement auctions. *The Rand Journal of Economics*, *36*(1), 1 – 15.

Cook, K. S., & Whitmeyer, J. M. (1992). Two approaches to social structure: Exchange theory and network analysis. *Annual Review of Sociology*, *18*, 109 – 127.

Cropanzano, R., & Mitchell, M. S. (2005). Social exchange theory: An interdisciplinary review. *Journal of Management*, *31*(6), 874 – 900.

Cuervo-Cazurra, A. (2006). Who cares about corruption? *Journal of International Business Studies*, *37*(6), 807 – 822.

Daboub, A. J., Rasheed, A. M. A., Priem, R. L., & Gray, D. A. (1995). Top management team characteristics and corporate illegal ac. *The Academy of Management Review*, *20*(1), 138 – 170.

Damania, R., Fredriksson, P. G., & Mani, M. (2004). The persistence of corruption and regulatory compliance failures: Theory and evidence. *Public Choice*, *121*(3-4), 363 – 390.

Darley, J. M. (2005). The cognitive and social psychology of contagious organizational corruption. *Brooklyn Law Review*, *70*(4), 1177 – 1194.

Davis, J. H., & Ruhe, J. A. (2003). Perceptions of country corruption: Antecedents and outcomes. *Journal of Business Ethics*, *43*(4), 275 – 288.

Davis, J. R., & Welton, R. E. (1991). Professional ethics: Business students' perceptions. *Journal of Business Ethics*, *10*(6), 451 – 463.

Davis, K. E. (2002). Self-interest and altruism in the deterrence of transnational bribery. *American Law and Economics Review*, *4*(2), 314 – 340.

Davis, W. A. (1984). A causal theory of intending. *American Philosophical Quarterly*, *21*(1), 43 – 54.

Dawes, R. M. (1980). Social dilemmas. *Annual Review of Psychology*, *31*(1), 169 – 193.

Dawson, L. M. (1997). Ethical differences between men and women in the sales profession. *Journal of Business Ethics*, *16*(11), 1143 – 1152.

Deflem, M. (1995). Corruption, law, and justice: A conceptual clarification. *Journal of Criminal Justice*, *23*(3), 243 – 258.

De George, R. T. (1993). *Competing with integrity in international business*. New York: Oxford University Press.

Delaney, J. T., & Sockell, D. (1992). Do company ethics training programs make a difference? An empirical analysis. *Journal of Business Ethics*, *11*(9), 719 – 727.

Deshpande, S. P. (1997). Managers' perception of proper ethical conduct: The effect of sex, age, and level of education. *Journal of Business Ethics*, *16*(1), 79 – 85.

Deshpande, S. P., Joseph, J., & Maximov, V. V. (2000). Perceptions of proper ethical conduct of male and female Russian managers. *Journal of Business Ethics*, *24*(2), 179 – 183.

272

Dholakia, U. M., & Bagozzi, R. P. (2002). Mustering motivation to enact decisions: How decision process characteristics influence goal realization. *Journal of Behavioral Decision Making, 15*(3), 167 – 188.

Diamantopoulos, A., & Winklhofer, H. M. (2001). Index construction with formative indicators: An alternative to scale development. *Journal of Marketing Research, 38*(2), 269 – 277.

Dollar, D., Fisman, R., & Gatti, R. (2001). Are women really the "fairer" sex? Corruption and women in government. *Journal of Economic Behavior & Organization, 46*(4), 423 – 429.

Dubinsky, A. J., & Loken, B. (1989). Analyzing ethical decision making in marketing. *Journal of Business Research, 19*(2), 83 – 107.

Dubinsky, A. J., Jolson, M. A., Michaels, R. E., Kotabe, M., & Lim, C. U. (1992). Ethical perceptions of field sales personnel: An empirical assessment. *The Journal of Personal Selling & Sales Management, 12*(4), 9 – 21.

Dunfee, T. W., & Warren, D. E. (2001). Is guanxi ethical? A normative analysis of doing business in China. *Journal of Business Ethics, 32*(3), 191 – 204.

Dunkelberg, J., & Jessup, D. R. (2001). So then why did you do it? *Journal of Business Ethics, 29*(1/2), 51 – 63.

Eagly, A. H., & Chaiken, S. (1993). *The psychology of attitudes.* San Diego, CA: Harcourt Brace Jovanovich.

Eberl, M. (2004). *Formative und reflektive Indikatoren im Forschungsprozess: Entscheidungsregeln und die Dominanz des reflektiven Modells.* (Schriften zur Empirischen Forschung und Quantitativen Unternehmensplanung, Heft 19). München: Ludwig-Maximilians-Universität München, Institut für Unternehmensentwicklung und Organisation. Retrieved September 22, 2005, from http://www.imm.bwl.uni-muenchen.de/dmdocuments/AP_efoplan_19.pdf

Ebert, G. (1992). Planspiel – eine aktive und attraktive Lehrmethode. In H. Keim (Ed.), *Planspiel, Rollenspiel, Fallstudie. Zur Praxis und Theorie lernaktiver Methoden* (pp. 25 – 42). Köln: Wirtschaftsverlag Bachem.

Edelhertz, H. (1970). *The nature, impact and prosecution of white collar crime.* Washington, DC: US Government Printing Office.

Eigen, P. (2003). Mit kraftvollen und kompetenten zivilgesellschaftlichen Organisationen gegen Korruption. In H. H. V. Arnim (Ed.), *Korruption. Netzwerke in Politik, Ämtern und Wirtschaft* (pp. 160 – 172). München: Knaur.

Eisenführ, F. (1974). Das Unternehmungsspiel als Instrument empirischer Forschung. In F. Eisenführ, D. Ordelheide, & G. Puck (Eds.), *Unternehmungsspiele in Ausbildung und Forschung* (pp. 269 – 299). Wiesbaden: Gabler.

Ekin, M. G. S., & Tezolmez, S. H. (1999). Business ethics in Turkey: An empirical investigation with special emphasis on gender. *Journal of Business Ethics, 18*(1), 17 – 34.

Eliasberg, W. (1951). Corruption and bribery. *Journal of Criminal Law, Criminology & Police Science, 42*(3), 317 – 331.

Emerson, P. M. (2006). Corruption, competition and democracy. *Journal of Development Economics, 81*(1), 193 – 212.

Emerson, R. M. (1972a). Exchange theory, part I: A psychological basis for social exchange. In J. Berger, M. Zelditch, & B. Anderson (Eds.), *Sociological theories in progress* (pp. 38 – 57). Boston: Houghton Mifflin.

Emerson, R. M. (1972b). Exchange theory, part II: Exchange rules and networks. In J. Berger, M. Zelditch, & B. Anderson (Eds.), *Sociological theories in progress* (pp. 58 – 87). Boston: Houghton Mifflin.

Emerson, R. M. (1976). Social exchange theory. *Annual Review of Sociology, 2*, 335 – 362.

Engerer, H. (1998). *Ursachen, Folgen und Bekämpfung von Korruption: Liefern ökonomische Ansätze bestechende Argumente?* (Discussion Paper No. 161). Berlin: Deutsches Institut für Wirtschaftsforschung. Retrieved January 20, 2005, from http://www.diw.de/deutsch/produkte/publikationen/diskussions papiere/docs/papers/dp161.pdf

Espejo, R., Bula, G., & Zarama, R. (2001). Auditing as the dissolution of corruption. *Systemic Practice and Action Research, 14*(2), 139 – 156.

European Commission (2004a). *Attitudes related to defrauding the European Union and its budget. Public opinion in the acceding and candidate countries, Candidate Countries Eurobarometer 2003/4.* Retrieved November 10, 2005, from http://europa.eu.int/comm/public_opinion/archives/cceb/2003/cceb_%202003.4_o laf_report.pdf

European Commission (2004b). *Attitudes related to defrauding the European Union and its budget. Public opinion in the member states, Special Eurobarometer 200 – Wave 60.1.* Retrieved November 10, 2005, from http://europa.eu.int/comm/anti_fraud/press_room/eurobar/memb_en.pdf

European Foundation for Management Development (2008). *EQUIS standards and criteria.* Brussels: European Foundation for Management Development. Retrieved April 30, 2008, from http://www.efmd.org/attachments//tmpl_1_art_041027xvpa_att_080404qois.pdf

Fan, Y. (2002). Guanxi's consequences: Personal gains at social cost. *Journal of Business Ethics, 38*(4), 371 – 380.

Fassott, G., & Eggert, A. (2005). Zur Verwendung formativer und reflektiver Indikatoren in Strukturgleichungsmodellen: Bestandsaufnahme und Anwendungsempfehlungen. In F. Bliemel, A. Eggert, G. Fassott, & J. Henseler (Eds.), *Handbuch PLS-Pfadmodellierung* (pp. 31 – 47). Stuttgart: Schäffer-Poeschel.

Ferrell, O. C., & Gresham, L. G. (1985). A contingency framework for understanding ethical decision making in marketing. *Journal of Marketing Management, 49*(3), 87 – 96.

Fiebig, H., & Junker, H. (2004). *Korruption und Untreue im öffentlichen Dienst: Erkennen – Bekämpfen – Vorbeugen*. Berlin: Schmidt.

Finney, H. C., & Lesieur, H. R. (1982). A contingency theory of organizational crime. In S. Barrach (Ed.), *Research in the sociology of organizations: A research annual* (pp. 255 – 299). Greenwich, CT: JAI Press.

Fischer, P. (1981). Korruption im internationalen Wirtschaftsverkehr im Zusammenhang mit der Tätigkeit transnationaler Unternehmen. In C. Brünner (Ed.), *Korruption und Kontrolle* (pp. 469 – 489). Wien: Böhlau.

Fishbein, M., & Ajzen, I. (1975). *Belief, attitude, intention and behavior*. London: Addison-Wesley.

Fisman, R., & Svensson, J. (2007). Are corruption and taxation really harmful to growth? Firm level evidence. *Journal of Development Economics, 83*(1), 63 – 75.

Fleck, C., & Kuzmics, H. (1985). Einleitung. In C. Fleck, & H. Kuzmics (Eds.), *Korruption. Zur Soziologie nicht immer abweichenden Verhaltens* (pp. 7 – 39). Königstein/Ts: Athenäum.

Ford, R. C., & Richardson, W. D. (1994). Ethical decision making: A review of the empirical literature. *Journal of Business Ethics, 13*(3), 205 – 221.

Fornell, C. (1985). *A second generation of multivariate analysis: Classification of methods and implications for marketing research.* (Working Paper No. 414). Ann Arbor: University of Michigan, Graduate School of Business Administration, Division of Research. Retrieved February 11, 2008, from http://deepblue.lib. umich.edu/bitstream/2027.42/35621/2/b1408124.0001.001.pdf

Fornell, C., & Bookstein, F. L. (1982). Two structural equation models: LISREL and PLS applied to consumer exit-voice theory. *Journal of Marketing Research, 19*(4), 440 – 452.

Fornell, C., & Larcker, D. F. (1981). Evaluating structural equation models with unobservable variables and measurement error. *Journal of Marketing Research, 18*(1), 39 – 50.

Forsyth, D. R. (1980). Taxonomy of ethical ideologies. *Journal of Personality and Social Psychology, 39*(1), 175 – 184.

Fraedrich, J. P. (1993). The ethical behavior of retail managers. *Journal of Business Ethics*, *12*(3), 207 – 218.

Frank, B. (2004). Zehn Jahre empirische Korruptionsforschung. *Vierteljahrshefte zur Wirtschaftsforschung*, *73*(2), 184 – 199.

Frank, B., & Schulze, G. G. (2000). Does economics make citizens corrupt? *Journal of Economic Behavior & Organization*, *43*(1), 101 – 113.

Frank, R. H., Gilovich, T. D., & Regan, D. T. (1996). Do economists make bad citizens? *The Journal of Economic Perspectives*, *10*(1), 187 – 192.

Frankfurt, H. G. (1988). *The importance of what we care about*. Cambridge: Cambridge University Press.

Freisitzer, K. (1981). Gesellschaftliche Bedingungen der Korruption. Versuch einer verhaltenswissenschaftlichen Deutung. In C. Brünner (Ed.), *Korruption und Kontrolle* (pp. 151 – 163). Wien: Böhlau.

Friedman, E., Johnson, S., Kaufmann, D., & Zoido-Lobaton, P. (2000). Dodging the grabbing hand: The determinants of unofficial activity in 69 countries. *Journal of Public Economics*, *76*(3), 459 – 493.

Fripp, J. (1984a). Business games can be educational too! *Journal of European Industrial Training*, *8*(1), 27 – 32.

Fripp, J. (1984b). Games for research. *Journal of European Industrial Training*, *8*(3), 17 – 22.

Fukukawa, K. (2002). Developing a framework for ethically questionable behavior in consumption. *Journal of Business Ethics*, *41*(1/2), 99 – 119.

Gardner, R. (2003). *Games for business and economics (2nd ed.)*. New York: Wiley.

Gatti, R., Paternostro, S., & Rigolini, J. (2003). *Individual attitudes toward corruption: Do social effects matter?* (World Bank Policy Research Working Paper No. 3122). Washington, DC: World Bank. Retrieved April 28, 2005, from http://econ.worldbank.org/files/29354_wp3122.pdf

Gaviria, A. (2002). Assessing the effects of corruption and crime on firm performance: evidence from Latin America. *Emerging Markets Review*, *3*(3), 245 – 268.

Geis, G. (1992). White-collar crime: What is it? In K. Schlegel, & D. Weisburd (Eds.), *White-collar crime reconsidered* (pp. 31 – 52). Boston: Northeastern University Press.

Geis, N. (1997). Korruption in Staat und Wirtschaft. In H. Reichmann, W. Schlaffke, & W. Then (Eds.), *Korruption in Staat und Wirtschaft* (pp. 47 – 60). Köln: Deutscher Instituts-Verlag.

Geisser, S. (1975). The predictive sample reuse method with applications. *Journal of the American Statistical Association*, *70*(350), 320 – 328.

Gelfand, M. J., Bhawuk, D. P. S., Nishii, L. H., & Bechtold, D. J. (2005). Individualism and collectivism. In R. J. House, P. J. Hanges, M. Javidan, P. W. Dorfman, & V. Gupta (Eds.), *Culture, leadership, and organizations: The GLOBE study of 62 societies* (pp. 437 – 512). Thousand Oaks, CA: Sage.

Gellerman, S. W. (1989). Managing ethics from the top down. *Sloan Management Review, 30*(2), 73 – 79.

Génaux, M. (2004). Social sciences and the evolving concept of corruption. *Crime, Law and Social Change, 42*(1), 13 – 24.

George, B. C., Lacey, K. A., & Birmele, J. (2000). The 1998 OECD Convention: An impetus for worldwide changes in attitudes toward corruption in business transactions. *American Business Law Journal, 37*(3), 485 – 525.

German, P. M. (2002). To bribe or not to bribe – a less than ethical dilemma, resolved? *Journal of Financial Crime, 9*(3), 249 – 258.

Getz, K. A., & Volkema, R. J. (2001). Culture, perceived corruption, and economics: A model of predictors and outcomes. *Business Society, 40*(1), 7 – 30.

Geuting, M. (2000). Soziale Simulation und Planspiel in pädagogischer Perspektive. In D. Herz, & A. Blättle (Eds.), *Simulation und Planspiel in den Sozialwissenschaften. Eine Bestandsaufnahme der internationalen Diskussion* (pp. 15 – 61). Münster: LIT.

Giddens, A. (1984). *The constitution of society: Outline of the theory of structuration.* Berkeley, CA: University of California Press .

Glynn, P., Kobrin, S. J., & Naim, M. (1997). The globalization of corruption. In A. E. Kimberly (Ed.), *Corruption and the global economy* (pp. 7 – 27). Washington, DC: Institute for International Economics.

Göbel, E. (2006). *Unternehmensethik – Grundlagen und praktische Umsetzung.* Stuttgart: Lucius & Lucius.

Goel, R. K., & Rich, D. P. (1989). On the economic incentives for taking bribes. *Public Choice, 61*(3), 269 – 275.

Gollwitzer, P. M. (1990). Action phases and mind-sets. In E. T. Higgins, & R. M. Sorrentino (Eds.), *Handbook of motivation and social cognition. Foundations of social behavior* (Vol. 2, pp. 287 – 312). New York: Guilford Press.

Gollwitzer, P. M. (1996). The volitional benefits of planning. In P. M. Gollwitzer, & J. A. Bargh (Eds.), *The psychology of action. Linking cognition and motivation to behavior* (pp. 287 – 312). New York: Guilford Press.

Gollwitzer, P. M. (1999). Implementation intentions: Strong effects of simple plans. *American Psychologist, 54*(7), 493 – 503.

Gollwitzer, P. M., & Brandstätter, V. (1997). Implementation intentions and effective goal pursuit. *Journal of Personality and Social Psychology, 73*(1), 186 – 199.

Gordon, K., & Miyake, M. (2001). Business approaches to combating bribery: A study of codes of conduct. *Journal of Business Ethics, 34*(3/4), 161 – 173.

Gorta, A. (2001). Research: A tool for building corruption resistance. In P. Larmour, & N. Wolanin (Eds.), *Corruption and anti-corruption* (pp. 11 – 29). Canberra: Asia Pacific Press.

Gottfredson, M. R., & Hirschi, T. (1990). *A general theory of crime.* Stanford, CA: Stanford University Press.

Goudie, A. W., & Stasavage, D. (1997). *Corruption: The issues.* (OECD Development Centre Working Papers No. 122). Paris: OECD Development Centre. Retrieved October 18, 2007, from http://caliban.sourceoecd.org/vl=1556691/cl= 17/nw=1/rpsv/cgi-bin/wppdf?file=5lgsjhvj7cxw.pdf

Graeff, P. (2004). Medien und Korruption: Die korruptionssenkende Wirkung der Mediennutzung und der "neuen Medien". *Vierteljahrshefte zur Wirtschaftsforschung, 73*(2), 212 – 225.

Graf, H. (2000). *Korruption. Die Entschlüsselung eines universellen Phänomens.* Egelsbach: Fouqué Literaturverlag.

Gray, C. W., & Kaufmann, D. (1998). Korruption und Entwicklung. *Finanzierung und Entwicklung, 35*, 7 – 10.

Greenberg, J., & Eskew, D. E. (1993). The role of role playing in organizational research. *Journal of Management, 19*(2), 221 – 241.

Grieger, J. (2005). *Corruption in organizations: Some outlines for research.* (Working Paper No. 2003). Wuppertal: University of Wuppertal, Department of Economics and Social Sciences. Retrieved July 31, 2007, from http://www.wiwi. uni-wuppertal.de/grieger/wp203.pdf

Guerrero, M. A., & Rodriguez-Oreggia, E. (2008). On the individual decisions to commit corruption: A methodological complement. *Journal of Economic Behavior & Organization, 65*(2), 357 – 372.

Gupta, S., Davoodi, H., & Alonso-Terme, R. (2002). Does corruption affect income inequality and poverty? *Economics of Governance, 3*(1), 23 – 45.

Habib, M., & Zurawicki, L. (2002). Corruption and foreign direct investment. *Journal of International Business Studies, 33*(2), 291 – 307.

Hacker, F. (1981). Sozialpsychologische Bedingungen der Korruption. In C. Brünner (Ed.), *Korruption und Kontrolle* (pp. 137 – 150). Wien: Böhlau.

Hägg, I., Johanson, J., & Ramström, D. (1974). Das Unternehmungsspiel als Forschungsinstrument – Experimente über die Wirkung empfangener Informationen auf den Entscheidungsprozeß. In F. Eisenführ, D. Ordelheide, & G. Puck (Eds.), *Unternehmungsspiele in Ausbildung und Forschung* (pp. 255 – 268). Wiesbaden: Gabler.

Hall, P. A., & Taylor, R. C. R. (1996). *Political science and the three new institutionalisms.* (MPIFG Discussion Paper No. 96/6). Köln: Max-Planck-Institut für Gesellschaftsforschung. Retrieved October 31, 2007, http://www.mpi-fg-koeln. mpg.de/pu/mpifg_dp/dp96-6.pdf

Hansmann, K., & Ringle, C. M. (2005). Wirkung einer Teilnahme an Unternehmensnetzwerken auf die strategischen Erfolgsfaktoren von Partnerunternehmen – Eine empirische Untersuchung. *Die Unternehmung, 3*, 217 – 236.

Hardt, B. (2001). *Korruption und Macht in der Organisation. Eine mikropolitische Analyse.* Universität Oldenburg: Dissertation.

Harris, J. R., & Sutton, C. D. (1995). Unravelling the ethical decision-making process: Clues from an empirical study comparing Fortune 1000 Executives and MBA students. *Journal of Business Ethics, 14*(10), 805 – 817.

Hasse, R., & Krücken, G. (2005). *Neo-Institutionalismus.* Bielefeld: Transcript-Verlag.

Heberer, T. (1991). *Korruption in China. Analyse eines politischen, ökonomischen und sozialen Problems.* Opladen: Westdeutscher Verlag.

Heberer, T. (2001). *Korruption als globales Phänomen und seine Ausprägungen in Ostasien. Korruption und Korruptionsdiskurse.* (Project Discussion Paper No. 9/2001). Duisburg: Gerhard-Mercator-Universität Duisburg, Institut für Ostasienwissenschaften. Retrieved January 24, 2006, from http://www.uni-duisburg.de/ Institute/OAWISS/download/doc/discuss9.pdf

Heckhausen, H. (1987a). Intentionsgeleitetes Handeln und seine Fehler. In H. Heckhausen, P. M. Gollwitzer, & F. E. Weinert (Eds.), *Jenseits des Rubikon: Der Wille in den Humanwissenschaften* (pp. 143 – 175). Heidelberg: Springer.

Heckhausen, H. (1987b). Wünschen – wählen – wollen. In H. Heckhausen, P. M. Gollwitzer, & F. E. Weinert (Eds.), *Jenseits des Rubikon: Der Wille in den Humanwissenschaften* (pp. 3 – 9). Heidelberg: Springer.

Heckhausen, H. (1989). *Motivation und Handeln* (2nd ed.). Berlin: Springer.

Hegarty, W. H., & Sims, H. P. (1978). Some determinants of unethical decision behavior: An experiment. *Journal of Applied Psychology, 63*(4), 451 – 457.

Heidack, C. (1980). *Planspiel-Praxis. Schwerpunkte der Methodik und Didaktik der Planspiel-Praxis unter besonderer Berücksichtigung des Verhaltenstrainings.* Speyer: Gabal.

Heidenheimer, A. J. (2002). Perspectives on the perception of corruption. In A. J. Heidenheimer, & M. Johnston (Eds.), *Political corruption: Concepts and contexts* (3rd ed., pp. 141 – 154). New Brunswick, NJ: Transaction Publishers.

Helmkamp, J., Ball, R., & Townsend, K. (1996). *Definitional dilemma: Can and should there be a universal definition of white-collar crime?* Morgantown, WV: National White-Collar Crime Center.

Henle, C. A. (2005). Predicting workplace deviance from the interaction between organizational justice and personality. *Journal of Managerial Issues, 17*(2), 247 – 263.

Henseler, J. (2005). Einführung in die PLS-Pfadmodellierung. *Wirtschaftswissenschaftliches Studium, 2,* 70 – 75.

Heuskel, D. (2004). Transparenz – moralische Forderung und unternehmerische Herausforderung. In A. Brink, & O. Karitzki (Eds.), *Unternehmensethik in turbulenten Zeiten. Wirtschaftsführer über Ethik im Management* (pp. 105 – 112). Bern: Haupt.

Hillgruber, A. (1912). *Fortlaufende Arbeit und Willensbetätigung.* Leipzig: Quelle und Meyer.

Hinze, H. (19.07.2005). Selbstbedienung in DAX-Konzernen – Korruption ist Chefsache. *Manager-Magazin.* Retrieved July 19, 2005, from http://www.manager-magazin.de/unternehmen/artikel/0,2828,365698,00.html

Höffling, C. (2002). *Korruption als soziale Beziehung.* Opladen: Leske + Budrich.

Hoffman, J. J. (1998). Are women really more ethical than men? Maybe it depends on the situation. *Journal of Managerial Issues, 10*(1), 60 – 73.

Hoffmann, J., Mokros, A., & Wilmer, R. (2008). *Der Psychologische Integritätstest PIT.* Düsseldorf: Wilmer & Hoffmann GbR. Website: http://pit-test.com/

Hofstede, G. (1980). *Culture's consequences: International differences in work-related values.* Beverly Hills, CA: Sage.

Hofstede, G. (1984). Cultural dimensions in management and planning. *Asia Pacific Journal of Management, 1*(2), 81 – 99.

Holtfreter, K. (2005). Is occupational fraud "typical" white-collar crime? A comparison of individual and organizational characteristics. *Journal of Criminal Justice, 33*(4), 353 – 365.

Homann, K. (1997). Unternehmensethik und Korruption. *Zeitschrift für betriebswirtschaftliche Forschung, 49*(3), 187 – 209.

Homans, G. C. (1961). *Social behavior: Its elementary forms.* New York: Harcourt, Brace & World.

Hotchkiss, C. (1998). The sleeping dog stirs: New signs of life in efforts to end corruption in international business. *Journal of Public Policy & Marketing, 17*(1), 108 – 115.

House, R. J., Hanges, P. J., Javidan, M., Dorfman, P. W., & Gupta, V. (Eds.) (2005). *Culture, leadership, and organizations: The GLOBE study of 62 societies.* Thousand Oaks, CA: Sage.

Huberty, C. J., & Morris, J. D. (1989). Multivariate analysis versus multiple univariate analyses. *Psychological Bulletin, 105*(2), 302 – 308.

Hulland, J. (1999). Use of partial least squares (PLS) in strategic management research: A review of four recent studies. *Strategic Management Journal, 20*(2), 195 – 204.

Hunt, J. (2004). *Trust and bribery: The role of the quid pro quo and the link with crime.* (IZA Discussion Paper No. 1179). Bonn: Institut zur Zukunft der Arbeit. Retrieved March 8, 2005, from http://dsl.nber.org/papers/w10510.pdf

Hunt, J., & Laszlo, S. (2005). *Bribery: Who pays, who refuses, what are the payoffs?* (William Davidson Institute Working Paper No. 792). Ann Arbor, MI: University of Michigan, William Davidson Institute. Retrieved November 24, 2005, from www.wdi.umich.edu/files/publications/workingpapers/wp792. pdf

Hunt, S. D., & Chonko, L. B. (1984). Marketing and Machiavellianism. *Journal of Marketing, 48*(3), 30 – 42.

Hunt, S. D., & Vitell, S. J. (1986). A general theory of marketing ethics. *Journal of Macromarketing, 6*(1), 5 – 16.

Huntington, S. P. (1968). *Political order in changing societies.* New Haven, CT: University Press.

Huntington, S. P. (1989). Modernization and corruption. In A. J. Heidenheimer, & M. Johnston (Eds.), *Political corruption: A handbook* (pp. 253 – 264). New Brunswick, NJ: Transaction.

Husted, B. W. (1999). Wealth, culture, and corruption. *Journal of International Business Studies, 30*(2), 339 – 359.

Husted, B. W. (2007). Agency, information, and the structure of moral problems in business. *Organization Studies, 28*(2), 177 – 195.

James, H. S. (2002). When is a bribe a bribe? Teaching a workable definition of bribery. *Teaching Business Ethics, 6*(2), 199 – 217.

Jarvis, C. B., MacKenzie, S. B., & Podsakoff, P. M. (2003). A critical review of construct indicators and measurement model misspecification in marketing and consumer research. *Journal of Consumer Research, 30*(2), 199 – 218.

Jayawickrama, N. (2001). Transparency International: Combating corruption through institutional reform. In A. Y. Lee-Chai, & J. A. Bargh (Eds.), *The use and abuse of power: Multiple perspectives on the causes of corruption* (pp. 281 – 298). Philadelphia: Psychology Press.

Johnson, S., Kaufmann, D., McMillan, J., & Woodruff, C. (2000). Why do firms hide? Bribes and unofficial activity after communism. *Journal of Public Economics, 76,* 495 – 520.

Johnston, M. (1989). Corruption, development and inequality. In P. M. Ward (Ed.), *Corruption, development, and inequality: Soft touch or hard graft* (pp. 13 – 37). London: Routledge.

Johnston, M. (2000, August). *The new corruption rankings: Implications for analysis and reform.* Paper presented at the World Congress of the International Political Science Association, Quebec City, Canada. Retrieved January 21, 2005, from http://departments.colgate.edu/polisci/papers/mjohnston/originals/Johnston IPSA2000.pdf

Jones, G. E., & Kavanagh, M. J. (1996). An experimental examination of the effects of individual and situational factors on unethical behavioral intentions in the workplace. *Journal of Business Ethics, 15*(5), 511 – 523.

Jones, T. M. (1991). Ethical decision making by individuals in organizations: An issue-contingent model. *The Academy of Management Review, 16*(2), 366 – 395.

Jong-sung, Y., & Khagram, S. (2005). A comparative study of inequality and corruption. *American Sociological Review, 70*(1), 136 – 157.

Jöreskog, K. G. (1970). A general method for analysis of covariance structures. *Biometrika, 57*(2), 239 – 251.

Jöreskog, K. G. (1979). Structural equation models in the social sciences: Specification, estimation and testing. In K. G. Jöreskog, & D. Sörbom (Eds.), *Advances in factor analysis and structural equation models* (pp. 105 – 127). Cambridge, MA: Abt Books.

Kant, I. (2002). *Groundwork for the metaphysics of morals* (A. W. Wood, Trans.). New Haven, CT: Yale University Press. (Original work published 1785)

Kaptein, M. (2004). Business codes of multinational firms: What do they say? *Journal of Business Ethics, 50*(1), 13 – 31.

Kaufmann, D. (1997). Corruption: The facts. *Foreign Policy, 107,* 114 – 131.

Kaufmann, D. (1998). Revisiting anti-corruption strategies: Tilt towards incentive-driven approaches? In United Nations Development Programme (Ed.), *Corruption and integrity improvement initiatives in developing countries* (pp. 63 – 82). New York: United Nations Development Programme.

Kaufmann, D., Kraay, A., & Mastruzzi, M. (2004). Governance matters III: Governance indicators for 1996, 1998, 2000, and 2002. *The World Bank Economic Review, 18*(2), 253 – 287.

Kaufmann, D., Kraay, A., & Zoido-Lobaton, P. (1999). *Governance matters*. (World Bank Policy Research Working Paper No. 2196). Washington, DC: World Bank. Retrieved October 18, 2007, from http://siteresources.worldbank.org/INTWBIGO VANTCOR/Resources/govmatrs.pdf

Kaufmann, D., Pradhan, S., & Ryterman, R. (1998). New frontiers in diagnosing and combating corruption.. *The World Bank PremNotes, 7*. Retrieved January 23, 2006, from http://www.worldbank.org/wbi/governance/wp-corruption.html

Kaufmann, D., & Wei, S. (1999). *Does "grease money" speed up the wheels of commerce?* (NBER Working Paper No. 7093). Cambridge, MA: National Bureau of Economic Research. Retrieved October 24, 2007, from http://www.nber.org/papers/w7093

Kayes, D. C. (2006). Organizational corruption as theodicy. *Journal of Business Ethics, 67*(1), 51 – 62.

Kern, M. (2003). *Planspiele im Internet. Netzbasierte Lernarrangements zur Vermittlung betriebswirtschaftlicher Kompetenz*. Wiesbaden: Deutscher Universitäts-Verlag.

Khan, M. (1996). A typology of corrupt transactions in developing countries. *IDS Bulletin, 27*(2), 12 – 21.

Khatri, N., & Tsang, E. W. K. (2003). Antecedents and consequences of cronyism in organizations. *Journal of Business Ethics, 43*(4), 289 – 303.

Khatri, N., Tsang, E. W. K., & Begley, T. M. (2005, August). *Dynamics of cronyist social exchanges across cultures*. Paper presented at the Academy of Management Conference, Honolulu, Hawaii.

Khatri, N., Tsang, E. W. K., & Begley, T. M. (2006). Cronyism: A cross-cultural analysis. *Journal of International Business Studies, 37*(1), 61 – 75.

Kidder, D. L. (2005). Is it 'who I am', 'what I can get away with', or 'what you've done to me'? A multi-theory examination of employee misconduct. *Journal of Business Ethics, 57*(4), 389 – 398.

Kidwell, J. M., Stevens, R. E., & Bethke, A. L. (1987). Differences in ethical perceptions between male and female managers: Myth or reality? *Journal of Business Ethics, 6*(6), 489 – 493.

Killias, M., & Ribeaud, D. (1999). Korruption: Neue Erkentnisse im Lichte quantitativer Untersuchungen. *Crimiscope, 4*. Retrieved January 25, 2006, from http://www.unil.ch/webdav/site/esc/shared/Crimiscope/Crimiscope004_1999_D.pdf

Kleinginna, P. R., & Kleinginna, A. M. (1981). A categorized list of emotion definitions with suggestions for a consensual definition. *Motivation and Emotion*, 5(4), 345 – 379.

Klitgaard, R. (1988). *Controlling corruption*. Berkeley, CA: University of California Press.

Klitgaard, R. (1998). International cooperation against corruption. *Finance & Development*, 35(1), 3 – 6.

Klitgaard, T. (1991). Gifts and bribes. In R. J. Zeckhauser (Ed.), *Strategy and choice* (pp. 211 – 239). Cambridge, MA: MIT Press .

Klochko, M. A., & Ordeshook, P. C. (2003). Corruption, cooperation and endogenous time discount rates. *Public Choice*, 115(3), 259 – 283.

Knack, S., & Keefer, P. (1995). Institutions and economic performance: Cross-country tests using alternative institutional measures. *Economics and Politics*, VII, 207 – 227.

Kochan, T. A. (2002). Addressing the crisis in confidence in corporations: Root causes, victims, and strategies for reform. *Academy of Management Executive*, 16(3), 139 – 141.

Köpf, P. (1997). *Auf unsere Kosten! Mißwirtschaft und Korruption in Deutschland*. München: Heyne.

Kohut, G. F., & Corriher, S. E. (1994). The relationship of age, gender, experience and awareness of written ethics policies to business decision making. *SAM Advanced Management Journal*, 59(1), 32 – 39.

Konovsky, M. A., & Jaster, F. (1989). 'Blaming the victim' and other ways business men and women account for questionable behavior. *Journal of Business Ethics*, 8(5), 391 – 398.

Kriz, W. (2005). Planspiel. In S. Kühl, P. Strodtholz, & A. Taffertshofer (Eds.), *Quantitative Methoden der Organisationsforschung. Ein Handbuch* (pp. 243 – 269). Wiesbaden: VS-Verlag für Sozialwissenschaften.

Krug, S. (1997). *Korruption in verschiedenen Wirtschaftssystemen: Eine komparatorische Analyse*. Wiesbaden: Deutscher Universitäts-Verlag.

Kubal, D., Baker, M., & Coleman, K. (2006). Doing the right thing: How today's leading companies are becoming more ethical. *Performance Improvement*, 45(3), 5 – 8.

Küchler, W. (1997). Korruption aus der Sicht eines Unternehmers. In H. Reichmann, W. Schlaffke, & W. Then (Eds.), *Korruption in Staat und Wirtschaft* (pp. 213 – 242). Köln: Deutscher Instituts-Verlag.

Kühl, S. (2005). Experiment. In S. Kühl, P. Strodtholz, & A. Taffertshofer (Eds.), *Quantitative Methoden der Organisationsforschung. Ein Handbuch* (pp. 213 – 242). Wiesbaden: VS-Verlag für Sozialwissenschaften.

Kugel, Y., & Gruenberg, G. W. (1977). *International payoffs: Dilemma for business.* Lexington, MA: Lexington Books.

Kwok, C. C. Y., & Tadesse, S. (2006). The MNC as an agent of change for host-country institutions: FDI and corruption. *Journal of International Business Studies, 37*(6), 767 – 785.

La Porta, R., Lopez-de-Silanes, F., Shleifer, A., & Vishny, R. (1999). The quality of government. *Journal of Law, Economics, and Organization, 15*(1), 222 – 279.

Laffont, J., & N'Guessan, T. (1999). Competition and corruption in an agency relationship. *Journal of Development Economics, 60*(2), 271 – 295.

Lambert-Mogiliansky, A. (2002). Why firms pay occasional bribes: The connection economy. *European Journal of Political Economy, 18*(1), 47 – 60.

Lambsdorff, J. G. (1999). *Corruption in empirical research – A review.* (Transparency International Working Paper). Berlin: Transparency International. Retrieved February 20, 2005, from http://www.transparency.org/working_papers/ lambsdorff/lambsdorff_eresearch.html

Lambsdorff, J. G. (2002). Making corrupt deals: Contracting in the shadow of the law. *Journal of Economic Behavior & Organization, 48*(3), 221 – 241.

Lambsdorff, J. G. (2003). How corruption affects persistent capital flows. *Economics of Governance, 4*(3), 229 – 243.

Lambsdorff, J. G., & Nell, M. (2005). Korruption in Deutschland: Reformmaßnahmen. *Wirtschaftsdienst, 85*(12), 783 – 790.

Lambsdorff, J. G., & Teksoz, S. U. (2002). *Corrupt relational contracting.* (Diskussionsbeitrag Nr. 113). Göttingen: Universität Göttingen, Volkswirtschaftliches Seminar. Retrieved March 8, 2005, from http://www.icgg.org/downloads/contribu tion09_utkuteksoz.pdf

Lane, H. W., & Simpson, D. G. (1984). Bribery in international business: Whose problem is it? *Journal of Business Ethics, 3*(1), 35 – 42.

Lapalombara, J. (1994). Structural and institutional aspects of corruption. *Social Research, 61*(2), 325 – 350.

Lederman, D., Loayza, N. V., & Soares, R. R. (2001). *Accountability and corruption: Political institutions matter.* (World Bank Policy Research Working Paper No. 2708). Washington, DC: World Bank. Retrieved October 2, 2007, from http://www-wds.worldbank.org/servlet/WDSContentServer/WDSP/IB/2001/12/ 17/000094946_01120404004589/Rendered/PDF/multi0page.pdf

Leff, N. H. (1964). Economic development through bureaucratic corruption. *The American Behavioral Scientist*, *8*(3), 8 – 14.

Leite, C., & Weidmann, J. (1999). *Does mother nature corrupt? Natural resources, corruption, and economic growth*. (IMF Working Paper No. 99/85). Washington, DC: International Monetary Fund. Retrieved September 26, 2007, from http://www.imf.org/external/pubs/ft/wp/1999/wp9985.pdf

Leonard, L. N. K., Cronan, T. P., & Kreie, J. (2004). What influences IT ethical behavior intentions – planned behavior, reasoned action, perceived importance, or individual characteristics? *Information & Management*, *42*(1), 143 – 158.

Leone, L., Perugini, M., & Ercolani, A. P. (1999). A comparison of three models of attitude–behavior relationships in the studying behavior domain. *European Journal of Social Psychology*, *29*(2/3), 161 – 189.

Levi, M. (2000). Shaming and the regulation of fraud and business "misconduct". In S. Karstedt, & K. Bussmann (Eds.), *Social dynamics of crime and control* (pp. 117 – 132). Oxford, UK: Hart.

Levine, D. P. (2005). The corrupt organization. *Human Relations*, *58*(6), 723 – 740.

Leyendecker, H., & Ott, K. (13.12.2006). Immer neue Namen, neue Zahlen, neue Tatorte – Ein Netz mit dicken Knoten. *sueddeutsche.de*. Retrieved January 12, 2007, from http://www.sueddeutsche.de/wirtschaft/artikel/858/94764/article. html

Li, H., Xu, L. C., & Zou, H. (2000). Corruption, income distribution, and growth. *Economics & Politics*, *12*(2), 155 – 182.

Lien, D. D. (1986). A note on competitive bribery games. *Economics Letters*, *22*(4), 337 – 341.

Lienert, G. A., & Raatz, U. (1994). *Testaufbau und Testanalyse* (5th ed.). Weinheim: Beltz.

Litzky, B. E., Eddleston, K. A., & Kidder, D. L. (2006). The good, the bad, and the misguided: How managers inadvertently encourage deviant behaviors. *The Academy of Management Perspectives*, *20*(1), 91 – 103.

Lloyd, D. C. F. (1978). An introduction to business games. *Industrial and Commercial Training*, *10*(1), 11 – 18.

Locke, E. A., & Latham, G. P. (1990). *A theory of goal setting and task performance*. Englewood Cliffs, NJ: Prentice Hall.

Loe, T. W., Ferrell, L., & Mansfield, P. (2000). A review of empirical studies assessing ethical decision making in business. *Journal of Business Ethics*, *25*(3), 185 – 204.

Löw, A. (2002). *Multiperspektivische Analyse der Wirtschaftskriminalität – Konsequenzen für die Gestaltung des Integrierten Risiko-Managements*. St. Gallen: Institut für Versicherungswirtschaft der Universität St. Gallen.

Lohmöller, J. (1989). *Latent variable path modeling with partial least squares*. Heidelberg: Physica-Verlag.

Loo, R. (1996). Utility and construct validity of an ethical dilemmas scale in management education. *Journal of Business Ethics, 15*(5), 551 – 557.

Loo, R. (2003). Are women more ethical than men? Findings from three independent studies. *Women in Management Review, 18*(3/4), 169 – 181.

Lui, F. T. (1985). An equilibrium queuing model of bribery. *The Journal of Political Economy, 93*(4), 760 – 781.

Lui, F. T. (1986). A dynamic model of corruption deterrence. *Journal of Public Economics, 31*(2), 215 – 236.

Lund, D. B. (2000). An empirical examination of marketing professional's ethical behavior in differing situations. *Journal of Business Ethics, 24*(4), 331 – 342.

Luo, Y. (2002). Corruption and organization in Asian management systems. *Asia Pacific Journal of Management, 19*(2,3), 405 – 422.

Lynch, T. D., Lynch, C. E., & Cruise, P. L. (2002). Productivity and the moral manager. *Administration & Society, 34*(4), 347 – 369.

Macrae, J. (1982). Underdevelopment and the economics of corruption: A game theory approach. *World Development, 10*(8), 677 – 687.

Maes, J. D., Jeffery, A., & Smith, T. V. (1998). The American Association of Advertising Agencies (4As) standards of practice: How for does this professional association's code of ethics' influence reach? *Journal of Business Ethics, 17*(11), 1155 – 1161.

Magidson, J. (1979). Introduction to Part II. In K. G. Jöreskog, & D. Sörbom (Eds.), *Advances in factor analysis and structural equation models* (p. 103). Cambridge, MA: Abt Books.

Mallinger, M., Rossy, G., & Singel, D. (2005). Corruption across borders – What are the challenges for the global manager? *Graziadio Business Report, 8* (2). Retrieved July 20, 2006, from http://gbr.pepperdine.edu/052/corruption.html

Manandhar, N. (2005). *Corruption and anti-corruption*. Kathmandu: Tansparency International.

Maravic, P. V. (2006). Korruptionsanalyse als Analyse von Handlungssituationen – Ein konzeptioneller Vorschlag. In K. Birkholz, C. Maaß, P. V. Maravic, & P. Siebart (Eds.), *Public Management – Eine neue Generation in Wissenschaft und Praxis: Festschrift für Christoph Reichard* (pp. 97 – 128). Potsdam: Universitätsverlag Potsdam.

March, J. G., & Olsen, J. P. (1989). *Rediscovering institutions: The organizational basics of politics*. New York: Free Press.

Marcus, B. (2006). *Inventar berufsbezogener Einstellungen und Selbsteinschät-zungen*. Göttingen: Hogrefe.

Martin, K. D., Cullen, J. B., Johnson, J. L., & Parboteeah, K. P. (2007). Deciding to bribe: A cross-level analysis of firm and home country influences on bribery activity. *Academy of Management Journal*, *50*(6), 1401 – 1422.

Mason, E. S., & Mudrack, P. E. (1996). Gender and ethical orientation: A test of gender and occupational socialization theories. *Journal of Business Ethics*, *15*(6), 599 – 604.

Mauro, P. (1995). Corruption and growth. *The Quarterly Journal of Economics*, *110*(3), 681 – 712.

Mauro, P. (1997). The effects of corruption on growth, investment, and government expenditure: A cross-country analysis. In K. A. Elliot (Ed.), *Corruption and the global economy* (pp. 83 – 107). Washington, DC: Institute of International Economics.

Mauro, P. (1998a). Corruption and the composition of government expenditure. *Journal of Public Economics*, *69*(2), 263 – 279.

Mauro, P. (1998b). Corruption: Causes, consequences, and agenda for further research. *Finance & Development*, *35*(1), 11 – 14.

Mayring, P. (2000). *Qualitative Inhaltsanalyse. Grundlagen und Techniken* (7th ed.). Weinheim: Deutscher Studienverlag.

McArthur, J., & Teal, F. (2002). *Corruption and firm performance in Africa*. (CSAE Working Paper No. 169). Oxford, UK: The Centre for the Study of African Economies. Retrieved October 23, 2007, from http://www.bepress.com/csae/paper169/

McCabe, A. C., Ingram, R., & Dato-on, M. C. (2006). The business of ethics and gender. *Journal of Business Ethics*, *64*(2), 101 – 116.

McDonald, G. (2000). Business ethics: Practical proposals for organisations. *Journal of Business Ethics*, *25*(2), 169 – 184.

McFarlane, J. (2001). Transnational crime: Corruption, crony capitalism and nepotism in the twenty-first century. In P. Larmour, & N. Wolanin (Eds.), *Corruption and anti-corruption* (pp. 131 – 145). Canberra: Asia Pacific Press.

McKendall, M., DeMarr, B., & Jones-Rikkers, C. (2002). Ethical compliance programs and corporate illegality: Testing the assumptions of the corporate sentencing guidelines. *Journal of Business Ethics*, *37*(4), 367 – 383.

Mele, A. R. (1995). Motivation: Essentially motivation-constituting attitudes. *Philosophical Review*, *104*(3), 387 – 423.

Merritt, S. (1991). Marketing ethics and education: Some empirical findings. *Journal of Business Ethics*, *10*(8), 625 – 632.

Merton, R. K. (1949). *Social theory and social structure*. Glencoe, IL: Free Press.

Michelman, J. H. (1983). Some ethical consequences of economic competition. *Journal of Business Ethics, 2*(2), 79 – 87.

Miller, W. L. (2006). Corruption and corruptibility. *World Development, 34*(2), 371 – 380.

Millington, A., Eberhardt, M., & Wilkinson, B. (2005). Gift giving, guanxi and illicit payments in buyer-supplier relations in China: Analysing the experience of UK companies. *Journal of Business Ethics, 57*(3), 255 – 268.

Mitchell, T. R. (1997). Matching motivational strategies with organizational contexts. *Research in Organizational Behavior, 19*, 57 – 149.

Mitchell, T. R., Daniels, D., Hopper, H., George-Falvy, J., & Ferris, G. R. (1996). Perceived correlates of illegal behavior in organizations. *Journal of Business Ethics, 15*(4), 439 – 455.

Mitchell, W. J., Lewis, P. V., & Reinsch, N. L,, Jr. (1992). Bank ethics: An exploratory study of ethical behaviors and perceptions in small, local banks. *Journal of Business Ethics, 11*(3), 197 – 205.

Mo, P. H. (2001). Corruption and economic growth. *Journal of Comparative Economics, 29*(1), 66 – 79.

Mocan, H. N. (2004). *What determines corruption?* Cambridge, MA: National Bureau of Economic Research.

Molm, L. D. (1994). Dependence and risk: Transforming the structure of social exchange. *Social Psychology Quarterly, 57*(3), 163 – 176.

Morgan, A. L. (1998). *Corruption: Causes, consequences, and policy implications. A literature review*. (Asia Foundation Working Paper No. 9). San Francisco: The Asia Foundation. Retrieved November 14, 2005, from http://www.asiafoundation.org/pdf/wp9.pdf

Münchau, W. (20.12.2006). Kultur der Käuflichkeit. *Financial Times Deutschland*. Retrieved December 20, 2006, from http://www.ftd.de/meinung/leitartikel/1435 51.html

Murphy, K. M., Shleifer, A., & Vishny, R. W. (1991). The allocation of talent: Implications for growth. *The Quarterly Journal of Economics, 106*(2), 503 – 530.

Murphy, K. M., Shleifer, A., & Vishny, R. W. (1993). Why is rent-seeking so costly to growth? *The American Economic Review, 83*(2), 409 – 414.

Murphy, P. R., Smith, J. E., & Daley, J. M. (1992). Executive attitudes, organizational size and ethical issues: Perspectives on a service industry. *Journal of Business Ethics, 11*(1), 11 – 19.

Mussel, P. (2003). Persönlichkeitsinventar zur Integritätsabschätzung (PIA). In J. Erpenbeck, & L. V. Rosenstiel (Eds.), *Handbuch Kompetenzmessung. Erkennen, verstehen und bewerten von Kompetenzen in der betrieblichen, pädagogischen und psychologischen Praxis* (pp. 3 – 18). Stuttgart: Schäffer-Poeschel Verlag.

Myrdal, G. (1968). *Asian drama. An inquiry into the poverty of nations*. New York: Pantheon.

Nagel, W. (2005). *WiN-ABSATZ*. Lörrach: WN-Learnware. service@wn-learnware. de

Nanus, B. (1969). Management games: An answer to critics. In R. G. Graham, & C. F. Gray (Eds.), *Business games handbook* (pp. 52 – 57). New York: American Management Association.

Near, J. P., & Miceli, M. P. (1985). Organizational dissidence: The case of whistle-blowing. *Journal of Business Ethics*, *4*(1), 1 – 16.

Neisser, U. (1967). *Cognitive psychology*. New York: Appleton-Century-Crofts.

Neugebauer, G. (1978). *Grundzüge einer ökonomischen Theorie der Korruption. Eine Studie über die Bestechung*. Zürich: Schulthess.

Noack, P. (1985). *Korruption, die andere Seite der Macht*. München: Kindler.

Noonan, R., & Wold, H. (1982). PLS path modeling with indirectly observed variables: A comparison of alternative estimates for latent variables . In K. G. Jöreskog, & Wold H (Eds.), *Systems under indirect observations: Causality, structure, prediction* (Vol. 2, pp. 75 – 94). Amsterdam: North-Holland.

Nunnally, J. C. (1978). *Psychometric theory*. New York: McGraw-Hill.

Nye, J. S. (1967). Corruption and political development: A cost-benefit analysis. *American Political Science Review*, *61*(2), 417 – 427.

O'Fallon, M. J., & Butterfield, K. D. (2005). A review of the empirical ethical decision-making literature: 1996-2003. *Journal of Business Ethics*, *59*(4), 375 – 413.

Ockenfels, W. (1997). Korruption als sozialethisches Problem. In H. Reichmann, W. Schlaffke, & W. Then (Eds.), *Korruption in Staat und Wirtschaft* (pp. 86 – 109). Köln: Deutscher Instituts-Verlag.

Organisation for Economic Co-operation and Development (2007). *Corruption – A glossary of international criminal standards*. Paris: Organisation for Economic Co-operation and Development. Retrieved February 5, 2008, from http://www. oecd.org/dataoecd/6/4/39968498.pdf

Osgood, D. W., Wilson, J. K., O'Malley, P. M., Bachman, J. G., & Johnston, L. D. (1996). Routine activities and individual deviant behavior. *American Sociological Review*, *61*(4), 635 – 655.

Paldam, M. (2001). Corruption and religion. Adding to the economic model? *Kyklos*, *54*(2/3), 383 – 413.

Paldam, M. (2002). The cross-country pattern of corruption: economics, culture and the seesaw dynamics. *European Journal of Political Economy*, *18*(2), 215 – 240.

Park, H. (2003). Determinants of corruption: A cross-national analysis. *Multinational Business Review*, *11*(2), 29 – 48.

Parker, D., Manstead, A. S. R., & Stradling, S. G. (1995). Extending the theory of planned behaviour: The role of personal norm. *British Journal of Social Psychology*, *34*(2), 127 – 137.

Pearson, Z. (2001). An international human rights approach to corruption. In P. Larmour, & N. Wolanin (Eds.), *Corruption and anti-corruption* (pp. 30 – 61). Canberra: Asia Pacific Press.

Pellegrini, L., & Gerlaugh, R. (2004). Corruption's effect on growth and its transmission channels. *Kyklos*, *57*(3), 429 – 456.

Pelletier, K. L., & Bligh, M. C. (2006). Rebounding from corruption: Perceptions of ethics program effectiveness in a public sector organization. *Journal of Business Ethics*, *67*(4), 359 – 374.

Perugini, M., & Bagozzi, R. P. (2001). The role of desires and anticipated emotions in goal-directed behaviours: Broadening and deepening the theory of planned behaviour. *British Journal of Social Psychology*, *40*(1), 79 – 98.

Perugini, M., & Bagozzi, R. P. (2004). The distinction between desires and intentions. *European Journal of Social Psychology*, *34*(1), 69 – 84.

Perugini, M., & Conner, M. (2000). Predicting and understanding behavioral volitions: The interplay between goals and behaviors. *European Journal of Social Psychology*, *30*(5), 705 – 731.

Peterson, D. K. (2002). Deviant workplace behavior and the organization's ethical climate. *Journal of Business and Psychology*, *17*(1), 47 – 61.

Pies, I. (2003). *Korruption: Diagnose und Therapie aus wirtschaftsethischer Sicht.* (Diskussionspapier Nr. 03-7). Wittenberg: Wittenberg Center for Global Ethics. Retrieved November 4, 2005, from http://www.wiwi.uni-halle.de/ linebreak4/mod/ netmedia_pdf/data/03-7.pdf

Pies, I., Sass, P., & Meyer zu Schwabedissen, H. (2005). *Prävention von Wirtschaftskriminalität – Zur Theorie und Praxis der Korruptionsbekämpfung.* (Wirtschaftsethik-Studie Nr. 2005-2). Halle: Martin-Luther Universität Halle-Wittenberg, Lehrstuhl für Wirtschaftsethik. Retrieved November 4, 2005, from http://www.wiwi.uni-halle.de/linebreak4/mod/netmedia_pdf/data/studie_2005_2.pdf

Pitt, L. F., & Abratt, R. (1986). Corruption in business – Are management attitudes right? *Journal of Business Ethics*, *5*(1), 39 – 44.

Pletscher, T. (1999). "Wie halten wir unser Haus sauber?" – Bekämpfung der Korruption aus Sicht der Wirtschaft. In M. Pieth, & P. Eigen (Eds.), *Korruption im internationalen Geschäftsverkehr: Bestandsaufnahme, Bekämpfung, Prävention* (pp. 275 – 289). Neuwied: Luchterhand.

Poirson, H. (1998). *Economic security, private investment, and growth in developing countries*. (IMF Working Paper No. 98/4). Washington, DC: International Monetary Fund. Retrieved October 18, 2007, from http://www.imf.org/external/pubs/ft/wp/wp9804.pdf

Poorsoltan, K., Amin, S. G., & Tootoonchi, A. (1991). Business ethics: Views of future leaders. *SAM Advanced Management Journal*, *56*(1), 4 – 9.

Powpaka, S. (2002). Factors affecting managers' decision to bribe: An empirical investigation. *Journal of Business Ethics*, *40*(3), 227 – 246.

Priddat, B. P. (2004). Verdeckte Geldgeschäfte, illegale Spenden, Bestechungen: "public-private-partnership" der anderen Art. In A. Brink, & O. Karitzki (Eds.), *Unternehmensethik in turbulenten Zeiten. Wirtschaftsführer über Ethik im Management* (pp. 113 – 128). Bern: Haupt.

Quah, J. S. T. (1989). Singapore's experience in curbing corruption. In A. J. Heidenheimer, M. Johnston, & V. T. LeVine (Eds.), *Political corruption: A handbook* (pp. 841 – 853). New Brunswick, NJ: Transaction Publishers.

Rabl, T. (2006, May). *Person-oriented components of corrupt action in and between companies – A research design*. Paper presented at the European Academy of Management Doctoral Colloquium, Oslo, Norway.

Rabl, T., & Kühlmann, T. M. (2006). What makes decision-makers in companies to act corruptly? An action model. *International Journal of Knowledge, Culture & Change Management*, *6*(2), 103 – 110.

Rabl, T., & Kühlmann, T. M. (2006, November). *A model of corrupt action in organizations*. Paper presented at the World Business Ethics Forum, Hong Kong and Macau.

Rabl, T., & Kühlmann, T. M. (2007, April). *Corrupt action in organisations – Does sex make a difference?* Paper presented at the 11th European Business Ethics Network-UK Conference and 9th Ethics and Human Resource Management Conference, Cheltenham, UK.

Rabl, T., & Kühlmann, T. M. (2007, September). *Understanding corruption in organizations – Development and empirical assessment of an action model*. Paper presented at the 20th European Business Ethics Network Annual Conference, Leuven, Belgium.

Rabl, T., & Kühlmann, T. M. (2008). Understanding corruption in organizations – Development and empirical assessment of an action model. *Journal of Business Ethics, 82*(2), 477 – 495.

Rabl, T., & Kühlmann, T. M. (2008, August). *Corruption in and between companies – An empirically validated action model.* Paper presented at the 68th Academy of Management Annual Meeting, Anaheim, CA.

Rabl, T., & Kühlmann, T. M. (2008, May). *Why or why not? Rationalizing corruption in organizations.* Paper presented at the 8th European Academy of Management Conference, Ljubljana and Bled, Slovenia.

Randall, D. M., & Gibson, A. M. (1991). Ethical decision making in the medical profession: An application of the Theory of Planned Behavior. *Journal of Business Ethics, 10*(2), 111 – 122.

Rauch, J. E., & Evans, P. B. (2000). Bureaucratic structure and bureaucratic performance in less developed countries. *Journal of Public Economics, 75*(1), 49 – 71.

Reasons, C. E. (1982). Crime and the abuse of power: Offenses and offenders beyond the reach of the law. In P. Wickman, & T. Dailey (Eds.), *White-collar and economic crime* (pp. 59 – 72). Lexington, MA: Heath.

Reichmann, H. (1997). Korruption – Einführung in die Problematik. In H. Reichmann, W. Schlaffke, & W. Then (Eds.), *Korruption in Staat und Wirtschaft* (pp. 8 – 11). Köln: Deutscher Instituts-Verlag.

Reinikka, R., & Svensson, J. (2002). Measuring and understanding corruption at the micro level. In D. Della Ports, & S. Rose-Ackerman (Eds.), *Corrupt exchanges: Empirical themes in the politics and political economy of corruption* (pp. 135 – 146). Baden-Baden: Nomos Verlagsgesellschaft.

Reinikka, R., & Svensson, J. (2003). *Survey techniques to measure and explain corruption.* (World Bank Policy Research Working Paper No. 3071). Washington, DC: World Bank. Retrieved February 8, 2008, from http://www-wds.world-bank.org/servlet/WDSContentServer/WDSP/IB/2003/07/08/000094946_0306210 4301451/Rendered/PDF/multi0page.pdf

Reinikka, R., & Svensson, J. (2006). Using micro-surveys to measure and explain corruption. *World Development, 34*(2), 359 – 370.

Renner, E. (2004). Wie lässt sich Korruption wirksam bekämpfen? – Empirische Befunde aus der experimentellen Wirtschaftsforschung. *Vierteljahrshefte zur Wirtschaftsforschung, 73*(2), 292 – 300.

Rest, J. R. (1986). *Moral development: Advances in research and theory.* New York: Praeger.

Riahi-Belkaoui, A., & Picur, R. D. (2000). Understanding fraud in the accounting environment. *Managerial Finance, 26*(11), 33 – 41.

Rigdon, E. E. (1998). Structural equation modeling. In G. A. Marcoulides (Ed.), *Modern methods for business research* (pp. 251 – 294). Mahwah, NJ: Lawrence Erlbaum.

Ringle, C. M. (2004a). *Gütemaße für den Partial Least Squares-Ansatz zur Bestimmung von Kausalmodellen*. (Arbeitspapier Nr. 16). Hamburg: Universität Hamburg, Institut für Industriebetriebslehre und Organisation. Retrieved September 26, 2005, from http://www.ibl-unihh.de/ap16.pdf

Ringle, C. M. (2004b). *Messung von Kausalmodellen – Ein Methodenvergleich*. (Arbeitspapier Nr. 14). Hamburg: Universität Hamburg, Institut für Industriebetriebslehre und Organisation. Retrieved September 22, 2005, from http://www.eco nbiz.de/archiv/hh/uhh/iindustrie/messung_kausalmodelle.pdf

Ringle, C. M., Boysen, N., Wende, S., & Will, A. (2006). Messung von Kausalmodellen mit dem Partial-Least-Squares-Verfahren. *Das Wirtschaftsstudium, 1*, 81 – 87.

Ringle, C. M., Wende, S., & Will, A. (2005). *SmartPLS 2.0 (beta)*. Hamburg: University of Hamburg. Website: www.smartpls.de

Robin, D., & Babin, L. (1997). Making sense of the research on gender and ethics in business: A critical analysis and extension. *Business Ethics Quarterly, 7*(4), 61 – 90.

Robinson, S. L., & Bennett, R. J. (1995). A typology of deviant workplace behaviors: A multdimensional scaling study. *Academy of Management Journal, 38*(2), 555 – 572.

Roozen, I., De Pelsmacker, P., & Bostyn, F. (2001). The ethical dimensions of decision processes of employees. *Journal of Business Ethics, 33*(2), 87 – 99.

Rose-Ackerman, S. (1975). The economics of corruption. *Journal of Public Economics, 4*(2), 187 – 203.

Rose-Ackerman, S. (1978). *Corruption. A study in political economy*. New York: Academic Press.

Rose-Ackerman, S. (1999). *Corruption and government: Causes, consequences and reform*. Cambridge: Cambridge University Press.

Rose-Ackerman, S. (2001). Trust, honesty and corruption: Reflection on the state-building process. *European Journal of Sociology, 42*(3), 526 – 570.

Rosenberg, R. D. (1987). Managerial morality and behavior: The questionable payments issue. *Journal of Business Ethics, 6*(1), 23 – 36.

Rotter, J. B. (1966). Generalized expectancies for internal versus external control of reinforcement. *Psychological Monographs, 80*(1), 1 – 28.

Roxas, M. L., & Stoneback, J. Y. (2004). The importance of gender across cultures in ethical decision-making. *Journal of Business Ethics, 50*(2), 149 – 165.

Rügemer, W. (1996). *Wirtschaften ohne Korruption?* Frankfurt am Main: Fischer-Taschenbuch-Verlag.

Ruegger, D., & King, E. W. (1992). A study of the effect of age and gender upon student business ethics. *Journal of Business Ethics, 11*(3), 179 – 186.

Sackett, P. R., & Wanek, J. E. (1996). New developments in the use of measures of honesty, integrity, conscientiousness, dependability, trustworthiness,and reliability for personnel selection. *Personnel Psychology, 49*(4), 787 – 829.

Sah, R. K. (Dec 1991). Social osmosis and patterns of crime. *The Journal of Political Economy, 99*(6), 1272 – 1295.

Salbu, S. R. (2001). Transnational bribery: The big questions. *Northwestern Journal of International Law & Business, 21*(2), 435 – 470.

Sandholtz, W., & Gray, M. M. (2003). International integration and national corruption. *International Organization, 57*(4), 761 – 800.

Sandholtz, W., & Koetzle, W. (2000). Accounting for corruption: Economic structure, democracy, and trade. *International Studies Quarterly, 44*(1), 31 – 50.

Sanyal, R. (2005). Determinants of bribery in international business: The cultural and economic factors. *Journal of Business Ethics, 59*(1-2), 139 – 145.

Sanyal, R. N., & Samanta, S. K. (2004a). Determinants of bribery in international business. *Thunderbird International Business Review, 46*(2), 133 – 148.

Sanyal, R., & Samanta, S. K. (2004b). Correlates of bribe giving in international business. *International Journal of Commerce & Management, 14*(2), 1 – 14.

Scharpf, F. W. (1997). *Games real actors play. Actor-centered institutionalism in policy research.* Boulder, CO: Westview Press.

Schaupensteiner, W. (2004). Korruption in Deutschland: Lagebild, Maßnahmen und Gefahren. In A. Schilling, & U. Dolata (Eds.), *Korruption im Wirtschaftssystem Deutschland. Jeder Mensch hat seinen Preis* (pp. 117 – 136). Murnau a. Staffelsee: Mankau.

Schein, E. H. (1988). *Organizational culture.* (Sloan Working Paper No. 2088-88). Cambridge, MA: Sloan School of Management, Massachusetts Institute of Technology. Retrieved April 11, 2008, from http://dspace.mit.edu/bitstream/1721.1/2224/1/SWP-2088-24854366.pdf

Schilling, A. (2004). Korruption im Wirtschaftssystem Deutschland: Auswirkungen, Präventionsstrategien und ethische Betrachtung. In A. Schilling, & U. Dolata (Eds.), *Korruption im Wirtschaftssystem Deutschland. Jeder Mensch hat seinen Preis* (pp. 15 – 102). Murnau a. Staffelsee: Mankau.

Schmidt, K. (2003). Korruption aus (vorwiegend) ökonomischer Sicht. In V. V. Nell, G. Schwitzgebel, & M. Vollet (Eds.), *Korruption. Interdisziplinäre Zugänge zu einem komplexen Phänomen* (pp. 87 – 98). Wiesbaden: Deutscher Universitäts-Verlag .

Schmidt, S. (1988). *Rollenspiel, Fallstudie, Planspiel.* München: Rainer Hampp Verlag.

Schmidt, S. (2004). *Korruption in Unternehmen – Typologie und Prävention.* Pforzheim: Fachhochschule Pforzheim.

Schneeweiß, H. (1991). Models with latent variables: LISREL versus PLS. *Statistica Neerlandica, 45*(2), 145 – 157.

Scholz, R. (1995). *Korruption in Deutschland. Die schmutzigen Finger der öffentlichen Hand.* Hamburg: Rowohlt.

Scholz, R. (1997). *Korruption in Deutschland. DPA-Hintergrund Nr. 3507.* Hamburg: Deutsche Presse-Agentur.

Schönbach, P. (1980). A category system for account phases. *European Journal of Social Psychology, 10*(2), 195 – 200.

Schriesheim, C. A., & Yaney, J. P. (1975). The motivation of business game participants. *Training and Development Journal, 29*(8), 11 – 15.

Schulze, G. G., & Frank, B. (2003). Deterrence versus intrinsic motivation: Experimental evidence on the determinants of corruptibility. *Economics of Governance, 4*(2), 143 – 160.

Schumann, P. L., Scott, T. W., & Anderson, P. H. (2006). Designing and introducing ethical dilemmas into computer-based business simulations. *Journal of Management Education, 30*(1), 195 – 219.

Schweitzer, M. E., Ordonez, L., & Douma, B. (2004). Goal setting as a motivator of unethical behavior. *Academy of Management Journal, 47*(3), 422 – 432.

Schwitzgebel, G. (2003). "Chefsache" Korruption – Instrumente der Unternehmensethik im Einsatz zur Prävention und Bekämpfung von Korruption im öffentlichen Raum. In V. V. Nell, G. Schwitzgebel, & M. Vollet (Eds.), *Korruption. Interdisziplinäre Zugänge zu einem komplexen Phänomen* (pp. 65 – 86). Wiesbaden: Deutscher Universitäts-Verlag .

Scott, M. B., & Lyman, S. M. (1968). Accounts. *American Sociological Review, 33*(1), 46 – 62.

Sellin, N. (1995). Partial least squares modeling in research on educational achievement. In W. Bos, & R. H. Lehmann (Eds.), *Reflections on educational achievement. Papers in honour of T. Neville Postlethwaite to mark the occasion of his retirement from his chair in comparative education at the University of Hamburg* (pp. 256 – 267). Münster: Waxman.

Semin, G. R., & Manstead, A. S. R. (1983). *The accountability of conduct: A social psychological analysis.* London: Academic Press.

Serra, D. (2006). Empirical determinants of corruption: A sensitivity analysis. *Public Choice, 126*(1-2), 225 – 256.

Shahabuddin, S. (2002). The causes and consequences of bribery in international business. *International Journal of Management, 19*(2), 366 – 376.

Sheeran, P., & Orbell, S. (1999). Augmenting the theory of planned behavior: Roles for anticipated regret and descriptive norms. *Journal of Applied Social Psychology, 29*(10), 2107 – 2142.

Shleifer, A., & Vishny, R. W. (1993). Corruption. *The Quarterly Journal of Economics, 108*(3), 599 – 617.

Shleifer, A., & Vishny, R. W. (1998). Corruption. In A. Shleifer, & R. W. Vishny (Eds.), *The grabbing hand. Government pathologies and their cures* (pp. 91 – 108). Cambridge, MA: Harvard University Press.

Shover, N., & Bryant, K. M. (1993). Theoretical explanations of corporate crime. In M. B. Blankenship (Ed.), *Understanding corporate criminality* (pp. 141 – 176). New York: Garland.

Simon, D. R., & Hagan, F. E. (1999). *White-collar deviance.* Boston: Allyn and Bacon.

Sims, R. L. (2002). Ethical rule breaking by employees: A test of social bonding theory. *Journal of Business Ethics, 40*(2), 101 – 109.

Sims, R. R. (1992). The challenge of ethical behavior in organizations. *Journal of Business Ethics, 11*(7), 505 – 513.

Smarzynska, B. K., & Wei, S. (2002). *Corruption and cross-border investment: Firm-level evidence.* (William Davidson Institute Working Paper No. 494). Ann Arbor, MI: University of Michigan, William Davidson Institute. Retrieved October 20, 2007, from http://wdi.umich.edu/files/Publications/WorkingPapers/wp494.pdf

Smelser, N. J. (1985). Stabilität, Instabilität und die Analyse der politischen Korruption. In C. Fleck, & H. Kuzmics (Eds.), *Korruption. Zur Soziologie nicht immer abweichenden Verhaltens* (pp. 202 – 228). Königstein/Ts: Athenäum.

Smettan, J. R. (1992). *Kriminelle Bereicherung in Abhängigkeit von Gewinnen, Risiken, Strafen und Moral.* Freiburg: Eigenverlag Max-Planck-Institut.

Smith, A., & Rogers, V. (2000). Ethics-related responses to specific situation vignettes: Evidence of gender-based differences and occupational socialization. *Journal of Business Ethics, 28*(1), 73 – 86.

Soon, L. G. (2006). Macro-economic outcomes of corruption: A longitudinal empirical study. *Singapore Management Review, 28*(1), 63 – 72.

Stanga, K. G., & Turpen, R. A. (1991). Ethical judgments on selected accounting issues: An empirical study. *Journal of Business Ethics*, *10*(10), 739 – 747.

Stauffer, J. M. (2003). An investigation into the effects of birth order, sex, and personality on the likelihood of engaging in unethical behavior. *ProQuest® Dissertations & Theses, AAT 3096338*. Norman, OK: University of Oklahoma.

Stead, W. E., Worrell, D. L., & Stead, J. G. (1990). An integrative model for understanding and managing ethical behavior in business organizations. *Journal of Business Ethics*, *9*(3), 233 – 242.

Steidlmeier, P. (1999). Gift giving, bribery and corruption: Ethical management of business relationships in China. *Journal of Business Ethics*, *20*(2), 121 – 132.

Steinrücken, T. (2004). Sind härtere Strafen für Korruption erforderlich? – Ökonomische Überlegungen zur Sanktionierung illegaler Austauschbeziehungen. *Vierteljahrshefte zur Wirtschaftsforschung*, *73*(2), 301 – 317.

Stitt, B. G., & Giacopassi, D. J. (1993). Assessing victimization from corporate harms. In M. B. Blankenship (Ed.), *Understanding corporate criminality* (pp. 57 – 83). New York: Garland.

Stone, M. (1974). Cross-validatory choice and assessment of statistical predictions. *Journal of the Royal Statistical Society. Series B (Methodological)*, *36*(2), 111 – 147.

Stoner, C. R. (1989). The foundations of business ethics: Exploring the relations. *SAM Advanced Management Journal*, *54*(3), 38 – 43.

Streißler, E. (1981). Zum Zusammenhang zwischen Korruption und Wirtschaftsverfassung. Korruption im Vergleich der Wirtschaftssysteme. In C. Brünner (Ed.), *Korruption und Kontrolle* (pp. 299 – 328). Wien: Böhlau.

Strina, G., & Haferkamp, S. (2003). Einleitung und Grundlagen der Planspielmethode. In K. Henning, & G. Strina (Eds.), *Planspiele in der betrieblichen Anwendung* (pp. 1 – 13). Aachen: Shaker.

Su, C., & Littlefield, J. E. (2001). Entering guanxi: A business ethical dilemma in mainland China? *Journal of Business Ethics*, *33*(3), 199 – 210.

Su, Z., & Richelieu, A. (1999). Western managers working in Romania: Perception and attitude regarding business ethics. *Journal of Business Ethics*, *20*(2), 133 – 146.

Sully de Luque, M., & Javidan, M. (2005). Uncertainty avoidance. In R. J. House, P. J. Hanges, M. Javidan, P. W. Dorfman, & V. Gupta (Eds.), *Culture, leadership, and organizations: The GLOBE study of 62 societies* (pp. 602 – 653). Thousand Oaks, CA: Sage.

Sutherland, E. H. (1940). White-collar criminality. *American Sociological Review*, *5*(1), 1 – 12.

Sutherland, E. H. (1949). *White collar crime*. New York: Dryden Press.

Sutton, R. H. (1997). Controlling corruption through collective means: Advocating the Inter-American Convention Against Corruption. *Fordham International Law Journal, 20*, 1427 – 1478.

Svensson, J. (2003). Who must pay bribes and how much? Evidence from a cross section of firms. *Quarterly Journal of Economics, 118*(1), 207 – 230.

Swamy, A., Knack, S., Lee, Y., & Azfar, O. (2001). Gender and corruption. *Journal of Development Economics, 64*(1), 25 – 55.

Sykes, G. M., & Matza, D. (1957). Techniques of neutralization: A theory of delinquency. *American Sociological Review, 22*(6), 664 – 670.

Szwajkowski, E. (1992). Accounting for organizational misconduct. *Journal of Business Ethics, 11*(5-6), 401 – 411.

Tanzi, V. (1995a). Corruption, arm'slength relationships, and markets. In G. Fiorentini, & S. Peltzman (Eds.), *The economics of organized crime* (pp. 161 – 180). Cambridge: Cambridge University Press.

Tanzi, V. (1995b). Corruption, governmental activities, and markets. *Finance and Development, 32*(4), 24 – 26.

Tanzi, V. (1998). Corruption around the world: Causes, consequences, scope, and cures. *International Monetary Fund. Staff Papers – International Monetary Fund, 45*(4), 559 – 594.

Tanzi, V., & Davoodi, H. R. (1997). *Corruption, public investment, and growth*. (IMF Working Paper No. 97/139). Washington, DC: International Monetary Fund. Retrieved October 18, 2007, from http://www.imf.org/external/pubs/ft/wp/wp97139.pdf

Taylor, S., & Todd, P. (1995). Decomposition and crossover effects in the theory of planned behavior: A study of consumer adoption intentions. *International Journal of Research in Marketing, 12*(2), 137 – 155.

Tenenhaus, M., Vinzi, V. E., Chatelin, Y., & Lauro, C. (2005). PLS path modeling. *Computational Statistics & Data Analysis, 48*(1), 159 – 205.

Then, W. (1997). Korruption im Unternehmen wirksam verhindern. Handlungsfreiheit und Glaubwürdigkeit für Unternehmen und Gesellschaft erhalten. In H. Reichmann, W. Schlaffke, & W. Then (Eds.), *Korruption in Staat und Wirtschaft* (pp. 69 – 76). Köln: Deutscher Instituts-Verlag.

Theobald, R. (1990). *Corruption, development and underdevelopment*. Durham, NC: Duke University Press.

Theobald, R. (2002). Containing corruption: Can the state deliver? *New Political Economy, 7*(3), 435 – 449.

Thibaut, J. W., & Kelley, H. H. (1959). *The social psychology of groups*. New York: Wiley.

Tirole, J. (1986). Hierarchies and bureaucracies: On the role of collusion in organizations. *Journal of Law, Economics and Organization, 2*(2), 181 – 214.

Tirole, J. (1996). A theory of collective reputations (with applications to the persistence of corruption and to firm quality). *The Review of Economic Studies, 63*(214), 1 – 22.

Transparency International (2000). *Transparency International Corruption Perceptions Index 2000*. Retrieved March 10, 2008, from http://www.transparency.org/policy_research/surveys_indices/cpi/previous_cpi__1/2000

Transparency International (2001). *Transparency International Corruption Perceptions Index 2001*. Retrieved March 10, 2008, from http://www.transparency.org/policy_research/surveys_indices/cpi/2001

Transparency International (2002). *Transparency International Corruption Perceptions Index 2002*. Retrieved March 10, 2008, from http://www.transparency.org/policy_research/surveys_indices/cpi/2002

Transparency International (2003). *Transparency International Corruption Perceptions Index 2003*. Retrieved March 10, 2008, from http://www.transparency.org/policy_research/surveys_indices/cpi/2003

Transparency International (2004). *Transparency International Corruption Perceptions Index 2004*. Retrieved March 10, 2008, from http://www.transparency.org/policy_research/surveys_indices/cpi/2004

Transparency International (2005). *Report on the Transparency International Global Corruption Barometer 2005*. Retrieved November 13, 2006, from http://www.transparency.org/policy_research/surveys_indices/gcb

Transparency International (2006). *Transparency International Corruption Perceptions Index 2006*. Retrieved March 10, 2008, from http://www.transparency.org/policy_research/surveys_indices/cpi/2006

Transparency International (2007a). *2007 Corruption Perceptions Index regional highlights: EU and Western Europe*. Retrieved March 10, 2008, from http://www.transparency.org/content/download/23977/358251

Transparency International (2007b). *Report on the Transparency International Global Corruption Barometer 2007*. Retrieved March 10, 2008, from http://www.transparency.org/content/download/27256/410704/file/GCB_2007_report_en_02-12-2007.pdf

Transparency International (2007c). *Transparency International Corruption Perceptions Index 2007*. Retrieved March 10, 2008, from http://www.transparency.org/policy_research/surveys_indices/cpi/2007

Treisman, D. (2000). The causes of corruption: A cross-national study. *Journal of Public Economics, 76*(3), 399 – 457.

Trevino, L. K. (1986). Ethical decision making in organizations: A person-situation interactionist model. *The Academy of Management Review, 11*(3), 601 – 617.

Trevino, L. K., & Brown, M. E. (2005). The role of leaders in influencing unethical behavior in the workplace. In R. E. Kidwell, & C. L. Martin (Eds.), *Managing organizational deviance* (pp. 69 – 96). Thousand Oaks, CA: Sage.

Trevino, L. K., Brown, M., & Hartman, L. P. (2003). A qualitative investigation of perceived executive ethical leadership: Perceptions from inside and outside the executive suite. *Human Relations, 56*(1), 5 – 37.

Tsalikis, J., & LaTour, M. S. (1995). Bribery and extortion in international business: Ethical perceptions of Greeks compared to Americans. *Journal of Business Ethics, 14*(4), 249 – 264.

Vahlenkamp, W., & Knauß, I. (1995). *Korruption – hinnehmen oder handeln?* Wiesbaden: Bundeskriminalamt.

Van Duyne, P. (1999). Combatting corruption: Acts and attitudes. In M. Joutsen (Ed.), *Five issues in European criminal justice: corruption, women in the criminal justice system, criminal policy indicators, community crime prevention, and computer crime* (pp. 22 – 60). Helsinki: European Institute for Crime Prevention and Control.

Van Duyne, P. C. (2001). Will Caligula go transparent? Corruption in acts and attitudes. *Forum on Crime and Society, 1*(2), 73 – 95.

Van Klaveren, J. (1989). The concept of corruption. In A. J. Heidenheimer, M. Johnston, & V. T. LeVine (Eds.), *Political corruption: A handbook* (pp. 25 – 27). New Brunswick, NJ: Transaction Publishers.

Van Rijckeghem, C., & Weder, B. (2001). Bureaucratic corruption and the rate of temptation: Do wages in the civil service affect corruption, and by how much? *Journal of Development Economics, 65*(2), 307 – 331.

Vaughan, D. S., Gleave, E. P., & Welser, H. T. (2005, August). *Controlling the evolution of corruption: Emulation, sanction and prestige.* Paper presented at the Annual Meeting of the American Sociological Association, Philadelphia. Retrieved Januara 19, 2007, from http://search.ebscohost.com/login.aspx?direct=true&db=sih&AN=18614682&site=ehost-live

Veiga, J. F., Golden, T. D., & Dechant, K. (2004). Why managers bend company rules. *The Academy of Management Executive, 18*(2), 84 – 90.

Vickers, M. R. (2005). Business ethics and the HR role: Past, present, and future. *HR. Human Resource Planning, 28*(1), 26 – 32.

Vitell, S. J., & Festervand, T. A. (1987). Business ethics: Conflicts, practices and beliefs of industrial executives. *Journal of Business Ethics, 6*(2), 111 – 122.

Vitell, S. J., & Grove, S. J. (1987). Marketing ethics and the techniques of neutralization. *Journal of Business Ethics, 6*(6), 433 – 438.

Vogt, A. O. (1997). *Korruption im Wirtschaftsleben. Eine betriebswirtschaftliche Schaden-Nutzen-Analyse.* Wiesbaden: Deutscher Universitäts-Verlag.

Vroom, V. H. (1984). *Work and motivation* (Reprint ed. with corr.). Malabar, FL: Krieger.

Warburton, J. (2001). Corruption as a social process: From dyads to networks. In P. Larmour, & N. Wolanin (Eds.), *Corruption and anti-corruption* (pp. 221 – 237). Canberra: Asia Pacific Press.

Wated, G., & Sanchez, J. I. (2005). The effects of attitudes, subjective norms, attributions, and individualism-collectivism on managers' responses to bribery in organizations: Evidence from a developing nation. *Journal of Business Ethics, 61*(2), 111 – 127.

Wedemann, A. (1997). Looters, rent-scrapers, and dividend-collectors: Corruption and growth in Zaire, South Korea, and the Philippines. *The Journal of Developing Areas, 31*(4), 457 – 478.

Weeks, W. A., & Nantel, J. (1992). Corporate codes of ethics and sales force behavior: A case study. *Journal of Business Ethics, 11*(10), 753 – 760.

Weeks, W. A., Moore, C. W., McKinney, J. A., & Longenecker, J. G. (1999). The effects of gender and career stage on ethical judgment. *Journal of Business Ethics, 20*(4), 301 – 313.

Wei, S. (1999). *Corruption in economic development: Beneficial grease, minor annoyance, or major obstacle?* (World Bank Policy Research Working Paper No. 2048). Washington DC: World Bank. Retrieved September 5, 2007, from http://www-wds.worldbank.org/servlet/WDSContentServer/WDSP/IB/2000/02/24/000094946_99031911113468/Rendered/PDF/multi_page.pdf

Wei, S. (2000a). How taxing is corruption on international investors? *The Review of Economics and Statistics, 82*(1), 1 – 11.

Wei, S. (2000b). *Natural openness and good government.* (NBER Working Paper No. 7765). Cambridge, MA: National Bureau of Economic Research. Retrieved January 26, 2005, from http://www.nber.org/papers/w7765.pdf

Wei, S., & Shleifer, A. (2000). Local corruption and global capital flows. *Brookings Papers on Economic Activity, 2000*(2), 303 – 354.

Wei, S., & Wu, Y. (2001). *Negative alchemy? Corruption, composition of capital flows, and currency crisis.* (NBER Working Paper No. 8187). Cambridge, MA: National Bureau of Economic Research. Retrieved October 20, 2007, from http://www.nber.org/papers/w8187.pdf

Weisburd, D., & Waring, E. (2001). *White-collar crime and criminal careers.* Cambridge: Cambridge University Press .

Weitz, B. O. (2000). *Planspiele in der ökonomischen Bildung.* Halle: Martin-Luther-Universität Halle-Wittenberg, Wirtschaftswissenschaftliche Fakultät.

Weitzel, U., & Berns, S. (2006). Cross-border takeovers, corruption, and related aspects of governance. *Journal of International Business Studies, 37*(6), 786 – 806.

Wellen, J. M. (2004, October). *From individual deviance to collective corruption: A social influence model of the spread deviance in organisations.* Paper presented to the Social Change in the 21st Century Conference, Brisbane, Australia. Retrieved September 27, 2006, from http://eprints.qut.edu.au/archive/00000649/01/wellen_jackie.pdf

Werts, C. E., Linn, R. L., & Jöreskog, K. G. (1974). Intraclass reliability estimates: Testing structural assumptions. *Educational and Psychological Measurement, 34*(1), 25 – 33.

Wheeler, D., & Mody, A. (1992). International investment location decisions: The case of U.S. firms. *Journal of International Economics, 33*(1-2), 57 – 76.

Wheeler, S. (1992). The problem of white-collar crime motivation. In K. Schlegel, & D. Weisburd (Eds.), *White-collar crime reconsidered* (pp. 108 – 123). Boston: Northeastern University Press.

Wiehen, M. H. (1998). Corruption in international business relations: Problems and solutions. In B. N. Kumar, & H. Steinmann (Eds.), *Ethics in international management* (pp. 183 – 211). Berlin: de Gruyter.

Wieland, J., & Grüninger, S. (2000). Ethik-Management-Systeme und ihre Auditierung – Theoretische Einordnung und praktische Erfahrungen. In T. Bausch, A. Kleinfeld, & H. Steinmann (Eds.), *Unternehmensethik in der Wirtschaftspraxis* (pp. 155 – 189). München: Hampp.

Williams, J. W., & Beare, M. E. (1999). The business of bribery: Globalization, economic liberalization, and the "problem" of corruption. *Crime, Law and Social Change, 32*(2), 115 – 146.

Williams, R. (Ed.) (2000). *Explaining corruption. The politics of corruption 1.* Cheltenham: Edward Elgar.

Williamson, O. E. (1975). *Markets and hierarchies: Analysis and antitrust implications.* New York: Free Press.

Wirl, F. (1998). Socio-economic typologies of bureaucratic corruption and implications. *Journal of Evolutionary Economics*, *8*(2), 199 – 220.

Wold, H. (1966). Non-linear estimation by iterative least squares procedures. In F. N. David (Ed.), *Research papers in statistics* (pp. 411 – 444). London: Wiley.

Wold, H. (1982). Soft modeling. The basic design and some extensions. In K. G. Jöreskog, & H. Wold (Eds.), *Systems under indirect observations, Part II* (pp. 1 – 54). Amsterdam: North-Holland Publications.

Wold, H. (1985). Partial least squares. In S. Kotz, & N. L. Johnson (Eds.), *Encyclopedia of statistical sciences. Vol. 6: Multivariate analysis to Plackett and Burman designs* (pp. 581 – 591). New York: Wiley.

Wood, J. A., Longenecker, J. G., McKinney, J. A., & Moore, C. W. (1988). Ethical attitudes of students and business professionals: A study of moral reasoning. *Journal of Business Ethics*, *7*(4), 249 – 257.

Wotruba, T. R., Chonko, L. B., & Loe, T. W. (2001). The impact of ethics code familiarity on manager behavior. *Journal of Business Ethics*, *33*(1), 59 – 69.

Wu, S. (2006). Corruption and cross-border investment by multinational firms. *Journal of Comparative Economics*, *34*(4), 839 – 856.

Yezer, A. M., Goldfarb, R. S., & Poppen, P. J. (1996). Does studying economics discourage cooperation? Watch what we do, not what we say or how we play. *The Journal of Economic Perspectives*, *10*(1), 177 – 186.

Zahra, S. A., Priem, R. L., & Rasheed, A. A. (2005). The antecedents and consequences of top management fraud. *Journal of Management*, *31*(6), 803 – 828.

Zekos, G. I. (2004). Ethics versus corruption in globalization. *The Journal of Management Development*, *23*(7/8), 631 – 647.

Zelditch, M. J., & Evan, W. M. (1962). Simulated bureaucracies: A methodological analysis. In H. Guetzkow (Ed.), *Simulation in social science* (pp. 48 – 60). Englewood Cliffs, NJ: Prentice Hall.

Zhao, J. H., Kim, S. H., & Du, J. (2003). The impact of corruption and transparency on foreign direct investment: An empirical analysis. *Management International Review*, *43*(1), 41 – 62.

Zimring, F. E., & Johnson, D. T. (2005). On the comparative study of corruption. *British Journal of Criminology*, *45*(6), 793 – 809.

Zinnbauer, M., & Eberl, M. (2004). *Die Überprüfung von Spezifikation und Güte von Strukturgleichungsmodellen: Verfahren und Anwendung.* (Schriften zur Empirischen Forschung und Quantitativen Unternehmensplanung, Heft 21). München: Ludwig-Maximilians-Universität München, Institut für Unternehmensentwicklung und Organisation. Retrieved September 22, 2005, from http://www. imm.bwl.uni-muenchen.de/dmdocuments/AP_efoplan_21.pdf

CURRICULUM VITAE

Tanja Rabl

University of Bayreuth
Chair of Human Resource Management
95440 Bayreuth
Germany

Tel.:   + 49 921 55 2953
Fax: + 49 921 55 2954
Email: tanja.rabl@uni-bayreuth.de
Web: www.hrm.uni-bayreuth.de

Personal Data

Date of birth	May 18, 1980
Nationality	German

Education

10/2004 – 07/2008	University of Bayreuth, Germany - Doctoral degree in Business Administration
10/1999 – 09/2004	Catholic University of Eichstätt-Ingolstadt, Germany - Diploma in Psychology - Major: Work and Organizational Psychology, Economic Psychology - Minor: Business Administration
10/2001 – 03/2002	University of Lancaster, Great Britain - Participation in the degree program „Master of Science in Psychological Research Methods"
09/1990 – 06/1999	Gymnasium Parsberg, Germany - Abitur (German high school diploma)

Professional Experience

10/2008 – present	University of Bayreuth, Germany - Assistant Professor at the Chair of Human Resource Management (Prof. Dr. T. M. Kühlmann)
10/2004 – 09/2008	University of Bayreuth, Germany - Research Assistant at the Chair of Human Resource Management (Prof. Dr. T. M. Kühlmann)

Marianne Schmid Mast

Gender Differences in Dominance Hierarchies

Men are said to organize themselves readily in hierarchies. But what about women? Do women build rank orders to the same extent as men or are women's groups structured in a more egalitarian way? In the present book, evidence from different disciplines pertaining to the topic are collected, existing theoretical models describing female rank orders are contrasted, and an empirical investigation with respect to rank structures in women and men is presented. 14 all-female and 14 all-male groups met three times in the same groups. By means of behavioral observation of different variables the degree of hierarchical structuring was determined for each group at different points in time. Results are discussed on the basis of the existing theoretical background and revealed that women built hierarchical structures comparable to men, however, in a later phase of the interaction. At the beginning of the interaction, all-men groups were more hierarchically structured than all-female groups. The presented study makes a contribution to the understanding of rank orders in all-female groups under a longitudinal perspective and in comparison to men.

148 pages, ISBN 978-3-934252-62-2, Price: 15,- Euro

PABST SCIENCE PUBLISHERS
Eichengrund 28, D-49525 Lengerich, Tel. ++ 49 (0) 5484-308
Fax ++ 49 (0) 5484-550, E-mail: pabst.publishers@t-online.de
www.pabst-publishers.de

R. W. Scholz, A. C. Zimmer (Eds.)

Qualitative Aspects of Decision Making

The volume *Qualitative Aspects of Decision Making* deals with three issues that may widen research on judgement and decision making. Firstly, the concepts and their formal or semantic relations in normative and cognitive modelling are addressed. Particularly *alternative representations of uncertainty* are treated which reflect different qualities of knowledge. Secondly, the meaning of the decision to the subject's world and its environment are treated. Thus *contextualizations* of the task and a theory of the subject task relation are discussed. Thirdly, the *complexity* of a decision task is conceived as a specific quality which, for example, requires multiple representations and strategies of knowledge integration.

All contributions are focusing on psychological models and theories. Empirical methods ranging from experiments through surveys to case studies are used. Theoretical and applied issues are dealt with. Applications and qualitative aspects are introduced from *economy, medical, legal and environmental sciences.*

188 pages, ISBN 978-3-931660-57-4, Price: 30,- Euro

PABST SCIENCE PUBLISHERS
Eichengrund 28, D-49525 Lengerich, Tel. ++ 49 (0) 5484-308
Fax ++ 49 (0) 5484-550, E-mail: pabst.publishers@t-online.de
www.pabst-publishers.de

M. Vartiainen, C. Antoni, X. Beaten, N. Hakonen, R. Lucas, H. Thierry (Eds.)

Reward Management – Facts and Trends in Europe

Reward Management - Facts and Trends in Europe covers a wide range of topics and perspectives that will help to understand the status and challenges of reward systems not only in Europe but also around the world.

This book is an outcome of the First European Reward Management Conference (RMC) held at Brussels December 17 -18, 2007. The book focuses on reward and compensation in Europe and the challenges ahead. Europe is large. This results in a variety of compensation, benefit and non-monetary reward practices, about which we know relatively little. Therefore, we need more debate about current issues in reward and compensation, both from a policy and practice perspective.

The book has thirteen chapters covering topics like: wages of young workers in Europe, employee ownership, differences between men's and women's perceptions and attitudes in pay-setting process, innovative compensation schemes, a new instrument (PReSS) to measure employees' satisfaction with psychological rewards, top management's (CEO) remuneration and how it is related to firm performance, the role of the first line manager in pay process, procedural and interactional justice in the performance appraisal process, employee benefits, differences of employees' reward preferences, the role of monetary rewards in innovativeness, and talent management.

PABST SCIENCE PUBLISHERS
Eichengrund 28
D-49525 Lengerich,
Tel. ++ 49 (0) 5484-308,
Fax ++ 49 (0) 5484-550,
pabst.publishers@t-online.de
www.pabst-publishers.de

300 pages, ISBN 978-3-89967-479-8
Price: 35,- Euro